What They Said

"Yesterday's news tomorrow."

—Yori Yanover's description of the Jewish Telegraphic Agency

"If you publish this, I will fuck you for the rest of your life."

—Malcolm Hoenlein to journalist Walter Ruby

"I guess it's new for a journalist to go in and treat a congregation journalistically."

—Stephen Fried, *The New Rabbi*

"If you believed in a God and a Final Judgment, would you have written the book the same way?"

—Rabbi Bradley Sharvit Artson, rosh yeshiva of the University of Judaism, to Stephen Fried

"Dear Mr. Ford; I did review your Web site, and find it imbalanced and toxic, particularly toward rabbis and Conservative Judaism. I am not willing to participate in your panel."

—Rabbi Artson

"Dear Mr. Ford: I do not wish to be included in your book. If there is anything negative about me or my family in your book you will hear from my attorney."

—Rabbi Sheldon Zimmerman, former president of the Hebrew Union College—Jewish Institute of Religion

"Dear Mr. Ford: I appreciate your interest, but I'd just prefer to pass on this."

—Seth Lipsky, former editor of the *Forward*

"I am annoyed at your annoyance, your presumption to tell me what I'm qualified to talk about when you don't even know me, your insinuations that I refuse to be 'transparent and accountable,' along with your slam on my trusted and most-valued colleague, Larry Stammer. He is not a 'crappy reporter,' as you put it."

—Teresa Watanabe, *The Los Angeles Times*

"You don't want Jewish journalism. You want an orgasm."

—Tom Tugend, *Jewish Journal*

"I am the moderator of the AJPA listserv and I will be sending out an email to all the editors later today to tell them of my unprofessional and discourteous experience with you."

—Benyamin Cohen, Jewsweek.com

"I don't understand what you are doing here. Who's your publisher?"

—Rabbi Shmuley Boteach, *Kosher Sex*

"Don't write about me!"

—Amy Klein, managing editor of the *Jewish Journal*

"We're all kind of mediocre."

—E.J. Kessler, deputy managing editor of the *Forward*

"Larry [Cohler] was essentially driven out. He found out that Gary [Rosenblatt] was without balls. Larry may sometimes be without brains but he is never without balls. Gary tends to be tame and timid."

—Dr. Michael Berenbaum, former director of the United States Holocaust Research Institute

"Of course Gary lacks balls. He's the editor of a Federation paper. If you want to keep these kinds of jobs, especially long-term, lacking balls is a requirement."

—Allison Kaplan Sommer, journalist

"The Jews who look to Jewish journalism tend to want to be anesthetized."

—J.J. Goldberg, editor of the *Forward*

"I'm not sure the Jewish community wants a compelling paper."

—Marc S. Klein, editor of *j. the Jewish news weekly of Northern California*

"Jewish men who are accused of kicking women are not popular."

—Dwight Owen Schweitzer, editor and publisher of the *Jewish Star Times*

"You want to be involved with Israel because it is a sexier, crookeder, funnier, nastier, more backstabbing, more backbiting, crazier, more psychotic place than Hollywood."

—Larry Yudelson, journalist

"I don't plant bombs but ideas."

—Rabbi Avi Shafran, spokesman for Agudath Israel

"The main problem with Jewish journalism is one organization runs almost the entire show. Almost an entire ethnic media is subservient to one organization."

—Steven I. Weiss, journalist

"As for the 'Kahanist rag' comment—obviously a retort made by a retard."

—Jason Maoz, editor of *The Jewish Press*

Yesterday's News Tomorrow

Also by Luke Ford

A History of X: 100 Years of Sex in Film

XXX-Communicated: A Rebel Without A Shul

The Producers: Profiles In Frustration

Yesterday's News Tomorrow

Inside American Jewish Journalism

Luke Ford

iUniverse, Inc.
New York Lincoln Shanghai

Yesterday's News Tomorrow
Inside American Jewish Journalism

All Rights Reserved © 2004 by Luke Ford

No part of this book may be reproduced or transmitted in any form or by any means, graphic, electronic, or mechanical, including photocopying, recording, taping, or by any information storage retrieval system, without the written permission of the publisher.

iUniverse, Inc.

For information address:
iUniverse, Inc.
2021 Pine Lake Road, Suite 100
Lincoln, NE 68512
www.iuniverse.com

ISBN: 0-595-33202-1 (pbk)
ISBN: 0-595-66768-6 (cloth)

Printed in the United States of America

For Cathy Seipp, my best friend

Contents

Foreword xv
Foreword II xix
Glossary & Cast of Characters xxi
Preface xxxi
CHAPTER 1   Stephen Fried 1
CHAPTER 2   Paul Wilkes 12
CHAPTER 3   Jonathan Tobin 18
CHAPTER 4   Ari L. Goldman 26
CHAPTER 5   Amy Klein 34
CHAPTER 6   Sue Fishkoff 40
CHAPTER 7   Stephen G. Bloom 48
CHAPTER 8   Jennie Rothenberg 60
CHAPTER 9   Steven I. Weiss 65
CHAPTER 10   Andrew Silow-Carroll 69
CHAPTER 11   Larry Cohler-Esses 76
CHAPTER 12   Sheldon Teitelbaum 81
CHAPTER 13   Gary Rosenblatt 86
CHAPTER 14   Michael Berenbaum 97
CHAPTER 15   Lisa Lenkiewicz 105

Chapter 16	Gene Lichtenstein	110
Chapter 17	Jonathan Sarna	123
Chapter 18	Rob Eshman	129
Chapter 19	E.J. Kessler	147
Chapter 20	Rabbi Avi Shafran	154
Chapter 21	Larry Yudelson	157
Chapter 22	Yori Yanover	167
Chapter 23	Benyamin Cohen	171
Chapter 24	Marc S. Klein	178
Chapter 25	Yossi Klein Halevi	184
Chapter 26	David Twersky	193
Chapter 27	Debra Nussbaum Cohen	197
Chapter 28	Steve Rabinowitz	201
Chapter 29	Tom Tugend	204
Chapter 30	J.J. Goldberg	209
Chapter 31	Wayne Hoffman	223
Chapter 32	Alana Newhouse	232
Chapter 33	Ami Eden	238
Chapter 34	Leslie Katz	243
Chapter 35	Robert Cohn	246
Chapter 36	Rabbi Shmuley Boteach	249
Chapter 37	Evan Gahr	254
Chapter 38	Debra Rubin	271
Chapter 39	Charles Fenyvesi	274
Chapter 40	Neil Rubin	281
Chapter 41	Walter Ruby	288
Chapter 42	Yosef I. Abramowitz	294

CHAPTER 43	Mark Silk	299
CHAPTER 44	Dwight Owen Schweitzer	302
CHAPTER 45	Jason Maoz	309
APPENDIX A	A History of Jewish Journalism in the United States	321
APPENDIX B	The Economics of Jewish Journalism in the United States	333
APPENDIX C	*New Jewish Times*	347
APPENDIX D	Jewish Sources For Journalistic Ethics	351
APPENDIX E	What *The New York Times* Tells Us About Ourselves	357
APPENDIX F	Eleven Problems With Jewish Journalism	361
Index		365

Foreword

By Robert J. Avrech

"*Every journalist who is not too stupid or too full of himself to notice what is going on knows that what he does is morally indefensible. He is a kind of confidence man, preying on people's vanity, ignorance, or loneliness, gaining their trust and betraying them without remorse.*"

—**Janet Malcolm**, *The Journalist and the Murderer*

Betrayal fascinates Luke Ford. It's his life.

Luke betrayed his father, a prominent Seventh Day Adventist minister, when Luke converted to Judaism.

Luke betrayed his second "father" when he sacrificed his friendship with Dennis Prager to work on an unauthorized biography of his hero.

Luke betrayed Judaism when he became lukeford.com, the preeminent journalist covering LA's sordid, mob-infested porn industry.

Luke betrayed his Orthodox synagogue when he lied about his work and told the rabbi that he was a "freelance journalist who writes about crime for a Japanese magazine."

I know all this first hand because I was and am a member of a shul that kicked him out when the truth of his work in porn came to light. Luke and I sat together in Daf Yomi, the page-a-day Talmud study class, for close to a year. All this is amply and honestly documented in Luke's second book: *XXX-Communicated: A Rebel Without a Shul*.

This book, *Yesterday's News Tomorrow: Inside American Jewish Journalism*, is a different matter entirely. When Luke told me what he was planning, I said a silent payer. Not for Luke—but for the poor unsuspecting journalists who were about to fall under the sniper lens of his scrutiny.

Luke has no interest in friendly, chatty dialogue. These are North Korean-like interrogations artfully disguised as interviews. Luke strives for maximum confrontation. Like a gifted major league pitcher, Luke throws a series of fastballs, followed by a change-up and then, zing! He lets loose with a knuckleball that sends the dazed subject diving to the dust.

There is nothing that raises Luke's ire as much as complacence. As you can see from the interviews, he is determined that journalists get a taste of their own medicine. It is, in all truth, deeply gratifying to see journalists squirm under Luke's relentless cross-examination. Clearly, they have underestimated him. They perceive Luke Ford as an infamous blogger who wrote about porn, converted to Judaism, and is a loose canon. He is someone these polite and well-bred people would *never* hire. Luke is far too disreputable for their august publications.

I can see the gears turning in their heads: *Ok, I'll give this nudnik an interview. He won't be any problem because all he really wants is a job.* They underestimate Luke Ford. They miscalculate his capacity for self-destruction. Luke Ford cares more about getting a good interview, then building the stone and mortar for his next job. They assume they can charm him. Wrong. Luke is king of the charmers. These good and well-intentioned journalists assume that Luke will extend them professional courtesy. Big mistake. Luke correctly sees professional courtesy for what it is: a polite way of lying. Luke comes on like Sherman marching thorough Georgia. And like the great Civil War general, he leaves ruin in his wake.

Luke Ford makes no pretence to "objective journalism." He knows that no such thing exists. Upfront about his conservative values, he writes, "I can't get through any pious story by a leftist. The *Jewish Journal* has way too much secular leftist piety—stuff about being kind to gays, that Jews are one people, we should take better care of the environment, we should talk through our differences…"

Luke establishes that most of the journalists he's dealing with are cut from the same political cloth: liberal Democrats, many former activists. He innocently queries if a paper would be better if there were a Republican on the staff. J.J. Goldberg admits that his paper, the *Forward*, would probably benefit from a dissenting political voice. And so, how many Republicans are there on Goldberg's staff? Zero.

And this is from the party which makes endless noise about diversity.

Rob Eshman, editor of the *Jewish Journal*, is an amiable gentleman who gives the most informative interview in the book. All the issues that bedevil Jewish journalism are considered from every possible angle. Luke tries to get Eshman to let down his guard, to name names, to admit that his Orthodox readers are by far the hardest to please. But Eshman knows Luke's game and we witness a friendly, but deadly serious, duel. Luke thrusts, Rob parries. Finally, an exhausted Rob Eshman expresses the central truth that any Luke Ford subject feels after undergoing the distinctive Luke Ford interview when he turns to his managing editor, Amy Klein, and says, "He's sucking me dry." It is my favorite moment in the whole book.

With disarming and refreshing honesty, Luke Ford blurts out his feelings. He adores Stephen Fried's *The New Rabbi*. For Luke, this book stands as the paradigm of what Jewish journalism should strive for.

With Ari Goldman, the former religion writer for *The NY Times*, you can feel Luke's respect for this thoughtful and sensitive man who gives an almost painfully confessional interview.

My favorite interview is with Benyamin Cohen. Cohen demands final cut over his words, and when Luke properly refuses, and then posts Cohen's somewhat hysterical response on the Web, Cohen goes to war. He tries to get other writers to stonewall Luke. The poor man does not realize that he is playing in Luke Ford's playground. How many journalists followed Cohen's lead? Few, if any. There is a deep feeling of satisfaction when an arrogant journalist gets a taste of his own medicine.

Luke Ford might be interested in betrayal, but he is also interested in truth. He wants to know why Jewish journalism is crammed with so much self-serving material. He wants to know who pulls the strings. He demands names, dates, places. He wonders why the brilliance that can frequently be found in the Beis Midrash is rarely evident in the Jewish newsroom. The key issue, Ford concludes, is the problem of reporting on a small group of which you are a part. More traditional minded journalists properly cite lashon hara, the biblical injunction against speaking evil or gossiping. For, if you take your Torah seriously, how can you in good conscience write a story about a rabbi who might be sexually abusing children? What happens if the charges are false? You have ruined a man's life.

In these interviews, as much as these good men and women try to stonewall and dodge the questions, the answers do arrive in a slow drip of truth.

It is a delicious and revealing irony that this minister's son from Cooranbong, Australia, turns out to be the one who burrows into the soft underbelly of the liberal Jewish elite. It is an unbearable paradox that this bad boy porn journalist advises these upright citizens that the job they are doing is simply not good enough. In fact, he hints, the writing is on the wall for traditional Jewish journalism. The Internet has given birth to a whole new brand of writing: Jewish journalism that is more personal and at the same time infinitely more honest, relevant and timely than anything these editors can put forward. I believe that they would be wise to scrutinize the world of Jewish blogs and the quirky Web sites that are proliferating, for if they are not careful, their familiar and comfortable journalistic worlds will evaporate, much like the old Yiddishists who dominated Jewish intellectual culture at the turn of the century.

I spend far too much time defending Luke Ford and his unique brand of journalism. People say he has no discipline. Not true. Luke has a puritan work ethic and no one I know labors as hard as he does. His discipline is of a different sort. Most journalists spend all their energy trying to write the perfect opening sentence. Luke could not care less about a zippy lead. He is after bigger game, the raw matter of truth. Luke is accused of being careless with facts, not checking his sources. Again, my experience is that when Luke makes a mistake, he cops to it immediately. Another complaint frequently leveled at Luke Ford is that he's not a "real journalist." He cuts and pastes, say his critics. My reading is of a different sort entirely. Luke Ford has invented a new form of journalism. Think of it as a fusion of traditional newspaper writing with an abundant dose of autobiographical musings. The stories, no matter what the subject matter—porn, religion, politics, Jewish journalism—always returns to a central core: Luke Ford and his unique worldview.

You can dislike Luke Ford and his particular brand of journalism, but in this day of Internet connectivity and the eventual primacy of the blog, it is foolish to dismiss him.

Luke Ford is a an old fashioned provocateur and in the end, he is entirely successful, for if you read these interviews closely you will discover that Luke Ford transforms the subjects of his interviews into mirror images of Luke Ford: journalists who betray journalism.

Robert J. Avrech is an Emmy Award winning screenwriter who lives in Los Angeles with his family. His first novel, **The Hebrew Kid and the Apache Maiden** *will be published by Seraphic Press in January 2005. For more information, go to www.seraphicpress.com.*

Foreword II

By Matt Welch

I'll never forget the first words Luke Ford ever spoke to me. "So Matt," he said, shaking my hand. "What do you like to think about when you masturbate?"

It would have been awkward in any context, all the more so because my beautiful wife Emmanuelle Richard was standing nearby, and I was dropping her off for a one-on-one interview in Luke's filthy studio apartment for an article about how he was the "Matt Drudge of porn."

That was the summer of 1998, and we've all gone through a lot of changes since then. For instance, Luke no longer automatically types up his memory of phone conversations with my wife onto his website, typos and accuracy bedamned. (Now he uses a tape recorder, and generally lets people know…or at least his friends are aware of the device in his pocket, and act accordingly.) Also, Luke no longer covers porn—at least not officially—and has instead focused his insatiable curiosity on Hollywood producers, Los Angeles journalists, his own conflicts as a porn-addicted Orthodox Jew, and now Jewish journalism. And he has had the good manners to turn his ever-gazing eye from me, and instead on my bosses—on my first day of work for the libertarian *Reason* magazine, for example, he cornered my editor Nick Gillespie and said "Do you realize you've just hired a liberal who's in favor of universal health care? Has he told you that?"

A year later, he cornered *Reason* publisher Mike Alissi and asked him for some scandal on his editor Nick. Not knowing who he was talking to, Mike said jokingly that Nick liked to bugger little boys. Luke promptly published the remark on his blog.

Luke's basic approach is the same as the one that led him to uncover important scoops ranging from the HIV crisis in Southern California's adult industry back in 1998, to private eye Anthony Pellicano's nefarious behavior in muscling the unfortunates who had the temerity to cross swords with C-actor Steven Seagal: Ask wildly impertinent questions, dump any and all source material—including interviews and cease-and-desist-letters—onto his Web site, and never shy away from embroidering the coverage with his own personal torments and conflicts.

The results can be thrilling, infuriating, hilarious, only occasionally banal, and unfailingly original. Luke may be a serial liar for all I know (it truly is hard to get a handle on a guy who is A) Australian, B) child of a strict Seventh Day Adventist, C) a failed actor, D) driver of one of the creepiest serial-killer vans in all of Hollywood, E) a porn freak, F) a converted and moralizing Orthodox Jew, and G) the voice behind several fictitious online characters, many of whom utter remarks that can charitably be described as borderline racist), and yet his work is almost chillingly honest.

Put simply, there is no journalist alive quite like him, and we are all richer for the output his mania produces. (Well, except for Hollywood producer J. Todd Harris, who told Luke, but not his wife, about borrowing $100,000 from their personal account to finance his film *29 Palms*.) Luke works in the vanishing tradition of journalists bored stiff by soft consensus, and who realize the point of asking questions is not to make the interviewer look good, but to make the subject squirm and react. At heart, he wants the world to be a more interesting place, and for its neglected corners to contain more light. In this book, he asks 50 reporters and editors literally hundreds of rude questions. Jewish journalists, and the rest of us, should be thankful. Or at least entertained.

Matt Welch is a columnist for **The National Post**, *writes a regular media column for* **Reason** *magazine, and operates a Web log at* http://mattwelch.com/warblog.html.

Glossary & Cast of Characters

Abramowitz, Yosef: Freelance journalist, CEO of Jewish Family & Life.

Agunot: Orthodox women who aren't granted divorces by their husbands.

Aliyah: To go up. (1) To be called to the Torah to recite a blessing. (2) To move to Israel.

Assur: Forbidden.

Baalei Batim: Constituents, congregants, laity.

Beit Midrash: Study hall.

Berenbaum, Michael: Holocaust scholar.

Besser, James: Weekly columnist out of Washington D.C.

Bima: Pulpit.

Bloom, Stephen: Author of *Postville*, a blistering critique of Lubavitchers taking over a small town in Iowa.

Silow-Carroll, Andrew: Editor of *New Jersey Jewish News*.

Boteach, Rabbi Shmuley: Author of the book *Kosher Sex* and America's best-known Orthodox rabbi.

Chabad: Lubavitch. A sect of Chasidic Judaism known for reaching out to non-religious Jews.

Challah: Braided bread used for Shabbat dinner.

Charedi: Fervently Orthodox.

Chumrah: Strict interpretation of Jewish law.

Chuppah: Canopy used at weddings.

Chutzpah: Arrogance.

Cohen, Benyamin: Editor of Jewsweek.com, creator of Jewishcontent.com.

Cohen, Debra Nussbaum: Wrote for JTA for almost a decade, now at *The Jewish Week*.

Eden, Ami: National editor of the *Forward*.

Eshman, Rob: Editor of the *Jewish Journal* of Los Angeles.

Cohler-Esses, Larry: Jewish journalism's premiere investigative reporter.

Farbrengen: Gathering of Chasidim.

Federation: "Massive nationwide fund-raising network, a Jewish United Way." (Stephen Fried)

Fenyvesi, Charles: *Washington Post, Washington Jewish Week, US News & World Report*.

Fishkoff, Sue: Author of *The Rebbe's Army*, a glowing portrait of Lubavitch emissaries.

Forward: American Jewry's premiere weekly.

Freedman, Samuel: Author of *Jew vs. Jew*, an acclaimed book on Jewish conflicts.

Fried, Stephen: Author of *The New Rabbi*.

Frum: Pious, a quality popularly associated with the Orthodox.

Galut: Diaspora, life outside of Israel.

Gan Eden: World to come.

Gedolei Torah: Giants of Torah.

Gedolim: Great ones.

Get: A divorce according to Jewish law.

Glatt: "Glatt is Yiddish for smooth, and in the context of *kashrut* it means that the lungs of the animal were smooth, without any adhesions that could potentially prohibit the animal as a *treifa*, an issue only applicable to animals, not fowl or non-meat products." (Rabbi Ari Z. Zivotofsky)

Goldberg, J.J.: Blunt leftist editor of the *Forward*, who has an encyclopedic knowledge of modern American Jewish history.

Goldman, Ari: Orthodox Jew, author of three books, former religion reporter for *The New York Times*. He's now an Associate Professor at the Columbia School of Journalism.

Goyim: Non-Jews.

Ha'aretz: Left-of-center Israeli paper with an online English edition.

Hadassah: Jewish women's philanthropy.

Hadassah **magazine:** Easy-to-read monthly.

Haftorah: Weekly reading from the Prophets.

Hakadosh Baruch Hu: God.

Halakha: Jewish law.

Halevi, Yossi Klein: Author of two compelling books as well as dozens of articles that probe the deepest parts of the Jewish soul.

Hashgacha: Kosher certification.

Havdalah: Saturday night ritual that marks the end of the Sabbath and the beginning of the new week.

Havurah: Hebrew for fellowship.

Hillel: (1) First Century Jewish sage. (2) A college campus organization.

Katz, Leslie: Wrote for the *Jewish Bulletin of Northern California* for more than a decade.

Hoenlein, Malcolm: Vice-Chairman of the Conference of Presidents of Major Jewish Organizations. He always wears a yarmulke and claims to be Orthodox.

j. the Jewish news weekly of Northern California: San Francisco's Jewish paper, one of America's top five Jewish weeklies.

Jerusalem Post: English-language daily.

Jerusalem Report: Jewry's premiere English-language biweekly.

Jewish Journal: Los Angeles weekly.

Jewish Telegraphic Agency: (JTA) Subsidized by the Federation, it seems to waste much of its resources providing stories already done better by the general news media.

Jewish Theological Seminary: Oldest American seminary for ordaining Conservative rabbis.

The Jewish Week: Establishment New York paper heavily subsidized by the Federation.

JSPS: Jewish Student Press Service. It was founded by Jewish antiwar activists in 1971.

Kaddish: Prayer said by mourners.

Kessler, E.J.: Best reporter on American Judaism in the 1990s.

Kiddish: Specifically, a blessing over wine on a holy day. Colloquially, the refreshments often served in synagogues after Sabbath prayers.

Klein, Amy: Managing editor of the *Jewish Journal*.

Klein, Marc: Editor of San Francisco's Jewish weekly.

Kipa: Head covering usually worn by men to show respect for God. In Yiddish, yarmulke.

Kishkes: Guts.

Kollel: A Talmudic academy for married men. They usually receive a stipend (about $40,000 a year at the LA Kollel).

Kosher: Fit. Permitted.

Lashon hara: Evil speech. Hurtful gossip. It's usually the first term to come to the lips of Jews protesting journalistic scrutiny.

Lenkiewicz, Lisa: Managing editor of *Connecticut Jewish Ledger*.

Lichtenstein, Gene: Founding editor of the *Jewish Journal*.

Lilith **magazine:** Feminist quarterly.

Lippman, Jerome: Editor/publisher of *Long Island Jewish World*, a writer's paper.

Macher: Big shot.

Maoz, Jason: Editor of the Orthodox weekly out of Brooklyn, *The Jewish Press*.

Mar'is ayim: Don't act in a way that could lead others to sin or to think that you have sinned.

Mark, Jonathan: Associate editor of *The Jewish Week*.

Menorah: Candlestick.

Meshuganah: Crazy.

Messiah: In traditional Jewish belief, one anointed by God to bring peace to this world.

Messianism: Belief that the Messiah has arrived.

Minyan: Prayer quorum. Traditionally has required ten men.

Mishegos: Craziness.

Moment magazine: Founded in 1975 by Elie Wiesel and Leonard Fein, *Moment* has the highest circulation of an independent Jewish periodical in North America.

Motzei Shabbos: After the Sabbath.

Muttur: Permitted.

Narischeit: Foolishness.

NCSY: Modern Orthodox high school group.

Neshama: Soul.

***New Jersey Jewish News*:** Plucky Federation weekly edited by Andrew Silow-Carroll.

Newhouse, Alana: Arts and Culture editor of the *Forward*.

Noahide Laws: Seven basic laws Judaism requires of Gentiles, such as don't murder, don't be cruel to animals, no incest or adultery or homosexuality, don't deny God's existence, don't worship idols, don't steal, and do set up courts of law.

Nudnik: Nut.

Oneg: Joy. Colloquially, snacks, treat, party in honor of the Sabbath.

OU: Orthodox Union. Provides kashrut certification and represents the modern end of the Orthodox spectrum.

Parsha: Torah section.

Parve: Neither meat nor milk.

Payos: Sidelocks.

Pikuah Nefesh: To save a life in Judaism, you are allowed to violate all its laws but three (against sexual immorality, public idol worship and murder).

Poskim: Deciders of Jewish law.

Protocols: www.protocols.blogspot.com.

Psak: Legal ruling.

Rachmones: Mercy.

Reform Judaism Magazine: Fun-to-read quarterly.

Rosh Hashanah: New year, ushers in ten days of repentance climaxed by Yom Kippur.

Rosenblatt, Gary: Mr. Jewish Journalism. Editor of *The Jewish Week*.

Rosh Yeshiva: Head of the yeshiva.

Rothenberg, Jennie: *Hadassah* magazine, *The Atlantic*, *Chicago Tribune*.

Sarna, Jonathan: Professor of American Jewish history at Brandeis.

Semicha: Rabbinic ordination.

Shabbat, Shabbos: The Sabbath, from sundown Friday night to sundown Saturday night. According to the Fourth Commandment, it is a holy day. No secular work is permitted.

Shafran, Rabbi Avi: Spokesman for Agudath Israel, a fervently Orthodox coalition.

Shochet: Religious Jewish slaughterer of kosher animals.

Ruby, Walter: *The Jerusalem Post, Forward, Village Voice, The Jewish Week.*

Shaliach: Emissary.

Shanda: Shame.

Shaygetz: Gentile man. Often used pejoratively.

Shiksa: Gentile woman. Literally means gentile abomination. Often used non-pejoratively by kindly folks such as myself.

Shiva: Mourning rituals for a death.

Shlichim: Emissaries.

Shochet: Ritual slaughterer.

Shtible: Tiny congregation. One room Chasidic synagogue.

Shul: Yiddish word for synagogue.

Shvartze: Yiddish word for black.

Strasser, Teresa: Controversial singles columnist.

Taharat hamishpacha: Laws of family purity.

Tallit: Prayer shawl.

Tefillin: Black boxes (containing Torah texts) and leather straps that religious Jews wrap around their arms and head every secular day, to literally bind God's word to themselves.

Tehillim: Psalms.

Teitelbaum, Sheldon: *The Los Angeles Times, The New York Times, Jerusalem Report, Premiere.*

Tikkun Olam: To repair the world.

Tobin, Jonathan: Editor of the *Jewish Exponent* out of Philadelphia, one of American Jewry's best weeklies.

Trafe: not kosher.

Tsures: Trouble.

Twersky, David: Veteran Jewish journalist, co-founder of the Jewish Student Press Service.

Tzadik: Righteous man.

UJ: University of Judaism.

UJC: United Jewish Communities represents 155 Jewish Federations and 400 Jewish communities across North America.

University of Judaism: A Los Angeles university and seminary affiliated with Conservative Judaism.

Weiss, Steven I.: Pioneering Orthodox blogger.

Wilkes, Paul: Roman Catholic author of *And They Shall Be My People: An American Rabbi and His Congregation*.

Yanover, Yori: Israeli stand-up comic turned American journalist.

Yarmulke: See Kipa.

Yasher Koach: Congratulations. More strength to you.

Yeshiva: Talmudic academy.

Yeshiva University (YU): Modern Orthodox university in New York.

Yom Kippur: Day of Atonement.

Yordim: Jewish immigrants from Israel.

Your Moral Leader: Luke Ford.

Yudelson, Larry: *Long Island Jewish World*. JTA.

Z"l: May his memory be a blessing.

Zaydeh: Grandfather.

Preface

May 2004

I make it a religious obligation to pray in shul several times a week, if not several times a day. But much of the time, I'm bored out of my mind. So, following the cues of my mentor Dennis Prager, I always take a book on Judaism with me to shul when the davening is going to last over an hour, and frequently finish several books a week while rattling off my prayers by rote.

A poor scribbler, I borrow most of my books from the Los Angeles Public Library. Once or twice a month, I check www.lapl.org and order in to my local branch all the new books on my religion.

On Friday night, January 3, 2003, I picked up Stephen Fried's *The New Rabbi: A Congregation Searches For Its Leader*. I was immediately mesmerized and I did not put the book down until I had finished it around midnight. It's the greatest work of Jewish journalism I've read.

I know that's not saying much. Jewish weeklies are often called "weaklies." Most American Jewish newspapers (the *Forward* is the big exception) suck. They're controlled by the Jewish Federation and their idea of reporting is printing safe news fed to them by their donors. I'd rather be sodomized by ten of the surliest inmates in the California Penal System than praise such crap.

As Fried writes in his prologue:

> When I was a kid, my parents had a Jewish bookshelf. On it were three kinds of books. There were, of course, prayer books and Bibles: some ours, some "accidentally" brought home from the synagogue and some-day to be returned. There were handsomely bound scholarly or historic books, most accepted as gifts and never read, except to look up something for Hebrew school. And then there were novels, like *The Chosen* and the *Tuesday the Rabbi* books and

even *Exodus*—the pulpit fiction of the day, where the struggle between religious life and real life was explored in language that anyone could understand: the human drama of the intersection of the divine and the secular, the battles between God and man and American culture, the searches for spiritual awakening and the perfect bar mitzvah caterer.

To broach these same subjects in non-fiction, especially the emotional and financial intricacies of American synagogue life, was considered dangerous, "bad for the Jews." And, to this day, that's still basically true. While Jewish bookshelves now teem with a new genre, spiritual self-help and how-to books, there is still very little journalism on the lives of American Jews as Jews. The scarcity is such that a recent book on American rabbis actually resorted to using many examples drawn from fiction—including quotes form fictitious rabbis—to illustrate points that everyone knows to be true, but almost no one dares to write down in narrative non-fiction.

On page 29, he writes:

My unusual request to observe the rabbi interviews and deliberations [at Har Zion] seems to have aroused equal parts of fascination and suspicion. Nobody says so, but it is clear that committee members are concerned about what an unchecked journalist would write about a Jewish institution. All the other volunteer work they do is covered solely by the local Jewish press [*Jewish Exponent*], which is published by the local chapter of "Federation." The Jewish Federation of Greater Philadelphia is part of a massive nationwide fund-raising network, a Jewish United Way, which takes great pains to make sure possible donors are never caused great pain by its Jewish media. Har Zion is one of the most charitable congregations in America, and its members are accustomed to being lionized for their good works. In fact, whenever the lay media cover anybody Jewish in anything but a congratulatory way, there is much tongue clicking.

As the *Columbia Journalism Review* put it in its January 2004 issue:

> Not only is much of the Jewish press in America lamely local—asking little more than the hard-hitting question, *Who was bar-mitzvahed this week?*—but, for the most part, their editorial line is filtered through one parochial prism: Is it good for the Jews? Bankrolled by local Jewish federations, the community weeklies lack the independence to report critically on the charities and institutions that make up Jewish organizational life. Dissent or even debate over Israeli policy is off limits.

June 17, 2004

Jewish journalist Allison Kaplan Sommer emails me:

> If you are really researching Jewish journalism, you should look up Larry Cohler, who now writes for the *New York Daily News*. He was the great "stir the pot" investigative Jewish journalist in the 1980s and 1990s—*Washington Jewish Week*, then *The Jewish Week* (NY), and some other places—who pissed off the establishment on a regular basis. Federation types used to turn green at the mention of his name.
>
> The basic problem in Jewish journalism, aside from Federation control, is making a living. People hit their 30s and need to support families. Therefore, they have to join the establishment papers—as editors if they want to make any kind of money, or move into better-paying work.
>
> Or, if they are excellent journalists, like Larry, they break out of the Jewish ghetto. Or, like the late Robert Friedman, they write about Jewish issues for the *Village Voice*, etc. I'm sure that someone like Steven [Weiss] is eventually going to stop being young and hungry and move on to the mainstream. He's already gotten stuff in *New York* magazine. Before him, Jeff Goldberg climbed from *The Jerusalem Post* to the *Forward*, to *New York*, to *New York Times Magazine* to *The New Yorker* (where he just wrote about...Israel).
>
> So you are left with few to no smart and talented people who, once they get the contacts and have the experience, are willing to work

indefinitely in the trenches of being a reporter for a Jewish paper. No Seymour Hershes. Hey, if you are willing to live in your hovel indefinitely, you're the man.

What's interesting is that there is occasionally some good critical journalism about the American Jewish community going on—by Israelis. In Hebrew, of course, though some of it is now translated into English by *Ha'aretz* and other places with Web sites. The advantage is that they are outsiders and not part of the community so they don't mind being critical. The downside is that they often aren't inside enough to get the stories, or to care deeply about them.

August 20, 2004

I tried and failed to get interviews with the following persons: Joseph Aaron, rabbi David Ackerman, rabbi Bradley Shavit Artson, Peter Beinart, David Biale, Wolfe Blitzer, Aaron Cohen, Vincent Coppola, rabbi Elliot Dorff, rabbi Hillel Goldberg, Jeffrey Goldberg, Eric Greenberg, Lawrence Grossman, Sue Grossman, Yossi Klein Halevi, Aron Hirt-Manheimer, Malcolm Hoenlein, Lisa Hostein, Phil Jacobs, Gershon Jacobson, Mark Joffe, Debbie Kalb, Marvin Kalb, Amy Klein, Neal Kozodoy, Jerome Lippman, Seth Lipsky, Arthur Maguida, rabbi Joel Meyers, David Myers, rabbi Perry Netter, Martin Peretz, Naomi Pfefferman, rabbi Perry Rank, Ira Rifkin, Jay Rosen, Jonathan Rosen, rabbi Jay Rosenbaum, Hershel Shanks, Ira Stoll, Teresa Strasser, rabbi Brian Walt, rabbi Arthur Waskow, Teresa Watanabe, Julie Weiner, Lauren Winner, Leon Wieseltier, rabbi Sheldon Zimmerman, and Nancy Zuckerbrod.

I've placed my part of the following interviews in bold. For longer versions of these discussions, see my Web site www.lukeford.net. You will also find there interviews with Dr. Edward Alexander, Sally Berkovic, James Besser, Matt Dorf, Eric Fingerhut, Samuel Freedman, Jonathan Friendly, Deborah Dash Moore, Gustav Niebuhr, and Ori Nir.

When my interviewees made questionable assertions about facts and persons, I checked their facts and reached out to the persons commented on for their response.

I've never attempted to write for any of the people I interviewed, nor for any Jewish publication ever (aside from two minor-league efforts in 1993, 1994).

In the course of writing this book, I did not socialize with any of my subjects (except Steven I. Weiss).

No animals were hurt in the production of this book, nor did I transgress any of laws of the Torah regarding forbidden relationships.

None of the leaders of the Jewish Telegraphic Agency (JTA) bothered to reply to my interview requests. It takes such journalistic giants as Mark J. Joffe (JTA executive editor and publisher), Lisa Hostein (JTA editor) and Michael S. Arnold (JTA managing editor), who demand accountability from others but flee from it themselves, to give us *Yesterday's News Tomorrow*.

1

Stephen Fried

Date: January 5, 2003

"I guess it's new for a journalist to go in and treat a congregation journalistically but this is what I do. I try to do investigative pieces for magazines and books in areas that haven't been subject to investigative reporting before. I found this in the fashion business. When I went in 15 years ago, they had never had a real journalist come in and write about them.

"People are happy if you do your homework. Much of what they are used to reading is opinion, very angered opinion at times. So they're happy to see someone come in and do the interviews, the fact-checking, and take the thing as seriously as they do.

"I would hope that my book will encourage people to start doing better journalism on religion. There's more to Catholicism than the priest-sex scandal and there's more to Judaism than arguments over Israel."

"Most Jewish newspapers make me want to hurl. They read like church bulletins."

"They're usually owned by the Federation and the Federation want to make sure that no one gets insulted and stops giving. I don't blame them. They are house-organs for a fundraising organization. They tend to ignore synagogue life because of the traditional church-state separation between Federation and synagogue. As to why there isn't more good journalism about Jews, I'm more likely to blame the journalists.

"I don't think there's a problem with coverage of Israel. The issue is does American-Jewish life get covered with the same kind of intensity. When you write about Jews, Jews really respond. People in the pharmaceutical business were nowhere near as welcoming when I wrote my last book about the pharmaceutical industry. Between the book fairs, the invitations to synagogues, the emails, it's been like one big bar mitzvah."

"No one has tried to clobber you with, 'You're a self-hating Jew'?"

"No. I haven't heard that once. I've heard complaints from rabbis who feel I was too open with their process. If anything, I could be accused of over-romanticizing synagogue life. 'Hey, when I go to synagogue, it's not this interesting and dramatic.' I've always had great passion for my religion. I've worked for self-hating Jews. There are a lot of self-hating Jews in the publishing business. Accusing people of being a self-hating Jew is more from the generation before me. I'm in my forties. People my age either opt out in a calm collected way or are still involved."

"It's impossible to do real journalism [without] those affected [crying], 'lashon hara.'"

"There will always be someone who will say that. One person's lashon hara is another person's good writing. There are some rabbis who are telling people not to read my book. Their definition of lashon hara is that I named the people who applied for a job."

"They will call lashon hara on any comment that makes someone look bad."

"A lot of that information came from the people it's about. They understood that it was in the context of someone trying to write a book to capture what was important about synagogue life and being an American Jew. I don't think anyone could mistake the context of this book. Even the people who've criticized it, have criticized certain parts, and then said otherwise they really liked it.

"The issues of lashon hara and journalism need to be discussed. If calling something lashon hara is keeping people from doing good journalism because they don't want to be criticized by their rabbis, I don't think that's good. Judaism believes in the truth and that there can be separate points of view. These things can be argued out. It's not a dogmatic religion.

"People are willing to print the most outrageous things, the most uninformed things, the most one-sided things, when it comes to Israel, but if somebody prints something truthful about their own congregation they go nuts.

"By dealing with the rabbis themselves, the leadership themselves, the search committee themselves, I did the best I could to make sure people would not say lashon hara. This information came to me on the record because the clergy at the synagogue cooperated, the Rabbinical Assembly cooperated, the leaders cooperated, some members of the search committee cooperated and because some members of the community thought this was an interesting project. Truthful information that comes journalistically to a writer who interviewed somebody on the record, I don't see how that's lashon hara.

"I would like to see people be less afraid of journalism. Journalism is a good thing. If it's unfair, it's not. A lot of things that happen in Jewish communities happen because of a lack of communication. Temple bulletins aren't great ways to communicate. Fiery emails aren't great ways to communicate. To me, every Jewish community should have a couple of good journalists that actually care and who are trying to figure out how to write about the most difficult sagas in the lives of these institutions. Everybody in town knows the stories anyway. They should at least know accurate versions of them because in many cases they are going to make decisions about their lives because of them.

"I've seen decisions in synagogue about rabbis, about the future of congregations, people withdrawing from congregations, when they didn't have the information to make the decision. Part of my goal for writing my book was to show how a congregation sticks together even through harsh difficult situations. This is a big intact powerful synagogue [Har Zion] that has survived many difficult times. That process is exciting. I think these institutions can take it. You're writing about stuff that they are already dealing with. The question is—if it's known to the public, will it be worse? In some cases yes, in some cases no. I look forward to the day when there's a more active Jewish press."

"Have any of the principle characters in the book told you that they regret talking to you?"

"No, although I can't say I've spoken to all of them. Whenever you are involved in a big journalistic project, the response of the sources and subjects changes over time. The year before my father died, I had written a long piece about him and about a fishing trip my brothers and I had taken with him. It came out and everybody loved it and he hated it because it read like his eulogy. He later came to like it. Sadly, it ended up being used at his eulogy. When someone writes about you in a long-form piece, your reaction to it changes over time."

"Rabbi Moshe Tutnauer? You called him a flake and an egotist."

"I hear from him a lot. He liked the book. We had several long email discussions about what egotism and flakery meant. Occasionally he will sign his emails to me, 'Love, the flakey egotist Moshe.' He's a smart funny guy and has been nothing but supportive. I only wish that we could be in the same city so we could play basketball.

"People are fascinated by the process of you turning them into a character in a book. A lot of these are public people who already see themselves as characters in books, they just assumed they would be their own books. You have people who are used to creating a certain world around themselves. Anything you interpret differently than they do they will make a big deal out of.

"I do see rabbis as heroic. I see the work of the synagogue as heroic. If I'm guilty of elevating the responsibilities of the synagogue president, cantor or rabbi, that's ok. This book romanticizes what clergy do. It makes it seem more important than what these people feel in their day-to-day lives."

"Rabbi Ackerman?"

"I have not spoken to him. I don't think he's all that thrilled. He did do the fact-checking for the book and everything that is in there about him, he verified. There are a couple of things he asked me to take out of the book and I did. People have told me he's upset. I heard an interesting story from the guy who is now the president of Rabbi Ackerman's synagogue. He came to one of my readings and said Rabbi Ackerman was upset with the book and that Rabbi Ackerman suggested to people that they shouldn't read it. The president told me, 'I've been telling people they should read it. I've told them that if they buy the book and they don't like it, I will buy it back from them. Fifteen members of the congregation have taken me up on my offer and no one has asked for their money back.'

"The things that the rabbi is going to be upset about in this book are inside-baseball sorts of things. I accurately portray a difficult point in his life. He wanted this job and ended up turning it down because he had to choose between his family and his career."

"Rabbi Joel Meyers, head of the Rabbinical Assembly [the Conservative rabbis union]?"

"I haven't spoken to him. I saw him respond in the *Forward*."

"Yeah, he said he'd heard from 40–50 colleagues, all with negative things to say [about the book]."

"I found that hard to believe because I know of a dozen people who have spoken to him with positive things to say. Look, a book like this is going to cause unrest in the Rabbinical Assembly for one big reason—because it accurately mirrors just how hard it is to be a rabbi. I swear that being a rabbi is the hardest job in America."

"When I read the *Forward* article about the complaints by rabbis about your book, I was furious. It represented how these guys are so protected in Jewish journalism generally that this is the first time they've had to deal with any real journalism. They've reacted angrily because for the first time they've been treated as the public figures that they are and they can't control their own image."

"Rabbis are public figures. A better conversation I haven't seen raised is whether a sanctuary service is open to the public."

"Of course it is."

"I think it is too but I would've been interested to see somebody raise the question of whether covering a bar mitzvah is cool.

"I think it depends on your journalistic ethics. If you go into a bar mitzvah and write about the excess of it without any real knowledge of what is going on, that's bad. I've read many stories over the years about congregations and bar mitzvahs that are written by people who really are self-hating Jews who go there and don't even know the people but are so upset because of the clothes and the cost of the catering. I don't care how much money people have. All the money in the world didn't help this congregation have an easier time picking a rabbi. And all the money in the world doesn't help you lead a more spiritual life. All the money in the world doesn't keep your dad from dying."

"You haven't experienced a backlash of people saying, 'Oooh, I'm scared to have you here at my bar mitzvah.'"

"I've lived my whole life with a certain number of people, just before saying something to me, saying, 'Oh geez, I don't know if I want to say that because I might see it in print somewhere,' starting with my mother. I've had more people say to me, 'Why don't you come write a book about my congregation?' than people say, 'Better not say that.'

"I try to make people understand when I'm working. If I'm going to write about something, I will go back to the person and say, 'Look, this happened in casual conversation but I want to write about it. How do you feel about that?' It rarely happens with me that people I interviewed step forward and say I did the wrong thing. I'm not somebody who sneaks around. I'm interested in doing the sort of projects that people cooperate with because you get a depth that you can't get any other way."

"Your book reminded me of *And They Shall Be My People* by Paul Wilkes. [Wilkes spent one year with Jay Rosenbaum, a Conservative rabbi.]"

"Ok."

"Didn't you see a lot of similarities?"

"Not really, because the guy who wrote it wasn't Jewish. To me, the books are only similar because they're both set in a synagogue. He came to that book because he's a writer about religion and this was his next religion to write about. I came to this book because my dad died and I began rediscovering my own religion and saw this as a way of doing journalism on that. The intents of the books are totally different."

"What's your critique of his book?"

"That he picked a congregation where not much happened. And because he wasn't Jewish, there were parts of the book that struck me as 'Margaret Mead among the Jews.'

"He was an outsider observing the mores, an anthropological study. He was only interested in writing a book about the life of a synagogue. A lot of my book is based on my own life and search as a Jew and my relationships with the people involved. They were different because I was a Jew coming back after mourning. A Christian journalist from *The New Yorker* is going to have a different way of doing things. I imagine he would be more likely to write a book like mine about his own religion.

"I remember the controversies about his book. People were amazed that his wife had spoken out so boldly."

"She was so bitter about the congregation."

"[Paul Wilkes] is a religion writer and I'm not. I had different goals than he did. But if people read my book and want to know more about synagogue life, they would be well-served by reading his book or *Kaddish* [by Leon Wieseltier]."

"I found *Kaddish* impenetrable. He's a terrible writer."

"I don't think he's a terrible writer. There are things in it that are wonderful and things in it that are difficult but I think it is an important book. I'd be lying if I said I read every word of it. His dad died about a month after mine. We started working on our projects about the same time. I was fascinated to see somebody do an exploration of Judaism in the aftermath of their father's death. I found it interesting to see where his mind went during minyan compared to where my mind went during minyan. Both these books grew out of the time you have during minyan thinking about things. He's read a lot more stuff than me and I've interviewed a lot more people than him."

"What did you think of Samuel Freedman's book *Jew vs. Jew*?"

"His book about the black church, *Upon This Rock*, is closer to the kind of project I did. Sam was the first person to agree to blurb my book. I'm teaching at Columbia now in part because of his support. Freedman blazed the trail for real journalism about Judaism and with *Upon This Rock* encouraged journalism about other religious organizations."

"**Did anyone give you a hard time on these seven words on page 93? 'In Judaism, belief in God is optional...'**"

"Those seven words have had more discussion than any other seven words in the book."

"**I about had a heart attack when I read that.**"

"I saw a sermon posted from an Anglican church last week in which those words were a jumping off point for his sermon. I've seen letters to the editor about those words.

"Most non-Jews don't understand that the concept of wrestling with belief in God is an important part of Judaism and you don't get excommunicated because you admit that you do it. Jews take that for granted. Most Christians would find that to be heresy.

"I came back to practicing Judaism when my dad died and I just happened to come to the right synagogue where I liked the rabbis, where I could ask stupid questions and nobody said that's a stupid question. I could've easily ended up at another synagogue where that was not the case. If I had only gone to that Orthodox minyan I wrote about...The guy who ran that minyan was typically Orthodox, judgmental. I remember getting into a fight with him once about who was a Jew. He didn't believe that people converted by Conservative rabbis were Jewish. He represented what I hate about Judaism or any religion—people telling other people how to be religious."

* * *

When I ask Conservative rabbis about Stephen Fried's book, they look like they want to cry.

I want to discuss *The New Rabbi* and its implications for Jewish journalism with leaders of the Conservative movement but they've all refused my interview requests.

Rabbi Jay Rosenbaum replies: "Dear Luke, I appreciate your asking for my opinion, but I'm regretfully have to decline. I learned quite a lot from working with Paul [Wilkes] and from the publication of the book. But, there were also some hard feelings created that took a long time to heal. Time to move on."

In their critical responses to the book, in their claims that release forms needed to be signed to permit the author to reveal embarrassing information, Fried's rabbinic critics reveal their own willful ignorance about journalism (which most rabbis seem to consume in enormous amounts). They expect to have the sole right to shape their own public image.

In an otherwise complimentary review, Rabbi Gerald L. Zelizer of Conservative congregation Neve Shalom, in Metuchen, New Jersey, writes in the December 30, 2002 *Jerusalem Report*:

> Fried's attempt to tell this story might have made an important contribution to the literature about rabbis and congregations. Unfortunately, his book is so encumbered by raw gossip and the unnecessary disclosure of confidential details about Wolpe's possible successors and colleagues, that the author sabotages his worthwhile objectives.
>
> Was it necessary, for example, to use the name of one leading candidate, who declined the job because Har Zion brought painful reminders to his wife of her late father's congregation, which treated her mother callously after her father's sudden death? What was gained by naming another rabbi dismissed from his congregation, who began a period of study and reflection, in order to be a more effective pulpit presenter—and who never even applied for the Har Zion position? Or another who left a large West Coast synagogue because he became involved with a congregant while still married to his estranged wife? (None of these rabbis signed waivers to allow the publication of this confidential information, all say they were embarrassed, and one even objected to the author.)
>
> In contrast, when describing the bar mitzvah of the child of a synagogue macher, an event that was sullied by an ugly public divorce, Fried utilizes pseudonyms in order to protect reputations. Why wasn't a similar courtesy extended to the many rabbis whom he depicted? This degree of raw tale-bearing would have been better placed in the gossip columns of the *New York Post* or *Yediot Aharonot*.

An informed observer tells me, "It's my hunch that many of the rabbis in Fried's book didn't understand they were dealing with an investigative journalist who was going to paint a warts-and-all portrait of them. They were used to softball Jewish press. It became confusing for them because they came to see Fried as a friend more than a journalist."

January 29, 2003

I meet Stephen at Sinai Temple in Westwood. He chews gum and doesn't wear a yarmulke until going on stage.

Rabbi David Wolpe opens the dialogue. "Before coming here, I was at a shiva house where I met a rabbi who said I could quote him by name, [University of Judaism rosh yeshiva] Brad Artson. I said to him, 'What should I ask Steve Fried?' [Rabbi Artson replied] 'If you believed in a God and a Final Judgment, would you have written the book the same way?'"

Laughter.

Stephen, taken aback: "Wow. That's the first question? When people are upset about a book and they come to talk to you, they expect that the point you brought up is one you haven't thought of. It doesn't occur to them that you might have thought of it, carefully considered it, and still made the same decision. I've been doing [journalism] for 20 years. I spent four years researching the book and I had a lot of time to think about what I could and couldn't do. I think that some of the people upset with the book are under the impression that this was done off the top of the head. It wasn't.

"I have this deep belief that a lot of things happen in life because people communicate badly. Every family would like a guy like me to come in and ask all the questions that they never got to ask so they can stop being upset about things. I started my career doing an investigative piece about a series of teenage suicides in a small town where the parents still didn't know anything about what their kids had gone through. It became my job to recreate the kids' lives and figure out what had gone wrong."

David: "My father said he personally had no complaints but had he known the synagogue was going to fall apart, 'I wouldn't have agreed [to cooperate with Fried] because it is painful for me to see this place fall apart and have it all documented so that everybody could read it.'"

Stephen: "One of the complaints that people have made is that rabbis should be different from everybody else who is hired in America. This is no different journalistically than covering who will be the next school board president or the next president of a major corporation. The process has value.

"One of the things the rabbis are claiming is baloney—that the search committees are private. Many synagogues put the pictures of the rabbi candidates in the bulletin. They come in and speak.

"I tried to be careful to deal with rabbis by the rules they lived by. I wasn't trying to trick rabbis into thinking I wasn't a journalist. When I talked to them, I always had a tape recorder or laptop. I was never trying to lull anybody into thinking I was just their pal and wasn't going to write a book.

"Some of [the rabbis] have had revisionist moments about whether they talked to me. I've heard people who [gave me] things to put in the book and then I hear from their colleagues that they are mad that it is in there. I don't blame them for that. It is a weird thing to be a character in a book."

David: "For anybody who has ever been quoted on anything, your words on a page always feel different from the words coming out of your mouth, so there's an initial shock, particularly for people who have not seen themselves quoted before."

Stephen: "Part of the problem here is that the Jewish press ignores rabbis except to write your commentaries."

David: "There's no reporting on them."

Stephen: "Because synagogue life is ignored by the Jewish press, rabbis are not used to the normal give and take that anybody else would have. Every rabbi I know is a voracious reader of the media. And when it comes to Israel, they are happy to see this level of journalism pushed to the Nth degree. I've had rabbis write that I needed their permission to print true things about them. Even public things about them, such as what their previous jobs were. This is a fantasy.

"One of the rabbis who has been the most voracious attacker of my book, who wrote a letter to one of the major Jewish newspapers that reading the book was immoral, is one of the people I took something out that he begged me to take out."

David: "There's a human desire to have your activities known, but not in a bad way. I read through the book. I thought it was fine. Yet, if you think that everything that was negative about [Wolpe's family] didn't strike me with a special force…

"The thing I resent most about the book is nothing that is in the book but it makes people come up to me and put their arm on their shoulder and say, 'Now I understand you.' And I just think, 'What page are they thinking of?'"

Stephen: "The thirst for information about the rabbi is unbelievable."

A few weeks later, I ask Conservative rabbi Perry Netter about *The New Rabbi*.

"I couldn't finish it," he says. "I read the part about my friend rabbi Rank and it was too painful."

He looks like he's about to cry. I ask him about *And They Shall Be My People*. He says it made him want to go home, take a nice warm bath, and open up a vein.

He says he will talk to me further about these matters another time. I should call him.

I call him and leave a message. No response. I write him. No response.

An assistant rabbi at Sinai Temple tells me *The New Rabbi* is filled with lashon hara but *And They Shall Be My People* was worse.

2

Paul Wilkes

Date: January 6, 2003

According to *Booklist*: "Wilkes, an award-winning writer and a Catholic, spent one year with Jay Rosenbaum, the 42-year-old rabbi of Congregation Beth Israel, a Conservative synagogue in an upper-middle-class community in Worcester, Massachusetts. Wilkes followed Rabbi Rosenbaum on his daily rounds—leading the services, performing weddings and conducting funerals, teaching children, and counseling couples. Wilkes interviewed the rabbi, the rabbi's wife, and some of the synagogue members. The rabbi had been at Beth Israel for six years, had started many new programs, and had begun to reverse the demographic trend, attracting younger families into what had been an aging synagogue. But he wanted his people to live more intensely Jewish lives."

"Stephen didn't see the resemblance with your book. You were different because you weren't Jewish."

"That did have something to do with some of the reception to the book. I gave a talk at the Jewish Theological Seminary after it came out and I was afforded 12-minutes at a lunch hour, while everyone was opening their brown bag lunches. I don't think it was taken kindly that I wasn't Jewish.

"It was taken as if I were an outsider taking potshots at Jewish life and of course that's not what I do. I try to do be as good as journalist as I can be and tell the story. I'm Roman Catholic and I write a lot about the Catholic Church. I just had a piece in *The New Yorker* a couple of months ago about a parish priest in Boston. It was a warts and all portrait. I'm critical of my own church as well as Judaism, if there's something to be critical about. Yes, I think there was resentment that a non-Jew would write about Jews.

"Within the Jewish community in America, there's always that feeling that a slight or epithet is [an example of anti-Semitism]. There's a wariness of the non-Jew, that you won't understand what we go through. You as a journalist and I as a journalist realize that if you are open to the experience, you can indeed come into the center of a story. I virtually lived as a Jew for a year. I wore a kipa all the time when I was with the rabbi. I went to Israel with him. I did a lot of reading on it. By the end of the year, I knew more about Judaism than 95% of my Jewish friends. Just by being there, not because I'm so smart."

"Were you invited by other Jewish organizations?"

"I gave a lot of talks after the book came out. I was certainly not invited to the rabbinical convention, the one that I wrote about."

"They didn't take kindly to your comments?"

"I don't think so. It was a case of we don't want to show anything untoward, unsavory or unpleasant.

"A funny thing happened at the end of the book. The *Worcester Telegram* did a big story on it and said it's amazing that this rabbi seems so wonderful yet at the end of the book the synagogue was not going to give him a raise. I guess that's in the epilogue. Then they gave him a big raise and a new contract. I don't think they really appreciated who they had until he became more of a public figure. He just got a congregation in Seattle [Herzl Ner Tamid]. His wife, a daughter of [Holocaust] survivors, always wanted to get back there. That book, if they ever wanted to do any investigation on a rabbi, here it is. Yet they hired him. That's a proof of something."

"He comes across well in the book."

"I think so."

"Though with some illusions about his ability to get people to become observant. Few Conservative Jews are observant of Jewish law."

"You're always looking for those moments in a story that give you insight. I think the whole thing over in Israel where his wife said, 'Let's make aliyah,' and he says no. In Israel they could be 110% Jewish, he says no. I always thought of that as a corollary to his people also saying, 'Yeah, I like the idea of it but I don't think so.'"

"What was the other fallout for him and his wife? His wife was quite bitter about the community."

"She's probably still angry about the book. She felt too exposed by it. Her weight problem. She was gaining weight and couldn't shop in the stores.

"Before the book came out, I gave the galleys to the rabbi. I told him, 'I don't want any corrections. I don't want any comments. You're not going to rewrite the book. Is it accurate? That's all I want to know. Do I have the Jewish stuff right?' He read the book before it was published so I felt perfectly ok about it."

"How did he react to the book?"

"I think he probably appreciated that he had his 15-minutes of fame, that he was a celebrity. I think he's doing a good job. I don't think he likes close scrutiny. Not too many people do. When he heard the reaction of other people to it, he probably thought, 'Oh boy, what did I do here?'"

"I take it you guys don't stay in touch."

"I've written 20 books. I've written about a lot of people. Some like me and some don't like me. Most feel fairly treated by me. We talked a couple of times since then. It wasn't like we were the best of buddies. I don't think we were the best of buddies during the book. It's always been cordial. I was asked to give some talks at Barnard College at a Jewish studies course. The rabbi never wanted to share a stage with me. That never happened."

"Have you stayed in touch with anyone from the book?"

"No."

"Anyone in the book get angry at you afterwards?"

"Yeah. The president of the congregation felt like I wasn't fair to him. To tell you the truth, I was probably more charitable than I needed to be. I didn't put everything in there that I knew. I didn't put in all the comments that his wife made about the congregation. If it didn't make sense for the story, I didn't put it in for the prurient interest of it. You're a journalist, you know. The people who are basically good people are going to come out ok and the people who are schmucks are going to come out like schmucks.

"Congregations tend to be tough on their rabbis and he needs to be his own man. The rebbetzin has to be her own woman or else they will eat you alive. The politics of it are tough. They are tougher in synagogues than in Catholic churches where guys are appointed by their bishop. In many Protestant positions, they are appointed also. I think it is much tougher in synagogues, and, sadly, not attractively so. I felt strongly that what they put [rabbis] through is not humane. It's not religious. It's not kosher to do that to somebody as if it's a business deal. This is a spiritual leader you're trying to find."

"Stephen Fried begins his book by deploring the low state of journalism in Jewish affairs. There's little narrative journalism of American Jews."

"That's exactly why my little venture was not warmly received."

"American Jewish journalism is so boring."

"I'm not a student of it. I stumbled into my book. You always stand the chance, especially as a non-Jew, of being considered anti-Semitic. I won't even look at that. It's not the way that I am. I'm going to call them the way that I see them with charity. I'm also Catholic. I'm a religious person. I'm not going to beat someone up just for a great anecdote in the book. If it doesn't make any sense, I'm not going to use it. If it does make sense, I have to."

"In the process of writing the book, did anyone try to make it difficult for you because you weren't Jewish?"

"No. I always felt like an outsider. Not only didn't I know the tradition, it wasn't in my bones like Catholicism is. People were fascinated that someone was doing a book. Nobody knows what it's going to be when you're doing it. When you're around and become like wallpaper, you become so ordinary that they don't realize that eventually there's going to be a book come out of it.

"I'm an easy-going guy. I like people and people sometimes like me. I didn't have any conflicts."

"I couldn't find any negative reviews of your book. Were there any?"

"Oh, praise God, I don't even know. I don't even read them. You've got to keep going. This book followed a book I wrote on a Catholic priest called *In Mysterious Ways*. That priest didn't even read the entire book I wrote on him. That's how much he cared about it. I'm sure Rabbi Rosenbaum read every word. I'm of the first category. I do the work and let other people say what they want to say."

"Are rabbis public figures and should they be subjected to the same level of scrutiny as leaders in other fields?"

"No, I don't think they are public figures. They're moral leaders. They're moral stature and moral vision should certainly be taken into account but they're not politicians where you have to scrutinize everything about them. They should stand for something. There's a New Testament quotation about if salt loses its flavor, what use is it? The same is true of a rabbi. God knows that many become salt-free. There's no bite anymore because they are afraid of alienating anyone, of making anyone angry. That's a pitiful state when that happens.

"I just gave talk to a group of priests in Minnesota. They were talking about their bishop. I said, 'Guys, if your bishop isn't calling you on the carpet at least once a year, you're not doing your job. You should be pushing the envelope.' The rabbi is not just a branch manager. You have to have a point of view, and sometimes it is not the point of view of your congregation. The perfect example is the craziness of this war that we're thinking of going into. I think this is a perfect time for someone to stand up and say, 'This is not something we should be doing.'"

"How did your wife like the book?"

"Her father is Jewish. She felt a little amazed that a Gentile could write about it. Your wife is always your biggest critic. She went to Israel with me. A lot of my Jewish friends read it and I didn't hear of any inaccuracies.

"That book started off as a profile for *The New Yorker*. Then Tina Brown came to town, taking over for Bob Gottlieb. Tina Brown was not interested in Conservative rabbis in Worcester, Massachusetts, so it never became a *New Yorker* profile and went right into being a book."

"Where are you on the Catholic spectrum?"

"Liberal is a bad word these days, so I would consider myself a progressive Catholic. I take Holy Communion at the hospital each Thursday here in Wilmington, North Carolina. I tithe. My boys went to Catholic grade school.

"I think Modern Orthodoxy has a great appeal to me. The black hats I don't feel the same way [towards]. Within certain parts of the Jewish community there's that exclusivity element, the 'I am and you're not.' I find that unattractive. I don't think anybody has the corner on the God market. We all ought to walk humbly before our God and not say we have the way and nobody else does.

"If I were not a Catholic, I would probably be a Jew. I would not be a Presbyterian or a Baptist. I think these are authentic substantial traditions that give you something to chew on and live by. The branch of Judaism that I found made the most sense was Mordecai Kaplan's Reconstructionist movement. While a small movement, it was spiritual and intelligent and the practice runs a range."

"What are your thoughts on the Conservative movement?"

"They say it's an Orthodox rabbi leading a Reform congregation. But I saw attractive elements in his synagogue in Worcester. People who were *Shomer Shabbos* (guardians of the Sabbath), living the righteous life, in the most simple and Godly ways."

"I've found many rabbis, like teachers and professors, are control freaks. They don't react well when they're not controlling their own image."

"I think you're exactly right. When I was at the Jewish Theological Seminary, they were talking about the old days when 'Our Torah scholars are going to be trained like scholars at Harvard.' This guy said, 'We trained generations of rabbis who loved Judaism and hated Jews.'

"That's a big part of it. Everybody loves being up on the bima [pulpit]. Everybody loves to be a center of attention at a bar mitzvah. But to get into the nitty gritty of people's lives. As Dostoevsky said, 'Love in practice is a harsh and dreadful thing.' Judaism in practice is a harsh and dreadful thing. It's very difficult. It's wonderful when you read about it but when you live it...... I'm not talking about kashrut [dietary laws]. I'm talking about living in community, being supportive of other people and their pilgrimage in life. That's the part that a lot of rabbis don't do as well."

"I think that's a particular weakness with JTS and its emphasis on scholarship and PhDs."

"If you want scholars, that's fine but if you want rabbis. To train a balanced person who has a home life and a sense of humor, who knows Torah but also can walk and breathe and live and isn't, as many rabbis were, these green hothouse plants."

3

Jonathan Tobin

Date: January 7, 2003

Philadelphia *Jewish Exponent* editor Jonathan Tobin writes in the August 7, 2002 edition of his newspaper about *The New Rabbi*:

> Who, for heaven's sake, would want to read such a book?
>
> There is plenty of lashon hara ("gossip") here, as some of the players in the transition took Fried into their confidence and dished as much dirt as they could. But none of it is juicy enough to fill a script of even the tamest of television soap operas.
>
> It is no slight to the members of Har Zion to relate that all of this blabbing to Fried creates a narrative that is less than scintillating. The life of their synagogue—and their rabbis—is just far too wholesome to justify this much investigation. And the work of the rabbinic-search committee and its conflict with the Conservative movement's Rabbinic Assembly is so intensely boring that it is almost fascinating to see how Fried puffs it all up into a 350-page book.
>
> The author fills the empty spaces in between the gripping accounts of the "Bat Mitzvah gone bad," the "High Holiday seating chart" and the low-intensity drama of rabbinic job interviews with himself.

"How is the book being received in your circles?"

"It's often the case when something has been puffed into a controversial incident, the farther you get away from it, the more fascinating it seems. Rabbinic turnover is a common thing. What was amazing about the book to me is that it takes a subject that is so boring that it is almost fascinating.

"It was promoted heavily in the Philadelphia region. His magazine [*Philadelphia*] featured it and everybody saw that. Certainly people at the synagogue weren't too thrilled. As is usually the case, the people who blabbed the most felt different once their quotes were in print."

"Is it the talking thing in Philadelphia Jewish life?"

Jonathan laughs. "Oh no. I'm sure that is Steve Fried's dearest wish. The book is what it is. I didn't get much negative feedback about what I wrote except from him and his publisher. I'm not in the business of feuds and nonsense.

"The book publishing industry is not that different from the rest of the world. If you get a major publisher behind you and have an air of seriousness and good intention, you're not likely to get anybody challenging it. There is reluctance in this world to call a bad book a bad book."

"And this is a bad book?"

"In my opinion, it is. I had many rabbis come to me and say, 'You hit that one on the nail.' They were unimpressed as well. If he gets it into paperback, there's subsequent news there. I wouldn't blame Steve Fried but a rabbi he admired and I do as well, Rabbi [Jacob] Herber's [situation] was certainly exacerbated by all the blabbing in that book and the focus it put on him."

"Where is Rabbi Herber today?"

"He's out of a job."

"You guys didn't write about it except in the review of the book."

"We will when do the round-up of all the rabbis coming and going, as we normally do as an annual thing. You want to turn that into hot stuff? I could give you six other synagogues in our region where there is rabbinic turnover. For the little community that's involved, it's a big deal. For the Jewish community as a whole, all right, let us know who's coming and who's going. Is that hot news? It's a monograph."

"Is this book bad for the Jews?"

"Only if they were forced to read it. Please don't inflate this into anything beyond what it is. It's a book. It's more about Steve Fried than it is about anything else. If you're really bowled over by his air of seriousness, then..."

"All the other reviewers were bowled over. What do you think of them?"

Tobin laughs. "I think they're wrong. Listen, I hope Steve Fried does well with it. I dare say it will probably be on the remainder shelves inside of a year. Frankly, his literary agent must be like the guy who got [baseball player] Alex Rodriguez $252 million if he got an advance to do a book about rabbinic turnover."

"It's not bad for the Jews. It's just a boring book."

"He presents in the prologue that his book fills a gaping hole in narrative Jewish journalism and implicitly you and your peers are responsible for this."

Tobin laughs. "Oh gosh. Then I guess he's performed a great service for the Jewish people. If he believes that, then fine. He's a Jewish hero. I'm not going to add to anything I say. I'm not going to detract from anything I wrote."

"Isn't there a point here? That there's a lack of hard-hitting journalism in Jewish papers?"

"There are many arguments about the things we cover and don't cover. I'll stand our newspaper up against any of the local alternatives. I'm not worried about the comparison. Jewish newspapers have been called 'weaklies,' for good reason, but obsessing over the minutiae of the Conservative movement's rabbinic selection committees is not one of our really great gaps. We've got other things. There are big issues in the Jewish community. Steve trips over them occasionally in the course of that book. Just enough to let us know that he knows something about it but not enough to do any good. I obviously don't think this is one of the great earthshaking issues that Jewish journalism has flubbed."

"I've got interviews coming up with Ari Goldman and Samuel Freedman."

Tobin laughs. "Oh good, they did the blurbs on the back [only Freedman did, though both are friends with Fried]. I wonder what they think."

"That's why you're such a find. You're the only one…"

"I wrote the piece. I don't want to get into any controversy. If Steve wants to milk it into something else to get somebody to buy the book, good for him."

"I found the book absorbing. I do find most Jewish newspapers boring."

"So do I and I see more of them than you do."

"I do think there needs to be harder-hitting Jewish journalism. I thought Seth Lipsky did a good job with the *Forward*."

"But what does that have to do with this book? It's hard-hitting Jewish journalism? Come on. I've got to run. You can call me tomorrow."

January 8, 2003

"What do you think is the state of Jewish journalism in America today?"

"If you took a historical perspective on where Jewish journalism was 20 years ago compared to where it is now, it's much improved. There are a number of fairly good papers, say ten to twelve, around the country that are worth reading. I don't want to be quoted as to which ones. There are more good people in Jewish journalism. The glass is half full. Are there shortcomings? Sure. It's harder to get good people into Jewish journalism.

"There are still constraints on the Jewish press, whether they are 'independent' or owned by Federations, to pull their punches on some issues. In the case of papers owned by the Federation, you don't report on your own publishers. That's true of Jewish papers and it's true of secular papers. Nobody at the *New York Post* reports about News Corp. Nobody at *The Philadelphia Inquirer* reports aggressively on Knight Ridder. It's more problematic with Jewish papers because Federations plays a large role in Jewish life. There's an expectation of a portion of our audience that is not used to seeing tough news coverage. I can give you plenty of examples from our own case where we've done stories on embezzlements in synagogues and crimes and people don't want to see that. People love to see negative news about somebody else, not themselves."

"Are you about the only non-liberal editing a Jewish paper?"

"No. Gary Rosenblatt at *The Jewish Week* in New York is not your garden-variety liberal. He doesn't stake out consistent positions ideologically. He's there in the center and you never know where he is going to come down. Most Jewish journalists are left-wing. Most journalists are left-wing. Certainly journalists in Israel are almost uniformly hard left-wing. That doesn't bother me and it doesn't make me feel like I've got a great niche. I lost my credentials as a real right-winger any number of times because I've taken stands on issues they disagree with. I've taken shots at the Right consistently when I think they're wrong. More consistently then when my colleagues on the Left take shots at the Left."

"Are you told what you can write about and not write about?"

"No. My greatest worry when I first came here to Philadelphia in 1998 [from] the *Connecticut Jewish Ledger* [was] editorial independence. Would there be pressure about my columns? Nothing has happened. My board hasn't hassled me one bit about that. They got a known quantity when they hired me and I've delivered what I promised. When it comes to covering some news stories, you get pressure like any newspaper gets pressure. Early in my tenure, when there was a different person running the Federation, we locked horns a couple of times. That isn't happening now.

"The people running the Jewish Federation in Philadelphia have bigger worries than the newspaper. They'd happily get out of the newspaper business if they could. Being a publisher involves different responsibilities than being a fundraiser. They're interested in narischeit (foolishness). They're interested in getting somebody's picture in the paper and making sure in the Federation section that all their people get proper credit.

"Where are you on the religious spectrum?"

"I am a lifelong member of the Conservative movement. Unlike most members of the Conservative movement, I actually believe in Conservative Judaism."

"Do you believe in God?"

Tobin, surprised: "Do I believe in God? I have to tell you. I've been interviewed many times. This is the first time anyone has ever asked me if I believe in God. That's a very unJewish unAmerican thing to do because we never talk about God. Do I believe in God? Yes, I believe in God. We get a paper out every week. How can I not believe in God?"

"Ari Goldman said that a major reason he left *The New York Times* as the religion writer was that he got so much tsures in shul from everyone coming over to him and telling him what to write and what not to write. Do you get a lot of tsures?"

"Those of us in print journalism, as my wife who is a lawyer would explain, we are limited-use public figures, under the *Times vs. Sullivan* libel laws as to who's a public figure and who's not. We're not television personalities. We don't get stopped at supermarkets wherever we go for autographs but to our reading public, we're a big deal. My picture appears in the paper every week with my column. For the 60,000 homes that get this paper, I got into their house every week and they feel entitled to call me by my first name and to let me know what they think wherever they are, whether it's in shul or at a New Year's Eve party or walking the dog.

"If you work for the *New York Times*, the Jewish community has serious issues about *The Times*...... The history of *The New York Times* and the Jews, people are very sensitive. It's a powerful institution. Being the religion writer at *The New York Times* is like being the White House liaison to the Jewish community. Utterly thankless job. You don't get to make policy but you get all the flak."

"Do you ever not write things because you don't want the tsures, even though you believe they are true and important?"

"Not really. There are certain sacred cows in the Jewish community. I'm not even going to tell you...... Those of us who work in the Jewish community know what they are and even if we respect and believe in them ourselves, we're sick of them. Sometimes we need a Shabbat from the Jews. I'm fortunate that I get to say what I believe. I write about 50-columns a year. Sooner or later, you say everything.

"I used to say that one of the shibboleths that I would never take on was the issue of [anti-Semitic 19th Century German composer] Wagner and the Jewish community. I always said that would be my last column in Jewish journalism to take on some of the inconsistencies in the way we view that issue. But I wound up doing that one anyway and maybe nobody noticed. The earth did not come down on me."

"What did you think of *And They Shall Be My People*?"

"I thought that it was interesting but not *War and Peace*. It was a monograph. There's a tendency in the Jewish community to god-up rabbis. Sportswriters like to say about godding-up athletes, turning them into gods. There's a portion of the Jewish community that will be so flattered by any book that talks about the minutiae of Jewish life that they'll think it's great whether it is good or not."

"He got a lot of negative feedback from Jews who did thought it was chutzpahdik of him a goy to write in detail about Jewish life."

"I don't think that's a serious complaint. Some of the best writing on Jewish history has been by non-Jewish historians and some of the worst has been done by Jews. The same is true of journalism."

"A lot of people at the Rabbinical Assembly were unhappy with the book."

"That's their union [of Conservative rabbis]. Interested parties are always looking to see how they look in the book. They might have felt that he was not sufficiently respectful of them.

"The best quote about Jews was when Edward Alexander said that 'Universalism is the particularism of the Jews.' That's true but we can be insular. Jewish communities can be like small towns and protective of their own wrongdoers and resentful of any scrutiny. That's the problem of journalism. All the problems of Jewish journalism are the problems of journalism per se."

"It seems that many of these rabbis are unaccustomed to such scrutiny."

Tobin chuckles. "Most people you cover, unless you're talking about politicians, movie stars or athletes, are not used to being covered. Most people are very happy to talk about themselves but very shocked to read it in print. Rabbis are second only to ballplayers in claiming that they were misquoted. The deal with rabbis is that many of them are goded-up by their congregants and they are not used to any sort of scrutiny. And many of them are not worthy of deep scrutiny. They are just workaday people, not wonder-working rebbes. Outside of the Chasidic tradition, that is not the way we view our religious leaders.

"It's a rare congregation that doesn't have internal politics where the rabbi isn't at war with the synagogue president or some members of his board. In our readership area we have 150 synagogues with 150 little dramas. Most of them are not worthy of that much scrutiny. They are not that big a deal. Gee, some people at synagogues don't like each other? That is not news."

"How do you feel about people who like gossip?"

"It's a rare person who doesn't. All journalism is really lashon hara. If you go by the Jewish traditions of the Chafetz Chaim, everything is lashon hara. You can find some friendly things in liturgy and in Torah that speak to the need of informing people. 'Don't place a stumbling block before the blind.' And the need to warn of wrongdoers. There's a rationale for journalism in Judaism but it's not an integral part of our historic traditions. Most of what passes for gossip in Jewish newspaper isn't really gossip, it's personal-mention columns. Who got what honor? We've got one, most newspapers have one. Some of them gussy it up by having some yenta write it."

"Was it unethical of you to break the publishing deadline on Fried's book by publishing about it August 8, 2002, two weeks or so before it even hit the shelves?"

"You've got to be kidding me. Three weeks before we ran our story and my review, lengthy excerpts from that book were published in *Philadelphia* magazine. More people read excerpts of that book in *Philadelphia* magazine than will ever buy that book. For his sake, I hope he sells a zillion copies. Yeah right. To speak of any embargo in those circumstances is absurd. It was impractical anyway because they placed their release date the week before Rosh Hashanah. There was no way we were going to devote our Rosh Hashanah issue to a major piece about him or about that book or frankly to allow *The Inquirer* to scoop us because we would have to wait two weeks to do it. So, sorry, I don't buy that for a minute. That book was all over the place, not to mention that almost everybody in the Jewish community had a review copy.

"I've heard secondhand they were in high dungeon at his publishers about that, but, believe me, if I had said what a great book it was, they wouldn't have been unhappy."

"What did you think of Ari Goldman's book *The Search For God at Harvard?*"

"It was interesting. He's another little Jewish media star. I don't want to get into it."

4

Ari L. Goldman

January 8, 2003

Ari has published two books, *The Search for God at Harvard* and *Jewish Practice*.

"I loved Stephen Fried's book."

"I thoroughly enjoyed it. It's a brilliant piece of reporting. He really gets into people's lives and tells about a community in crisis. It's an exciting book to read. My one criticism of it is that he hurts a lot of people along the way. While it's good journalism, it's not always good from an ethical point of view. I know some of the people he writes about and a lot of people are going to have to live down a bad sermon, a slip of the tongue, some other embarrassing moment in their life. It's fair game if you're writing about politicians but I don't know that rabbis are politicians in the same way."

"You sympathize with the critics and the Perry Ranks?"

"Yes. I read the article in the *Forward*. I've heard some of the criticism. I think the same good reporting could've been done while protecting people. One of the people interviewed for the book was blindsided by the final product, saying, 'He told me he was writing a profile of Gerald Wolpe and instead...'"

"Rabbi Ackerman?"

"No. That chapter 'Waiting For Ackerman' is one of my favorite chapters. He's a good writer and a fine reporter and I'm impressed how much he learned about the observant Conservative community."

"If you ever do any good journalism, you are going to be hurting people's feelings right, left and center."

"I don't think that's necessary. I think you could tell the same story and manage to protect people's dignity."

"Is that something you were concerned with when you were working for *The New York Times*?"

"Of course. I write books and I'm conscious of that when I write, the effect of what I say could damage someone's reputation, could embarrass them. Lately I've been writing a lot of obituaries for *The New York Times*. What's great about that is that you are only embarrassing dead people.

"You worry a little bit about the survivors but in an obituary you can say nice things. In every other kind of journalism, they press you to find something bad to say.

"I teach journalism. Let's say a student is writing a profile. And I'll say, 'Go talk to a critic. Go show this guy's failings.' These profiles aren't believable unless you can see the human frailty. In my journalism, I don't shy away from being critical. You do it for balance and when it's relevant, but there's a sense in [Fried's] book that a lot of this is just gossip. Here's some juicy gossip."

"It's delicious dish."

"It is delicious dish. The whole Leonid Feldman…"

"Oh, I loved that. Yummy!"

"There was nothing new in there. It was all in *The Palm Beach Post*."

"I never knew of it. I was like, wow! This is great!"

"But it was irrelevant to Har Zion."

"But it was fun as hell to read. I was telling my friends at my Orthodox shul and it just confirmed all our worst suspicions about the Conservative movement. I told my rabbi friend at shul and he loved it because he hates the Conservative movement."

"You should give the movement its dignity too. This basketball game with the rabbis after shul on Shabbos. It's not the Judaism I grew up with."

"Now let's get to your premise. Is there a dearth of good Jewish journalism?"

"This sort of dish."

"I don't know. Look at Gary Rosenblatt and the Baruch Lanner story."

"The Orthodox rabbi molesting kids at NCSY [National Council of Synagogue Youth]. That was a rare story. Normally Jewish journalists are lapdogs."

"Yes. That was courageous. Did that story hurt people? Absolutely. There's an example of a case that was necessary. Yes he hurt people and yes he got people fired and he got somebody who ended up in jail. You can make a good argument that that needed to be told. Whether Perry Rank is bald and where he wears his yarmulke on his head. It was a good story but it could've been told anonymously."

"But it would've lost its punch."

"In some regards but I don't think it would've been totally denuded. Also, there's the problem of Stephen Fried. I like him. I know him. I had breakfast with him two weeks ago before I read the book. He gets into the mind of the selection committee. This is what they were thinking. Number one, he wasn't even in the room. He got this from his sources. Was that the most outstanding characteristic [of Perry Rank]? His preaching on Bob Dylan and his crooked yarmulke? It seems gratuitous.

"I wouldn't paint [Fried] as the paradigm of reporting in the Jewish community. I don't know that we need more reporting like that. We need more examination of issues that make us uncomfortable—dissent on the Israel question, the question of gays in the synagogue and pulpit, intermarriage. I think there are tough questions to explore but gossip is not one of them.

"There's stuff worth exposing and then there's stuff better left anonymous. You should question at every turn, do I need to embarrass this person? Is it worth it?"

"Would your criteria be different if your subject were a non-Jew?"

"If you look at Fried's earlier books, he's written about the fashion and pharmaceutical industries. He's bringing the skills that he developed writing secular books to the Jewish story and applying the same standards. To an extent, I think that's fair and admirable. We should be able to withstand that kind of grownup journalism.

"I'm not against the book as a whole. Rabbi [Gerald] Wolpe went in with his eyes open. Jacob Herber cooperated. Those central characters, you had to use their names. But whether Ackerman's wife's mother got cheated out of a house because of a selfish congregation, I don't know. I hear that people [in that allegedly selfish congregation] are saying, 'How embarrassing!' When he starts getting into the cousin's mother's uncle's son.... He opens up the pot with all the garbage in it and flings it around."

"How did you feel about him going into synagogue and taking notes and evaluating whether the rabbi gave a good sermon or not?"

"If you want to get to the sleazy line, when Herber catches him taking notes, he says, 'You can't do that. It's wrong.' He comes on Rosh Hashanah with a tape recorder [in his tallit bag].... Here's a guy who opens up to you and is honest and is your friend. He's screwing him left and right."

"That's what journalists do. That's quintessential journalism, it just so happens to take place in our sacred spaces. If it was any other goyishe situation, we'd say, 'Wow, look at his spunk.' But he's violating God's law."

"I'm uncomfortable with a lot of that. He successfully captures [Rabbi Gerald] Wolpe, the congregation's inability to replace a leader of that magnitude, the only one they know. It's an impossible task. Nobody can replace that kind of leader who's developed relationships with people at life cycle events over the generations. There's some powerful stuff in there."

"Where do you find compelling writing on Jewish life as lived as you experienced it?"

Ari, ten second pause: "I could start with my own books."

"You got some stiff criticism for your memoir, *The Search For God At Harvard*."

"I did go outside the bounds [of Orthodox Judaism]. I was criticized by the Orthodox community and embarrassed some people. I'm not so holy here. I just wonder about the limits of it.

"Sam Freedman in *Jew vs. Jew* applies the same sort of journalistic techniques that he learned in writing about schools and politics and the black church. Sam and I work together. I know his method. Before he publishes a book, he shows it to the people he wrote about. If he did a chapter on Luke Ford, he would run it by you and say, 'You're not my censor, I want to make sure that I got this right. I want to make sure that I'm not hurting you. I want to make sure I didn't do anything under false pretences.' Now, that's not common journalistic practice."

"You're right that's not common journalistic practice. We wouldn't do that with the goyim."

"But he did it with the goyim. He did it on his church book and on his education book. Not for approval, but he didn't want to say something in book form that was inaccurate."

"Fried checked his facts. They hold up. He just went for the same details in synagogue that he'd use in the fashion industry."

"I think you put it well. This is our sacred space. I think it has to be treated a little more respectfully. I think the tape recorder is a good example of violating a trust.

"I teach my students that when you do an interview or write an article, you go into a relationship with someone. You trust that they are giving you good information. They trust you that you will be accurate, fair and kind, and not trash them and get something over at their expense. I think he does that. I read it to the last page but it left me feeling guilty. I didn't want to see all these people humiliated but it is so much fun."

"So many of the rabbis I know are control freaks and used to controlling not only their own shul but with their image generally and I found this book refreshing that they had to deal with the same type of scrutiny as any other public figure. Do you think rabbis are public figures and accountable to the same sort of scrutiny we'd give other public figures?"

"Yes, I think rabbis are public figures. Once you take that job, you live a public life. I've participated here on academic searches to bring in new professors and new deans and new presidents of the university. Confidentiality of that process is sacred. Ninety nine out of 100 people you talk to are not going to get the job and that they are looking for a job could hurt them in their current position. You have to be sensitive in who you are talking to about who's good at the interview and who's bad. For all this to be made public, I'm not sure of the benefit of saying that this rabbi couldn't say a d'var Torah (teach a passage from the Bible) off the cuff or this rabbi was having a bad day.

"I don't think anything would've been lost if he had protected a few people. Maybe it is time for him to turn his attention away from the Jewish community. Maybe the Catholic Church could use a Stephen Fried."

"Where does this concern for not hurting people come from? Is it primarily a Jewish thing or an American thing? I know British and Australian journalists don't have that compunction."

"In my life, and I've hurt people, it comes out of my Jewish education. In our secular society, it comes more out of our libel laws. You don't want to get sued. For me, it's an ethical issue. I remember years ago, I wrote an article about a major Reform Jewish leader. In the eighties, there was a lot of discussion about denominations getting along better. There were Orthodox and Reform rabbis talking. I did an article about the difficulties of bridging the gap.

"I quoted a Reform rabbi who made an off-the-cuff comment to me after dinner one night. I didn't have my notebook out. He said to me, 'I'd give up eating lobster if sometimes they didn't wear a yarmulke.' I wrote this news analysis and then my kicker quote was from this rabbi. A few days later, I get a note from the Reform rabbi and all it says is, 'Ari, how could you?' He was indignant. No rabbi wants to be known as the lobster-eating rabbi in *The New York Times*. Did I really need to name him? Could I have fudged it? Could I have said something else? I was young. I don't think he really ate lobster."

"That's a delicious quote. I love it."

"I can tell which side of the debate you're on. Every journalist has to ask, is it worth the laugh for someone's reputation. What did he really mean? Rabbi Herber talks too much about the [New York] Islanders [hockey team]. I don't know."

"Were you prepared for the hostility you got for your memoir from the Orthodox community?"

"Yes, I think I was prepared for it. I'm a product of that community and I know how vicious it can be. What surprised me even more was the sympathy and support I got. Many Orthodox Jews said, 'I cut corners too. I don't talk about it. But behind closed doors, I do the things you did and you were courageous for making them public and struggling with them.'"

"People put tremendous effort in the Orthodox community into maintaining appearances."

"I felt that if I was going to be a journalist and write honestly about other people, I would have to apply the same standard to myself. I don't know that Stephen Fried did that.

"I'm not sure he applied the same level of scrutiny to himself that he does to everyone else. He emerges one-dimensional as a character in his return to Judaism. He left it for 20 years. What was that like? How honest is he in now saying I'm back, I'm a member of the club, I can judge everyone else. I think he needed to acknowledge that he left the club and he's not quite in the position to judge these rabbis who, flawed as they are, are in positions because of their scholarship and talent and their ability to work with people. You have to apply that critical standard to yourself as well as to the people you write about and he doesn't seem to be terribly self-critical."

"What did you think of Paul Wilkes' book *And They Shall Be My People*?"

"That book's a little too soft, a little too loving, a little too positive."

"Fried says that because Wilkes is not Jewish…"

"It insulates [Wilkes] from the kind of criticism that Fried's vulnerable to. In a way, [Fried] took advantage of Wolpe's relationship with his family. I admire what Fried did but something made me uneasy about reading this book."

"Does one need to be Jewish to capture the dynamics of Jewish life?"

"I don't think so. It would be wrong for me to say that because I've written a lot about the Catholic Church. It takes a while to get that insider-feel."

"Did you get accused of *lashon hara* with your memoir?"

"Not really, more in my journalism writing for *The Times*. I didn't name names in my memoir. I see *lashon hara* as directed more towards an individual.

"I don't mean to sound haughty, but the person who the most *lashon hara* is told about in my memoir is myself. I talk about having premarital sex, eating non-kosher food and desecrating the Shabbos. I'm the victim.

"I violate a lot of other laws. *Mar'is ayim*. When people see you doing something and then conclude it's ok if Ari Goldman can eat trafe. I'm setting a bad example. I was certainly accused of setting a bad example. Who am I to bend the laws with using a pencil on Shabbos?"

"They are not so upset that you did it but that you admitted it publicly."

"Right. I don't think Fried does the kind of soul-searching and self-criticism necessary before you go attack others."

"It's hard in Orthodox Jewish life to step outside the circle and just be a responsible journalist, particularly with Jewish issues. The community exerts tremendous pressure on you. Your second book was much more gentle than your first."

"There too I bend the rules a bit and talk about different approaches to *halakha* (Jewish law) and the different ways people practice, as if everything they do is kosher. I got some criticism for that. The worst thing for any author is to be ignored and I didn't get attacked enough [for that book]. I should've been sharper.

"It's been almost ten years since I left, and people still come up to me and say, 'That *New York Times*.' There's no escape."

September 9, 2003

I talk with Ari about his memoir, *Living a Year of Kaddish*.

"As with my first book, I wanted to hold on to the experience. Being a mourner was not something pleasant, but something significant in my life.

"Some family members are not happy with my portrayal of events. I have my interpretation of what happened. Writing this book was cathartic. This isn't anybody else's memoir. I will put up with the tsures from family."

"It wasn't a crippling thing as you were writing it? Oh no, what will Uncle Joe or cousin Sarah say? Did you have to fight that fear?"

"I thought it was important to make my points without unnecessarily hurting people. I did tone things down. I left some stories out. I write about the uncle [at the funeral] who forgets to mention me in a eulogy for my father. At first I wrote his name. At the request of one of my cousins, I took it out. I thought that story was emblematic of when there's a divorce in the family, some people pretend it never happened. That the issue [children] of that marriage is not worth mentioning."

"How many people did you seek permission to write about them or to check their recollections of events?"

"I showed it to various family members as I was writing it. Some corrected me. Some said I was way off the mark. Some asked that I not publish the book. I tried to be sensitive to their feelings but I felt my own inner-need to say this overrode anybody else's feelings."

"How has your life been affected since your book came out?"

"It's been out two weeks. Overwhelmingly the response has been good. There have been a few unhappy people, but I didn't write it for them. I've gotten responses that the book was helpful, comforting. And there was the Christian friend who said the book was about forgiveness. I don't think I intended it that way."

"Christians love that. Everybody sees the book through their own prism."

"I found that comforting. Yes, it is about forgiving my father and forgiving myself for not being the son I could've been. It's about coming to terms.

"What I do here is validate an Orthodox practice. On the other hand, traditionalists might take offense at my reasoning. The traditional Orthodox point of view on the Kaddish might be—it is not for you. It is not to make you feel better. It's the halakha, you have to do it. It's not about trying to say Kaddish, it's about saying it. It's not about going once a day, it's about going three times a day."

5

Amy Klein

March 17, 2003

Everywhere I go, I run into people who point at me and say, "Don't write about me!"

Tonight is no exception. And journalists, far from being an exception to this rule, are about the group most afraid of being written up.

I am at a Purim party thrown by Sinai Temple.

I see the young female managing editor of the *Jewish Journal*, Amy Klein, dressed as a black cat. I wave at her and she waves a reproving finger back. "Don't write about me on your blog!" she says.

Rabbi Wolpe walks by. Amy says to him, while pointing at me, "This man is dangerous. He has this blog where he writes about people." Rabbi Wolpe gives me a searching glance.

June 30, 2003

Project Next Step (an Orthodox Jewish outreach organization funded by the Simon Wiesenthal Center) gets its biggest crowd ever for Amy Klein.

Over 100 people (normal crowd is about 30) pack the room as Klein, who has a haunting sadness in her eyes, and Rabbi Yitzchok Adlerstein discuss objective journalism vs. personal narrative.

A few weeks ago, the *Jewish Journal* published Amy's cover story on her adventures on Jdate.com. She intended the piece for *Moment* magazine because she didn't want it to affect her Los Angeles search for a husband.

Then she allowed her editor, Rob Eshman, to talk her into putting it in the *Journal*.

A week ago on my Web site, I threatened to bonk Amy on the head with a heavy book on Jewish culture and drag her back to my Aborigine-style hovel and make her mine. I figure that tonight there are enough people around that she won't feel threatened by me. My only weapon this evening is a slim volume on kabbalah scholar Gershom Scholem. I could only land a frail chick with a whack from this book. Amy's more substantial. Nothing less than a Talmudic tractate will knock her out.

Tonight's program is billed: "Is the personal printable? Journalists who tell all."

There's a whisper in the room that Amy wants us to sit in a circle.

Amy sits with the rabbi at the front. She's dressed in black. I've only once seen her in a skirt and that was at an Orthodox synagogue on the Sabbath. According to Jewish law, women are forbidden from wearing pants in public (though there are Orthodox rabbis who dissent from this). She uses minimal make-up. She's a straight forward, no nonsense, what-you-see-is-what-you-get, surprisingly shy woman.

She says she's more comfortable writing than speaking. It's true. When you see her out, she keeps to herself and to people she knows.

Amy says she doesn't believe in objective journalism. No human being is capable of complete objectivity. What journalists should strive for is balance.

I find this discussion tiresome and I fear the evening is going to be a complete bore.

Then Amy gets personal and my interest perks up. She was the humor editor of her elementary school yearbook and she wrote what she thought was a funny send-up of her history teacher. He did not find it amusing. Amy found the experience so traumatizing, she abandoned journalism until college.

Klein, who is left-of-center, wrote for *The Jerusalem Post* (center-right) for seven years. She found that her personal stories got the most response. The only negative response came from her family who didn't like the way they were portrayed.

"When I came to the *Journal*, I was supposed to write the singles column. But I was also supposed to write news stories and we realized it would be hard to have credibility writing about Israel, etc, and also writing about my dating life."

So she chose the editorial over the personal.

I can't get through most of Amy's (or Rob Eshman's) non-personal columns because they are too pious.

I can't get through any pious story by a leftist. The *Jewish Journal* has way too much secular leftist piety—stuff about being kind to gays, that Jews are one people, we should take better care of the environment, we should talk through our differences, we need to be more innovative with Judaism to attract the young people…

Amy says she got such an enormous response to her JDate article that she wondered why the paper ever wrote on serious topics.

Rabbi Adlerstein responds. As usual, he tries to show how Jewish law is superior to secular law. Rabbi Adlerstein says that unless a journalist is objective, he shouldn't report a story. Objective journalists shouldn't taint themselves with writing personal pieces.

Then the program opens up to comments and questions. It gets boring fast.

Too many people falsely believe they can write a book, host a talk show and edit a newspaper. It seems like everyone in the crowd has an opinion on journalism, most of them far a field from tonight's topic. I don't hear anything I haven't thought through.

One man, dressed casually and not wearing a yarmulke, says, "Torah is the manual for my life. There's a ton of garbage out there, like the *Jewish Journal*, that I don't care for."

His sentiments largely reflect Rabbi Adlerstein's (who writes for the paper) views, though the rabbi would never be so boorish in expressing them. Rabbi Adlerstein's long despised the *Jewish Journal*. I've heard him say that you can read it in the bathroom. The question is whether you can read it outside the bathroom.

Another guy says that every time he reads Teresa Strasser, he wants to kill her.

If the cliché is true that if you are getting attacked from all sides, you are doing something right, then the *Journal* is doing something right.

I've seen the exhaustion from dealing with such whining Jews written across Amy's face at many LA Press Club events. Tonight she is again a punching bag.

Amy says the *Journal* does not have many guys write about dating because few can do it articulately.

Why is this? One, males are less interested in writing about such matters. Two, our culture frowns on men who spill the beans on women. If a man wrote the identical article Amy did about JDate, he'd look like a cad. In 21st

Century America, it's fine to evaluate male weaknesses in detail, but you can't do the same to women. For this reason, almost all sex columnists in college papers are women. If it were men talking about their sexual lives, it would seem crass.

Also, men complain less. If a man were to write about women the way the female columnists of the *Journal* write about men, he'd be lynched. Men usually just take it when they're ridiculed. Women have higher barriers of sensitivity. They are more likely to go ape over a slight. You can't josh with most women.

Look at the differing receptions to the book *Cad: Confessions of a Toxic Bachelor* by Rick Marin, and *Sex in the City* by Candace Bushnell. When men talk about their sex lives, they're scorned. When women do it, they're applauded for their bravery.

Amy says she's offered many of the men she's dated the chance to write about their dating experiences for the *Journal*.

I doubt the *Journal* is going to publish any accounts by men of disappointing dating experiences with Amy.

One guy in Amy's article complained he was unfairly depicted. Another guy, who Klein claimed had blown her off, had not intended such, and they're going to give things a second try.

Amy says she couldn't date a hardcore Republican.

It speaks well of the *Journal* that it constantly puts itself into the community to answer questions about itself. Klein, Eshman and company truly listen to their critics.

Then they go back to their headquarters and produce another dull issue. So what's the point of all this dialogue?

November 18, 2003

I'm getting blowback from the prissy chicks at the *Jewish Journal* who say I'm a stalker.

Your Moral Leader is used to these kind of attacks, all aimed at destroying his unimpeachable credibility.

A friend writes: "The last thing you are is a stalker. You have too much pride. Too much dignity. What you are is romantic. You tend to fall deeply in love with every pretty woman who gives you the time of day."

An ex-girlfriend writes: "You never stalked me but then again I live in Long Beach and you never wanted to drive that far."

I call my buddy Fred.

"This woman I want says she was warned that I'm a stalker."

"Stalking chicks? You're guilty of banging chicks, but stalking chicks? You're the opposite of a stalker. The first sign of rejection, you're out of there."

"How do you think I feel to hear I'm a stalker?"

"You've got to talk to chicks about this stuff rather than email. How can you possibly read what she's feeling or thinking?"

"Dennis Prager says email is an excellent way to communicate. It's just that none of my girls have ever thought so. They always say, 'We should do this on the phone.'"

"Dennis Prager hasn't been searching for a woman in almost 20 years. Email is not appropriate for matters like this."

"I prefer email."

"At least she could hear that you're a real caring person and that you really care about her feelings and don't want to write anything controversial anymore."

"So what did you say?"

"Baby, I love your way.

"I just got my CDs. Here, let me put on my Air Supply.

"I'm disappointed with my Best of Supertramp. I only like half of their songs."

"Half? Considering what I remember of Supertramp, that's good."

"I haven't listened to Barry Manilow's Greatest Hits yet."

"Wouldn't it be funny if you had a woman and you managed to keep her even though she knew all about your past and then she found out about your record collection and she left you."

"What if she had the same type of collection?"

"That's like her telling you—Oooh, I went into your closet and it's just like mine."

"Even the nights are better now that we're together."

"Oh, please God. Oh, no, no, no."

"I'm just lost in love and I don't know much."

"Who wrote Mandy?"

"Barry Manilow."

My Air Supply CD comes on. I turn it up and put the phone to the speaker.

"I obviously have to repent. When you come before the great scorekeeper in the sky and he asks you about this…. I can't see how liking Air Supply is going to help you. It's so gay."

"Most girls like them."

"Of course they do."

"I'm romantic. I'm not a stalker.

"Lift your eyes if you feel can…. And I'll show you the way."

"Lift your eyes? Who said that?"

"You know you can't fool me. I've been loving you too long."

"Ok."

"It started so easy. I want to carry on."

"Drop dead."

"Carry on."

"You're not the most romantic guy in the world. It's not that you fall in love with every woman who gives you the time of day. It's that you want to bang every woman who gives you the time of day. But you're not a stalker. You have no history of wanting to be one. You'd rather run if you're rejected. Sometimes you used to be pretty aggressive when rejected initially but…. I'll talk to her."

"I'm lost in love and I don't know much."

"So what about the other six women?"

"They don't mean much to me."

"Seriously? Is one of them the 19-year old?"

"I've been crying myself to sleep, waking up lonely."

"About the Cowboys? What's the Cowboys' record?"

"7-3.

"I needed someone to hold me, whoa ooh.

"The *Journal* wants to do a profile of me but the women on the staff hate me, so no go."

"Have you had experiences with these women on the *Journal*?"

"Social ones, not sexual ones."

"Sad, obviously."

6

Sue Fishkoff

June 25, 2003

I slip into the AJPA (American Jewish Press Association) conference to find my new friend Sue Fishkoff, author of *The Rebbe's Army* (about Chabad emissaries).

Sue barely has time to greet me before we're barreled over by members of the Jewish press eager to get a free book.

I look at them grabbing at freebies and realize why Jewish papers are so dull. They are products of dull minds.

I'm feeling all haughty when organizer Natasha Rosenstock (the only person aside from Sue who greets me all afternoon) says hi. I tell her my name and that I'm a friend of Sue and that I'm here to give her emotional support. Officially, I should not be here. This is a conference that Jews are paying $300 to $500 each to attend and I've snuck in for free.

Natasha says I'm welcome to help myself to the snacks. She welcomes me to the conference. She has a good sense of humor. I ask her if people crowd around her in bars when she mentions her role with the AJPA.

Sue appears exhausted. She paints on a big plastic smile. I tell her she missed her calling. She should be a used car salesman. She leaps away from me and back to her desk and I fear I've wrecked a budding friendship.

I must remember that one cannot josh with women.

Fifteen minutes later, the attendees are herded like sheep by Natasha into the panel discussions next door. Sharp people don't like to be herded. Many of the attendees appear on their last legs. Others appear to be housewives whose experience with journalism doesn't extend beyond publishing bake sale schedules.

Give us compelling Jewish journalism in our time, oh Lord.

It reminds me of a conference of church bulletin writers. What a wild thing that would be.

There are hundreds of people working on Jewish publications represented at the conference, living lives around this crap, on advancing up the chain of mediocrity, and impressing their friends with photos of Joey at his bar mitzvah. The most read parts of Jewish papers are the pictures of kids getting bar mitzvahed, and of oldies attending testimonial dinners for Sam and Sarah Feinsmith, who've attended this synagogue for 40 years and paid their dues on time.

The conference agenda, to put it charitably, is uninspiring. Nobody wants to shake things up by examining such questions as—why are we so dull?

July 1, 2003

"You write gossip on all the writers, right?"

"That's what it is."

"You're so funny about trying not to stalk Amy."

"I've got Amy Tourettes. Maybe there's a medication for it?"

"If there is, don't take it. Were you at her birthday party on Saturday or didn't you get that invite?"

"I didn't get that invite."

"You should complain about it in your next column."

"So how did you enjoy the AJPA conference?"

"Am I on the record?"

"Yeah."

"It was ok."

"Was it invigorating to be around the best and the brightest of your profession?"

Sue, long pause: "Invigorating?"

"Were your nerve endings tingling?"

"Yes, because I was sitting next to Amy Klein."

"How did the subjects of your book react to it?"

"With shock and awe? Not with shrapnel bombs at least. Clearly the emissaries, the shlichim, were happy to be in the book and the ones that I heard from were generally happy. Their whole life is about promoting their message.

And if there's no publicity, they haven't promoted their message. That there's a book explaining what they do and people are reading it validates their entire mission."

"What percentage of them were happy and what percentage of them were not happy with the book?"

"Eighty six point four percent were happy and the others I haven't heard from. I have been getting angry calls from other Lubavitchers who weren't in the book or who were messianists who said I didn't understand and I've been getting calls from unidentified Jews in Brooklyn who say that I don't understand how Chabad is trying to take over the world and they are very evil. I get between five and ten hate calls a day.

"If you want to see something mean that I wrote, look for my story in *The Jerusalem Post* when the Skirball Museum opened. I was writing as a high-on-the-horse Zionist just moved back from Israel, and I wrote that American Jewish history shouldn't end with the big Statute of Liberty, as it does at the Skirball Museum. I thought it was too parve an exhibit and too America-centered. Now I really like the Skirball."

"I'm looking in your prologue where you write that you aren't looking for scandal."

"You hate me for that, don't you?"

"I do."

"You're such a mean person. All you care about is scandal."

Sue writes: "There's a lot that this book isn't about. It's not about what's wrong with Chabad. One can find criminals and ne'er-do-wells in any group. Chabad is no exception."

"Why would you ignore the criminals and ne'er-do-wells in Chabad if they were shlichim?"

"Why did I ignore shlichim in 45-states?"

"Because you didn't have time."

"And because it was not necessary for the purposes of my book. Why didn't I write about the theology? The history of the movement?"

"I'm just interested in the scandal here."

"But it's the same answer. My answer to why I didn't talk about Pinchas Lew [Chabad criminal immortalized in *Postville*] because that was not my thesis."

"Did you turn a blind eye to wrongdoing that you witnessed?"

"I didn't witness anything. I'm sitting in somebody's house for three days. If any of the shlichim had committed a murder while I was there, for sure I would've written about it. That would've been fascinating. That would've been within the scope of my story. My story was about what I saw visiting the shlichim. When I was doing extra research, that was to support what I found in my reporting.

"I happen to think the whole chapter on menoras got into what you might call scandal. By you it's not a scandal because nobody got murdered.

"Coming into a community, steamrolling in, stealing lists of Federation donors, calling them up and saying, 'Give to my Chabad house.' It's not pretty but I was happy to write about it because it was part of the story. There's no sex and no murder and I do apologize for that."

"You received universally glowing reviews."

"Glowing but most of the reviews do say what they wish I had done differently."

"Was there anything common to that?"

"The *Forward* and *The New York Times*, the two reviews I take the most seriously, both wished I had talked more about specific conflicts in local communities and I agree with that. Both of them suggested I was too close to my subjects and was not critical enough. I do agree with that too. It was a first impressions book."

"And you're also a nice person, right?"

"I'm a very nice person."

"You're not dying to take scalps."

"No. I'm dying to get married. That's why I'm such a nice person."

"Did you find any potential mates in your research?"

"No, and I begged every single Chabad shaliach to find me somebody. But have they helped me? No."

"Why are you living in Monterey when you could be living in Los Angeles and mixing with the hundreds of thousands of Jews here, getting married and having 12 children?"

"Because I never thought of it in quite those terms. Because my family lives here and it's good for birthday parties."

"Were you changed by your research?"

"Yes. I used to be a man.

"This is more fun than the AP interview I did yesterday."

"I bet *The New York Times* didn't criticize you for lack of sex?"

"Many people think that the Lubavitchers do not have sex. That's erroneous."

"How were changed by researching this book?"

"I feel much more at home in the overall Jewish community. I feel comfortable in an Orthodox crowd. I feel comfortable walking through a street of Chasidim. I feel more of a sense of kinship around other Jews I felt awkward around before. It's been said that the Lubavitchers actualize the Jewish values many of us talk about. I've found myself lately being aware of lashon hara and making shivah (comforting those who mourn) calls to people I do not know. I'm subject to this same American attitude towards death that most of us have. I shy away from it. If you don't know the family well, you think that they won't want to hear from you. It feels awkward to send a letter to a family you don't know to say how much their son or daughter meant to you. I've been doing it lately and hearing back from the families. That is something I would never have done before. I would've thought—that is not my place. I should stay away. Now I reach out, and that's because of Chabad."

"There's a widespread perception that Chasidim are dirty. Can you speak to that?"

"It's a stupid perception."

"What about the hole-in-the-sheet perception?"

"I didn't check their sheets."

"Did you ever talk about it?"

"No, because I know that is not true with Lubavitchers."

"What about other Chasidim?"

"That may be true. Certainly the story came from somewhere and it wasn't entirely invented but I'm not sure specifically which groups might engage in such perversion. It sounds like a form of bondage. Maybe it makes sex more exciting. I have never tried it."

"Which reactions to the book have most surprised you?"

"That the reviews are so positive and there has been so much interest in the book from the media. I expected it to be more of a small niche book. Once *The New York Times* review came out, which stunned me because it was so positive, that gave legitimacy to the book and other people started reviewing it."

"What do you love and what do you hate about the book?"

"I love the cover. I hate that I didn't have another year [to work on it]."

Fishkoff devoted 18-months to the book.

"What were your biggest obstacles in writing this book?"

Sue pauses. "I'm hesitating because the absolute honest answer to that I don't want in print. It's too personal. The biggest obstacles to the book were all inside my head."

"Your own feelings about the subject matter?"

"Yes, and about writing a book and being lonely and shutting myself up in a room for half a year to write it. And feeling that I'm not an expert and didn't have any business writing a book like this. Even though the publisher said to me specifically that was why she wanted me to write it. Because I was coming at it as a reporter and not as a self-proclaimed expert. I felt the lack of my own background and knowledge was an obstacle."

"Were most of the emissaries believing in the rebbe as moshiach?"

"Few of them did. Messianism was more widespread during the rebbe's illness. Since he died, it's been decreasing, but decreasing much more sharply among the emissaries than among Lubavitch communities. That is a function of class and of education as well as these are the people who are out in the world. Few emissaries are messianists. Of those who are, few of them will say it out loud. One who did say it out loud, who was shaliach at New York University, has resigned. No coincidence in my opinion. At any rate, what somebody believes in his heart isn't as interesting for my purposes as what they're proclaiming."

"So David Berger is hysterical over very little?"

"For him, it's a matter of life and death because he believes in a flesh and blood Messiah. For him, it's very important what an individual Jew believes in his heart. And that a shochet who's slaughtering a cow should not believe in his heart that the rebbe is Messiah. For David Berger, that is of monumental importance. Me, I don't care."

"At what points did your own thoughts and feelings rise up and you had to battle them to do your job?"

"The only times I got close to that were at some classes where they were talking about the Afterlife in front of people who'd just converted. According to Orthodox Jews, and Orthodox Jews don't like to talk about this, in the Messianic times, all Jews will be resurrected along with the righteous Gentiles. That means there are non-righteous Gentiles who dissolve into the mists. Some of the converts were saying, 'How will I know if I'm going to be in Heaven with my family?' Being a convert [Orthodox] myself, that whole conversation appalled me. That reminded me of the ugly underbelly of Orthodox Judaism that we don't talk about—that Jews are a Chosen People who have an additional soul that enables them to be a holy people. All of that ugliness touches a bad chord in me."

"In Orthodox Judaism, it's difficult to do anything with non-Jews except business, except to make money off them. You can't eat with them or drink with them unless it is on your own terms."

"That's absurd for you to say. Orthodox Judaism does not restrict interaction with non-Jews only to making money off them. Chabad shlichim do outreach to non-Jews and teach them about the Noahide laws."

"Did you ever find yourself getting into arguments with the shlichim?"

"Sure. About Israel and Palestine, a lot. I'm very left-wing on that and they tend to be very right-wing."

"Was writing the book a harrowing experience?"

"Horrible."

"What was hardest? The writing or the research?"

"The loneliness.

"Chabad doesn't keep its own history. I had to collect the background orally from various people and compile the stories into a coherent history. It was difficult to start from ground zero, sitting in a little bedroom in Washington D.C."

"How did your friends react?"

"A couple of people tried to talk me out of it at the beginning. They said it would only bring me heartbreak. They knew it would be hard."

For the past ten minutes, Sue has been speaking in a whisper. "But most of my friends and family were much more positive about it than I was."

"Was there a difference between the way your Jewish and your non-Jewish friends reacted to the project?"

"My non-Jewish friends were completely positive. The Jewish reaction was more mixed."

"Do you believe in God?"

"Yes."

"How long have you been Jewish?"

"Twenty six years."

"What did you think of the book *Postville*?"

"It was a fascinating lurid read, filled with stereotypes and lies."

"What were the lies?"

"A lie by omission. The town [of Postville] and the Lubavitchers reached a modus vivendi, an agreement, before he turned in the final manuscript, but he chose to end his story while they were still at loggerheads. That was deceptive. He could've at least put that in the epilogue."

"Anything else?"

"That was the only lie. The stereotypes were almost anti-Semitic in his depictions of the fat, sweating, sloppy, Chasidic Jewish butchers."

"You don't think they could've been accurate?"

"They could have been accurate but the deceptive part of it was presenting that as a picture of Chasidic Jewry. If you go to a slaughterhouse in Chicago and you talk to the workers and you present that as a picture of Americans, that's no more or less deceptive or accurate. Yes, probably those descriptions of those particular people were accurate but it was the context that was misleading."

"So you didn't frequently encounter the Chasidim he depicts in your travels?"

"No, because who was I interviewing? The best and the brightest at the top of the food chain. I would've encountered the same people he did if I had written his book. That said, it's a fascinating book. I read it all in one night. He's a very good writer."

After thinking a second, third, and fourth time about our interview, Fishkoff has me delete more than ten paragraphs.

7

Stephen G. Bloom

July 2, 2003

"I haven't read [Sue Fishkoff's] book. I read Samuel Freedman's review of her book in *The New York Times* Book Review, in which he cites *Postville*. He says her book is an interesting read but it's a valentine. It doesn't really deal with some of the more complex issues of the Lubavitchers.

"You're a good journalist for trying to pin her down when she says it's filled with stereotypes and lies. What were the lies? She sort of backtracks and says a lie by omission.

"I am in contact with many people in Postville on a weekly basis. The town of Postville and the Lubavitchers have never reached an agreement. I turned the manuscript in in mid-2000. There was not an agreement reached in mid-2000. There is not an agreement reached in the summer of 2003. I am not sure what she's talking about. I go up to Postville and talk to people in Postville and there's still a civil war being waged in Postville. I can give Sue Fishkoff, you, or anyone else, the names of dozens of people who will tell you that they want the Lubavitchers out. That the Lubavitchers have ruined that town.

"She also talks about the stereotypes are almost anti-Semitic. I don't think so. My job is to report. My job is to go up there, open my eyes, and write what I see. If I see people who are sweating, doing a difficult job that requires a strong back and a strong stomach, I'm going to write that. That they are Jewish, should that enter into some kind of self-censorship? Absolutely not.

"Then she backtracks and you smartly say, 'Don't you think those descriptions could've been accurate?' She says they could've been accurate but the deceptive part was presenting that as a picture of Lubavitch. No way. This book is about Chasidim in a tiny town 23-miles west of the Mississippi River, in a corner of Iowa sandwiched between Minnesota and Wisconsin. It's not about Chasidic Jewry. It's about a town. The name of the book should tip off Sue Fishkoff that this book is not about the Rebbe's army. It's about Postville.

"Postville is a tiny town of 1400 that suddenly changed when 150 ultra-Orthodox fundamentalist Jews came and opened up a slaughterhouse.

"To the larger question you raise about reactions and social standing, did you read the epilogue in the paperback version?"

"Yes. You talk about two Chasidic women who congratulated you on the book."

"I've spoken in a lot of public places. It's rare when I'm in a metropolitan venue and someone doesn't stand up and scream something like, 'Shame, shame, shame. For a Jew to say this about other Jews, shame on you.' I'm not going to surrender my role as a journalist based on erroneous inferences that some may draw that this is a story about Jews in general.

"I spoke in Chicago to the American Jewish Congress. I was introduced as a culinary Jew, as a lox and bagels kind of Jew. That did not sit well with me. It made me think that there is some kind of pecking order. That there are certain Jews who are less Jewish than other Jews. That if you keep kosher, you are a better Jew than others. If you go to synagogue every week, somehow you are a better Jew. It was a rating game. I didn't like being relegated to the bottom of that rating card. I think that fractures the collective nature of what it is to be a Jew."

"I know you emotionally didn't like it but didn't you intellectually realize that there was something to it, in that only the people who observe Jewish law are going to perpetuate Judaism and the Jewish people?"

"No. If you and I were together, I'd probably be grabbing your shoulders right now and shaking you. Absolutely not. It's not in an intellectual way, it's in a visceral way that I found that offensive. My son Michael, his Hebrew name is Moishe, was just bar mitzvahed two weeks ago. To say that because I like lox and bagels that I'm not going to carry on the tradition of Judaism, shame on you. Shame on anyone. That's like the Orthodox saying, 'The Conservatives are the goyim.' That's like the Conservatives to the Reform, 'They don't know anything.' No, that's a bunch of bullshit. My kid is just as Jewish as any of those kids in Postville. And my kid read his parsha [Torah section] without mistake. My son wore a tallit and was able to carry a Torah around a synagogue. And to say that somehow because I don't keep kosher, I'm less committed to carrying on a Jewish tradition. No, that's the height of hypocrisy."

"Do you believe there's excellence in being Jewish?"

"I don't understand the question."

"There's excellence in journalism. You can be a good journalist, a bad journalist, or a mediocre journalist. You can be a good pianist or a bad pianist. You can be a good football player or a bad football player. Can you be a good Jew or a bad Jew?"

"Yeah, and it has nothing to do with how often you go to synagogue. It's something to do with what I believe Doc Wolf epitomized in the book [a Jew who did not practice Judaism and kept quiet about being Jewish]. The Chasidim confuse faith and religion. They believe if you know the 613 rules, you are a better Jew. No, no, no, no, no. If you precut toilet paper because you are not supposed to rip anything on the Sabbath, that means you are a better Jew? No. What makes you a better Jew is a sense that you are one of the Chosen People. Meaning, that way back Jews assigned themselves the role of being a model in their actions. That means that Jews ought to make this world a better place for those who follow us. All of those who follow us, not just Jews.

"My family and I take seriously the concept of repairing the world. Many of the Lubavitchers I met in Postville don't give a rat's ass about anyone else in the world except fellow Jews. I was a good person to write this story because I was allowed into the Lubavitcher family because my mother is Jewish. The Lubavitchers believed that I needed to be proselytized. Lubavitchers believe it is a mitzvah to make a Jew turn into a very observant Jew. That wrapping tefillin is a mitzvah.

"In the five years I did this book, I interviewed 350 people in Postville. I learned that the Lubavitchers in Postville didn't care about the non-Jews. They look through the non-Jews. And it burned me because that is not what a righteous Jew is supposed to do. The world is larger than Jew vs. non-Jew. It hurt me deeply as a Jew to see my fellow Jews not even acknowledge the locals, 'the goyim.'

"Even the word goyim makes my stomach burn. I'm repulsed by that."

"How about the word shiksa?"

"I'm repulsed by the word shaygetz, shiksa."

"Schvartze?"

"Particularly schvartze. Jews of all people ought to know that they don't use words that are exclusionary. I remember the first reading I gave of Postville took place in Postville. We had a standing-room crowd only. I took to task the Chasidim for using the word 'goy.' A Chasidic woman raised her hand and again shouted shame, shame, shame. She addressed the crowd, explaining that in Hebrew, 'Goy means nation. We don't mean anything by that. They are not of our nation.' I said, 'They are of your nation. You're in fricken America.'

"There was a farmer who came up to me afterwards. He was too laconic and shy to say this in public. 'When that lady said we're the goyim, it reminded me of those who said in the south, niggers. When you say to them, 'Don't use that word!' The good ol' Southern boy will say, 'We don't mean anything by it. That's just how we talk." It does make a difference.

"I don't think Jews of all stripes need to use words like schvartze. I know it means black in German. It's a divisive term that subjugates people."

"Do you think it is wrong of Lubavitchers to ignore non-Jews?"

"They can do what they want. I want to include people. There are too many bountiful things in this world for me to put blinders on so I can't allow myself to say hello to somebody on a Saturday morning in the middle of Iowa because his mother isn't Jewish. No, that's what you call racism. It's based on blood. Lubavitchers don't even see the guy on the sidewalk because to acknowledge him would be the beginning of assimilation. Then his children will play with my children and that's the end of our faith. I don't think it is the end of my son's faith if he plays stickball with Hispanic kids. I want him to do that."

"How would you feel if he married a non-Jew?"

"That's his decision. Isn't it presumptuous for me to tell my son to marry somebody based on solely on who somebody's mother is?

"Most rabbis [that] have written me [say] they're tickled by the book. They think the book took guts to write and needs to be out there.

"I want to address the issue of does the book spur anti-Semitism. It's why the book has received favorable comments from many rabbis. If there is anyone who is creating anti-Semitism in Postville, it is not the Steve Blooms who are going in there and observing, it is the Lubavitchers who are not wanting to fit in in any way, shape, or form to that community. It's the Lubavitchers who are cutting into line at the Post Office because, perhaps, that's what they do in Crown Heights.

"When I first got up there and I tried to connect to both sides of the story, it took a New York second for Sholom Rubashkin to acknowledge who I was. The first thing he said wasn't, 'You're Stephen Bloom,' but, 'You're a Jew.' It took two years for the locals to muster enough moxie for them to backdoor into the issue. It was Ida May Olsen and Clifford Olsen who, apologetically, said, 'Are you Jewish, Stephen?' For most of the Postville locals, there was no vision of what a Jew is, except perhaps *Seinfeld*. They'd never met a Jew before. And in come 150 ultra-Orthodox Jews, many of whom are very obnoxious, who essentially flip the bird to the locals. If Postville people were different people, they'd think that's what all Jews are like. People have told me that my entry into this theater of sorts gave them optimism that all Jews were not of that ilk.

"The book has never been acknowledged by the institutional body of Judaism. It was never really reviewed any of the Jewish magazines like *Reform Judaism* or *Moment*. I thought that was peculiar. It's one of the first books that takes to task a group of Jews.

"About a year and a half ago, I got an email from *Hadassah*, saying that *Postville* had been picked as one of the six books that *Hadassah* was going to urge all of its members to read. It's a congratulatory email. They wanted to know if I had a reader's guide to the book. I was surprised but proud that *Hadassah* could be open and large enough to accommodate a book like *Postville*.

"A week later, I get another email from *Hadassah*. 'Mr. Bloom, we're sorry. We made a mistake. *Postville* isn't one of the books.'"

"**Any explanation?**"

"They said it was a clerical mistake."

"**Yeah, right.**"

"*Hadassah* is the only Jewish magazine to review the book. They said it was a great book but at the end of the review, they say that Mr. Bloom is a self-loathing Jew.

"This was not an easy book to sell. I have an agent in New York City. We had a literary auction. There was someone interested from the Free Press. He'd read the proposal and he wanted to interview me. He said, 'First off, I'm uncomfortable with your conclusions. The Jews come out the bad guys.' I said, 'This book is not for you,' and hung up.

"There were 18 publishers who had the chance to bid on this book and only two bid on it. I ended up with Harcourt, who were terrific.

"When I handed in the manuscript, the editor said two things to me: 'One—this is terrific. Two—I'm really glad you're Jewish, because I don't think we would be able to publish this if you weren't.'

"Most journalists would parachute into Postville, hang out for a day or two, go back to Chicago and write their story. It would be a 'Golly, gee whiz' story. That's the story I did write. Postville began as a piece in the *Chicago Tribune* Sunday magazine. I wrote 8,000 words and it was 'Golly, gee whiz, who would've thunk it?' Wow, Chasidic Jews, guys with hats and beards, in a state that has ten times as many pigs as people.

"There was something about that story that propelled me deeper and deeper into Postville and also into myself. It initially hurt me when I would read flippant comments about the depth of my observations.

"*Postville* is painful because it is me, my family. I put it all on the line.

"The hatchet pieces were in Orthodox Jewish newspapers. There was a newspaper in Chicago where the review began, 'This is the worst book I have ever read in my life.' The Lubavitchers in their own organ said that I should convert to Protestantism. They said that I should not be welcomed in any synagogue. So they're the only righteous Jews?

"When I report, I never use a tape recorder. I always use a notebook. I keep it in my back pocket. I get people comfortable with me. About the sixth or seventh time, I start taking notes. It's a time-intensive, labor-intensive business. It's not, 'Gee whiz, tell me what you've got,' and then leave."

"Why don't you use a tape recorder?"

"It inhibits people. I find that 97% of what people say is background information and is not quotable. How old are you?"

"I'm 37."

"I find that in the newsroom, there's a line of demarcation at about 45. People over 45 do not use tape recorders. People under 45 do.

"It's difficult to have a conversation with somebody with the tape recorder rolling. I don't like tape recorders and often times they don't work. Are you taping this?"

"Yes."

"That's fine. I'm a writer who is particularly interested in language. I want to listen to how the Chasidim and the locals express themselves. There's a great line in the book when Clifford Jay Olsen says about the locals, 'The Jews are coons on a hound's back.' I always think that quotes are for opinion, not for recitation of fact. The only time I would use a tape recorder is when I only have one opportunity to interview a person, if I am interviewing a Colin Powell or a jury foreman at a press conference after a murder conviction."

"Did you notice a difference in reactions to your book from Jews and non-Jews?"

"Three groups of people didn't like the book. Many academics did not like it because I put myself in it, there are no footnotes, and it sold well. It was nontraditional research. I do not look at myself as an ethnographer. I look at myself as a journalist. There's a piece in *The Chronicle of Higher Education* that takes some cheap shots at the book.

"There are a lot of Iowans who don't like the book because they think I take cheap shots at Iowa. They say I make people believe that everyone is a country bumpkin who just fell off the turnip truck but these are my perceptions coming from San Francisco, where I lived for a long time. Interestingly, former Iowans love the book.

"Then the last group being those who claim that I am anti-Semitic. Many ultra-Orthodox Jews. I don't get many emails from them. Ninety nine percent of the emails I get are wildly enthusiastic. Many rabbis have written me, praising the book. Many Conservative and Orthodox rabbis, who don't like the Chasidim for their heavy-handed tactics, have written me to praise the book."

"You mention that crime has gone up in Postville. Is it the Lubavitchers?"

"No. When I was doing the research for Postville, the Chasidim would not hire Mexicans. That changed after I wrote the book because the labor shortage was so acute. The crime rate has increased in Postville based on a couple of things. One, that there is a slaughter house and they employ 500 people at that slaughterhouse. You don't need much to work at a slaughter house except a strong back and a strong stomach. Most of the men who work at the slaughterhouse are there alone. There's no family support system. So the liquor store is popular on payday. When you mix single men, no family support system, and alcohol, there's a higher evidence of crime."

"These generally aren't Jews working these manual jobs? These are immigrant laborers?"

Steve struggles. He hates to answer in racial terms. "Yeah. There have been several incidents of high profile crime in Postville. One incident involved two Hispanics. One involved a Russian and Ukrainian, both non-Jews. There was an attempted murder committed by a Jew on another Jew. So it's not exclusive to non-Jews.

"This is a self-selecting population. Jews who would go to Postville are not typically scholars. They're butchers. There are two no-goodniks, two bad [Jewish] guys in *Postville* the book, Stillman and Lew. If you have a problem kid, and you live in Brooklyn or Crown Heights, what better place would there be to send him than a Lubavitcher community in North Eastern Iowa?"

"Do you have any Lubavitch friends?"

"No."

"Nobody in the Lubavitch community in Postville is talking to you today?"

"Nobody from that community is talking to me today.

"A lot of people said to me, 'Wow, this would make a great movie. It's like *Witness*. We could call it *Vitness*.'

"Well, the Jews come out as the bad guys. It can't be made into a movie for a lot of good reasons. Who's going to make it into a movie? Look at Hollywood.

"If you run that, people are going to say, 'Gee, is he talking about the Jewish conspiracy, a cabal that runs Hollywood?' No. But a lot of Jews make influential and important decisions in Hollywood and this would make a tough sell.

"I devour a lot of Jewish publications, like *Reform Judaism*, a great magazine. But when it comes to discussions of Israel and meaty issues like the Chasidim, no, there's a complete boycott of those kinds of articles."

Steve praises his friend Samuel Freedman and his book *Jew vs. Jew*.

"It's a safer book than yours. He doesn't blow any covers."

"I don't think it went far enough but I'm not Sam Freedman. A lot of people have read *Postville* and said, 'Wow, that's a gutsy book. You lay it on the line.' I always looked at it as reporting and stumbling on the social laboratory called Postville and doing my job.

"People have used this book as a touchstone for their own personal situations. I've gotten many emails from gay men who have looked at the book and seen themselves as being persecuted, as the Postville locals look at themselves, by this powerful group of brokers. A lot of feminist women have written me, like Susan Brownmiller, who talks about how courageous the book is and how it should be viewed as a book about oppression of people who do not belong. Those who don't belong in this topsy turvy world are the locals."

May 13, 2004

I read in the *Forward* about a glowing documentary on Postville by Hallmark—*The Way Home: Stories of Forgiveness*.

"The producers wanted a blurb from me extolling the virtues of the show," says Stephen.

I laugh.

"Do you think they read your book?"

"No. I was the one responsible for Hallmark going to Postville. I got a phone call from an independent producer who was contracted by Hallmark [to Faith & Values Media, a coalition of feel-good Jewish and Christian groups]. He'd been asked to come up with several different story ideas.

"They said they'd read my book and the story interested them.

"I said, 'This is not a story about reconciliation. This is more like a civil war saga.' That was the last I heard from them.

"The initial people I talked to bowed out of the project. Hallmark got involved. They did go to Postville. It's one of three episodes on this hour-long documentary.

"It was terrible.

"It's interesting how the press works. Why is there this sudden revival of interest in Postville? Because *Hadassah* magazine (April) has a cover story on Postville [by Jennie Rothenberg] saying things are just so great up there. It's like the United Nations. I thought the story bordered on being unethical. The reporter talked to me a long time ago.

"It's what we call in the business agenda-journalism. *Hadassah* had an agenda. And this reporter fulfilled that agenda. I wrote a letter to the editor attacking the piece. I don't think they'll ever print it [they don't].

"After *Hadassah* run this piece, the *Washington Post* runs a story on Postville.

"The reporter called me. Frankly, I wasn't impressed by the reporter. She didn't ask informed questions.

"The JTA story appeared because they'd seen the *Washington Post* piece. It's dominos.

"Because the JTA piece appeared, I get a phone call from the *Forward*. None of these pieces refers to the preceding piece.

"The [Hallmark] video is an embarrassment. It's contrived. It's an audio-visual Hallmark card. It's cheery, upbeat, positive.

"Ever since *Postville* has come out, I've been interested in what the Japanese call Wa—how Japanese society is run. It means harmony. In Japan, Wa is very important. It's rare in Japan for a vote in a corporation or the parliament that is not unanimous. All the differences are aired in private. By the time the public is clued in, everyone is on board, even the most vociferous critics.

"It's most important to live in a harmonious society where disagreement is eliminated. In America, journalism is generally opposed to the Wa. We journalists look at issues and we don't say, 'George Bush is doing a great job.' That is not a news story. We say, 'George Bush is screwing up big time.'

"There seems to be a tremendous attempt by the Jewish community, as prompted by the *Hadassah* piece, JTA, *Forward*, and this Hallmark presentation, to say that two different communities can flourish in America today. Postville is an example of that. There's a tremendous sense that readers and viewers need to come away with a feel good response. 'That stuff that Stephen Bloom did is water under the bridge. That was a long time ago. That was terrible. But now there's been forgiveness, reconciliation and harmony.' That's what the [Hallmark] show is all about.

"They make up a story line that when the Gentile head of the slaughter house, Donald Hunt, who's in my book. I call him a Caesar Romero lookalike. He died about a year ago. His death brought together the distinct factions in Postville and began to heal the wounds. There's footage of Hunt's funeral and locals as well as Lubavitchers at the funeral. They use that as a point of entry for establishing a premise that things are going along just great.

"The people I talk to in Postville say things are not going along great.

"This latest skirmish is the slaughter house dumping some 30 tons of salt a week into the aquifers of ground water.

"There seems to be a journalistic mandate to remind everyone that Postville has reached Wa status. That's not what journalists do. Journalists are supposed to afflict the comfortable and comfort the afflicted.

"There have been some courageous [almost all liberal] places that have invited me to speak. I spoke at a Reform synagogue in New Brunswick, New Jersey. It was a huge crowd. People were enthusiastic about my book. There's a tremendous backlash among progressive Jews about the Lubavitch and what they're doing.

"Even at Reform synagogues, I still get people screaming at me, 'Shame, shame, shame. For a Jew to say this, shame on you.'"

"Do you have any reason to believe that the situation in Postville has significantly improved from the latest version of your book?"

"No. The people I talk to in Postville are waving a white flag. They've lost. There's nothing they can do. The slaughter house is the industry in town. There used to be a turkey processing plant. It burned down. Agriprocessors [owned by the Chasidim] is going great. You've got to get with the program.

"There was a small piece in the *Chicago Tribune* December 26 about discontentment in Postville. The Chasidim were up in arms because the local merchants [and/or city council] laid out about $10,000 for non-sectarian holiday decorations in the downtown. There were no crèches. Jesus Christ was not on every lamp post. And the Chasidim said no. We want menorahs up. If you are going to put up what we perceive as religious, then we want menorahs up.

"After the story appeared, the one city council member, Ginger Medberry, who spoke out against the Chasidim in Postville was reamed. She was censured for speaking negatively to a reporter. She was hung out to dry. Her fellow council members crucified her.

"Isn't it interesting that in the Hallmark video, there is no mention of alcoholism. No mention of crime. The liquor store is doing box office business. When people leave their job, they just anesthetize themselves with alcohol. But we don't talk about that with *Hadassah*. We don't mention that in the Hallmark show. We don't mention the attempted murder in Postville by a Chasidic man [convicted]. This isn't even on the radar of *Hadassah* or Hallmark."

"This [*Hadassah*] writer, Jennie Rothenberg, is a regular contributor to *The Atlantic*."

"She sent me an email a while back. She was a graduate student at the University of California at Berkeley. She wanted to know if she would have access to the Chasidim. But she never called me back.

"Before I came to the University of Iowa, I worked for *The Sacramento Bee* in San Francisco. One of the reasons I left that newspaper is that I was asked to do all these agenda-journalism pieces. Tell us what a weird, wacky place San Francisco is. How it's Sodom and Gomorrah falling off into the ocean. Why Sacramento, implicitly, is such a great place.

"Minnesotans have jokes about Iowa. There's always a stupid pecking order. Don't let the truth get in the way of the story is what *Hadassah* is suggesting.

"My wife worked at the *San Francisco Chronicle* for many years. Her favorite saying was, 'Check 'em and lose 'em.' You check the facts and you lose the story. So let's not check 'em. There was no attempt by *Hadassah* and Hallmark to do a truthful story.

"I believe there is a difference between truth and accuracy. Truth is of a higher order than accuracy.

"There's an old expression—is it good for the Jews? Sandy Koufax. Good for the Jews? John F. Kennedy. Good for the Jews? For a lot of good reasons, those words have stuck. I guess *Hadassah* feels it is not in their purview to run a story that gets at larger more important issues.

"It's just easier [to wimp out]. My aunt, 82, alerted me to the *Hadassah* story. She said, 'I'm glad to read that things are copasetic now. When you were out there, things were different but now things seem better. I feel better about it now.'"

8

Jennie Rothenberg

May 14, 2004

"Stephen Bloom traces a flurry of what he would call 'valentines' to your article in the April *Hadassah* magazine."

"That's flattering but I don't think that is the case."

"How did you come to write that article for *Hadassah*?"

"I was in Iowa at that time [Jennie did her undergraduate degree in English Literature at the Maharishi University of Management] and I'd always been intrigued by Postville. I'd never been there. I didn't think there was a whole lot going on in Jewish life [in Iowa] at the time other than Postville."

"Bloom called it agenda-journalism. Did *Hadassah* only want a feel-good piece on Postville or is that what you genuinely encountered?"

"I think both things are partly true. I don't think *Hadassah* told me they wanted a feel-good piece but if you are writing for different kinds of audiences, different things will be an issue. There's investigative reporting where you go into the slaughter house and look at what is going on. My piece was on the school.

"I did go out of my way to get many sides of the story. I spoke to the local superintendent and to a teacher. They found it difficult to work within the Jewish system. I spoke to some high school kids who said the Jews kept to themselves. I included all of these viewpoints in my article.

"Because Stephen Bloom so covered one angle of this, it frees other journalists to look at other angles. Anyone who goes in there will have read his book."

"Did you want to feel good about what was going on in Postville or is this primarily a reflection of what you encountered?"

"I want to live in a world where everyone respects each other but if I felt that the people there were causing strife, I wouldn't feel comfortable reporting that in a positive way. If I had found that people had not nice things to say, that would not have been something I could've covered up in a story.

"I was happy to find that things have improved. When Aaron Goldsmith [first Chasidic Jew to sit on the city council]. At the time of his campaign, there was a lot of hate mail sent to residents of Postville by a neo-Nazi group. That crystallized things. People in the town felt that they weren't just operating in a bubble but were on a world stage and had to overcome a lot of the pettiness happening on both sides.

"I don't know if Bloom has such a high opinion of Aaron Goldsmith but I think [Goldsmith] did a lot to bridge the gaps in the town. Before he came, there were two distinct groups that hadn't really met anyone like the other before.

"Chasidic Jews do keep to themselves. They are not politically correct modern liberal people. I didn't feel the need to harp on that. The readers of *Hadassah* tend to know that. They are not going to be Chasidic Jews. They're going to be Reform or Conservative. I wouldn't say that I came there and found Chasidic boys dating Iowan girls. There's also a kosher issue. [Chasidic Jews] can't eat at [the houses of people who do not keep kosher].

"A lot of it is urban vs. rural. Iowans have a different social fabric. The Jews in Postville are fast talkers. They're New Yorkers. They're businessmen. You wouldn't expect to see them bonding but they seem to be getting along all right. There's a range. Some Jewish people are more worldly and some are more sheltered.

"I wanted to find out what makes these people tick. I explored some avenues that were just not as interesting to Stephen Bloom because that is not his personality. I'm more philosophical. I found it interesting to have long discussions with people and to find out what their beliefs were."

"How much do you think who we are influences the stories we write?"

"Absolutely. My story is not the most positive one [on Postville] to come out. There are people who come out with a completely rosy picture and don't interview any naysayers. Every story is so complex. Even if you spent 15 years living with a group of people, someone else could come in and see a completely different side that you did not focus on. Sometimes, the longer you are with a story, the more you form your hardened crystallized ideas and you just continue in that track for the rest of your exploration. We need lots of different perspectives on any story, whether it is this or the Iraqi prisons."

"Have you ever felt like you owned a story and then you resented when other people came in and did not do it as well as you thought you had?"

"No. I haven't gained the kind of high profile that Stephen Bloom has. I can imagine that he would probably feel that way."

"Was it hard to get access?"

"No. Lubavitch of Iowa publishes a calendar and sends it to everyone they can find who's Jewish in Iowa. In almost every square, there's a family that wants to invite you to come to their home in Postville."

"Did Stephen Bloom's book make it difficult for you to follow in his footsteps?"

"I had a lot of people ask me if I had read his book. They were suspicious."

"They wanted to know your reaction to it before they spoke to you?"

"Yes. I told them the truth. That I felt he had explored one aspect of it.

"I had other experiences writing about communities where a group comes from the outside, like a university vs. the local town community. You can always find some shocking story. In his case, he wrote about these two Chasidic boys who came for a summer and committed a crime [attempted murder]. Obviously, that makes for a better story, but I'm not so sure that reflects what is going on. I'm not sure the people there can be held responsible.

"I told people that he presented things in a certain way that made for an interesting story but…"

"Sensationalized?"

"You could say that. I think he was trying to prove a point. He was trying to show a connection between people committing that crime and people turning up their noses at their neighbors. I'm not so sure that connection can be drawn, to merit two chapters in the book about the crime.

"He spent a lot of time on Doc Wolf [secular Jewish doctor who lived and died nearby]. Some of the families who had gone to Doc Wolf's bedside had a very different impression of what Doc Wolf's desires were at the end of his life [from what Bloom described]. I met some of the boys who had gone there as teenagers and I didn't get the impression they had gone there with an agenda. They did have an agenda to bring him closer to Judaism at the end of his life but I don't think they were trying to win people over for the vote coming up in town [as Bloom's book suggests].

"I think *Postville* was a good read. I don't feel it was the complete story. I wanted to be extra conscientious not to just stand on his shoulders and use his book as my manual for what happened in Postville. I went the extra distance to form my own opinions.

"Chasidic Jews are mystical. I had a fascinating conversation with one of the Rubashkins. I have more of a philosophical background and I love going into the kabbalistic issues and the subtle aspects of their beliefs and traditions.

"It does rub me the wrong way if anybody does not relate to other people as human. [Many of the Chasidim] did not think about non-Jews as part of their world. I would like to see that change. But in general, I don't have any anger towards them.

"My focus was on the school. It would've been outside of my story to investigate crime rates and all that. I didn't write about the Mexican or Ukrainian immigrants.

"I'm a vegetarian. I've never [intentionally] eaten meat in my life. In the '70s, my parents became interested in health.

"I didn't want to have anything to do with the slaughterhouse. If I had seen one slab of meat hanging.... That took a lot for me to accept that they could have other beliefs [about eating meat]. They have this kabbalistic belief that it elevates the animal for them to consume it. I don't feel that. I felt that was a test of my own journalistic maturity to let that part go.

"I wonder what Bloom expects other journalists to find when we go there. It's part of our natures to want other people to have the same impressions we do. I get the impression from his letter that he would've only been satisfied with a piece that reported all the same things he found. We all know about those things because he wrote about them. We all read his book cover to cover."

"Is there a particular tone to your work? Do you prefer cheery and winsome?"

"If there's conflict, I prefer to go one level deeper and get to the source. I think journalism has a two part role: One, to inform people. Two, to influence the world in a positive way.

"I think Bloom honestly feels that his book did good and it may well have. It may have made some people more open and tolerant. I didn't feel that was so much needed now. I didn't feel like it was my role to go and do a huge expose. My skill as a journalist is getting into the subtleties of people's thinking and their psychology more than to go through all the records and find scandals.

"I have written grittier pieces. I won't say that I didn't enjoy the fact that I found nicer people and nicer situations than I expected.

"When people are very strong in their religion, in one sense it is the most beautiful, because they are vibrant and get to the deeper levels. On the other hand, they are more narrow. They close themselves into that world more. That's the challenge in Postville and why so many people have written about it."

We chat about befriending the subjects of our stories.

"I had a lot of professors [at UC Berkeley journalism program] who prided themselves on, for example, spending quality time with Hillary Clinton, going on tour with her, becoming her best friend, then blasting her in *Vanity Fair*. In that case, it seemed frivolous. It didn't seem like people's lives were going to be improved. It was just that she got a good story.

"If you are going to spend time with people on a personal level you owe it to them to present some of the subtle nuances of their life. If you are going to stay in someone's home, you're going to show that he is at least a complex individual who has sides to them. Not just spend time with him, disregard everything that is positive and only write the negative.

"I grew up in a world that journalists liked to ridicule [a community where everyone practices Transcendental Meditation]." People would come in and go out of their way to find the one person who would say something negative. I went to Israel with my father when I was younger and watched the press interview him.

"One man interviewed him and wrote in the first draft of his article that he was a fancy doctor swilling research papers out of a leather briefcase. My father commented that he did not have a leather briefcase. He had a canvas blue bag from Lands End. In the final draft, he was a hippy swinging a blue jeans pack over his shoulder. The journalist was determined to ridicule him no matter what.

"I'm extra sensitive not to do that whenever possible. I'm not the type to go for the jugular."

After reading my interview with Jennie, Stephen Bloom emails: "Luke, another interesting take on the evolving story of Postville, journalism, writers' perceptions. I enjoyed Jennie Rothenberg's comments. She really presented herself in a strong and (to me) fascinating manner. You got at the difference between her mission as a journalist and mine."

9

Steven I. Weiss

June 15, 2004

"I used to feel that I was going to change the world. That I should bring about a messianic utopian age. I could see things coming to a head and I wanted to be part of that. I'd always assumed that the Jewish messianic age would come before my grandfather died. That didn't happen, and I remember being kind of surprised at that reality when he died.

"The First Cause idea is a compelling philosophy. Monotheism is compelling. That God would communicate with people seems compelling."

"Do you care whether women get aliyot (called to the Torah on Shabbos mornings and festivals)?"

"I'm agnostic on a lot of these questions. Other than outright abuse, I don't care that much about what happens in Judaism. As far as friends go, I'm good. As far as the community goes, I've been kicked out of so many things, that I can take it or leave it. As far as where it goes, I'm agnostic. These things don't keep me up nights. Ritual will figure itself out."

"How did you meet the other elders on Protocols?"

"From the editorial board of the *YU Commentator* (student newspaper), Yehuda Kraut, Pinchas Shapiro, and Sam Singer. I always wanted to get Jason Cyrulnik, editor-in-chief of the *Commentator* in Volume 65, which was '00–'01. I wanted it to be like Oxblog. Oxblog is a group of guys from Oxford who are smart and funny and got together to talk about cool issues, and that was something I wanted to have among my friends, in part to preserve the dialogue that I couldn't participate in anymore because I was expelled and broke.

My friends and I had these late-at-night discussions all the time during layout, and I thought it'd be great if we could continue them on a blog like OxBlog and show people what we were made of. [YU rabbinical student] Avraham Bronstein was reading when Protocols started and was sending in suggestions and links and comments, providing more content than the other Elders, so pretty quickly he came on-board, and soon after that it was essentially a two-man show.

"I wanted Protocols to be us taking on the world. The name Protocols was a joke but it was also meant to mean something. Soon enough we started focusing on Jewish stuff. Bronstein and I did most of the posting with occasional help from Singer and Pinchas and almost never from Kraut. But we were still this island in the blogging world, not really interacting with anyone. I remember when we first started interacting with other J-blogs. We got into this raging vitriolic argument with Jewschool. It was the coolest thing in the world. It was like Robinson Crusoe discovering the footprint on the beach. Everything changed after that."

"Why did Avraham leave?"

"I'd helped report on a book that had come out of Lakewood that was being called racist, that talked about the relative status of Jews and non-Jews, and then I got calls from people about an article in YU's rabbinical journal, *Beis Yitzchok*, about the Noahide Laws and the prohibition against murder and how there may be a difference between Jews and non-Jews. I couldn't get into YU to buy the journal, and I was busy with other stuff, so I put up a post saying something like, 'Word has it that there's a controversial article in the new *Beis Yitzchok* about the Sixth Commandment and how it applies to non-Jews.'

"Chakira [Josh Harrison] posted the relevant portion and translated it. That led to the longest comments thread we'd had. Chakira got a lot of heat for translating it, but it's not like he could've posted it in the comments in Hebrew. All of a sudden, a lot of people in the [YU] rabbinical school, started paying attention [to Protocols]. People in the kollel were sitting there with printouts of the comments from Protocols. Some of the comments became embarrassing for Avraham.

"There were various people leaning on him who changed him as a person and a blogger. He asked if we could moderate the comments. I said no way.

"I had a long talk with a rabbi, Ezra Schwartz, one of the rabbis in the big kollel at YU, and we were talking about this situation. And he was saying that it's good to discuss these issues, but that they have a proper venue, and blogging wasn't it. That the Orthodox Forum [convened yearly by Rabbi Norman Lamm] was where these things should be sorted out.

"When something happens and you are called by the world or by the community to take part, you don't get to choose the forum. If thousands of readers are saying, this is the issue, it's easy to say that you are going to lock yourself up in the Orthodox Forum, or in the beis medrash, and say that 'blogging is not my medium.' But you're failing those people as a communal leader. It's not ok to say no comment on an issue when tens of thousands of Jewish readers care about it, and it's not ok to say that blogs are not a proper forum when that's where the Jews are asking questions. Even if the older rabbis don't plug into it because they are completely computer illiterate, a fair number of the middle-aged and younger rabbis already are, and that's a good thing and that's what they should do. And if you have an issue with the discussion in the comments there, that's your problem, because this is your community. And you are part of the problem of why the comments are what they are.

"Protocols was about the only completely unmoderated forum for discussion of Jewish issues. If you don't like the discussion there, you can fix it. People tend to know when they can't hold up their end of the argument against an expert, when they are at a conversational disadvantage. If you set yourself to raising the level of discussion, those people will self-censor, in deference to you.

"There was a shift in Protocols from primarily me to primarily you. In some ways, the response was justified. There are a lot of better things to focus on than what is going on with Luke Ford to what is Luke Ford observing in the Jewish community. If you stopped writing in the first person, I think you'd find some good stuff.

"My writing and thoughts are an open book. My work is uncommon. I do good work. I work hard. I'm very serious about my work, whatever work I choose to do. People who tried to do what I was doing failed."

"What are the principle obstacles you face in doing good Jewish journalism?"

"The bad Jewish journalism out there."

"Who's particularly horrible out there? *The Jewish Week*?"

"It's easy to bash *The Jewish Week*. The only thing they do that is actively bad is when they get basic elements of Judaism wrong.

"The main problem with Jewish journalism is one organization [the Jewish Federations who fund most Jewish newspapers] runs almost the entire show. Almost an entire ethnic media is subservient to one organization. They don't even go looking there for stories. They want to have friendships with these people. A lot of these Jews in journalism want to be friends with their sources and their sources' friends and with their communities when they go home. The way they go about it creates bad journalism.

"Comps are a problem with a lot of Jewish journalists. Major Jewish journalists get major comps. Free cruises. Free trips and hotel accommodation.

"I know of a journalist who approached a major Jewish organization for a comp. They said no way. He then went on to write a story bashing that organization without mentioning the comp.

"The weeklies receive almost all the money and all the attention of the older generation while actively failing to capture the younger generation. One of the few things that allow these papers to maintain any relevance is Shabbos, when many people will sit down with the paper, but that will only last as long as people are willing to read week-and-a-half-old JTA stories, in print, as their primary Jewish news consumption."

"What can blogging do to change Jewish journalism?"

"You can reach your sources in Jewish journalism. You can go talk to these rabbis and communal leaders. There's rarely sophisticated PR and that can you usually be gotten around. It becomes a problem when the Jewish journalist becomes one of the guys and not one of the people trying to get the truth. That's why bloggers can take over. There's no huge gap like there is in reporting on federal politics or other issues where the sources are so far away."

If Steven had not brought me on as a guest blogger on Protocols in May 2004, and then inspired me with his vision for Jewish journalism on his trip to Los Angeles two weeks later, I would never have written this book.

10

Andrew Silow-Carroll

June 18, 2004

"If your goal every week is to muckrake and to uncover a scandal," says Andrew (editor of *New Jersey Jewish News*), "you have to assume there are a lot of scandals that are going under the radar. I'm not sure how true that is. One judge of Jewish journalism is not just covering a community's bad news but making sure the debate about Jewish life reflects a broad range of opinions. Jewish journalism is doing a better job of that over the past ten years than it ever did. Partly because when Rabin came to power, it broke down the taboo on the right of criticizing Israel.

"Let's separate the reporting from ideas journalism. There are definitely more ideas in play in Jewish journalism than there have been in the past. The ZOA (Zionist Organization of America) is glad to criticize the Sharon government as harshly as ten years ago Peace Now criticized the Shamir government.

"Yeah, there's probably not enough hard news investigative reporting in Jewish journalism but that doesn't mean that Jewish journalism is a rubber stamp for some of the biggest ideas in Jewish life."

"Is the *New Jersey Jewish News* owned by the Federation?"

"It is. It is an obstacle. It puts a constraint on us and the things we can report about. Within the world of Federation-owned newspapers, my Federation tries to extend as much independence as possible. I get to write my editorials. I don't have to submit them to an editorial board. I don't have to submit my articles to an editorial board. I do have to have a consulting relationship with them that I would rather not have. About half of Jewish newspapers are in that boat. Being independent doesn't mean you're a good paper and being with the Federation doesn't necessarily mean that you're bad. When you're independent, it doesn't mean that you don't have constraints coming from advertisers and your owner. I've worked for individual owners who sometimes have more axes to grind than the community boards that run or advise a Federation paper.

"It is up to a good editor to see that a full story is told. We've been able to tell stories honestly, though sometimes not with the telling detail that I would prefer. You start thinking, can this story be told without embarrassing the participants more than they need to be embarrassed? Can the story be told without doing damage to the institution itself beyond the damage it deserves? I'm not embarrassed by this restraint. We're a small paper serving a small community which is a small subset of a small ethnic group. We have a kind of responsibility that you don't have if you have a big wild and woolly city weekly that doesn't have to worry about the sensibilities of a small voluntary community. I have 45,000 subscribers."

"What were the benefits and costs in journalism of moving to your present position?"

"Benefits: You have a nice intimate relationship with your readers who are rooted in their geography and want to know about their friends and neighbors. The *Forward* is a national paper that sets an agenda for the organizational world but you don't meet your readers beyond the board rooms of the big organizations. The down side is independence. Independence is nice at the *Forward*. It's nice to be able to say that the only thing that matters in this story is—is it true? Is it fair? Is it accurate? At some level, every good journalist should ask, is it serving a purpose? You don't have to ask: Whose ox is being gored? What are the prices of a volunteer philanthropist not liking the story? That's liberating. Because it's a national newspaper, every week the *Forward* can go out and find the 15–20 best stories in the country. I'm a local weekly. I have to find the best things that are happening in my geography. Some weeks are interesting and some weeks are pro forma."

"Where did you begin in Jewish journalism?"

"I go back to the late '80s at the *Jewish Exponent* in Philadelphia. I was a freelancer. I got hired by the *Jewish Telegraphic Agency* (for 30 months). Then I was at the *Washington Jewish Week* (for 30 months). I became editor. I had a great staff, including Larry Cohler. We had an independent owner [Dr. Leonard Kapiloff] who was erratic but gave us latitude to write some interesting things. We built up an interesting reputation for telling the truth at a time when that was not that accepted in the Jewish world that you would write something that would not reflect well, especially on Israel.

"I resigned after my late boss demoted me, ostensibly because I was too young (I was in my early 30s), but at the same time AIPAC was distributing a memo saying I was a leftist who shouldn't be editing a Jewish weekly. Apparently an AIPAC 'monitor' caught a speech I gave at a picnic for Washington-area left-wing groups, and alleged that by my speaking at a picnic for left-wing groups, I was endorsing their agenda. I spoke everywhere I was invited—that's one of the responsibilities of being an editor. My boss went through about ten editors in twelve years.

"My life has moved on. AIPAC has changed its stripes because suppressing debate now means suppressing the right. Norman Podhoretz wrote as soon as Rabin came to power that it's ok to criticize Israel. It's ok to criticize the Left. It put AIPAC out of their control-the-message business.

"In all my years with Larry [Cohler], I never remember printing a correction, clarification, or retraction. What AIPAC hated at the time, and what they still hate about the *Forward*, is that they don't think these things should be written about. They make the case that we need a unified voice when it comes to Israel because we are a beleaguered people. By reporting on dissent in the community, you give fodder to Israel's enemies.

"But consensus in the Jewish community does not exist. By not providing a voice to those who dissent, you disenfranchise a large part of the community. The Conference of Presidents can say, why are you printing these guys who have no standing in the community? Well, they have no standing in the community because they lost the vote. It doesn't mean they are not dues-paying members of the community. We need to be a voice for both.

"Malcolm Hoenlein (executive vice president of the Conference of Presidents of major American Jewish Organizations) recently spoke to the American Jewish Press Association on the topic of dissent in the community. He seemed to be troubled by articles that report dissent in the community. I think he had the *Forward* in mind. Jewish newspapers go to reliable people knowing they will disagree with the mainstream. And that's not responsible, according to Hoenlein. If the Conference of Presidents comes to a consensual idea, it's not responsible to go to *Tikkun* for a contrary opinion."

"You don't have any time for that view, right?"

"Who am I to read *Tikkun* out of the communal debate? If Bush doesn't get 30% of the [Jewish] votes come November, nobody is going to be surprised.

We've known all along that he still has vulnerabilities in the Jewish community.

"Republican Jews, to take another example, are a minority in the Jewish community, but we are obligated to publish their views.

"I'm not even sure what Malcolm would expect of us. Just to report Conference of Presidents proceedings as is without hinting about the debates that roil beneath the surface is a false picture of Jewish life."

"People like him who consume an enormous amount of journalism really don't have the first clue about it."

"Quite the opposite. Malcolm is a savvy player. He knows full well what we do. He thinks Jewish journalism has a different responsibility than mainstream journalism. And it is true: There is an advocacy part of what we do that demands that we work closely with the greater aims of the Jewish community. Then the debate comes who sets those aims. Malcom feels that as the professional at a group that represents consensus among the presidents of the top 52 Jewish organizations he's the closest you are going to get to it. They set the advocacy agenda. Jewish journalism should not undermine that agenda. It's a point of view about journalism. I think he understands journalism entirely."

"That's not journalism. That's *Pravda*."

"Umm, maybe. I won't go that far. I just know it's a different view of what we should be."

"You can't hold any truck with that."

"I tend not to. This is not to say that we don't think about a responsibility to Jewish life. We do have an advocacy role to play. I'm not neutral on Israel. I'm proudly pro-Israel. If there's a point of view expressed in the Israel Knesset, it's probably fair to have it expressed in the American Jewish community. There's Tommy Lapid, Ariel Sharon and Yossi Beilin. These are all good Jewish Israelis whose opinions should be expressed in our paper. It doesn't mean we'll print everything. It doesn't mean that I don't weigh the effects of what we do on Jewish well being."

"Is there much self-hating Jewish stuff written anymore?"

"I don't think there ever was. I don't buy that *Portnoy's Complaint* was self-hating. Where the self-hating stuff is supposedly going on today is on the far Left of the mainstream political debate. You've got a lot of Jews involved in the *Nation* magazine and [the anti-globalization and anti-Iraq war movement]. They are very critical of Israel. Tony Judt, who wrote that piece in the *New York Review of Books* questioning Israel's legitimacy. They have been described as self-hating. Not about American Jewry, but about Israel. I hate the term. I'd prefer to debate people on the stands they take, rather than delve into their psychologies."

"But they're not funny."

"Most of the interesting Jewish literature now is being written by the more observant core Jews. Roth and Wallace Markfield (*To an Early Grave*) were writing in reaction to assimilationist tension. Now the interesting stuff is by Allegra Goodman, Nathan Englander, who are looking at what is happening among Jews who are religious and involved. The assimilation thing has been played out. There is less reason for self hatred. The self-haters, if there ever were, opted out of Jewish life and the ones who stayed in are getting ever more Jewish."

"What did you think of *The New Rabbi*?"

"I think it is a terrific book. I belong to a Conservative synagogue. I can look out from my pew and see some of the people named in the book. I'm surprised by the reaction from all the Conservative rabbis about the damage he did. I thought it was a pro-rabbi book. It showed that lay leaders can be incredibly petty. It showed how difficult it can be for a rabbi to be a politician who has to please an entire congregation. The famous stuff about Perry Rank [that he wore his kipa side-saddle] made the synagogue look bad for focusing on such superficial things. It didn't make me think less of Perry Rank. I'm baffled [at the accusations that] Fried spoke lashon hara in this book. He did a lot of homework, got the cooperation of most of the people in the book, and told a useful story. I wouldn't want to be a rabbi and not read that book."

"**I was ticked off at the criticism by so many Conservative rabbis. These guys must be incredibly thin-skinned and control freaks.**"

"There's a certain amount of self importance in the role. It's one thing for you and I and Stephen Fried and Ari Goldman to agree that rabbis are public figures. If they don't see themselves as such, however, there's going to be a period of transition where they don't fully understand their role as public figures. They may find themselves saying things that a public figure would not. I don't know how much education is going on in the Jewish Theological Seminary about press relations. If you come up as a politician or a civil service executive, you have a press office.

"In community journalism, we say you're a public figure, whether you're the head of a pre-school or a day school principal, but they don't see themselves as such, so they're not savvy with the newspaper. They can get screwed. They don't know how to play the game. I tell my reporters all the time that we have some responsibility to tell them that we are going to be writing about this.

Think about how you want to message this. Make sure you are speaking for the synagogue and not just yourself."

"Is there good American Jewish journalism by Israeli papers?"

"Not much. I haven't been that impressed. The Israelis take a patronizing tone to nutty American Judaism, meaning Reform and Conservative Jews. Israelis don't have a grasp of American diversity.

"Federation papers can do a good job. The serious people you want to attract to Jewish causes are not going to be attracted to a newspaper that is pediatric or geriatric. If they see themselves and their concerns and their dissent reflected in the pages of the paper, they're more likely to respect the community and take part. That's how I sold myself to my current position and I think they buy it."

"Any reflections on your time guest-blogging on Protocols?"

"You're talking to the inside of the inside. Really smart people. I get a lot of ideas from them. They're insiders who are talking out of school every now and then. In between the rumors, there are the germs for a good story."

Andrew writes me later:

> Maybe the primary obstacle to a robust Jewish journalism is that there may not be a constituency for tough, iconoclastic reporting. I suspect that most of our subscribers, and subscribers to Jewish weeklies, do not want a newspaper that makes them feel uncomfortable about aspects of Jewish life. They feel we have a role to play as advocates, as comforters, as entertainers, and bulletin boards, but not as gadflies or the "afflicters of the comfortable." When we were publishing good investigative stuff at the *Washington Jewish Week* in the early 1990s, I felt there was a small elite of readers who appreciated what we were doing (the kinds of readers who gravitate to Protocols and the woefully under-subscribed *Forward*), a similarly-sized clique that felt we were bad for the Jews, but a remaining majority that didn't care much for that kind of reporting and flipped quickly to the recipes, synagogue announcements and wedding notices.
>
> It's a divide within religious life as well—there are many folks, and I'd guess they are the majority, who take part in religious life as if they were slipping into a warm bath, looking for comfort, solace, and reaffirmation of their basic beliefs and prejudices. Only an elite takes part to be intellectually challenged and spiritually discomfited. (I think this is true in all the movements.) That's not to say that the

complacent crowd is neither intellectual nor up for a challenge—only that they seek those challenges outside of affiliated Jewish life.

The question for me as an editor is, do I lead or follow? I think I try to split the difference—gently and responsibly lead them to uncomfortable places, but also provide the kind of stuff that affirms their basic commitment to their Jewishness. Does that sound wiggly? Perhaps. But I don't think there is an editor in the country, at any newspaper or media outlet, who doesn't weigh the platonic ideals of the journalist's profession against what he sees as the appetites of his community of readers.

Finally, the talent pool in Jewish journalism. Journalism and the media are already 'Jewish' professions and serve as magnets for the best and brightest of our community. Papers like mine are small, alternative, fairly low-paying—and unable to provide the prestige and opportunities available in the mainstream. That doesn't mean that I haven't worked with talented people—and still do. But the reality is that we're less able to compete for the 'major league' talent, and on the whole the product suffers as a result.

11

Larry Cohler-Esses

June 20, 2004

"I went to the University of Illinois. I majored in Anthropology. I went to the Journalism school for my masters degree [a thesis on the Jewish Defense League in Brooklyn], graduating in 1982. I became the editor of the Jewish Student Press Service (JSPS). It was founded by Jewish antiwar activists to be a Jewish students' forum for all the stuff going on on campuses. J.J. Goldberg, Lisa Schiffren (the woman who wrote Dan Quayle's speech about *Murphy Brown*), Aron Hirt-Manheimer (editor of *Reform Judaism* magazine), Yossi Klein Halevi, Larry Yudelson, who was the editor after me.

"Then I started working for the *Long Island Jewish World* (which employed Walter Ruby, Yossi Klein Halevi, and Sue Grossman, who became one of the first female Conservative rabbis). It was a writers' newspaper. It paid very little and it let you write what you want. You could go out and report and write without fear or favor.

"In 1986, the editor made an arrangement with eight different Jewish newspapers to send me down to Washington D.C. I got picked up by the *Washington Jewish Week* (1986–93). Then I was at *The Jewish Week* (NY) from 1994–2000."

"I hear you pissed off the establishment on a regular basis."

"I'm glad to know that. I didn't know that then because they didn't talk to me much."

"What are the principle obstacles to doing good Jewish journalism?"

"Money. Not meaning only salaries, but money to support the expenses involved in going to places and reporting firsthand. The censorship or influence of the owners of the papers. The self-censorship that people employ when they sense what the boundaries are. The expectations of readers. People don't read Jewish newspapers for the reason they read regular newspapers. People read regular newspapers to get information, whether they agree with the paper or not. People read Jewish newspaper to affirm their sense of identity. Often that means you are writing articles that people don't particularly want to know about.

"If you want to know to know about Israel, you can get most of your information from *The New York Times* and the *Washington Post*. You read the Jewish newspapers to get your sense of Israel's rightness in the world affirmed."

"What's your view of the way AIPAC attempted during your tenure [at the *Washington Jewish Week*] to keep the Jewish press in line?"

"It was atrocious. That's not their mission. Their mission statement doesn't say anything about them mucking around in Jewish newspapers. AIPAC tried to get me fired, Andy [Silow-Carrol] fired [from the *Washington Jewish Week* in 1992]. They never came to me with complaints about my coverage (with one or two exceptions). They didn't even go to the editor. They went to the owner.

"There was an AIPAC conference where James Baker (US Secretary of State under George Bush Sr.) called on supporters of Israel to give up on their dreams of a [territorially] greater Israel. In interviewing members of the audience after the speech, I talked to an AIPAC macher from Iowa. I quoted him accurately saying, 'That speech was garbage.' It went in the newspaper. I never heard anything until the owner of the paper, Dr. Leonard Kapiloff, called me into his office, showing me a letter from [AIPAC leader] Tom Dine, passing on a letter from this Iowa macher that not only is that quote not correct, Larry Cohler never even interviewed me. It's fabricated. Dr. Kapiloff had enormous respect and admiration for Tom Dine. He made it clear that the burden was on me.

"Fortunately, I had run out of notepaper that day. So the fellow I'd interviewed had given me his business card. So I had put my notes containing the key quote scribbled on the back of his business card. And I still had it. I showed that to the owner and that mollified him.

"The letter from Dine said this is an example of why we have a problem with Larry Cohler. I would like you and me to have dinner to discuss this problem.

"I remember once I was in the Israeli embassy with a couple of Israeli diplomats. One of them, who hadn't been in Washington that long, was talking freely to me. He said he was giving me this stuff because I'd know what to do with it. We were on the same team. The other diplomat, who'd been in Washington a while and knew my writing, said, no, no, it's not that way. You should treat it the same way as if you were talking to an Israeli reporter.

"I had good fortune in working for Dr. Kapiloff. He had a strong self image of being independent and iconoclastic. For reasons I never quite understood, he looked at me in an avuncular and almost paternalistic way. He thought I was a foster son of his. Especially after the Tom Dine incident convinced him that I was a diligent and conscientious reporter, he defended me. Because he got so much flack over me, and he didn't want to fire me, he fired editors. All the stories in question were about me. I felt like I was walking over bodies while leading a charmed life.

"The only legal threat I ever received came from AIPAC. They wanted me off the AIPAC beat. The counsel for AIPAC (the late David Ifshin) called [editor] Andy [Silow-Carroll] and hinted there could be legal problems. He said they were going to go over my articles with a fine-tooth comb and look for grounds for a lawsuit. They never sued.

"I had more freedom then than I have now [at the *New York Daily News*]. I was the first and only journalist from a Jewish newspaper to get a visa to go to Syria. I spent a week reporting from Syria. I went to Yemen. In 1988, he sent me to Tunis, where the PLO was then in exile. I did a series of interviews with the mastermind of the Munich Olympics massacre.

"This was the Jewish newspaper that members of Congress and the State Department see. It wasn't the type of stuff you normally find in a Jewish newspaper.

"I was very happy from a journalistic point of view. The salary was low—$35,000 annually when I left in late 1993. I made about $70,000 when I left *The Jewish Week* in NY in 2000. Only editors made more. I think the managing editor made $70,000 when I arrived.

"I wrote some stories about New York state Assemblyman Dov Hikind. It led to him being indicted along with three others for bribery. He was a member of the Jewish Defense League under Meir Kahane. He retained a lot of connections to that crowd. They tried to intimidate me during the trial. The judge had to call in an FBI agent to interview me to find out who had verbally threatened me in the court room.

"When I went to attend a press conference in which Hikind defended himself in Borough Park, a lot of people threatened to beat me up and I was hustled away. Dov Hikind was close to Governor Pataki. But he was not a favorite of the Jewish Establishment. The Jewish Establishment was probably as pleased as punch that I wrote those articles."

"Any prominent leaders in Jewish life refuse to talk to you?"

"The board members of AIPAC would never agree to speak with me (with a couple of brief exceptions when I caught them on the phone at home)."

"How much freedom did you have working for *The Jewish Week*?"

"It was pretty good. There were some boundaries. Gary Rosenblatt was sensitive to writing about Federation agencies in a critical fashion. He didn't prohibit it. He was just very sensitive about it. If I came to him with such a story, it had to be very good and meet a high standard."

"What do you miss and what do you not miss about working in Jewish journalism?"

"I miss engaging in issues that I cared about at the level of my own sense of identity. I don't miss the lack of resources. The *New York Daily News* has an editorial staff of about 200. I was like a farmer from Iowa who was trying desperately to look like the big city didn't phase him. There was a whole staff of librarians waiting at my beck n'call to search for me. From real estate databases to how to locate people with unpublished numbers to doing LexisNexis searches."

"Do you have more status in shul working for the *New York Daily News* or *The Jewish Week*?"

"The Bible of American Jews is *The New York Times*. My wife is a Conservative rabbi. Through her, I'm a member of a couple of overlapping spiritual communities. If it were not for her, I would not be a member of any minyan or spiritual community.

"As far as status, I might as well be writing for the *Buenos Aires Daily Herald*. It's not what they read. I more frequently heard about what I was writing when I was *The Jewish Week* than at the *Daily News*."

"Have you studied what Judaism says about Judaism and has this created any conflicts for you in how you practice your craft?"

"No. I don't think it has much relevance to me. It would have some academic interest. I am aware of real problems and conflicts that could exist between journalism and the injunction against lashon hara. I've always considered my standard for journalism to be secular."

"Do you ever have any discussions with your wife on these themes of Judaism vs. journalism?"

"In the beginning we did. She saw my investigative journalism as a Talmudic thing, because a lot of investigative journalism involves close reading of texts. But that's different from what I think you are getting at—the difference between Jewish ethics and journalism. I don't think we ever discussed that as a Jewish issue."

Larry married in 1996 and became Larry Cohler-Esses.

"Did you have a lot of stories that you couldn't publish?"

"I got to publish pretty much everything I had to say. There were a few occasions when the editing prevented me from saying it in the way I wanted it said."

In early 1996, Larry discovered that Malcolm Hoenlein of the Presidents Conference had a secret slush fund of almost a million dollars. Malcolm threatened Larry's editor Gary Rosenblatt that he would financially destroy *The Jewish Week* if it reported on his secret fund. So Gary held off on the story for 18-months before finally burying it in the August 8, 1997 issue.

While Gary sat on the story, Larry fumed. He went on an unofficial strike for 18-months, refusing to do further investigative journalism. As Larry pushed Gary to act, it destroyed his friendship with his editor and made it inevitable that he would one day leave the paper.

12

Sheldon Teitelbaum

June 21, 2004

"I got my first job in the US within a week of arriving. Tom Tugend, whom I knew from my work at the Jerusalem Post, told me they were starting up a new Jewish paper and were looking for writers. I had spent several years at the Post, writing investigative features, working on the night desk alongside (newly appointed Post editor) David Horovitz and (controversial Israeli historian) Benny Morris, sometimes editing copy by Wolf Blitzer, then the Washington correspondent. I met Gene one fine November morning at Federation HQ and he hired me on the spot. There was only one thing bothering him, he said, shuffling through my resume, looking quite troubled. How could I justify, morally, having served in the army of a foreign country—I had volunteered five years as an IDF officer—notably Israel?

"I was dumbfounded, absolutely thunderstruck. For one thing, I was not an American citizen. So unless Gene was representing Canadian Foreign Affairs, the question was moot. Twenty years in this country—and I am still not an American citizen—and no one ever asked me anything remotely like that. I worked for seven years on a high profile US government project, where my associations with Israel were well known, and no one there ever said a word to me critical of my dual citizenship. For the editor of the Federation-funded house organ of the second-largest Jewish community in North America, though, Israel was a foreign country and my service made me suspect.

"I quickly learned that Gene had no feeling for Israel at all. Moreover, he labored under the initial impression that most of his readers had little or no interest in the country either. Now I am not a card-carrying member of AIPAC—if anything, I joined the mammoth protest against the Lebanon War in Tel Aviv after returning home from a stint in southern Beirut and doffing my uniform. But this was like showing up for work at the News York Jewish Press and finding out that Noam Chomsky had been appointed editor. He described his view of Israel, which he had never visited prior to taking up his position, as "Hobbesian." Talk about projecting!

"Gene and I experienced any number of blowouts pertaining to the paper's coverage of Israel. I used to digest Hebrew news in translation. I ran an item culled from *Ha'aretz* about female Syrian Army recruits who went through an induction ceremony that involved biting the heads off snakes. We had these amazing pictures—it sure beat swearing over a rifle and Bible, per IDF practice. Gene came back to me complaining that the photo and caption I ran were racist. The fact that the caption dryly described what had transpired was immaterial—depicting Syrians as snake-biters was racist. Another time, I ran a short piece about an Israeli journalist who, 10 years after Entebbe, found himself on the tarmac at the site of the famed rescue operation. 'I just don't see the point of the story,' Gene said. 'What's the big deal?'

"Now admittedly, none of us at the paper (with the exception of Gene's lapdog, Yehuda Lev) came out of the American Jewish journalism world. Tom Waldman, who went on to become chief of staff for Congressman Howard Berman, came out of the USC School of Journalism with an MA. His interests were California politics and rock music. Steve Weinstein wanted to write fiction and went on to cover radio and TV for the Times. Joe Domanick, who was not Jewish, joined us soon after. He eventually authored, *To Protect and to Serve: The LAPD's Century of War in the City of Dreams, Cruel Justice: Three Strikes and the Politics of Crime in America's Golden State* and is now a senior fellow at USC Annenberg's Institute for Justice and Journalism.

"Gene had been an editor at *Esquire*. He was your basic New York Jewish intellectual. He swore by the *New York Review of Books*, he worshipped Phillip Roth and Anne Roiphe, and he almost never changed his sweater. He'd never belonged to a synagogue. He vacationed in Germany. He had no sense of the Jewish community, and no interest, he insisted, in cultivating one. It was almost a point of honor. Helming the paper for what—a dozen years—he kept his word.

"Within my first month, I wrote an article about Dennis Prager, who was the head of a major program at Brandeis Bardin. I remember Gene coming back to me that he had run into Barbie Weinberg (one of the machers at the

Federation who helped, I think, start the paper). She'd read my piece and insisted that it was not possible that whoever made whatever quote was made. I explained to Gene that I had learned early in my career never to go anywhere without a tape recorder. I immediately come home after an interview and transcribe it. I never use a notepad. I find that it helps with accuracy. When you interview someone, you're not always listening. Your mind is racing. You're dealing with noise. You're thinking of your next question. I found it is helpful to listen a second time.

"I told Gene that I had the tape. I have the transcript. His response was that it was not the truth or accuracy that he was interested in, it was the impression I made in the community. I was hostile. On the tape, though, I was just having a nice chat. He would not check it. His line from then on, 'I'm more interested in the impression you make in the community than in your craft or your veracity.' He said that people had complained that I seemed to be more interested in winning a Pulitzer than anything else. As if that was a terrible thing for a reporter to aspire to.

"Early on I did a story about the dearth of contacts between the local Jewish and Arab-American community. I was interviewing Casey ("America's Top 40" radio show host) Kasem, and he told me he had long wanted to reach out to his Jewish counterparts but he had no idea where to find them. It was no big mystery—most of them, I said, were holed up at 6505 Wilshire, the old Federation HQ. The rest, I said, were listed in various published directories. Kasem called up David Lehrer of the ADL and a few others and invited them for breakfast at Nibblers. My God, you'd have thought I'd set up a tryst with George Habash! The "feds" complained to Gene that I had crossed the line from reporting the news to creating the news. This merely by pointing Kasem (who later set up a long-lived Jewish-Arab outreach group called the Cousin's Club because of this effort) to a phone book. Gene, of course, intoned that once again, the facts of the matter were of no consequence. Hell of a way to run a paper.

"Gene wouldn't mind rocking other boats he didn't have a foot in. With impunity, he could've run pieces against Marvin Hier and the Wiesenthal Center. He could've written critically of Chabad. Nobody [at the Federation] would've said a word. But there were things that were the bailiwicks of the machers. The paper's independence was nonsense. It was never independent. The Federation put up the money and agreed to buy a set number of issues.

"There was a time that I couldn't bear to read the paper because I thought it was a crock of shit.

"I had a visceral response to Gene's refusal to back us. I had just come out of the Israeli army, where your commander (and I had experienced this at both ends) says "follow me!" He doesn't send you ahead of him. He sets the tone and pulls you forward. He's responsible for you if you cut your finger. And nobody's left behind. That was the credo I internalized during my five years in the army and afterwards in the reserves. It shocked me to see an editor of a major Jewish paper, in the first month, not only fold in front of the community, but offer up his own people as sacrificial lambs. I was gone within eight months. I got an offer from USC that paid better and generated less aggravation. You could say I ran screaming into the night.

"Tom and I did a piece in 1991 for *The LA Times* Sunday magazine on Rabbi Marvin Hier. One of the people that Tom interviewed was Stanley Hirsh, who at the time was the president of the Federation. There was a story about Yitzhak Shamir coming to town. Stanley said, and I salute his political impulses, 'I don't want to meet that fucking dwarf.' Tom quoted it in the piece.

"*The LAT*'s fact checker called Hirsh and he denied it. Even though we had it on tape, *The LAT*'s didn't want to hear the tape. They didn't want the aggravation. So it wasn't just the *Journal*.

"Stanley later boasted, 'Of course I said it. What do you think? I'm going to admit it to *The Times*?' This is the kind of thing that went on all the time and it drove me crazy—a fundamental cynicism and lack of integrity than ran throughout the leadership.

"The religious community hated the *Journal* from day one because it wasn't religious. Gene didn't have any feeling for Orthodox or Conservative Judaism. The only one who used to write about it was Yehuda Lev, who was to the left of Tommy Lapid [an opponent of Orthodox sway in Israeli politics].

"The Orthodox were understandably never favorably disposed towards the Federation. So the thinking [at the *Jewish Journal* under Gene Lichtenstein] may have been, why cover them if their people do not donate on Super Sunday? The Federation's main interest in funding this paper and anything else it does was to get people to donate funds to cover its overhead, and to do good works. In which order of priority I can't say."

"Rob Eshman has bent over backwards to reach out to the Orthodox."

"Rob Eshman has bent over backwards in any way he could think of to reach out to people estranged from the paper. He cares about the quality of the writing he runs. That's rare in the Jewish journalism world. I don't think he has any axes to grind. I don't think he has a mean-spirited bone in his body.

I think he delights in the pluralism of this community. I don't think he's the least interested in shutting people out of the paper.

"Hershel Shanks asked to do a profile of Michael Lerner for *Moment* magazine. I talked to many people. I wrote a long piece balanced between his detractors, who were vituperative, and his defenders, who were passionate. I got a phone call from Hershel—he really liked the piece. Then I got a call a week later from Hershel. He didn't like the piece. He felt I had been too soft on Lerner. He sent back a version of the piece in which every single statement that might have mitigated a negative profile had been removed. It was a hatchet job. I said to him, if you're going to do that, you're going to have to take my name off. He said fine. He put his name on the piece. Michael Lerner was furious with me. He felt I should've know that was what was going to happen ultimately. It was my worst nightmare. I couldn't believe that anyone would do such a thing. On the other hand, I cashed the check. Shame on me!"

"Jewish journalism does not attract our best and brightest."

"Do you think there is a writer for any of these papers who wouldn't rather be writing for The LA Times or a major magazine? Present company included? The best and the brightest may use it as a stepping-stone. I've written for any number of front-ranking American, Canadian and Israeli publications on subjects as disparate as film and TV, telecommunications, science and travel. But I keep coming back to covering Jewish life. The irony, I suppose, is that I left Israel convinced that there was no future in English-language journalism there, and none for me in Hebrew-language journalism. So here I am in Agoura Hills, a staff senior writer for a major Israeli newsmagazine and, 20 years after arriving, continue to write for the *Jewish Journal*, the *Forward* and various other Jewish periodicals. Go figure."

13

Gary Rosenblatt

June 24, 2004

From the *Columbia Journalism Review* November 2000 issue:

> Public beratement, private pressure, advertiser ultimatums—such is the usual scenario when an ethnic news organization exposes a scandal within the ethnic community it serves. And so it was for New York's *Jewish Week*, whose June 23 edition carried a disturbing front-page special report. "Stolen Innocence," by editor and publisher Gary Rosenblatt, documented a long and longtime record of allegations that Rabbi Baruch Lanner, a revered educator in the Union of Orthodox Jewish Congregations who worked closely with its teenage members for more than three decades, had sexually, emotionally, and physically harassed and abused scores of youngsters in his care. More unnerving—and embarrassing—still, was the further revelation that the Orthodox Union, fully aware of Lanner's behavior, had chosen to avert its gaze. On learning of the newspaper's investigation—which included dozens of on-the-record interviews with Lanner's victims—OU officials, invoking the Jewish law against "malicious gossip," pressed Rosenblatt to keep the matter private. But Rosenblatt's better journalistic angel prevailed, and *Jewish Week* went to press. This is what happened after that: the OU forced the rabbi to resign as director of regions of its youth organization, and commissioned an independent inquiry; two congregations suspended their OU membership in protest of the cover-up; more vic-

tims came forward and filed complaints with local prosecutors; two rabbis used their pulpits to castigate the paper; a major advertiser threatened to lead a boycott; and readers showered *Jewish Week* with letters of praise.

A former stand-up comic and a dynamic public speaker, Gary Rosenblatt, editor of *The Jewish Week*, sounds half asleep, partly distracted and somewhat medicated when we chat by phone.

"I sometime describe our ongoing dilemma this way—a Jewish journalist works with two competing mandates. The first commandment for journalists is to probe, explore and uncover and all the things people expect when they pick up their daily paper. On the other hand, one of the commandments in the organized Jewish community is the opposite, to cover-up and create a unified front, and not present any negative impression to the outside world. The Yiddish expression, *shander fer de goyim* (scandal for the goyim). You're always walking that tightrope—doing the job of a journalist and being a responsible part of the Jewish community.

"We're like the Rodney Dangerfields of Jewish life. We don't get any respect. On the other hand, it is incremental in building respect. I think it can be there. It depends on the paper and the individual. It is too easy to hide behind the notion that there is some inherent part of our job that makes us not respected by the community. If you do a good job, you are respected by the community.

"One of my first jobs was with *TV Guide* (sports editor from 1970–72). If you get a high from writing for a big audience, that was great. Now I get to combine my love of journalism with Jewish life. The downside is the same. Sometimes it can be dispiriting when you see the pettiness of the community you really care about. People you admire until you meet them. See their egos and the things that motivate them. Sometimes you wish you had just known them from a distance."

"How do you deal with threats, such as threats to the financial survivability of the paper if you publish something that a powerful person does not want?"

"It is part of the nature of the job. I remember in Baltimore, we did a story about Israel bonds. We were told that if that story appeared, it would not only hurt that local bonds drive, but the state of Israel was going to suffer. They both survived.

"That doesn't mean I'm dismissive of what you'd call a threat, which is a pretty strong word. A cautionary message. I try to take them all seriously and not be so cavalier as to not think about the consequences of things we write. My experience has born out that the sun will still come up the next day. I have yet to see the kind of article that would be so destructive. There are threats of boycotting the paper and boycotting our advertisers but it hasn't gone anywhere."

"**Your paper was famous for its investigation of [Rabbi] Baruch Lanner and the abuse situation. Many people think that have you information about other rabbis who were similarly abusive. You even wrote a column about information pouring in to you. But you didn't seem to go on to investigate other rabbis with the same zest you applied to Lanner?**"

"I don't think that's accurate. I have a lot of files. One rabbi in particular I've been trailing for over three years. I've talked to many dozen people. I have to apply the same standards as I would for the Lanner story. We have done stories about other rabbis and other cases of abuse. Until it meets that bar, I have continued to pursue some of these stories.

"I think the Lanner stories have had a corrective element. I've written that I don't think that the newspaper should be the mechanism for dealing with these issues. There should be communal mechanisms. The reason people come to us is that they have struck out everywhere else in the community. They come to us out of frustration and desperation."

"**How would you rate the quality of Jewish journalism done on the Federations?**"

"It depends on city to city, newspaper to newspaper, issue to issue. If I pick up a Jewish newspaper from different parts of the country, I sometimes wouldn't know what community I was reading about if I covered up the masthead. It's a lot easier to run a JTA story about what is going on in Israel than to send a reporter to cover a conflict in your own neighborhood. It's cheaper and safer to run the JTA."

"**Are there any individuals in the Jewish Establishment who you would regard as the greatest threats to Jewish journalism because they're bullies?**"

"Yeah. I wouldn't name them. I've met some national Jewish leaders who've told me, not in a bullying way, that they believe that the role of Jewish newspapers is to promote Israel and the Jewish community and to unify the community and not to write critical articles about the community. I differ with that. The best way to educate, enlighten and involve people in the Jewish community is to tell them what is really going on. If we tell them we are one, all we do is lose our credibility. I don't think we are one is a goal."

"How often do you encounter bullying?"

"There are varying degrees of it, from canceling subscriptions to stopping advertising to getting my friends to do those things."

"What's the biggest hit you've taken for publishing a story?"

"It's hard to measure. When the Lanner story first broke, we were threatened with institutions pulling their advertising. We didn't see it happen."

"What are the joys and tribulations of being a Federation paper?"

"We do not consider ourselves a Federation paper. We have no formal ties with the UJA Federation. There was a time when the UJA were ex-officio members of the board of *The Jewish Week* but that stopped about eight years ago. They buy subscriptions for people who give $50 or more to UJA."

"Does that make them the dominant force behind the paper?"

"Yeah, in that sense, sure. Then we have close to 30,000 subscribers directly."

"How many papers does the Federation buy?"

"Between 55,000 and 70,000."

"If they are buying about twice the number of papers than subscribers, could not the paper be fairly called a Federation paper?"

"I don't think so. We have no formal ties. They don't have any say in editorial or financial matters. It's their choice. They think it serves them well to supply their donors with a Jewish newspaper.

"Some of the pressure I got in Baltimore, where we were an independent paper, was just as strong as the pressure I get here. From the Federation and the establishment."

"If you wrote a memoir, would you have a pile of stories you weren't able to work into the Jewish papers you've worked on?"

"I have a file I keep called, 'My Last Issue.' Not necessarily a tell-all memoir, I'd just like to deal with some of these issues."

"There isn't a market for hard-hitting muckraking Jewish journalism for a Jewish audience?"

"Jewish readers tend to be very bright, well-read, sophisticated people, and if you present them good journalism, I think they will want to read it."

"What did your father the rabbi think of your going into journalism?"

"He was proud of me. He used to tease me that if I stayed away from the rabbinate because I saw you live in a glass house, he'd say he only had his congregants giving him a hard time while I had everybody giving me a hard time. But they don't pay my salary directly."

"How do you think the Internet and blogging is affecting Jewish journalism?"

"I always wonder who has the time to read a lot of these blogs. I don't get the impression that those audiences are wide but I guess they're pretty deep. It does give me a lot of pause because I think it has the potential to reach as many people as standard journalism but it doesn't have the checks and balances and an editing process that more normative journalism has. That's something to worry about."

"You think that's more of a downer than a good sign?"

"It's certainly worrisome. People can come home late at night and write anything off the top of their head and send it out and it's out there."

"Is that scary?"

"It can be."

"Do you think we have too many checks and balances in Establishment Jewish journalism?"

"No. They are the same checks and balances you have in any professional journalistic enterprise, maybe with an added element of sensitivity, which I don't think is a bad thing. I don't think it is a question of whether or not you do a story but how you do a story. I don't see any stories that are absolutely verboten, but it depends on how you treat it."

"You should be sensitive to save people's feelings?"

"You should be aware of feelings. At times it is inevitable you will hurt people's feelings, say a rabbi who's losing a job. You have to weigh that against what you owe the readers in the larger community. Those are tough calls. I don't think there are clear definitions. They are ad hoc and made as much from your kishkes as from your brains."

"Did you read the book *The New Rabbi*?"

"Yeah. There was a lot that I admired and I think he went a little too far sometimes in exposing people, specifically embarrassing them in ways that he could've handled a little more indirectly and gotten the same message across and not be as hurtful."

Gary wouldn't answer any of my tough questions, nor would he send me any of his old columns when I requested them.

In my interviews, I never found a journalist (except for Yossi Abramowitz, who Gary has blacklisted from his paper, and Jason Maoz of *The Jewish Press*) who was willing to criticize Gary on the record. Most of them wanted to be friends with Gary. They regarded him as Mr. Jewish Journalism.

I was anonymously mailed some revealing correspondence in and out of Gary's office.

> April 21, 1997
> From: Gail J. Hyman
> Group Vice President Marketing & Communications
> UJA-Federation of New York
> To: Mr. Gary Rosenblatt
>
> I wanted to put in writing our growing concern over the continuing lack of presence for UJA-Federation we feel in the page of *Jewish Week*.
>
> Despite several regional pieces that ran last week on agency activities and the Joint Passover story on page 44, it is still difficult to locate UJA-Federation's name or communal role in the paper. Only a thorough read of all editions of the paper uncovers our identity; there remains no visible presence for us organizationally.
>
> I bring this perspective to your attention because our leadership's increasing frustration and dissatisfaction with *Jewish Week* is at an all time high. Coverage of UJA-Federation, even as we engage in dialogue with you to change the situation, remains inconsistent. It is no longer sufficient to tell our leadership we are making progress when the newspaper demonstrates otherwise. It would seem that unless improvement in coverage of UJA-Federation is immediately forthcoming, meetings with the new subcommittee will not be of any use.
>
> Gary, it would seem that based on the paper's track record in recent weeks, your commitment to assuring a consistent presence for UJA-Federation is in question.

....

From Gary Rosenblatt:
Dear Mr. and Mrs. [Lawrence] Tisch [of Rye, NY 10580]:

I have been told that you were hurt by my column in last week's issue of *The Jewish Week* and for this I sincerely apologize.

My intention was not to cause you embarrassment but to highlight some of the complex issues involved regarding Jewish views on smoking.

This unfortunate incident reminds me of the moral of a story my late father, who was a rabbi in Annapolis, MD, for 40 years, used to tell. It is about a man who went to his Chasidic rabbi to ask how he could undo a hurtful comment he had made in public about a neighbor. The rabbi told him to go home, take a feather pillow, rip it apart out in his yard, and then return for further instruction. After the man did as he was told, the rabbi told him to go home and bring him all of the feather from the pillow, for only then would he be forgiven.

I am particularly mindful of that lesson now, and if I had it do over again, I would have tried to express my views in the column without bringing specific names into it.

In writing columns and editorials in Jewish community newspapers for more than 20 years, I have always tried to be sensitive to those I write about. But in these last few days I have come to appreciate that I can never be too attuned to people's feelings and I will strive to be more diligent in the future.

Perhaps I had come to think of your family as an institution rather than consisting of real people with real feelings. In any case, please know that I have the greatest respect for you and your good works and hope that in that spirit you will understand, if not forgive, my words from last week.

....

August 31, 1995
Draft Letter To All *Jewish Week* Board Members
[From Richard L. Hirsch, president, cc'd to Gary Rosenblatt, Richard Waloff]

By now, most of the Board members are probably aware of the controversy that erupted following publication of Gary's column "Where There's Smoke" in our August 18th issue. The Tisch family [which owns Lorillard Tobacco Company] and Lester Pollack took umbrage at the criticism leveled therein and, not surprisingly, UJA took up the cause in defense of their honor as major philanthropists. On August 24th, a meeting between representatives of *The Jewish Week* and UJA was held, yielding two outcomes:

1. An oversight had occurred and the Board expressed regret along with unwavering support of *The Jewish Week* staff. Gary on the one hand, and Mort and I on the other, would send the Tisch family and Lester Pollack conciliatory letters to smooth over any offense that might have been taken.

2. This relatively small controversy—which for the most part has been resolved—has further galvanized UJA's desire to dissolve its formal association and financial ties with *The Jewish Week* over a shorter time period than previously agreed upon.

The second point above is the larger issue which we at *The Jewish Week* need to focus on. The Board has courted this matter over the years but the time has come to address it proactively.

I believe that we must tread cautiously in these discussions, but at the same time be sensitive to the position of UJA. *The Jewish Week* has a terrific staff and an excellent product and we must protect not only our financial investment but, most importantly, the *Week*'s raison d'etre.

....

To: *The Jewish Week*'s Board of Directors
From: Louise Greilsheimer, Stephen D. Solender [Federation machers, this letter was composed on Gail Hyman's computer]
Date: April 7, 1997
Re: Strengthening the UJA Federation/*Jewish Week* Relationship

While we recognize and take great pride in our longstanding and generally positive relationship with *Jewish Week*, we also acknowledge that there is a need to improve it. Indeed, at times, the relationship between UJA-Federation and *Jewish Week* has been a difficult and ambiguous one. We wish to clarify and strengthen it by each of us committing to our shared long-term goal of providing the Jewish community with news about it and the work of UJA-Federation, its campaigns and agencies.

To that end, UJA-Federation will continue to make its donor list available to *Jewish Week* for subscriptions so long as *Jewish Week* provides UJA-Federation with the regular "presence" it needs.

While we recognize *Jewish Week* as a quality paper in which we can all take pride, we believe it can maintain its quality while also fulfilling UJA-Federation's need for presence.

We are suggesting that a joint group of UJA-Federation and *Jewish Week* leadership be formed to regularly monitor the agreed upon goals and execute the plan as detailed in this memorandum. As was stated in the UJA-Federation Board of Directors resolution of February, 1994:

"WHEREAS, a fundamental principle governing UJA-Federation's consideration is that it remains committed to having a Jewish newspaper reach all of our donors so that issues concerning the Jewish community, including the message of UJA-Federation's campaign and the story of our agencies, is told and a sense of commitment and community is developed among our donors at the lowest possible cost…"

We are committed to assuring that this resolution be realized through our strengthened relationship.

RECOMMENDATION: To clarify UJA-Federation's relationship with *Jewish Week*, we recommend that the following statement be included in the paper's staff box: "*Jewish Week* is an independent community newspaper. UJA-Federation buys subscriptions for its donors to assure that they are informed of news of the Jewish community. UJA-Federation bears no responsibility for the news or editorial material contained herein. Any positions reflected are solely those of the *Jewish Week*."

The Executive Committee of UJA-Federation recommends the following changes to increase coverage and give UJA-Federation presence both graphically and editorially.

* Priority changes proposed by UJA-Federation's executive committee.

* EDITORIAL: Train and sensitize *Jewish Week* reporters and editors to UJA-Federation as a resource and seek out its perspective on important stories. (EXAMPLE: The December 27th issue, UP CLOSE section, "Target Practice." We would have preferred more opportunity to help shape the piece, as well as provide more balance through either a sidebar or column.)

* UJA-Federation's role should be integrated into any featured story concerning one of its agencies. Encourage reporters to use UJA-Federation professional staff as key resources to help shape agency-based stories from our perspective, with our insights.

* Develop one UJA-Federation cover story per month in all editions (12 a year).

* LEADERSHIP COLUMN: Arrange for a monthly column by a broad representation of UJA-Federation leadership. Columns would be assigned to appropriate leadership and scheduled to address timely and important organizational efforts/issues.

* ADVERTISING: UJA-Federation should be the first full-page ad; UJA-Federation should develop an ad to conform with the space of the inside front cover page.

* Greater sensitivity of all UJA-Federation ad placements that should emphasize not only which page the ad appears but what sections its appears in (i.e. Israel Experience ad should have appeared opposite Israel page).

* OTHER PROPOSED CHANGES: In addition to the above stated priorities we recommend the following changes be made to assure UJA-Federation's presence in the *Jewish Week*.

* EDITORIAL: Use the first 15 to 20 pages in the general N.Y. section (in all editions) to find ways to feature UJA-Federation programs and events (as done in the Dec. 20th issue). Also, in those pages, provide greater UJA-Federation presence in headlines or kickers—including our name whenever possible.

* Use cover-page teasers to UJA-Federation stories, including the UJA-Federation name whenever possible.

* Wherever possible or appropriate, augment *Jewish Week* human-interest stories with a UJA-Federation perspective (via box or sidebar of our programs). Encourage *Jewish Week* to share with UJA-Federation professional staff, on a weekly basis, stories that they are working on. This weekly story development list would provide UJA-Federation the opportunity to assure that its perspective be included in more stories.

* Seek ways to incorporate UJA-Federation role in the first three to five pages of the paper, "In the Beginning" section (see Dec. 20th issue, page four—New World Symphony photo, NYANA, with no mention of UJA-Federation).

* Create special UJA-Federation mission calendar in travel section, update quarterly.

* Major post-event UJA-Federation stories should be covered, whether through a story or photo, in all editions, not limited to the calendar pages of one edition (Lawyers Division dinner photo in Dec. 20th issue deserved better placement, and its relevancy transcended the borders of the Manhattan edition where it appeared).

14

Michael Berenbaum

June 25, 2004

"I am still an observant Jew. I do not use denominational ties but we daven [at a Conservative temple]. I was ordinated [Orthodox] by Rabbi Yaakov Rabin zt'l [at age 23].

"I was ordained because of Vietnam, but it proved to be one of the most important things in my life. It imposed upon me a responsibility to the Jewish past—and the Jewish future—and to become a producer of Torah and not just a consumer."

A Holocaust scholar, Dr. Berenbaum is a part-time professor at the University of Judaism. Married for the second time, he has four kids, aged 31, 26, 5, 4.

As I sit on Michael's couch, his five year old boy asks him, "Who's that man?"

"He wants to interview me," says the professor.

"Are you going to be on television?"

"I don't know."

Two minutes later, the boy asks his father again, "Are you going to be on television?"

A minute later, I begin.

"Could you sketch your Jewish journalism career?"

"I got into it by accident. Dr. Leonard Kapiloff, who had just bought *Washington Jewish Week*, asked me to edit the paper."

A journalist writes me:

> In [November 1984,] the then book-editor of *Washington Jewish Week*, Michael Berenbaum, reported the ongoing secret rescue of thousands of Ethiopian Jews from refugee camps in Sudan on page one of the paper. *The New York Times* had also been aware of the rescue, known as Operation Moses. But it had acceded to an urgent request from Jewish leaders and Israel to delay publishing until it was finished. Once Michael published his story, *The Times* considered itself freed from the embargo and published the next day.
>
> This ultimately to overthrow of Sudanese President Gen. Jaffar Numieri, who had cooperated with the plan at U.S. behest. I do not doubt that people in the camps died as a result.
>
> Michael decided to run with the story, which he, like *The Times*, had been sitting on, after he saw that The Jewish Agency had put news about it in one of their press releases. They did so in order to brag about their role. Hardly anyone actually read their propaganda, which they issued by the bushel. Michael did. In fact, some Federations even took out ads in Jewish newspapers alluding to the rescue as part of their fundraising pitch. The Agency was chaired at the time by Arye Dulzin. It was he who made the decision. Israeli Ambassador Meir Rosenne called [editor Charles Fenyvesi] at the printing plant in Gaithersberg as the paper was going to press to beg him to kill the story. But he refused.
>
> Michael defended himself by citing the standards of secular journalism. If the quasi-governmental agency participating in the Jews' rescue wasn't embargoing the news, why should a newspaper? After all, it was in a press release. It didn't matter. The calumny of the entire Jewish world stormed down on Berenbaum's head. He was effectively a murderer of Jews.
>
> Dr. Kapiloff publicly defended his editor against the hail of charges raining down on him. But after a decent interval, Michael [and Charles Fenyvesi were] quietly shoved aside.
>
> Michael, who had substantial scholarly credentials, went on to become content designer for the now famous Washington Holocaust Museum. Later, he directed the Shoah Oral History project established by Stephen Spielberg.

Michael's editor was Charles Fenyvesi. An erudite Hungarian Jew, Fenyvesi published a story by one of his reporters that revealed to Washington a reality widely known, and already reported on Israel: The then-Israeli envoy to Washington, Meir Rosenne, was considered a nonentity in Jerusalem. Israel's leaders routinely bypassed him to go directly to the US leaders with whom they wanted to deal and threw his cables into the wastebasket. He was considered ineffective and irrelevant.

The story caused a storm at the embassy. It was one thing to have this kind of thing published 10,000 miles away. But now everyone in Washington knew the truth. Rosenne retaliated with the harshest penalty at his command: He imposed a ban on embassy staff from talking to *Washington Jewish Week*. Worse, he banished Dr. Kapiloff from admission to all embassy functions.

This was very painful for Dr. Kapiloff. He deeply treasured the contacts and connections to Israeli movers and shakers that his ownership of the paper facilitated. He didn't seem to care too much about criticism, but being thrown out of the room altogether was something else. Once again, he did not fire Fenyvesi immediately. But after a decent interval, Charles Fenyvesi was fired—ostensibly for refusing to give up a regular gardening column he wrote for the *Washington Post*. Dr. Kapiloff said it was a conflict of interest.

"What are the obstacles to doing good Jewish journalism?"
"There are many pressures to not doing good Jewish journalism. The first pressure in those days was—you're not supporting the state of Israel if you tell any bad news. The second is that you will weaken the community. You're doing a disservice to hardworking wonderful volunteers. Why not only tell the good story? Why not only give a good book review? Why not only give a good opinion?

"Journalists, by their nature, should be standing apart. You have to be prepared to be critical, to make some enemies, and to say some tough things. We ran a story shortly after I left, but it started when I was still editor, on the bypass of Meir Rosenne. There were a series of meetings at the White House at which Meir Rosenne was not represented. That turned out to be the key to understanding the Iran-Contra story because they [Israeli government] deliberately kept Meir Rosenne out of the loop because the Israelis didn't want to ruin the ambassador as they were raising the issues of the Iran-Contra story. Remember, they were trading arms for hostages.

"The ambassador protested. The embassy was livid. When the *Washington Jewish Week* puts that on the front page, it weakens the Israeli ambassador, at a time when he needs to be strong. Israel's in danger. In the same way that Gary Rosenblatt got tremendous pressure when he had his greatest moment in Jewish journalism with the Baruch Lanner story. That's the moment he entered Jewish journalism. Nobody else could've made the case. It's a shanda fer de yidden. It's a shanda fer de goyim. How can you embarrass [Lanner]? You're indicting the Orthodox infrastructure. You make a series of enemies and you pay a price. The community is trying to raise funds. Institutions are trying to survive. Israel is in a precarious situation. Soviet Jewry is in danger.

"To be a journalist, there has to be streak in you that values truth-telling over other things. Institutions are better if they have to fear the press and behave appropriately lest X, Y or Z happen. I conduct my personal affairs as if they could appear on the front page of the *Washington Post* and I could hold my head high. I've seen too many people get into trouble, like this guy [Jack Ryan] in Illinois today who had to drop out [of a political race]. The fear of the press is like the fear of the wrath of God. The press finds out what we'd like to hide and God apparently knows what we'd like to hide."

"Tell me about your story on Operation Moses."

"Nothing happened after we ran the story except we got a ton of heat. Nothing happened after *The New York Times* ran the story. It was about ten weeks later that the Israeli government confirmed the story. After they confirmed the story, the rescue of Ethiopian Jewry stopped for a period of time, and then it resumed clandestinely. We reported something in the story that ended up making the organized American Jewish community look terrible.

"It was not a secret story. Leon Dulzin [head of the Jewish Agency, which feeds and rescues needy Jews] had told it to all of the people at the GA [General Assembly of Jewish groups]. He told 3,000 people sworn to secrecy because he wanted to convince them that their new campaign was for the rescue of Ethiopian Jewry, which was not the case. The American government had allocated $85 million for the rescue. If the Jewish Agency was going to be responsible for anything, it would be for the resettlement of Ethiopian Jewry, which is significantly less sexy than rescue."

"Did any part of you die during that experience?"

"Was I upset by it? Absolutely. Did I relish being called a murderer of Jews? Absolutely not. I had devoted my entire career to the rescue of Jews and the preservation of the remnants of Jewish communities. I've been active in the rescue of Soviet and Ethiopian Jewry. I traveled to the Soviet Union a half dozen times on quasi-clandestine things.

"I ended up being disinvited from a couple of forums. My income suffered significantly. Prior to that, I spoke for Federations routinely. I did not speak for Federations for years thereafter. I became persona non grata but that's the price you pay for doing what you do."

"Do you have any regrets about the article?"

"Had I known all the elements involved in that, I'm not sure I would've run the article. In one sense, it wasn't worth the costs that it had to my life, Fenyvesi's life, Kapiloff's life, and to whatever indirect role we had, if any, in the decision of the Israeli government to release the information on the rescue of the Ethiopian Jewry.

"If anything, the heat should have gone on Arye Dulzin. If you are doing clandestine operations, you don't reveal it to 3,000 people. You don't put ads in a newspaper. You don't issue a press release.

"We had an independent owner. Most Jewish journalists are supported by a Federation. Therefore, there are limits on what they can say. They know those limits. You can count on two hands the number of independent Jewish weeklies and journals.

"Gary Rosenblatt knows how to walk the line, how to not go outside the consensus."

"Are there any Jewish publications that you would regard as a riveting read?"

Long pause. "That's a good question. There are sometimes things in the *Forward* that I like reading. I read *The Jewish Week*, not because I regard it as a riveting read, but because it is a temperature of the community. I read the local *Jewish Journal* because I feel I have to be part of this community. I used to read *Sh'ma* regularly in [rabbi] Eugene Borowitz's day. The first time I published was in *Sh'ma*. Gene had a unique capacity to have Jews listen to a variety of points of view in the Jewish community. It was a lively exchange. It's had a difficult time after it lost Gene's voice. *Moment* had a difficult time after it lost Leonard Fein's voice. Hershel Shanks is a good friend of mine but he doesn't have enough of a driven voice to give the magazine passion. He's too even-keeled and it comes out parve. I don't read *Tikkun* or *Commentary* regularly.

[Michael is on *Tikkun*'s editorial board. On its Web site, the magazine incorrectly describes him as Orthodox.]

"J.J. Goldberg was under enormous pressure years ago, when he was a columnist, for some of the stuff he was writing against Morton Klein, who can't even read Hebrew. He's a holier than thou returnee, not to Judaism, but to a certain type of political Zionism. The *Jewish Exponent* dropped [J.J.'s] column. I thought the *Forward* in Seth Lipsky's [Seth's paper, purportedly right-wing, endorsed Bill Clinton twice and David Dinkins for New York mayor in 1993] time was vicious, inaccurate and irresponsible.

"I sit on a foundation board and interview people who get fellowships. One of the persons applying wrote about how she covered a *Tikkun* convention in New York and how Lipsky rewrote her story to be vicious and hard-hitting against Lerner, when she was impressed by the Jewish energy in the room. She had submitted an essay on her cowardice. She didn't fight for her story. I wouldn't let a guy do that to me. I would've stormed out of there. Even though her essay was well-written, it confirmed everything I knew about Lipsky. I didn't understand how this woman representing her cowardice was going to be her way of getting a fellowship.

"My most important involvement with the *Forward* on that was on the John Roth story. He was named as my successor as director of the Holocaust Museum. The *Forward* issued an attack on his writing. They misquoted him completely. Roth and I have written a couple of books together. He's one of my best friends in the world.

"I put a $10,000 check on the table [with the author of the *Forward* article, Ira Stoll]. I said, 'If you have quoted him correctly, you can keep this check.' Ira Stoll had quoted him from a Harry Jaffe article that had misrepresented the essence of Roth's remarks and left out a series of qualifiers. It was the act of ultimate irresponsibility. He had used the Net, a right-wing paraphrase, as though Roth had compared Hitler to Reagan.

"Roth then said forget it. Roth was a tenured full professor at Claremont. He thought, why the hell do I want to go into a political sewer?"

"What's your critique of J.J. Goldberg and the *Forward*?"

"First, I don't think he has yet established an Op/Ed page that reflects dramatic opinion in the [style of] *The New York Times* and *Washington Post*. That you have an understanding of the issues and you shape an agenda. There are enough people writing enough powerful stuff that the *Forward* should be able to do it. There are usually two or three good stories each week and the rest of the paper is not worth reading. The Culture section is sometimes very good."

"What's your critique of Gary Rosenblatt and *The Jewish Week*?"

"Gary earned his place in Gan Eden [world to come] by virtue of what he did on the Lanner thing. He's too tame. He often comes off as if he is ball-less. When he had some good journalists working for him, he restrained them from covering anything too controversial. He had Larry Cohler. I helped train Larry. You've got to let him do his stuff and stick by him and 99% of the time you will end up with something of worth. Larry was essentially driven out. He found out that Gary was without balls. Larry may sometimes be without brains but he is never without balls. Gary tends to be tame and timid.

"*The Jewish Week* doesn't have a good Arts section or a good book review section. Jewish life in its intellectual sphere is flourishing. How a paper like that in New York isn't covering books and literature and arts and dance and theatre at the center of where that is exciting, I don't understand. I don't understand that with my friend [Rob Eshman] at the *Jewish Journal*. How can you not cover this? Stuff gets covered in *The New York Times* book review or the *New York Review of Books* but *The Jewish Week* doesn't say a goddamn thing about it. The *Jewish Journal* doesn't say a goddamn thing about it.

"For example, compare the review of David Myers' book [*Resisting History: Historicism and Its Discontents in German-Jewish Thought*] by Rabbi Daniel Bouskila in the *Jewish Journal* with the way [Samuel Moyn] from Columbia reviewed it in the *Forward* and you see the difference between something that is serious and something that is not serious. In the areas I know well, these guys are not committed to it. Even if you were Gary and you wanted to play it safe, you could raise every issue you wanted to raise through the book review section that you don't want to review elsewhere."

"**How much status do journalists for Jewish media have in Jewish life?**"

"Jewish journalists who want to write on Jewish issues and want to have an impact and earn money are better off going mainstream and writing occasionally on Jewish issues. They get greater freedom, exposure, and financial incentives. Take Tom Friedman, Richard Cohen, Wolf Blitzer. Wolf began writing as the Washington correspondent for *The Jerusalem Post*. He used to work for me. I used to pay him $25 a week for his column. Wolf wasn't even that good of a journalist. Wolf got one piece of luck. He went to work for CNN during the Gulf War. He knew all the weaponry because of what he'd covered for Israel. He knew the Pentagon and the Middle East better than anyone else."

"**Professors have more status in Jewish life.**"

"Professors can wrap themselves around a specific expertise. They know something. A good journalist should know how to know something. The Jewish community likes people who are credentialed in the secular world."

"What have you learned about journalism from being a subject of it?"

"The more I know about a field, the less a journalist is accurate. I suspend my belief that they know something in fields that I do not know.

"Journalists in Israel fuel the debate. They shape the government. They shape the perceptions of society in the same way that mainstream American journalists do. People don't do that in the Jewish world. They're not regarded as having that status."

"Would you agree or disagree with the adjective dull applied to most Jewish journalism?"

"How could you disagree with that? It's a fair judgment."

Jewish journalist Allison Kaplan Sommer writes me:

> Of course Gary lacks balls. He's the editor of a Federation paper. If you want to keep these kind of jobs, especially long-term, lacking balls is a requirement.
>
> Just like if you want to set up an independent Web site covering the porn industry and pissing off very scary people, having massively oversized balls and being slightly insane is a requirement.
>
> It takes all types to make a world, even in journalism. Would the papers be better if they employed a series of editors with journalistic balls, each of whom got fired after three months on the job?
>
> The question isn't whether the Federation rags are journalistically daring or not, the question is whether there are alternatives. Till the *Forward* and the Web publications and blogs came along, there weren't alternatives. And frankly, there would be no *Forward* if there wasn't a very rich Jewish macher [Michael Steinhardt] who is willing to bankroll a paper that is critical of, among other things, rich Jewish machers.
>
> It's all about the money—or lack thereof. That's why the Internet is a boon, because the start-up and support costs are so low.

15

Lisa Lenkiewicz

June 24, 2004

I chat with Lisa, the 47-year old managing editor of the *Connecticut Jewish Ledger*.

"It is difficult to be part of the Jewish community yet report on the Jewish community as an independent journalist. There is a concept in Judaism of *lashon hara* (evil gossip). Many news stories get put through the filter of—is this good for the Jews? Another newspaper would not even consider that. Are we a Jewish newspaper or are we a newspaper for Jews? What are our boundaries? What will cause harm in the Jewish community? Do we have a responsibility not to cause harm in the Jewish community? Are Jewish newspapers communal institutions? Or are you independent?"

"**What do you think is the best Jewish newspaper?**"

"*The Jewish Week*. I think the writing is of a high quality. It is on the cutting edge of trends. It does a good job of covering New York."

"**I don't think I ever recall a negative book review in *The Jewish Week*.**"

Lisa laughs. "I don't either. The *Forward* is very intellectual and has a whole literary section. *The Jewish Week* can't do that but at least they inform people about the hot Jewish books out there and interview authors."

"**Would you call it a compelling read?**"

"I think Jonathan Mark is a wonderful writer. I think it is a must read if you are interested in Jewish journalism."

"**Would you call it a Federation paper?**"

"Yes. You don't like *The Jewish Week*?"

"I think it's dull."

"One of the criticisms you hear about Jewish newspapers in general is that they are dull. They are not exciting reads. That is a challenge to all of us editors.

"What are you looking for? What are you going to find that is not there?"

"We're not all hip young magazines. We're Jewish newspapers. What do you think is missing?"

"It is so sanitized. I know Jewish life. I know about the egos and peacocking and scamming and posturing that go on but I don't read about them in my Jewish newspaper, the *Jewish Journal*."

"But is that news? That there's backstabbing and infighting?"

"I don't recognize the Jewish life that I participate in when I read the *Jewish Journal* or any other Jewish paper, but I do recognize it when I read *Postville* and *The New Rabbi*."

"I found *The New Rabbi* a good read. A number of people were furious with him. But it was juicy gossip."

"**It was delicious.**"

"It was complete and total gossip in that book but it totally shed a light on the whole rabbinic search process. It was wonderful."

"**That book got me excited. I realized that Jewish journalism can be exciting.**"

"You are right. The feedback I got was that it was pure gossip. I know rabbis who know rabbis and those people are greatly hurt by what was written about them."

"**Well, tough.**"

"A tremendous amount of damage."

"**That's what Gary said.**"

"That's what you hear from everyone."

"**They didn't get to set their own image this time and it was shocking for them.**"

"No question."

"**They're control freaks.**"

"You take a rabbi, a nice guy like Perry Rank, and your heart goes out to him. That these people said X, Y, and Z about him. I think it made them look bad."

"Yeah, I think it made them look bad."

"Yeah, but his [relatives] who live here, they were just mortified to see their private life exposed like that. I kept saying, it makes everyone else look bad. Not Perry. It still didn't matter. It was very hurtful."

"I find it amusing that these rabbis who are such enormous consumers of journalism, guys who read *The New York Times* every day, but as soon as soon as some regular journalistic techniques are applied on them and their friends, they go ballistic."

"Yep. Except, when it happens to you, you don't want to see your life dragged out in front of everybody.

"I can't disagree in many instances with your assessment that Jewish newspapers are too dull. We work hard here to get away from the 'Who poured the punch at the Oneg pictures.' We've gotten away from being a shul bulletin. We're doing nice features. We write about wonderful people doing wonderful things. There is that pressure to write about the Federation annual meeting. Because of the ebb and flow of the Jewish news cycle, it's the same Rosh Hashanah and Passover stories. I like to think we are always looking for fresh angles on things. Where Jewish newspapers fall down is that we don't have the resources to do a good job in investigative journalism."

"Do you think there's a generation gap?"

"There is. Our readers are 60 and above. They don't want to see anything bad about the Jewish community. All of us have recognized that if we don't start reaching out to a different generation, there won't be a Jewish newspaper to wrap their fish in. I'm relatively young in the Jewish newspaper world. At the *Ledger*, we run events for singles. We have dances, lectures, speed dating, a night out at the ball park. We've had over a dozen marriages."

"When did you begin in Jewish journalism?"

"I went to the *Washington Jewish Week* in 1982. I moved to the *Ledger* in 1992."

"Did you see big stories you couldn't get into the paper?"

"Oh, sure. An executive director for 40 years here is dismissed from a synagogue. He comes to us and says he was dismissed for age discrimination. He's going to file a lawsuit. Then the rabbi calls you up and says, we would greatly appreciate it if you would not run that story. And the publisher says ok. Or a rabbi is dismissed from the synagogue for abusing the discretionary fund account. I call the rabbi. He says, I won't speak to you. This is a legal matter. You are not to print it. You are not able to get anything on the record, no cooperation from anyone in the synagogue or the community and you're not able to run the story. Or, the Jewish Federation executive director settles with the Federation. People come forward and say he's verbally abusing women. The board decides to pay him off and ship him out. And you can't get the story."

"According to the Awareness Center, there are a lot more abusive rabbis than just Lanner."

"I called the women who had run-ins with [the executive director]. They hung up the phone on me. Or said they were scared and wouldn't talk to me. The Federation officials wouldn't talk to us. There were several stories that were vital to do and I am disappointed that we didn't do them. A funeral home gets a fine from the state for malpractice and bilking people and we get beat by *The Hartford Courant*. They got the information first. Eventually we got to run the story, but some major advertisers came in here and said they would pull their advertising. We sat down with them. We heard their side. We eventually got to do their side but we were completely beat by the secular press on this. What is it about Jewish newspapers that they don't have the staff, the resources, the money, and the ability to be ahead of these stories?"

"What about the status? I've had journalists complain to me that journalists for Jewish papers get treated like teachers in the community."

"As managing editor, I get treated nicely by the people in Connecticut. I always feel that people want me to speak and want to be in the paper. I just got an honor from some kashrut commission for my community service of twelve years. True, they were trying to fill their brunch. I don't always feel like a second-class citizen to the people we cover. Yet the first inclination is to say, I'm not talking to you. And pressure is put on you to not write stories that could harm the Jewish community."

"Do you really think the Jewish community would be harmed if these stories ran?"

"Not me. I wouldn't be in this business if I thought that. I keep trying to make the point that the Jewish community can only be strengthened if we are accurate reporters of what is occurring. Not just on what our Jewish institutions are doing but on what's doing at our Jewish institutions.

"People want to open up a Jewish newspaper and feel good. They want to see all the good works that they are doing. They want to hear about their neighbor. They want to see the awards. When I go out speaking, I find that the most popular part of the paper is the obituary page. Then they want to see the engagements, the weddings and the life cycle events. It's that insular feeling of community that they are interested in. If they want to read investigative journalism, they'll go to *The New York Times*.

"I keep saying that Jewish newspapers should start a gossip column. That would really sell newspapers. So-and-so sold their house for this much and they're moving to Florida. This is what people are talking about.

"Most Jewish journalists don't want to go to *The New York Times*. They like their hometown paper. They feel like they are making a difference.

"Larry [Cohler-Esses] tried for so long to break into non-Jewish journalism. I remember when Larry got an interview with Mike Wallace of *60 Minutes*. [Larry does not recall this, he thinks Lisa may mean Tom Friedman.] Mike told him that he was the best Jewish journalist in the country but you've got to get out of Jewish journalism and get some daily experience. And it was years before Larry was able to get out of Jewish journalism.

"Charles Fenyvesi was at the *Washington Post*, then the Bnai Brith magazine, then *Washington Jewish Week*, then he got a job at *US News & World Report*. That was our big excitement. One of ours made it into an important magazine. It doesn't happen that often.

"You need a section in your book on Jewish editors who've been on the job a long time. Robert Cohn, 35 years in St Louis. Marc Klein in San Francisco. This is more than a job for them. You may say it's boring but they really believe in what they're doing. I would say that most of my peers are happy with their job. We wish the salaries were higher. For full-time reporters at our paper, the salary range is between $20–30,000. The pay scale is pretty similar in the secular world. But how do you entice someone coming up in the world of journalism to choose this path? Gary has worked hard to attract young Jewish journalists with seminars and internships."

16

Gene Lichtenstein

June 25, 2004

I run down my list of previous interviews, including Gary Rosenblatt.

"I would think that Gary is as knowledgeable as anyone."

"Yeah. He also gave me the least. He gave me nothing. It was a complete wash, but it's a good get. I didn't get any information from him, but yeah, I can tell everybody that I interviewed Gary."

"If you interview Gary, all the doors will be open."

"Even though he might as well have just spoken about the weather for 30 minutes. It was the worst interview I've done."

"I'm willing to be interviewed but I am not a good yardstick of Jewish journalism. All of the editors of Jewish newspapers I know are all Jewish in a way that I am not. They're observant Jews. They live in a Jewish world. All their friends are Jewish. All the people they see at parties are Jewish. Their wives are Jewish. They look at Judaism and Israel and being a Jew in America from a different perspective than I do. I don't belong to a synagogue. I never have. My children were not bar mitzvahed. I don't belong to Jewish organizations and I don't live in a Jewish world. Gary is Orthodox. They all go to synagogue on Yom Kippur. I don't. They are all committed to Judaism and I'm not. I'm not even a rebel. It's just a fluke that I edited a Jewish newspaper."

July 1, 2004

Gene's hands move constantly during our interview, gesturing, scratching, emphasizing points.

He talks about his time creating the *Jewish Journal* of the North Shore for a Boston-area Jewish Federation (1983–85). "I had enough run-ins with the Federation and with a couple of people on the board who were ardent Zionists. I'm not a Zionist."

"Would you prefer a binational state?"

"I don't know. I'm certainly opposed to what Israel is doing. If I had to choose between a Jewish state and a democratic state, I'd choose a democratic one.

"I was at an 84th birthday party for Stanley Sheinbaum. I was sitting at a table with bright liberal Jews. We were all with Peace Now. Soon we were talking about this issue. I said something about in America, do you think of yourself as a Jew first or an American first? This smart young woman who'd helped run Tom Hayden's campaign and was in Peace Now as an activist, said, I'm a Jew first. I almost fell out of the chair. I said that I think of myself first as an American.

"That question assumes that I have a stake in Israel and I don't feel like I have a stake in Israel.

"When I started the *Jewish Journal* of Los Angeles, I did not know Jewish Los Angeles. The paper was controversial. One, my stance on certain issues was not something the community accepted. I was more interested in foreign, national, political and cultural issues. I was not interested enough in local news. If you look at the *Jewish Bulletin of Northern California*, you'll see that that's a local paper. And that's what the community expected.

"Also, I was naive about certain issues. I remember devoting an early issue to intermarriage. I thought it was a joke. I couldn't imagine that in 1986, people would take intermarriage seriously. I had a great Roy Lichtenstein-style cartoon with balloons coming out and a story that made a joke of the whole thing. The publisher said, boy, you really put your foot in it.

"I was up front with my lack of knowledge of Judaism. He said, we'll get you up to snuff. Well, I learned pretty fast."

"What did you get the most hate mail over?"

"Not attacking the Palestinians. The first Intifada occurred. There was a small Peace Now demonstration and Orthodox Rabbi Abner Weiss led a counter-demonstration with placards and drowned them out and wouldn't let them speak. A lot of people said the Peace Now people should keep quiet and not criticize Israel. I wrote an editorial saying that silence was a form of speech. And that's everything that America is opposed to. If you felt Israel was wrong, not to speak to was to join the other side and to give up your responsibility as a concerned citizen to exercise your voice.

"The paper got known to be too liberal. I didn't think it was liberal at all. I would always publish other views. Rabbi Harold Schulweiss wrote this piece attacking me. I published it. He later called me and said, 'My wife says you were right.'

"Yehuda Lev had been considered for the editorship of the paper and almost got it. I hired two people who were up for the job—Yehuda and Marlene Marks. Yehuda couldn't get over that I had hired the competition.

"Yehuda was liberal and left. He was against bureaucracy and authority. He was very critical of Jewish organizations. He often got his facts wrong. I didn't know that at first. I learned the hard way. But he was a good writer. I got pressured to fire him. Finally, the implication was fire him or you go, but I didn't fire him."

"What about hiring Teresa Strasser?"

"That was my idea. Teresa had lived in San Francisco and done book reviews and pieces for them. She came down here and was looking for something. I said, why don't you write about being a single Jewish woman in LA. She said, can I really do that? I said of course. But I want to give you the first three subjects. Write about your mother. So she wrote this piece about her mother taking her at age 14 to get fitted for a diaphragm. We got a lot of mail for that."

Gene laughs. "More con than pro. I thought her stuff was so good, other newspapers would pick it up. I paid her more than I could afford. I told her, I know you can't live on what we pay so I'm going to give you double. But when we sell it, I want a little back. She said fine. Well, no paper would print her. They all said, what's so Jewish about this?

"We wrote a piece about Israel Bonds and we got a lot of antagonism for that. It was mostly the stuff on Israel that got most of the complaints.

"When Salam-Al Marayiti, the head of the Muslim Public Affairs Council, was selected [around 1999] by Richard Gephardt to serve on the anti-terrorist committee, the Jewish community exploded. I called Salam and interviewed him. I wrote a piece that he reflected a Muslim perspective and there's nothing wrong with that. And for the Jewish community to object was unfair. We should endorse it. We were the only Jewish newspaper that said so. And Gephardt yanked him.

"I learned about Judaism. I went to Israel every year and interviewed Peres, Sharon, Rabin.

"My criticism of Jewish organizations and Jewish identity issues was that American Jews thought of themselves too often as victims. They were sold this to solidify the community.

"When I grew up, you did not apologize for being an anti-Semite. That was given. Jews were outsiders. True, but I was never a victim. I was never willing to concede that I couldn't move freely and compete. Jewish community papers too often confirm that sense of victimhood. I saw my role as leading the Jewish community into America. You could still live in a Jewish community but not be too distrustful of Americans. You could move freely back and forth. I chose to live freely. Most of my readers chose to live in the Jewish community. That's fine. I just wanted them to feel that the doors were open.

"I had a series of lunches with a wealthy powerful Jewish realtor in LA. He was at the center of the Jewish community. He told me at one of these lunches that if Hubert Humphrey had won [in 1968], he would've been the first secretary of HUD. He'd been very critical of the paper and tried to shut it down and almost succeeded [circa 1995]. He brought it up at the Federation."

"His primary problem with the paper was?"

"Israel. He said to me at lunch at the Beverly Wilshire Hotel, you can't have confusion. You can't have different views. You can't have them question. In the end, you can't trust the Gentiles.

"I almost fell out of my chair."

"Did he say goyim or Gentiles?"

"I don't know. I hate that word goyim, so I block on it."

"Do you hate the word shiksa?"

"Yeah, I do."

"Shaygetz?"

"Yeah, I do not like those words."

"Kike?"

"I do not like that. Schvartze. I do not like that. Never use those words.

"I heard that [you can't trust the Gentiles] again and again from wealthy self-made Jews in LA. I opposed that view. You can't trust some Gentiles but I can say the same thing about Jews. That was the central clashing point. I saw my role as educating the reader so that he could see America as a safe open place with some anti-Semitism.

"Anti-Semites are now the people out of power. They lack the education and the skills. They're not modernists. Society has bypassed them."

"How much of your vision did you get to fulfill?"

"It was in the paper most issues. My being a psychologist helped. I didn't try to be politically didactic. I'd write something agreeing with the people I disagreed with. It's called feeding the symptom. Yes, this is the way people feel. And then the hook.

"It's ok to be frightened of elevators or to fear that your next-door-neighbor is out to get you. He often is. So it's sensible.... It's called paradoxical intervention.

"If the consequence of your fear is that you never go outside your house, perhaps it would be better to find a way to go outside your house and at the same time understand that your neighbor may not like you.

"Paul Conrad of *The Los Angeles Times* did a series of cartoons [against Israel during the first Intifada]. The Federation and the synagogues ordered a boycott of *The LA Times*. I didn't know Conrad. I went down and spent an afternoon interviewing him. In the next issue of the *Jewish Journal*, Conrad's cartoons were on the cover of the paper. I wrote a piece about Conrad saying he was a populist from the Midwest and how incensed he was at social injustice and civil rights. How he drew cartoons against anti-Semites and anti-Blacks. He saw Palestinians vs. Israel as a civil rights issue. He saw the Palestinians as the blacks. He was not an anti-Semite. Boycotting *The LA Times* was foolish and Conrad was getting a bad rap.

"The Federation had a meeting with *The LA Times* a week or so later and *The Times* editor pulled out the *Jewish Journal* and said, well, not everyone in the Jewish community feels that way.

"Stanley Hirsh became the publisher when Ed Brennglass died (1999)."

"What were the dynamics behind Stanley giving you the hook?"

"Stanley was like a bull in a china shop. A self-made man, he was aggressive and sensitive and defensive about the other presidents of the Federation who were lawyers, accountants and doctors. In cultural class and manner, Stanley was roughhewn and he boasted about that. I was defined by him, correctly, as an intellectual. That was negative from his point of view.

"When he became publisher, I thought it wasn't going to work. To my surprise, it worked well. Ed Brennglass ran a tight ship. Stanley asked me what we need. The paper had become profitable and all the money had gone to charity. I said we can't go on this way. We have to pour some of the money back into the paper. I want raises for the staff and hire a couple of people. He said, do it.

"We spent the money. The next year, our expenses zoomed. He said, you've got to cut back. I found ways to cut back $100,000, which is what we had ballooned up. In January 2000, he came to me, liking the kudos the paper had received. He said the paper is a success due to you. I'm giving you a $10,000 raise. I'd put in requests for raises for everyone and he had been tight on that. I was putting in for $500, $1000 and $2000 raises for the staff but not me.

"Then, over the next six months, how do I say this? Two things happened. Critics of the paper who said we weren't covering the community well enough reached him. He felt that. Second, he wanted editorial control. He'd say, I want this on the cover. Why don't you do this story? He was a forceful personality. He wanted to demonstrate that he was the boss of the whole thing. It came out in ugly ways at meetings in our office. He did get out of control."

Stanley, who was married, wanted to impress a woman on the *Journal* staff that he was the true boss of the paper.

"Did he think Rob would be more malleable?"

"Stanley called me in and fired me in September 2000. He said, it isn't working out. You don't listen to my orders. It's not a community newspaper. I said, you gave me a $10,000 raise six months ago. What's changed? Has the paper changed in six months? No. So, we haggled over what he would give me as a severance. This was in the middle of the week. He asked me to clear out my desk by Friday. I said I'd rather do it on Saturday. He said fine.

"On Sunday, I get a call from Stanley. He wanted to meet. I said ok.

"He'd called Rob down on Friday about becoming the editor. I thought Rob would become a great editor.

"Stanley said, I want to change my mind. So you want to stay until the new year? The same terms of severance will stand.

"I said, why? He said, well, Rob came by the office on Friday. And he's worse than you are. He wants his own way. I'm going to hire someone else. I thought about it for a day. I called Rob to ask what was going on. Rob told me. He went down there and told Stanley that he wanted a raise and he wanted to do this and that. I thought Rob deserved it. I thought he could do the job and do it well. He had a different approach from mine. He was a part of the community. Even at the end of 16 years, I was not really a part of the community. I still didn't belong to a synagogue. His wife was a rabbi.

"I felt like without Rob or me, he could not put out a paper.

"I called Stanley on Monday and said no. I did have an ace in the hole. I had gotten a call that weekend from J.J. Goldberg. 'I hear you're leaving and would you cover the presidential elections for me.' He wasn't going to give me my [*Journal*] salary but it was something.

"He couldn't fire Rob. Rob said, if he doesn't make me the editor, I'm quitting. He had to hire Rob. He couldn't deal with shutting down the paper. The word would've gotten out that he had fired me and Rob. Rob's parents belong to the Hillside Country Club. His father was an advertising executive. Yeah, they're wealthy."

I give Gene my Sheldon Teitelbaum interview.

"That was the second or third issue of the paper. Brandeis-Bardin had been the institute that everyone on the board [of the *Journal*] had become a member of. Shlomo Bardin had gotten them interested in Judaism. It was their alma mater. Sheldon's piece attacked Prager and the Bardin board for letting him go on and not wanting to air the dirty linen of Prager being a terrible head of Brandeis Bardin.

"So Barbie, a member of the four-member editorial board, was hostile. She wanted me to kill the story or hear the tapes. I asked Sheldon about the tapes. I was getting a lot of heat on that piece. I said to her, I have the tapes. She said, I want to listen to them. I said why? I can't allow that. She got very angry and offended. I stood up to them. She then demanded at the editorial board to be able to read my editorials and any piece that they wanted prior to publication. I said no. If you do that, you don't need me. You need an efficient managing editor who can process the paper. So you should let me go. That was my way of saying I was going to resign.

"They took a vote. They came down on my side. She resigned.

"I listened to the tape. I told Sheldon that his questions were very aggressive and very hostile. I said to him that I'd interviewed many people and been in on many interviews, but I had never heard any interview as hostile and aggressive as that. I think you ought to change your way of doing it.

"He didn't hear me.

"I found his writing dense. Because of my experience at *Esquire*, I was much more interested in good writing than in journalism. Steve was a wonderful writer. Yehuda was a good writer. Tom Waldman was a decent writer. Sheldon, a reporter, was too dense and I had a hard time getting through his pieces. Too many facts compressed. You had to get into it and push and it was too much work.

"He was very ambitious. He wanted to do everything. He said, I want to write a column about Israel. I said great. He'd say, I want to do this. I'd say great. He'd say, I want to do that. I'd say great. I'd read the material and say, this doesn't work, and I began to peel back.

"He came into my office one day. I think he lasted about a year. He said, I'm having a problem with you. I said, let's talk about it. My office is always open. What is it?

"He said you let me do this and then you don't run it. I said, I'm having a hard time with the writing. You get a lot of facts and you're really energetic but you're writing is too dense. It requires too much editing time for me. They're very hard to edit. I'm doing this alone. I don't have the time to give it the editing it needs.

"It is true that I did not want him to rock the boat, but when he did, I really stood up for him. And this happened with other stories.

"The paper was independent. I ran a lot of stories the board objected to. We ran a piece critical of Marvin Hier and the Wiesenthal Center by Yehuda Lev. Marvin was furious. I offered to come down to meet him. He read me the riot act. A lot of members of my board were on the board of the Wiesenthal Center.

"I listened and said, you're telling me that this is wrong and this is wrong and this is wrong in the article, as well as the tone. He said yes. I said, let me check. I went back and checked. The tone was hostile but the facts were wrong. I called him and apologized. You're absolutely right. It's my fault. I should've checked. I want you to promise to call me every time we run a piece on the Wiesenthal Center to let me know if the facts are right.

"**Did you go to any AJPA meetings?**"

"Yeah."

"**What adjectives would you use to describe them?**"

"They were sort of dull."

"**Terribly dull.**"

"There were about a half dozen people I liked. The rest of the people represented small town community papers and I felt their views were dominant because there were more of them. That was not what I was interested in. Marc Klein put out a paper in San Francisco that I didn't like. Their interests and my interests were not congruent. I'm not sure I was right. I felt we didn't do a good-enough job publishing community news.

"We published wedding announcements when people married non-Jews. That was controversial."

"**Were there any great stories during your tenure that you couldn't get in the paper?**"

"There was one story that I killed [circa 1990] but not through pressure. My killing it was unpopular. Naomi Pfefferman, who I had hired, had done a long piece about the University of Judaism. There was a female professor there, a poet [Marsha Falk], who was popular among the students and had published a lot and had a PhD. When it came time for tenure, the president David Lieber, vetoed her tenure. He was popular and he was leaving. He was a humane decent man but he had a hard time with women. The faculty had been for her. There were some ugly incidents concerning students who had protested. Naomi had done a terrific job. We had the story. I regret that we didn't run it.

"I got calls from people on the board of the University of Judaism. Kill the story. They hadn't read it.

"I did some background. He said to me, 'I can't bear this woman. She was obnoxious.' If we ran the story in its entirety, we would've had to come out with the reason she was denied tenure—that the president and some of the faculty found her obnoxious. They didn't want her as a colleague.

"I should've run it but I didn't want to hurt her feelings."

"She didn't realize that?"

"No. Nor did Naomi. People thought I was knuckling under. The poet had had dinner at my house. In fairness to David Lieber, I would've had to say that, so I killed the story. If I were working at *The New York Times*, I wouldn't have killed the story, but I felt that a community newspaper has an obligation to people in the community to not hurt them unnecessarily. That is not a journalistic view."

Dr. David Lieber writes me:

> ...[A]n academic review committee of her peers, including a distinguished professor in her field from another university, voted unanimously not to recommend her for tenure.
>
> Mr. Lichtenstein was a very competent editor. The same cannot be said of many of his "journalists," most of whom were part-time and did not know how to research a story. Thus the writer in question never interviewed either me or the dean of the school in which the professor taught, nor did she inquire about the circumstances of the professor's leaving the university at which she taught prior to coming to the University of Judaism.

"I changed one story. I ran a story about a rabbi [Robert Kirschner] who had been in San Francisco and had been caught out sexually. He came down one summer to teach at HUC. It turned out the dean at HUC and he were buddies. That nobody on the faculty nor the students had been consulted. So we wrote the story outing him and the dean. They rescinded the offer or he backed out.

"Then, about three years later, when he was at the Skirball, [a Jewish journalist] did a series on sex and the rabbinate. About five pieces. We ran them as one long piece. There was a lot about him. We had already run that in the HUC story. We mentioned him in passing but we didn't replay.

"The author [who says she does not remember communicating with Gene on this] sent me a hot letter that we had knuckled under to the Skirball, which was not true. I called her, you're wrong. She said, why wouldn't you run it? I said, we already did it. I didn't see the need to shoot him again. He has a full-time job. She said, no, you're just chicken. You're just knuckling under. I said, why are you so aggressive on this point? She said, well, I'm the voice of his wife. I'm speaking out in defense of his wife.

"I said, boy, who appointed you to that job. She said, you don't understand. I said, let me suggest something to you as the defendant. If he doesn't have a job at the Skirball, he's living with his mother because he's paying everything in alimony, his wife's income is going to be cut. As her defendant, you should think about that. She didn't reply.

"I didn't knuckle under. I'm sure I toned some things down when pressure was applied. But on major issues, we ran the stories."

Gene writes me later:

> Thank you for not asking me, 'What do you think of [Rob's] editorship of the *Journal*,' which is not an infrequent question. For the record, I think he's a terrific editor and is doing a great job.
>
> Good writing was the central focus of the *Journal* when I started it. My judgments may have been faulty, but the concern was paramount. Steve Weinstein, for example, was a writer, not a journalist. He was lured away from the *Journal* within a year by *The LA Times* to write features about popular culture; Joe Domanick had no reporting experience either, but turned out to be an exceptionally good reporter and magazine writer. He was pulled away by the *LA Weekly* and *The LA Times*.
>
> Columnists were seen by me as writers who would serve as the spine of the paper. I started with Yehuda Lev, who was a wonderful

writer. By the time he moved to Rhode Island, he was old and tired and spent, though occasionally produced something wonderful. Marlene Marks, who had wanted to be the editor of the paper, came by about a year after we had been publishing. Her husband had just died. She wrote two rather boring, sophomoric pieces about Judaism and the community, which I turned down. I told her to write about being in the hospital when she heard that her husband had died, and her anger at the doctors and rabbi, etc. She did, and was off and running. Her columns were about herself and women and being a single mother in LA, and in the first few years they were terrific. Later she became a celebrity and her columns were a bit ponderous and full of herself. During the last year that I was at the paper, I couldn't bear to read them and asked Rob to take over the responsibility (this was before she developed cancer).

Anyway, I could cite many other writers—Stephen Leder, David Margolis, Dov Aharoni, J.J. Goldberg, Teresa Strasser, Rob Eshman, Eric Silver, Helen Davis—all of whom I brought to the paper because of their writing. Stephen Leder, who is rabbi at Wilshire Blvd. Temple, was then an assistant rabbi who wrote the Torah Portion, which had been guarded by the Board of Rabbis, who zealously made sure every rabbi who wanted got a shot at it. Most of the writing was dreadful until Leder came along; at which point I dispensed with the Board and signed him on. Read some of his columns; they were very good. The Federation, the Board, the publisher of the newspaper all pressured me to rotate, but I stayed with Steve until he had to bow out because of time.

The same thing applied to Dov Aharoni, an extreme right wing Orthodox rabbi. I don't think he and I agreed on a single issue; but he was a wonderful writer. The Federation in the person of Stanley Hirsh, who was also a member of the newspaper's board of directors, pressed me not to run him: He was too extreme, too divisive. We kept publishing him until he withdrew to attend law school. Even when it came to hiring reporters, such as Naomi Pfefferman and Julie Fax, good writing was a central factor.

I approached J.J. Goldberg and asked if he'd write for us if I could put together a consortium of Jewish newspapers to pay him a decent salary. He agreed and I called David Twersky, who then edited the

NJ newspaper, and asked him to help line up some papers. That's how J.J. came to write a column.

On the other hand, Dennis Prager, who has a large following in LA, asked if he could write a column for us. I had published a few pieces by him, but found his writing pompous, overblown and boring. I turned him down because of the writing, though he was convinced it was because I disagreed with him about policy. What he didn't understand was that I was desperate for good writers on the right (Aharoni was a case in point), but unwilling to publish bad writing.

"Publisher Stanley Hirsh wanted a gossip column. Why did you not give him one?"

Several reasons: First, Stanley was always pressing to put his foot in the editorial door, usually by floating suggestions that were passed along to him by friends at lunch. I was chary of encouraging this.

Second, his suggestion did not necessarily exclude people who were his friends or acquaintances, of whom there were many. More than once he pushed me to run an interview with someone he knew, or to whom he owed a favor, and he wanted that story published in a favorable light. Ted Stein, an ambitious opportunist, was one example. Stanley was after me to get a story that showed all the good things he did for the Jewish community. That was just one example. But it was his mantra—stories about people who make a contribution to the Jewish community. Happy stories for happy people is the way I thought of them, and I tried my best to resist.

Third, behind the notion of a gossip column was his idea that this would win friends and influence people in the community; namely, it was meant to be a feel-good column; who was seen at which parties. I had told Deborah Berger—she was a psychologist who wrote our advice column—that I did not want a lot of one-upsman psychologizing in the column, and that she should tell readers, when appropriate, to pull up their own socks. If we ran a gossip column, I wanted it to have a bit of a sting. That was not what Stanley (or the newspaper's board) wanted. I just saw him calling me all the time and telling me which parties were taking place and to send someone over. Not for me.

Finally, no one on the staff could do it properly; or had the contacts (maybe Tom Tugend, but it was not something he would want to do, and besides he was married and on a low half-time salary). So it meant hiring someone with money we did not have.

17

Jonathan Sarna

June 28, 2004

"Would you be surprised if leaders of the Jewish Establishment threatened to destroy a paper if it published something they didn't like?"

"It's a very old story, and not a particularly Jewish one. If you read the history of journalism, often big corporations would threaten to destroy a paper. They would withdraw advertising. Jews too engage in this. Many Jews stopped contributing to NPR because they felt NPR was biased.

"There's a tension inherent in journalism. On the one hand, you need to serve your reading public. If you antagonize them, you go out of business. On the other hand, you have a certain obligation to journalistic standards, which may antagonize some of your readers. You may report some things that make them angry and they make take their anger out against the messenger. Jewish journalism is not that different from Catholic journalism or even small town journalism in this battle between interest groups that want to shape the news and journalists that want to expose the 'truth.' Probably it is a healthy tension.

"When *The Jewish Week* exposed the scandal at NCSY [Rabbi Baruch Lanner], because they knew how their readers would view it, they were extraordinarily careful. It was written in careful language. They'd done an immense amount of research. Those who threatened to withdraw their support for *The Jewish Week* found themselves ridiculed in the community.

"Some Jewish newspapers have cleverly managed to pit wealthy Jews against one another, so that if one threatens, the other defends. Nevertheless, there are many cases where Jewish newspapers have engaged in self-censorship. As a result, readers truly interested in what is going on in the Jewish world, look elsewhere. They look to *The New York Times*. That's where they'll really find out what is going on. You won't, for example, hear much about Jews and slavery in Jewish newspapers. Even in the time of the Civil War, that was too hot to handle.

"I remember in the 1980s a rabbinical student in Cincinnati was on trial for sexually molesting a child at a summer camp. He was eventually found innocent. While this trial was on the front page of the newspaper day-after-day, the Jewish newspaper was reluctant to print the story. When it did print a bit about the story, the newspaper was bitterly criticized.

"You won't find much in Jewish newspapers about the Rosenberg trial [American couple who were executed in 1953 for spying for the Soviet Union]. Take out the American Jewish Year Book and you would think it wasn't big news. It's hardly there. Again, the Jewish community didn't want to give [it] publicity lest people feel that all Jews are communists.

"I think we look back at these moments in the way *The New York Times* looks back at its coverage of the Holocaust. With some substantial shame and a vow to do better. But when difficult matters come up, it is still difficult. Perhaps what we need is the equivalent of what *The New York Times* ombudsman now does. Somebody who would stand back and write reflectively to readers about these issues.

"Take Yossi Abramowitz's series on the Jewish National Fund. He took on a real icon of the community. Many people argue that there were all sorts of practices at the JNF that were unethical, maybe worse. By exposing them, Abramowitz [created] change. On the other hand, there are people who argue that the JNF never recovered from the scandal. Here was an institution raising large sums for Israel, full of people with high-minded ideas. The journalist, by tarring the whole institution, destroyed it.

"I'm not here to judge. My job is to remind reporters how difficult their job is. I have more respect for the Rosenblatts of the world, who agonize, who feel responsible for their community, but also have a strong sense of the role of the journalist, then I do for journalists who feel that they have no responsibility at all for their community.

"You talk about Stephen Fried. There was a fine debate at Brandeis in which Fried spoke about that book and the role of journalists. There were many journalists there who did not agree with everything that Stephen Fried did, who argued that future journalists were harmed by his naming so many names of people who thought they were confidentially interviewing for a rabbinic position. They argued that never again would a synagogue trust journalists. Journalism depends on a certain amount of trust. If I talk to a journalist and I say that this is on the record, this is off the record, I assume that my wishes will be honored. Even if the journalist doesn't like it, there has to be a certain degree of trust. The candidates interviewing assumed that a confidential process would remain confidential.

"These aren't easy issues. The important thing is to have an open debate, and to have journalists who are simultaneously committed to journalism and journalistic ethics, and at the same time care about their communities, and weigh their sometime conflicting responsibilities."

"Your critique of *The New Rabbi* is?"

"Stephen Fried has a more extreme view of the role of the journalist than I do and he is suspicious of all things confidential. I think his book is wonderfully written and accurate. I knew some of those details first hand. On the other hand, it was not clear to me that the story would've been one whit less powerful if some confidentiality had been preserved, especially when he mentioned names of candidates for the position [of rabbi of Har Zion]. Does the Jewish community suffer when no confidentiality is maintained because many people will not apply for positions if they can not be assured of confidentiality? Government has suffered. We are no longer getting some of the Jeffersons to go into politics because there is a sense of no confidentiality.

"On the one hand, nobody will probably go into a search for a new rabbi without reading that book. On the other hand, I do worry that that book made it more difficult for journalists. Now the first thing you do when you run a search is ban any conversation with a journalist. Even more so, it may have made it more difficult for congregations to sound out rabbis at other places because people will say that they can't risk having their name exposed to the press."

"Rabbis tend to be among the most voracious consumers of journalism. I find it humorous that when some elementary techniques of journalism are finally applied to them, they squeal like stuck pigs."

"That is not a complaint unique to rabbis or to Jews. On the one hand, everybody is interested in the private business of the president and of pop stars. We peep in. We have television shows wholly dedicated to uncovering other people's most private affairs. On the other hand, everybody wants to guard his or her own privacy. The Jewish case is simply a reflection of a larger case of social hypocrisy. Rabbis are no different from average citizens in this respect."

"**Did you read *Postville*?**"

"Yeah. *Postville* I liked a lot less than Stephen Fried's book. The reporter was not objective at all. At a certain point in the story, the reporter decided he didn't like these guys [Chabadniks]. His book became a vendetta against them. It happens a lot in journalism. The journalist is not a dispassionate objective reporter of events but the journalist, like so many of the European journalists, is really an activist who is putting on the guise of objectivity hoping to delude the public away from the agenda that the journalist actually has. A bunch of Middle East journalists are like that. If you speak to the journalists privately, they have strong agendas. They pretend to be objective, but their anti-Israel bias inevitably shows through. The same thing happened in *Postville*.

"I don't think the reporter of *Postville* started that way, but at a certain point, he had an agenda. I found the book much weaker because his dislike of the Chasidim came through. His book would have been much stronger had he helped the Chasidim and the town understand each other better on their own terms.

"Second, the reporter didn't know much [about Judaism]. Therefore, there were all sorts of mistakes in the book, some of them hilarious, which cause one to cast doubt on the journalist, because his facts are wrong. He, for example, quotes a Lubavitcher telling him to put on tefillin three times a day, which no Lubavitcher would have ever said [tefillin are only put on once a day]."

"**Which Jewish publications do you regard as riveting reads?**"

"I don't regard any publication as a riveting read. At times, I read riveting articles in Jewish newspapers."

"**Which Jewish publications do you regard as the most interesting?**"

"If someone were to ask me what do I have to read to be aware of what is going on in the Jewish world, I would list four—*The Jewish Week*, the *Forward*, *The Jerusalem Report*, and the JTA. Sometimes they are not riveting. Sometimes I think they're irresponsible. Sometimes I think I know the story on the inside and I think they're wrong. Nevertheless, they have the highest commitment to presenting us with the story of the Jewish community as it really is."

"**How accurate do you think the adjective 'dull' is when applied to American Jewish journalism in general and *The Jewish Week* in particular?**"

"I do not find *The Jewish Week* dull but that's because my local Jewish weekly is [Boston's] *The Jewish Advocate*. Compared to many of the other weeklies, *The Jewish Week* seems to be a model of what a Jewish weekly can be.

You only have to compare it to its predecessors to see what a wonderful job Gary has done.

"I think the dullest articles we tend to read are the articles from Israel. They are dull because by the time we read the articles, we're already read *The New York Times*."

"**What do you think of the book review section of *The Jewish Week*, which has not published a negative review in my lifetime?**"

"I think you're being a bit harsh. I don't think I look to *The Jewish Week* to get a sense of Jewish books. Do I think it matches the *Forward*? The answer is no. Under Jonathan Rosen, the [*Forward*'s] Culture page was remarkable and set a standard rarely equaled in Jewish journalism.

"We haven't talked at all [about] the role of the Jewish newspaper as an educational vehicle for the Jewish community. It's no different from the goal of *The New York Times* in presenting science news, where much of that is simply informing a public that is ignorant about science. The Jewish newspaper has an education function that may stand in tension with its critical function. In this case, the goal of *The Jewish Week* seems to be to inform readers concerning the best and most important Jewish books that are published."

"**The *Forward* vs. *The Jewish Week*? Which is more fearless and a better paper?**"

"I think the *Forward* has become much less objective. It has declined under its new regime. I found it more compelling under the previous regime. There are stories that you find in the *Forward* that you find nowhere else. On the other hand, I find stories in *The Jewish Week* that I don't find well done in the *Forward*. I think *The Jewish Week* does a much better job of preserving a sense of objectivity whereas the *Forward* is taking a liberal party line approach. For example, its reporting on Israel reflects a certain point of view, one that is clearly opposed to Prime Minister Sharon.

"The reporting on the National Jewish Population Survey was also skewed to support the editor's unique and unsubstantiated theories concerning the survey and the previous survey. Almost none of the scholars of the NJPS buy into J.J. Goldberg's conspiracy theory about the survey, nor do most of us buy into his view that intermarriage is not a significant issue. I do not think there was any conspiracy in the NJPS. There may have been mistakes. There are grave problems today with telephone surveys as a genre. I do not think the *Forward* did a good job of explaining that. *The New York Times* did.

"We have not seen anything that resembles Eve Kessler's articles on Jewish religious life [under the Lipsky regime] in the new *Forward*. She's still working there but she has a different beat. They never replaced her with someone who was investigating our religious institutions in quite so serious a way. They don't even have such a correspondent. The reason is simple. The current editor is not very interested in Jewish religious life. It's not what he thinks the American Jewish community cares about. I think he's wrong.

"I found the *Forward* more riveting under Seth Lipsky. I respect Seth for creating a new vision of what Jewish journalism could be. I understand he ran afoul of the people who were paying the piper and that J.J. is more in tune with the folks who are from the old *Forward* and have a certain political [socialist] perspective taken from the old Yiddish *Forward*. I don't happen to share that politics. It's not surprising that I find the slant of the *Forward* less to my liking. Seth opened up stories that we have not seen before or since.

"There is nobody I respect more in the field of Jewish journalism than Gary Rosenblatt."

"What do you think of the *Jewish Journal* of Los Angeles?"

"I don't read it unless I'm out there.

"I read the *New Jersey Jewish News*, which I thought David Twersky significantly improved [until] he fell afoul of his baal habaatim. I think it is unfortunate that a community the size of Boston doesn't have a Jewish newspaper that reflects the high standards of the community or even its voices. The gap between *The Jewish Advocate* and those other papers is much wider than the gap between the *Boston Globe* and *The New York Times*."

18

Rob Eshman

October 8, 2002

The *Jewish Journal* of Los Angeles tends to be fair and balanced. It's responsible. It supports the Jewish community. It reads like a synagogue bulletin. 'Let's all pitch in and bring something to the bake sale Sunday so the women's club can buy new tablecloths.'

The *Jewish Journal* avoids yellow journalism. It does not sensationalize. It probably has high ethical standards for its writers. It does not needlessly provoke readers. It doesn't scream for attention. It tries to give everybody in the Jewish community a voice, from the ultra-Orthodox (it won't even use this term because if offends religious Jews) to leftist homosexual activists.

But with the exception of columnist Theresa Strasser, it is BORING! It is PIOUS! It is unctuous. It is pointless. It never stirs the pot.

I don't want to hate the *Jewish Journal*. I don't want to admit my strong feelings. I'm embarrassed about them. I even admitted in therapy that I'm unfathomably filled with rage each time I pick up this gentle well-meaning weekly.

I don't hate everything Jewish. I support Israel. I keep the Sabbath. I push myself to date Jewish women, even when they're frizzy-haired and 30 pounds over weight. I study *Portnoy's Complaint* and *Bava Metzia*. I long for the day when people of color are no longer oppressed and queers can walk hand-in-hand down the street without being afraid.

I read the *Jewish Journal* every week without fail. It's filled with useful information. It tries hard to serve its readers. I like most of the people who work for it. Yet I hate the paper so much. I shake with anger when I read it. Not because it's slanderous or unbalanced but because it's dull. It's everything I'm against. It's nice and mature and grown up and reserved and balanced and ethical and pious and smug and superior. And a real snooze. It reminds me of *The LA Times.*

I wonder if part of the reason there's almost no intellectual excitement in Jewish life these days is that Jewish publications, with the exception of the *Forward* and a few interesting writers like Strasser, are so dull.

March 6, 2004

My journalist friend Cathy Seipp calls. "If you were nicer to Rob Eshman [editor], you could get these things in the *Jewish Journal*."

"Why would I want to be in the *Jewish Journal*? It's a dull paper."

"You secretly love the *Jewish Journal*. You'd love to be in the *Jewish Journal*."

"I don't think so. If I wrote for them, I'd have to stop writing about how much I hate the paper."

"So give it up."

"That's not authentic."

"I think it is. You say you hate it but you really want to be in it, like your deal with women."

"I don't really hate them. I just want to be in them?"

We dissolve in laughter.

May 12, 2004

I run into Rob Eshman at the University of Judaism debate on same-sex marriage.

"Are you living with Cathy Seipp?" he asks.

"No, but many people think that. We're best of friends."

Dennis Prager walks up. He spots me, has a start of recognition, and ignites into a huge smile.

"So where are you theologically?" he asks. We shake hands.

"I [affiliate] Modern Orthodox. Just like baseball has rules, I accept that Orthodoxy defines the rules for Jewish life."

"You won't like our cover story on gay marriage then," says Rob. It's by the kindly Julie Fax (Orthodox), who has amazing access across the spectrum of Los Angeles Judaism.

Rob says the only reason he feels safe setting foot in the UJ is because of his good relationship with its head of adult education, Gady Levy, who organized tonight's event.

The *Journal* recently lost $60,000 in Chabad advertising when they ran some ponderous stories on a financial dispute in Marina Del Rey over a Chabad shul.

May 13, 2004

Cathy Seipp writes on her blog:

> I realized the other day that I hadn't seen Luke Ford in a couple of weeks. That's because he's been busy. Usually his bad behavior is confined to raiding dessert tables at various functions around town, being pointlessly rude to the *Jewish Journal*, and drooling on his blog about girls he wants to sleep with…or (more accurately) girls he wants me to think he wants to sleep with. Lately, though, he's been working overtime: committing felonies; working himself into a self-righteous lather when people point out that he's committed felonies; imagining nasty, tasteless "satires" about pederasty; asking fans to write endless epilogues to his memoir (I believe he's collected 37 so far); accusing his betters of being "fat assholes" in blog comments sections; fiddling with the lithium dosage; and guest blogging on a group site [Protocols] run by a bunch of frum Jews, most of whom probably don't know what hit them.

June 30, 2004

I sit in Rob Eshman's office in Koreatown. He wears jeans, a long-sleeve shirt and a tie. He chews gum.

We chat about his childhood.

Rob grew up rich, secular and loved in the San Fernando Valley. His family went to Stephen S. Wise temple on Yom Kippur. He majored in Anthropology at Dartmouth, graduating in 1982. After two years of living in San Francisco, he moved to Israel.

"I'd always been attracted to Judaism but felt like I was always getting a watered-down version. After my bar mitzvah, I stopped going [to temple]. I just didn't find it compelling.

"The rabbi at Dartmouth was Michael Paley, a dynamo. He got me interested in Judaism as an intellectual pursuit, where you could put the words 'passion' and 'Judaism' in the same sentence.

"In Israel, I supported myself as a counselor and doing freelance journalism for everyone who would pay. I wrote some pieces for the *Jewish Journal*. I came back to LA and kept doing journalism.

"I married in 1991. Gene [Lichtenstein] called me. I worked freelance for two years and went full-time in September 1994. My son was born in July.

"I felt like this was the junk bond of the Jewish community. It was an undervalued institution and under-used. It had enormous potential. I became editor in 2000.

"I want it to be a picture of Jewish LA. I understand that some things are more important. I don't read anybody out except Jews for Jesus. We don't accept their advertising. We do write stories about their recruitment efforts. We don't ignore them. We will print letters to the editor from them.

"I approach it anthropologically. If you had asked me at Dartmouth, will you become an editor of a Jewish newspaper, I would've said, 'Are you high?' But if you looked at what I was doing at Dartmouth, studying ethnography and doing journalism, that's what I'm doing. I'm interested in intellectual and spiritual issues."

"Were you thrilled to become editor?"

"Yeah, I was ready. I had specific ideas of where I would take the paper, like every managing editor does. I'm sure Amy [Klein] does. The way it happened. Gene was hurt in the process and it would've been better if he weren't."

"What are the biggest obstacles that you've had to face to do quality work?"

"The same as every other paper—time and money. The more time and money we put into any article, the better it is.

"We really want to reach every Jew in the city. If you do it through any one organization, there's the appearance that you belong to that organization. LA Jews are different. They don't go to shul that often. They don't go to Jewish places. There are distinct Jewish neighborhoods here but they are comparatively small compared to the enormity of the Jewish population. Our idea was to throw the paper out there, do controlled-circulation (around 60,000), which means to give it away. It coincided with the Federation needing to cut its budget.

"Our support comes from our advertisers. We've just begun to mine that market. By going out on the street, we've attracted a lot more advertisers to the *Jewish Journal* from people who didn't know it existed. It was going to homes [of people who gave over a certain amount a year to the Federation, though in 2005 the Federation will buy zero papers]. Our advertising reps would call people and ask if they wanted to advertise and they'd say they'd never seen it. Now people see it, so they call us. We've also started some other products, such as the *Jewish Family Life* of the Conejo Valley, a featurey glossy. It's a quarterly going monthly. We have *Orange County Jewish Journal* (monthly). We have separate revenue streams. It dissipates the effect of any one advertiser."

"So you really aren't a Federation paper. I've lied about you."

"We've never shared payroll. None of their people have ever sat on our boards or had any role in decision making here. We were started by former [machers] of the Federation because they felt an independent paper was the best thing for the community. To their credit, they hired Gene. To his credit, he fought like a bear to keep the independence of the paper against the powers that be. He infused that feeling in me and the other people here, making it much easier for me to fight those fights, which are rare now.

"I appreciate all the good work Federations and their agencies do. They are major players in Jewish communal life for good reason. But precisely because we saw the journalistic and mutual financial downside of Federation-dependent newspapers, we have worked hard and taken huge financial and editorial risks to secure and maintain our independence. People can have opinions about our Federation coverage (some think it's too kind; some think it's too harsh; I think Marc Ballon, our senior writer, who was 10 years at *Forbes* and *The LA Times*, is terrific) but that's all opinion. The fact is we're a non-profit news weekly that answers to a diverse, thoughtful and independent board of directors.

"It is a level playing field here. We do want all Jewish voices in the paper so long as they can write well. We do want every good Jewish story in the paper. We've had some big advertisers read us the riot act but I am not going to name them. But think of every big Jewish institution in town, at one time or another, they either pulled [ads] a little bit, pulled back, or threatened to start their own paper...

"When you look at [sex-abuse] scandals in the Catholic church and how the Catholic press handled it, and how sex abuse was handled in the Jewish press, whether it was Gary's piece on Lanner or the tons of pieces that we have done investigating sexual abuse, there's no comparison. That's one example of where an independent Jewish press contributes real value to the Jewish community. Controversy makes us stronger. Debate makes us stronger."

I laugh.

"That sounds lame."

"Your coverage of abuse stories never seem to go beyond the pro-forma. You get the police report. You interview the protagonists and the critics."

"You'd have to look at all the stories we've done. Some have been done in depth and some have been pro forma. At one point, Julie Fax pleaded with me to get her off the sex abuse beat. She's the religion editor but there are so many of those stories out there, she found herself going from one sex scandal to another. It was ecumenical. It was Reform, Conservative and Orthodox. I know that some of those won us awards. I know that they were more than pro forma. What's the sex scandal of this week? In the Orange County paper, there's a piece about a rabbi who was reprimanded formally by the UAHC."

"Where have you done good and where are you frustrated with your own performance?"

"There's good writing in the paper. We have good columnists. We have good feature stories. I'm happy with our reporters. If there's one piece that's missing from the paper, and that we're always working on trying to get into the paper, is Jewish life as it is lived in LA. That raw Wolfe-ian sense of..."

I start bellowing and jumping up and down in my seat.

"Yeah. Yeah. Scene-by-scene construction. Status details."

"Publisher Stanley Hirsh, a big macher in town, a cantankerous fascinating guy, wanted that. 'Get the gossip in the paper. I want a gossip column.'"

"Lashon Hara Corner."

"He wouldn't have known that [term]. We'd talk to Gene about it and he'd say, Stanley says he wants it but he really doesn't want it. Stanley only wanted it about the people he wants it about. He didn't want it about his friends. Nevertheless, no Jewish paper does it. Bloggers do it but without fact-checking.

"Luke, you have to question why your standard for true Jewish journalism is revelatory personal details. Yossi [Klein Halevi] took you to task for this, correctly so. I'm all for including them when they are relevant, but to only be concerned for those kind of stories means you miss or demean very important communal stories that feature no sex or violence. For every Kabbalah Centre or ecstasy investigative piece, we've done pieces like the recent one on the Federation's $20 million pension shortfall or the JCC's, pieces that affect many lives here but certainly are the opposite of sexy, and that make us no friends among the establishment. I like sex as much as the next guy, but I don't look to my community Jewish paper for a dependable source of titillation.

"We are the Jewish institution that more Jews participate in each week than any other aspect of Jewish life. We have a circulation of 55,000, with a pass-around-rate of three times that many, which is approaching a majority of English-reading Jewish adults in Los Angeles."

In my ten years in LA, I don't recall a lot of people passing around the *Jewish Journal*. Walking home from shul on Friday nights, however, I sometimes see copies of the *Journal* blowing in the wind down Pico Blvd. I guess that boosts the pass-around rate.

"I think we'd have to get up to 100,000 to really shmear the community. That's our goal, by the end of 2006. Where you can't avoid it, whether you want it or not. We pass out papers around the city and we have a two-three percent return rate. Meaning that two percent of the papers that we pass out for free come back to us. The industry standard, I understand, is ten percent. We want to get to ten percent. We want a lot of papers returned to us so we know that we're saturating the community.

"What else do 150,000 Jews do every week as Jews? They don't celebrate Shabbat.

"It's an enormous responsibility. It gives us this power, this potential grasp of the gestalt of the Jewish community, which I don't yet feel satisfied is reflected in the pages of the paper in an ongoing engaging way."

"Because there are so few writers that can do it?"

"I've talked to a lot of really good writers in town who I think could do it. Many of them make millions writing for movies. They say they'll do it and they might write for us once or twice a year. People like Michael Tolkin. But every minute he spends writing for us is money out of his pocket. He's better and more involved and committed than most."

"He's only done polemical stuff for you."

"Yeah. He hasn't done *The Player* stuff. I've spoken to him about.

"I've looked for younger people starting out who I feel could do that. It hasn't gelled for us yet. I'm thinking the Internet could be the place where that really happens for us. A section of the paper online on Jewish life as it is lived in LA. It's the anthropology part of me. In a given day, I can go from little Russian shteibls in Fairfax to the backyards of these massive homes in Bel Air. In the course of a week, I'll see the highest, the lowest. The most religious, least religious. I'm just amazed by it. Sometimes I will come into our editorial meetings on Tuesday and be frustrated. Where is that [diversity] in the paper? We have those dutiful articles that nobody else will have. An article on a rabbi accused of [sexual abuse]. This week we have an article on a kid who's suing his school in Canejo Valley because his coach has slandered him.

"You have to have the letters to the editor, because that's the community's voice in the paper. The opinions are important. The singles section is the second most popular part of the paper, sometimes the first. You've got to have obits, the second or third most popular part of the paper."

"Why do you run all the JTA, James David Besser and [days-old Israel stuff]?"

"I'm a James Besser fan. He's got a specifically Jewish take on national politics. JTA is a more valid point. The JTA boilerplate pieces on Israel we tend not to run. The Leslie Susser pieces we do run."

"Why would anyone go to the *Jewish Journal* for Mideast analysis?"

"I think it's good analysis. Can you imagine a Jewish newspaper that didn't run anything on Israel? Leslie Slusser is better than a lot of stuff on CNN and MSNBC and as good as a lot of stuff you'll see in *The New York Times*. If I don't learn anything from it, I don't put it in the paper. Could I be more defensive?"

"Does Besser ever break a story or did that stop in the '80s?"

"When did you stop beating your wife? Do you know him? He's a tremendous guy."

"His peers say he doesn't break stories anymore. He's writing for so many different people he doesn't have time to break stories."

"I can't think of the last story he's broken. We don't run him every week. I run him when I think there's something fresh there. This week he has a piece on neo-cons."

"When's the last time Sandee Brawarski…"

"Hated a book? I can even finish your questions for you. Look, those shelves, those are the books that have come in in the last couple of weeks. There are so many books out there. If we have one page for a book review every week, sometimes we don't have that much space for a book review, do I want to use that page to slam somebody or to draw people's attention to a book they should be reading? I don't have a lot of space in the paper. The *Forward* has a lot of space and they do a good job with it and they lose a couple of million dollars a year. I can't. I don't lose any money."

"But she's never written a negative review since *Mein Kampf*."

Rob laughs. "She gets tons of books."

"Of course. They know they're never going to get a negative review. I'd send her my books too."

"I know there's a blood sport to [writing bad reviews] but I don't have the space. It's not that it is unfair to the person who wrote the bad book but it is unfair to the person who wrote the good book."

"You ran a story about the male administrator [Dr. Amnon Finkelstein, dean of admissions] at the UJ who fell out of the window with a naked female student. Why didn't you name names?"

Long pause. "We've since found out all the sordid details, the names, everything, but at the end of the day, was this a Jewish community story or a story of three people who are Jewish having wild sex? We don't do stories on every Jew booked down at the County jail, or every Jew who commits adultery.

"We just moved on to other things. Gaby Wenig's story reflected the larger implications of the story—when big institutions that promote Torah values have to deal with scandals that oppose Torah values. The police blotter.... It was certainly salacious and would've gotten a lot of people to read the paper but at the end of the day, it was not the story. Now, if it were a UJ rabbi…

"Yeah. We've done stories where we've let all the details hang out…"

"Such as?"

"A shooting at Chabad in the Marina. Chabad's a big advertiser. We put Gaby on that story and she and we took nothing but grief.

"So how would you have done it [UJ scandal]? Why didn't you? You have a blog. You can do what you want."

"I did do it."

"You did the Milken High [porn] video scandal?"

"[I did it a week before the *Journal*.] You ran such pious New Age quotes from the administration about the students' self esteem. This video circulated for a year. What does that tell you about the huge disconnect between the people running the school and the students?"

"When a Jewish newspaper takes on any subject like that, we're already on somebody's shit list. Just for that first phone call. Every parent calls you and pleads with you [not to do a story]. Every administrator calls. When that doesn't work, the heavy guns come out. The people who think their money runs the town. They say, 'How is this building community? How is this helping the Jews? Do you know what kind of pain this is going to cause?'

"I think about all these things, the last being most important. I live in this community. The thing about Jewish journalism is that you shit where you eat. You do things that the stupidest animal in the world knows not to do but the Jewish journalist makes his living that way. You have to go back to the same well for the next story. You're always coming face-to-face with these people on a personal level."

"Shabbos dinner."

"Forget Shabbos dinner. How about the men's room at Temple Beth Am? You try to sneak out of services and catch a break at the urinal and some guy says, 'I didn't appreciate that last comment in that article.' Or you get pitched on something, which is constant.

"It's rare that we find details germane to a story that we don't report."

"Does that mean you don't have good reporters?"

Rob laughs. "People call us with crap on everybody. The community that wants only the best [dishes crap on others]. 'I don't see why you do negative stuff on us. You should be doing it on Chabad. How does it help the community to be so nasty to a Jewish institution? Meanwhile, did you hear what the UJ's doing?' We do collect the Jay Edgar Hoover files on people. But a lot of it is just rumors and lashon hara.

"The thing that differentiates a newspaper from a blog is that we bring journalistic standards to bear. Things have to be multi-sourced. We try to get things on the record. Lots of verification.

"Every day I get people with funny accents giving deep dark information. Sure, we could be that kind of paper 24/7. There are intellectuals who want us to be *Commentary West*. There are literati who want us to be *New York Review of Books West*. But our audience is everybody. Six hundred thousand who are a city unto themselves. When people say, 'Why can't you do such-and-such in the *Jewish Journal?*,' what they really mean is, 'Why can't you reaffirm my sense of what Jewish life is? Why can't you reaffirm my Jewish existence for me in every one of your 60 pages?' Everybody, in every single issue, is going to read something that bores them, interests them, offends them and excites them. What's so funny with Jews is that they have this sense of entitlement with their community paper. It should be their paper. When they get *The Wall Street Journal*, do they expect every page they turn to be intensely interesting? I don't. When I read the *Jewish Journal*, there are stories that bore me but I expect that."

"Remember that cover story you did a few months ago about eight new rabbis in town? There were no telling details in the whole piece."

"I can tell you about a lot of stories that didn't live up to expectations but we put out a paper a week. Any good stories?"

"I love Teresa Strasser stories. Joel Kotkin. Umm…"

"I don't want to bust your brains coming up with good stories. I can tell that your ears are steaming. I can see that this is way too strenuous for you."

"How is the Internet and Jewish blogging affecting Jewish journalism?"

"I don't think anybody knows. It's another source of information distribution and we're in the information distribution business. At some point, we're going to have to figure out how to get that information distribution into the life of the *Jewish Journal*. Blogging is here to stay. Some of it is interesting. I think you told me that it is parasitic on real reporting on real Web sites. I hope people understand that blogs aren't reporting. Sometimes it is just a shadow of other reporting and sometimes it is just made-up shit. The people who are smart understand this and the people who aren't aren't going to get it anyway. It has the luxury of space. We run 50/50 every week between ads and copy. In the summer, when we're in advertising doldrums, it means we're going to have a 40-page paper. That means a 20-page newspaper, with about six pages for news.

"We've done hard-hitting stories. I know. You're going, hard-hitting stories in the *Jewish Journal*? We did hard-hitting stories on the Wiesenthal Center and how much money [Rabbi Marvin] Hier is getting."

"You mean the story that broke in the *LA Weekly* and you followed up on it [with defensive explanations for the Hier-family salaries]?"

"Yeah, but we had raised some of those questions previously."

"Do you really think your story on salaries at the Wiesenthal Center was hard-hitting? Was there anything new in it from the *LA Weekly*?"

"Did it hit them [Wiesenthal Center] hard? Yes. Was it hard-hitting? I don't know.

"Tom did interview teachers at YULA [affiliated with the Wiesenthal Center, where R. Hier is the dean] and people who had specific complaints about not getting supplies.

"The Wiesenthal Center doesn't advertise in the *LA Weekly* and their contributors don't read the *LA Weekly*. They read the *Jewish Journal*.

"The JCC [branches closing around LA] story broke with us and then we followed it into the grave."

"Oh God, did you…"

"You and Amy. It affects a lot of people. It doesn't affect you. I felt it was a huge mistake the Federation was making."

"You wrote several columns about that."

"We really ran it into the dust according to people who weren't interested."

"Did you read *The New Rabbi* or *Postville*?"

"I read large parts of both. I just didn't finish them. My take on *The New Rabbi* was that it would've been a compelling 20-page article in *The New Yorker*. I just felt that he kept trying to establish why it was such a big story. And if you have to try to do that, it weakens it. A Tracy Kidder, John McPhee, or even a Sam Freedman in *Jew vs. Jew*, you don't have to tell the reader why this is such a big story. Fried kept putting that in and it annoyed me. I found it hard to believe that it was interesting to non-Jews and I find it hard to believe that the book did that well. Critically it did well but I don't think it sold a lot of copies. It didn't have much resonance outside the Jewish community.

"He kept trying to tell people what was at stake. I think he consciously decided that this was a microcosm of this macrocosm and I just didn't buy it and eventually I lost my interest. I know David [Wolpe] and I read a lot of it with that in mind.

"Postville I thought would've been a great movie. I was fascinated by the whole slaughterhouse thing. I liked *Jew vs. Jew*. He tells each story completely. He gets into the characters. He establishes the conflict and plays it out. I thought the conflict was genuinely reflective of conflicts in Jewish life. I brought Sam out here to talk to our staff about that kind of writing."

"Did it do any good?"

We laugh. "I don't know. We try our best. It's so unseemly to toot our own horn. We get more awards than we've ever gotten before."

I suppress my need to burst out laughing. Awards from the AJPA [American Jewish Press Association]. Big deal.

"From other boring journalists," says Rob.

I burst out laughing and Rob laughs too.

"How did you know [what I was thinking]?"

"You've got the worst poker face I've seen."

"What's that horrible group, the American Association of…"

"AJPA?"

"They are not our best and brightest."

Rob laughs. "I'm on the board. Look, I think Jewish journalism is in an interesting spot now. Our goal is to be the best Jewish paper in America. To be the best weekly in America. Why not?"

"Better than *Time*, *Newsweek*, *The New Yorker*?"

"Why not? *Commentary* started somewhere."

I burst out laughing.

"Why shouldn't we aim high? We have amazing talent in this town. It might take a different format, a different editor. There is no reason that a paper devoted to Jewish life that has the resources of Jewish talent can't have great aspirations. Some say a Jewish journal should only talk about Jewish stuff. I say a Jewish journal should talk about stuff of interest to Jews."

"Wouldn't it be great if you had Sam Freedman writing for you?"

"Time and money. I'm looking for the next Sam Freedman. It's hard to find a Sam Freedman in LA. Most of those really great Jewish journalists who live and breathe the Jewish beat don't live in LA. Marlene Marks (managing editor who died of lung cancer a few years ago) was one of them."

"How much of *The Jewish Week* do you find a good read?"

"I find Gary a good read. Jonathan Mark. They do a good job covering their swath of the community. They have a smaller swath than we do. They tend to the more traditional swathe and we do everybody. I don't think Gary would put gay marriage on the cover. We get no credit from you for that. No matter the amount of shit we took. It was exciting. We don't do it to shock. We think these are important issues for the Jewish community to face. Some people think the *Jewish Journal* is not the place to face them. I don't know where else is. Certainly *The LA Times* is not going to deal with gay marriage from a Jewish perspective.

"In 1998, I did a cover story on the Kabbalah Centre. Only *New York* magazine had done a cover story on them."

"That was a hard-hitting piece."

Rob smiles. "Boy, I'm really flattered. I'm offended and flattered that you remember the pieces that could've been better."

"You reported the details of R. Avraham Union getting a slaughtered lamb's head left on his door. [It arrived the day before he was going to mail all the rabbis in town a devastating letter on the Kabbalah Centre. After the head, he did not send out the letter.]"

"First."

"Yasher koach."

"And all the people you quoted who thought the *Jewish Journal* wasn't hard-hitting wouldn't talk on the record about that because they were worried about a sheep's head."

"Who wrote that?"

"Me."

"Oh, God bless."

"Boy, I actually get a compliment out of you.

"The Kabbalah Centre never stopped advertising. They've been a steady advertiser over the year. We did a story where we took their bottled holy water and had it analyzed for content, and made a mockery of their claims, and they still advertise. I think they understand that we're doing our job, they're doing their job. And we all meet together in the *Jewish Journal*."

"Which segment of the Jewish community is the surliest?"

"Like I'm going to answer that? They all have their moments. You could fill the *Jewish Journal* with the worst of the Jewish community every week. I think that's better left for blogs."

"Who do you think complains the most about the *Jewish Journal*?"

"You."

I collapse into my chair laughing.

"It's flattering. I read your piece. Somebody sent me your interview with Jonathan Sarna. He goes into this long critique of Jewish papers. You ask him if he reads the *Jewish Journal*. He says, when I'm in LA. Here's a scholar proffering a scholarly opinion on American Jewish journalism, who then admits he only reads the *Journal* maybe twice a year. It was offensive. How do you talk about the state of Jewish journalism without taking into account the second largest Jewish newspaper in the country."

"Same way that nobody on the East Coast ever talks about *The LA Times*."

"No one in East Coast Jewry talks about West Coast Jewry. I don't think in his book *American Judaism*, Los Angeles is mentioned once in 500 pages. I don't think the West is mentioned. You didn't bust him on it either."

"Do you think that he doesn't read the *Jewish Journal* reflects more on him or on you?"

"If he wants to have an opinion, it reflects on him. Don't you? What do you think?"

"Yeah. I just found it funny. When people accidentally tell the truth."

"You got him on that. He reads *The Jewish Week*, the Boston paper, which has a ways to go, the Connecticut paper which tries hard but is a Federation paper, New Jersey, Federation paper. We get written off by people here as a Federation paper. It would be nice if they were informed. I'm glad that we do our job more carefully."

I make a guilty laugh.

"I think the Orthodox community gives you the hardest time."

"I think the Orthodox community has the hardest time with us. They don't always give me the hardest time. I get along with them. I have good relationships with Rabbis May and Muskin and Chabad and others. I know Amy is really close with Rabbi Adlerstein. I have tons of respect for Danny Korobkin and Yosef Kanefsky.

"I think they [Orthodox] take a lot of this stuff harder than anyone else. What most Jews consider normative like gay Jews. There are two major gay Jewish synagogues in this town. There's major gay Jewish money that supports major institutions in this town. Our job is to reflect the Jewish community as it is, not as one portion of it wants it to be. They have a hard time that we put men seeking men ads in the paper. That we put gay marriage announcements in the paper. Gene was incredibly courageous to start that. Long before it was a twinkling in the eyes of *The New York Times*. Gene fought big battles over that. It's a huge credit to our board that they support us in these things. It's ideal."

"What do you clash with the board most?"

"Nothing. We're better off financially than we've ever been. We've doubled our circulation in the past four years. When I took over, the median age [of readership] was 49. Now it's in its early 30s, I'd say. We've kept a core of wealthy older Jews who are major contributors to the community. It's a balancing act in every issue to appeal across the board and move the conversation along. You want people to be arguing about the *Jewish Journal* at your dinner table."

"How often does a macher in the community threaten to go on a financial jihad against you?"

"At least every year, someone threatens to or starts another Jewish paper. The last one was in the Valley. They told me they were finally going to publish a paper from the Orthodox Republican perspective."

I ask Rob if he's a cheerleader for LA Jewish life. He says yes. "Jewish life here is fascinating. The level of scholarship here is astonishing. The level of political activity is historic. The level of Jewish innovation is groundbreaking. Sarna completely missed this in his book."

I complain about plodding cover stories, such as the recent one on Mare Winningham, the actress who converted from Catholicism to Judaism.

"You missed the part about her being a serial killer? You read too fast."

"I want something to surprise me. I knew it all just by the cover headline."

"You've got a high standard. You need a money shot. Sometimes you don't get that. You've still got to go to press."

"Has Naomi Pfefferman (Arts editor) ever written a critical celebrity story?"

"I don't know. Probably not."

"What does that mean?"

"That Naomi has never written a critical celebrity story."

"**If some Jew has a movie or TV show coming out and they are profiled in the *Jewish Journal*, I know it is going to be a positive profile.**"

"So give me the model of the negative story you'd like to see?"

Amy Wallace's takedown of Peter Bart in *Los Angeles* magazine, the result of months of exhaustive reporting, which the *Jewish Journal* could not afford.

"**The abominable behavior that goes on routinely in Hollywood. [Drugs, whores, egotism.] Death threats.**"

"You have a much more difficult time with your sources.

"I think there are places for that in journalism. I'm not sure there's a place for that in every 1100-word profile that is mostly fulfilling that information need. These are no less hard-hitting than the celebrity profiles in *Vanity Fair*. Entertainment journalism tends to be profoundly positive. I defy you to find a critical piece on a celebrity because that is the last interview that reporter is ever going to get with a celebrity."

"**That's why you guys have such great access.**"

"Naomi has amazing access. In 18-years, one person has said no to us. That was Al Franken when his first book came out. The second book he said yes. I can't think of one person we can't reach."

"**Because they know that you'll be nice.**"

"No. Hier and Cooper and Federation people and politicians we haven't been nice to will come on the phone. At the end of the day, the dust settles and they realize we've told another side of the story and the world hasn't collapsed around the Jews. If there were three Jewish newspapers in town, there would be more [powder puff journalism]. It's very expensive to put out a paper. It's easier to be independent and tough when you are the only Jewish paper in town.

"Say we're not at the quality Luke Ford wants, but say we're at an above-average quality. We provide advertisers with access to an upscale, educated and involved demographic, unique in this region. Everybody here gets a good wage. We're at the industry standard. Nobody is being screwed here because they're part of the Jewish community and have the honor of working here. We try to pay writers what is standard for freelancers. We're self-sustaining. We provide a weekly service to readers for free or for a minimal subscription cost. Thanks to our business staff, it works without us having to be beholden to any one communal interest."

Rob is called away. As he walks out, he hands me *Los Angeles* magazine. "If you want hard-hitting…. What's their excuse?"

Three minutes later, he returns.

Managing editor Amy Klein walks in. "I'm sorry but…"

"He's sucking me dry," smiles Rob.

"I know," she says. "But we need to go to press and I need you to…"

"I've looked at everything."

"Your editorial?"

"Yep."

She leaves.

"When you're at the AJPA, do you feel like you're with a sharp crowd?"

"You're with your peers. A lot of it is some whining, kvetching, drinking, talking shop about advertising rates, software. These are your cousins."

"Your retarded cousins?"

We laugh.

"Some are really bright. I defy you to find many journalists in this country who are as good as Andy Carroll."

"What happened to the part of you that wanted to publish all the salacious details?"

"I get accused of always doing it. People pick on me that I am only interested in sex. I think in some ways we're pussycats.

"*The Jewish Week* and the *Forward* would never run Teresa Strasser. Meanwhile, she's won all sorts of awards and her career's taking off and she's a terrific writer. But she writes about making out with a guy at 3 a.m. in a strip joint in Hollywood. I get all the time, how does that build Jewish community?"

[Eve Kessler from the *Forward* writes: "That's false. We have run personal essays about women and sex that were just as pungent as Teresa's. I don't know if Teresa ever pitched anything to us. If so, we would only take it if it was exclusive. I'm a fan of her's, actually, having met her many years ago when she was at the *Jewish Bulletin of Northern California*. But the idea that he's the only one who would run a cute, light chick column about sex is just bunk. We ran an interview with a Jewish stripper on page one probably 11 years ago."]

"Do you get more hate mail over her?"

"We did, but it's like *The Simpsons* and Howard Stern. What started out as anti-establishment and everybody hated it, now I get 80-year old grandmothers coming up to me and complaining that there's not enough Teresa Strasser in the paper.

"We're doing a better job than any other institution in town reaching younger people.

"All our male writers get married within two weeks of writing a column. These women could write singles columns for 30 years…. They can get a lot of dates because of it but they won't find a guy."

Our last hour together is largely off-the-record chitchat. When I give Rob some grudging accolades for his work, he says, "No, no. Stick to your guns. 'It's a boring paper.'"

Rob encourages me to pitch him with suggestions on how to make the *Journal* a more exciting paper. I think I'd rather stay a part of the problem rather than part of the solution.

All I want from my Jewish paper is peace in the Middle East and a peak experience. Is that too much to ask?

When I read an article in the *Jewish Journal*, I want to feel my whole body convulsed by tension, climaxed by a satisfying conclusion that makes me scream, "Oh my God. Oh my God. That was the best ever." Is that too much to ask?

I want to leave my tawdry life while reading the paper and float in an ethereal world. Is that too much to ask?

Each time I open up the pages of the *Journal*, I expect my experience to usher in a messianic age. Each time I'm disappointed. It makes me very very angry.

19

E.J. Kessler

July 1, 2004

"I didn't set out to be a journalist. I was in Zionist activism from the time I was a child. I went to Barnard College majoring in English. I graduated in 1982. I wanted to reconnect with my Judaism. I lived in Israel for most of 1985. I got in my head that I wanted to solve the Arab-Israel conflict. I went to the Columbia School of International Affairs for a masters. I wanted to be a policy analyst. I studied the Middle East and took courses in the journalism school. I graduated in 1989.

"The cold war ended. There were fewer jobs for policy analysts. I still had the question of what was I going to be when I grew up. My professors encouraged me to get a PhD. I wasn't interested in staying in academia because I was interested in getting married and starting a family. I knew I wanted to marry a Jew.

"I took a job as the editor of a magazine for an international Jewish women's organization, ORT [original Russian acronym].

"I was becoming more religious. I lived on the Upper West Side. I was getting swept up in the whole religious revival. I wasn't becoming Orthodox as much as I was becoming Sabbath observant. I was hanging out with a bunch of single Jewish intellectuals in their late 20s, early 30s. Our social lives centered around these elaborate Sabbath lunches we would make at various people's homes. We'd shul hop. It was there that I met my husband. I had kids.

"The *Forward* was launched in 1990 in English by Seth Lipsky. The *Forward* is a tradition in newspapering. It's 109 years old. In the 1920s, it was a

Yiddish daily that reached a quarter of a million people, which was more than *The New York Times* at the time. *Forward* was what our grandparents read. It was part of a whole wave of Jewish working-class activism.

"I called up Jonathan Rosen and asked him if there was anything I could do for him. He assigned me a book to review. It was one of those fateful things that starts you on an intellectual journey. It was probably the single most life-changing piece I ever wrote. *The Voice of Sarah: Feminine Spirituality and Traditional Judaism* by Tamar Frankiel.

"It's not that the book was so great. It was a middling book. But it started my writing about Judaism. I was practicing Judaism but I had never approached it from an intellectual vein.

"I started reviewing books and writing about religion. I started writing about what my life was about.

"In 1996, I was living in Palo Alto. I was the mother of two. They invited me to become a staff writer. I moved back to New York. They turned me into a full-time reporter."

"When did you get pulled off the religion beat?"

"I took myself off the religion beat. It's about what happened in 2000 when Lipsky and the *Forward* Association had their falling out. They hadn't yet hired a replacement. They asked me to be the acting editor. I'm the only female editor-in-chief the *Forward* has ever had. That's my footnote in history. I'm a footnote."

She laughs.

"When J.J. came in, he needed me to edit the Op/Ed page. I felt like an era had closed. I started writing about politics."

"What were the principle obstacles you faced to doing good Jewish journalism when you were the reporter?"

"You can say this about the Jewish world generally. They're not used to being reported about critically. None of the Jewish institutions are. They don't like it. Because for the lay people, it is their avocation, something they do from their heart, they don't understand that someone would look at this and critique it in the same way that *The Wall Street Journal* would critique their finance company. The professionals who work in these institutions haven't had a whole lot of professional press scrutiny."

"Because the Jewish press is so dull."

"Yes. Because a large part of it is a kept press. It is not independent. Because it is sponsored by the Federation, it doesn't report critically about hardly any institutions.

"I was persona non grata for two years at the Jewish Theological Seminary. They declined to speak to me…for reporting on an [Ismar] Schorsch speech in the Midwest. I reported that some Conservative lay people didn't like speech. Nobody had ever seen anything like that."

"Is there any group that is more thin-skinned and control-freaked than the Conservative rabbinate? Look at how they went nuts over the book *The New Rabbi*."

"I'm not willing to say that any one institution is more paranoid or sensitive to criticism. They all are. When you have a response by any institution that's like that, it's because the institution is hunkered down in some way and in trouble. Confident institutions don't react that way. Ok? I don't want to say anything specifically about them.

"Lipsky used to publish all sorts of things that Federations and UJA didn't like. The various powers that be had all kinds of tiffs with him.

"In American life since the 1960s, elite institutions have taken a drubbing. There's been a questioning of authority across the board. It's not simply Judaism."

"What's your critique of *The Jewish Week*?"

"It waxes and wanes. It got better under Gary when he first took over. It was not a good paper under Phil Ritzenberg."

"Is it still a good paper?"

"We used to compete directly with *The Jewish Week* under Seth because he was interested in the New York story. He was interested in the charitable and Federated story. He was interested in the power brokers, many of whom were aligned with *The Jewish Week*, which had Federation subsidy for a long time. We had a newspaper war. Seth believed that subsidy created an un-level playing field in the New York market. He editorialized against that practice. He competed with them as a business for advertising and journalistically.

[The *Forward* is subsidized by its own foundation and loses millions of dollars every year.]

"I don't know that anyone was going to win that war. The Anglo-Jewish press is an undeveloped market. The *Forward* as a national Jewish newspaper is a dicey idea. You discover when you live outside of New York that all Judaism is local. People look to their local Jewish paper. They don't understand that there can be meta-discourse and not just JTA dispatches from Hungary, but a paper that talks about American Jewish life. That national market hasn't been established and it is hard to newspaper for a market that has not been established. Newspapering is a local craft.

"One reason I so enjoyed reporting from Palo Alto is that Jewish practices were so ad hoc. You had these Orthodox women who were basically synchretizing Californian New Age practice with Judaism. It was interesting to go to a placenta planting ceremony in the backyard of an Orthodox synagogue."

"Do you find *The Jewish Week* a compelling read?"

"Graphically, it leaves something to be desired. I don't think its headlines are smart. It has some good reporters. The whole package could be updated."

"The quality of the writing?"

"It's ok."

"The arts and books coverage?"

"I don't read them. Do you?"

"It's a horrible paper. Did Gary run out of steam years ago? Is there something about that institution that just sucks life out of you?

"Do you ever read the *Jewish Journal*?"

"Only when I have some reason, such as when I'm reporting about California."

"Unless you have to, you don't read it."

"No. Why would I read it?"

Beats me.

"It's not a national product. It's not offering me anything."

"What are the most compelling reads in Jewish journalism?"

Eve sighs. "Oh God..."

"If any?"

"I don't read a lot of Jewish journalism anymore."

"You would if there were compelling reads out there."

"I suppose. I don't read any Jewish magazines though I did when I had to report on the movements."

"What do you think of James David Besser's work?"

"He's a decent reporter."

"Do you remember when he last broke a story?"

"Look. My comment is that he's a decent reporter."

"Are there any book-length works of Jewish journalism that have really impressed you in the past few years?"

"Jewish journalism?" Her voice rises high. She's disbelieving what she's hearing. Impressive book length works of Jewish journalism? What am I? Meshuganah?

Long pause. Clarifying questions. Then, "There was really nothing I felt I had to read."

"Anyone on secular papers doing a bang-up job on American Judaism?"

"Nope. Religion reporting in general in the elite papers sucks."

"It goes to the dullest reporters."

"The paper that pays the most attention to religion in an inquisitive way is *The Christian Science Monitor*. *The New York Times* hasn't had any decent religion reporting in years, since Gus Niebuhr hasn't been around. Even he wasn't on fire. They have Laurie Goodstein on the beat, but she doesn't appear to be fulltime. She seems to know more about Catholicism than she does about Judaism.

"When I was asking [Jewish religious leaders] close questions about what they were doing, they suddenly had to take a step back and think about it more. I felt like I was affecting them for the good. I felt like I was sharpening their thinking because suddenly they had to explain to someone who wasn't one of them."

"What do you think of Jewsweek?"

"It's a little derivative of what we do. You can see that it's edited by someone who's Orthodox. It's the same thing as the JewishWorldReview. People who are frum-from-birth and create publications like that, they put their mark on it."

"Have you discovered any great talent in the blogosphere?"

"I don't get that far into the blogosphere. I'm reading political blogs more than I'm reading Jewish blogs. My husband complains that my Jewish practice has become attenuated since I'm not reporting so much on Judaism. I used to know everything because I was up on the rabbinic debates. That's not true anymore. A lot of the debates, frankly, haven't progressed that far in the four years that I haven't been reporting on them.

"The *Forward* under J.J. has become much more oriented towards the diplomatic and Arab-Israel thing."

"How come there isn't more scene-by-scene construction and focus on status details?"

"The medium is the message. The function follows the form. The *Forward* is a broadsheet. It's not big. Articles in the *Forward* do not tend to be longer than 1500 words. It's difficult to do that kind of journalism in *Forward* because of what we are. We're not the *Village Voice*, which is a tabloid. We have traditional notions of what is a beat reporter. We're not New Journalists. We were hired to report the news. Better that we should do that well than try this other thing which is entertaining and wonderful when it is well done in *The New Yorker* or *Esquire*. It's more of a magazine form. It's not our enterprise.

"I've had almost every job you can have here. It's a small shop. It's like improvisational jazz. One time when I was features editor, someone wrote a personal essay. By and by, she mentions it was like giving blowjobs. It's part of my daily speech, so it totally flew by me and landed in the paper. Seth was like, 'BLOWJOBS?' He pulled up his glasses. 'Seth, I didn't notice.' It was so natural in the flow of the piece that it didn't register. We're a family newspaper. We're not supposed to say that.

"There is a virtue to being small and obscure because you have more freedom. We printed [cartoonist] Art Spiegleman's comment on the shadow of the two towers [of the World Trade Center]. *The New Yorker* turned it down because they knew it would be full of outré stuff that would antagonize people. He gave us his comic. In one frame, it had George Bush holding a box cutter to the neck of the American Eagle. We lost subscriptions because of this. There was a lot of wicked left-wing stuff that he drew. We were willing to do it.

"There's stuff I've said about American political figures because, who am I? I'm nobody. For instance, I wrote that the Hebrew spelling of Kerry—kuf, resh, yud—in the Talmud means an unwanted seminal emission."

"Anyone try to bribe you?"

Eve laughs. "We're so important that someone is going to want to bribe us? It's an absurd notion."

"Which practitioners of your craft do you admire the most?"

Long pause. "Look." A little frustrated. "I don't exempt myself when I say we're all kind of mediocre.

"I put my intellect in the service of my [Jewish] community, otherwise I'd be out there seeking to maximize my income. I'm connected with the Jewish story. Lipsky used to say it's the best story of the last 5,000 years.

"My colleagues are as dedicated to this story as I am. Some are more talented than others. We're all trying. Do we succeed as a group? No. I include myself in that group.

"I was once invited to a seminar on Jewish journalism at Brandeis. I told the assembled Federated paper types that we were mediocre because we are a 'kept press'—which I thought was the most obvious observation. But I never was invited back."

"How much status has your hard work gained you in Jewish life?"

"When I reported about the rabbinate, my husband used to say that I was like a minor Jewish celebrity because rabbis and Jewish academics were highly interested in what I was doing. We'd meet a rabbi at a bar mitzvah. I'd introduce myself and he'd be like [with awe], 'Oh, you're E.J. Kessler?' My husband got an inflated idea of who I was. I had a following. I enjoyed that. I'm not sure that there is quite as large a group in the general Jewish community for my political stories although I get nice comments from political insiders. It's more important to me that my work be appreciated by other journalists than by [the hoi polloi]."

"Would you like to see American Jewish journalists get the same influence that their Israeli counterparts have?"

"It's not possible. Israel is a well-developed market for news."

"Have you been impressed by Israeli journalism on American Jewish life?"

"Nope. I don't think they have any insight into our community. They come at it with a bunch of Israeli prejudices. I don't think we have any insight into their community either.

"The subject I least enjoyed writing about was Jewish divorce. People would give me their divorce papers, which were filled with ugliness. Sometimes I would cry all night because of the pain in them."

20

Rabbi Avi Shafran

July 2, 2004

Rabbi Shafran has been the spokesman for Agudath Israel (right-of-center Orthodox group) for a decade. He writes a weekly column widely printed in the Jewish press.

"I'm something of a journalism junkie."

"Do you find it a good experience to interact with the news media?"

"I'm not usually happy when I interact with the general press. I find that reporters often miss important nuances.

"There are, though, good reporters out there. I particularly liked the work of Gus Niebuhr, who was the religion editor of *The New York Times*. He's now teaching at Syracuse. He was an open-minded, fair-minded, perceptive, reporter. And, unfortunately, he apparently didn't like his job at *The Times*.

"I've been impressed as well by Dan Okrent, the ombudsman at *The Times*. I've interacted with him considerably."

"Are there any Orthodox Jews working the secular news media that you know of?"

"Not that I know of."

There are such people but they are few. Jewish laws about forbidden speech (*lashon hara*) make it difficult for a Torah Jew to work as a journalist.

"Are there things the Orthodox community has been doing that discourage Jews from going into journalism?"

"It is a problem. I was heartened that the most recent issue of *The Jewish Observer* (published by Agudath Israel) took to task the state of secular education in some Charedi schools, that secular studies are not taken seriously enough in some of our yeshivos. It seems that we subtly send the message that these are not important things. And that's not right. First, they are required by American law, which should take the issue off the table. Communication skills are the most valuable things a Jew can have. We're all about communication, study, arguing, investigating.

'It's not surprising that our focus has been somewhat limited until now. The last 40 years of American Orthodoxy have largely been all about recovering from the Holocaust. We've rarely had the chance to settle down and set forth a positive agenda."

"Do your fellow [Charedim] give you a hard time about your column and work with the secular news media?"

"Not really. I have a good relationship with my community. Sometimes I will get scathing letters about using big words. I also get criticized for referring to Reform and Conservative [clergy] as rabbis."

Rabbi Shafran's formal secular education ended when he graduated high school.

"What kind of journalist do you write out of your Rolodex?"

"Someone who makes no effort to be objective. When words are taken out of context. Ideas are skewed and not rendered the way they are given over, and it happens eight or nine times with the same person, I become disillusioned. There's only one reporter, though, whom I've written out. Not to say that there aren't others I'm cautious about."

"What's your critique of the *Forward*?"

"The *Forward* is generally a fascinating paper. It fills a niche. It's independent and cheeky and undaunted. I've been happy with the way its editors have responded when I've had criticism of the way a particular thing has appeared in the *Forward*. When I've requested Op/Ed space to reply to something, they've been forthcoming. In one case, I skewered the paper for a blatantly hypocritical position. They had editorialized about the need to take care of America's underprivileged children no matter whose fault it is that they are underprivileged (referring to the urban communities). Then, a while later, they blasted the Israeli Charedi community for having so many children and asking the government to help support them.

"It was to their tremendous credit that they published my piece, and without any editorial response. They gave themselves a black eye. When I asked J.J. Goldberg for permission to reprint it, he even said to me, 'It is one thing to let you do what you did in our pages, but to have you do it in other papers, we'd prefer you do not.' I respected that sentiment, but took it as a compliment.

"On the other hand, I think there have been times when the paper has been too anxious to score a scoop, and in the process has trampled objectivity."

"What did you think of Gary Rosenblatt's famed investigative series on Baruch Lanner?"

"Gary has said that he consulted with rabbinic authorities about what to do and presumably he followed what they told him. To me, that's the bottom line determinant of whether it was proper or not."

"Are you comfortable with Rabbi Shmuley Boteach being the best known voice for Orthodox Judaism in North America?"

"There are other Orthodox voices that should be better known. He's written some fine things. I don't want to get into his past and some of the people he's rubbed elbows with. I think he's often written responsibly. He took Madonna to task. I don't know if I wouldn't have done it so harshly. To lay bare some of the emptiness of the secular world, I respect him for that. I'm not enamored, though, with his focus on things sexual. I don't know that he's written anything halakhicly outrageous, but there's a certain concept in Judaism called *tzniut* (modesty). That one does not flaunt issues that are best kept in the private realm. I don't know whether he's guilty or not of having done that. I'm not intimately familiar with what he's written but placing sex repeatedly in the spotlight is not something I can endorse."

"Do you wish you were as famous as Rabbi Boteach?"

"No. I get my kicks out of seeding minds. I like to put ideas out there for people to get upset at or to just tweak them. I'm a sort of terrorist. I don't plant bombs but ideas, to try to get people talking. I'm gratified when I can get minds to focus on something. I don't want to see my face in *The New York Times*. I'd rather get some thoughts that I've put forth become discussed in the public sphere. That's my darkest desire."

21

Larry Yudelson

July 4, 2004

"I got the journalism bug early, with the elementary school paper. In high school [Chafetz Hayim Yeshiva in Rochester], I was the NCSY newspaper editor and designer. In college, I went to Yeshiva University (on the secular side compared to my high school, though not compared to my upbringing) and worked on the school paper (*Hamevaser*) before graduating (with a degree in computer science) in 1985.

"Larry Cohler got me into Jewish journalism as a career. In 1984–85, he was at *Long Island Jewish World*, and I was picking up *The Jewish Week* and the *Jewish World* every weekend. He had a couple of outstanding articles on halakhic issues. Rumors would fly around YU about various issues. He sat down and made phone calls. The most incredible article was about women's prayer groups. Rabbi Louis Bernstein, then head of the RCA, had asked the RIETS rosh yeshiva for a psak (legal ruling). It was assur (forbidden). Larry called, spoke to them, and they were caught honestly saying what they thought, and they were caught being total fools. This is why they don't talk to the press anymore. One rebbe said, I don't need to speak to the women. I know their types. Just a mass generalization and mass ignorance. Nothing of surprise to anyone who goes to their classes but this was in public.

"His article wasn't just 500 words of 'he said it isn't ok, she said it is ok.' Larry put the whole thing together. It was fascinating to see what journalistic technique can do to halakhic stories.

"Flipping forward to 2004 with this water issue in New York [Rav Schachter has reportedly ruled that filters must be installed to strain out bugs], the blogs are doing it. But nobody is asking hard questions of the poskim [deciders of Jewish law]. Poskim say they don't need to be asked hard questions. They need to answer why is this water different from Reb Moshe Feinstein's [leading decider of Jewish law in the 20th Century] water? I'm waiting for Steven Weiss to ask people that but they don't want to speak to him. If they were the honest Gedolei Torah [giants of Torah] that they claim to be, they would answer the question.

"Anyway, in college I was running with this crowd who wanted to become rabbis and high school principals. Twenty years later, they're all rabbis and high school principals. I wanted to make a mark on the Jewish community through journalism.

"At age 21, I decided to do an article about Jewish journalists. I called Larry Cohler and I asked him all these questions. Being a senior and lazy and under pressure, I didn't make any more phone calls. Then I get a phone call from Larry Cohler right after I graduate. He said he was on the board of the JSPS and they were interviewing for new editors. I go to the interview. I'm asked for my philosophy of Jewish journalism. I give him a whole spiel. Back on the street, I realize that I had almost word-for-word regurgitated what Larry had told me three months earlier. So, he liked it.

"Working at JSPS was a phenomenal education. I edited writers who were worse than I was. Editing people is a good way to learn how to edit yourself. Larry started assigning me freelance stories. I went to conferences of Reform, Conservative and Orthodox rabbis. I got an education in American Judaism.

"One person who inspired me was Rifka Rosenwein. She wrote for *The Wall Street Journal* and did a wonderful center column piece on Coca Cola getting OU hashgacha (kosher certification) finally. She subsequently became my editor at JTA. She died in November 2003. She was in-and-out of Jewish journalism. She would be drawn to Jewish journalism because that was her community and those were the stories she wanted to tell, but bringing in outside experience in serious journalism.

"Then I did a year at the *Long Island Jewish World*. Jerry Lippman let people commit great journalism. He was an old school editor. Always screaming. I had nightmares for a few months after I stopped working there. I had to run away from this guy who was yelling at me every Tuesday night. I went to Israel and stayed for a couple of years and wrote for a consortium of Jewish papers. I was edited by Marty Pomeranz [editor of the *Washington Jewish Week* who was later outed by his staff as a serial liar].

"I came back to America and a after a year of freelancing, got hired at the Jewish Telegraphic Agency. I was one of their two New York reporters. Debra Nussbaum Cohen had seniority, so she got to cover religious issues. My beat was politics and organizations. She got God; I got Malcolm Hoenlein.

"There's a power to Jewish journalism. When you choose to write about something and push it forward, it makes a difference. You can try to move a community from one centered on fear to one concerned with the content of Judaism. You can have ripple effects.

"The bad of Jewish journalism is that you don't have any editors who are pushing a story forward. If Eve Kessler is a deputy managing editor and Debra Nussbaum Cohen is spending more time with her family and there are stories that aren't getting written as a result, that's not an indictment of Debra or Eve. But these people have editors and it is the job of the editor to make sure that the story doesn't get lost. Jewish newspapers generally are not well edited. A great newspaper reflects a great editor.

"If I can sit around the table and come up with ten stories that nobody has written about, and you can come up with ten stories for the *Jewish Journal* that haven't been written, then that is the editor's fault.

"What's the mission of a newspaper? That was the problem with JTA. Was it a wire service or a publicity release or a way to get copy for the *Jewish Bulletin of Northern California*? News for Jews who hadn't read *The New York Times*. This was silly in 1995. In 2005, if you want to know *The New York Times* news, you'll read it online.

"When we cover Jewish organizations, is it our job to make people like Jewish organizations? Or is to help Jewish organizations do a better job spending their money?

"Journalism can serve its community. It can create a community. Look at trade publications. Look at *Printing Press Monthly*. A monthly magazine for people who buy and sell high-end printing equipment. Jewish publications should be trade publications but they're not.

"Let's say I create a dream publication that goes to people who give more than $1,000 a year to the Jewish community. If I say Israel Bonds is bankrupt and is a waste of money, am I taking money out of the Jewish community? No. I'm having it go more effectively to the Jewish community. My loyalty is not to an organization but to the broader community.

"Are the day schools working effectively? Are people in Los Angeles happy with their day schools? How come *The Los Angeles Times* runs a better story on Jewish day schools [long piece on the Modern Orthodox Shalhevet school by Barry Siegel] than the *Jewish Journal*?

"The LA Jewish community spends maybe $100 million a year on Jewish education?

"My sister spends thousands of dollars a year on my niece's education (whatever amount gets negotiated between her, and her accountant and the financial aid committee of her day school). The *Jewish Journal* speaks nothing to her. Why don't they start covering the schools? How many parents in [LA Orthodox schools] like that their kid's class isn't coed in second grade? Where's the voice of the parents in the community? That should be the newspaper's job.

"Newspapers, instead of covering day schools, are covering institutions in the President's Conference, which is a 1950s model of a Jewish organization. I gave a pitch once to a Jewish editor to come on board as an education reporter. If it paid the mortgage, I'd be happy to do it. This is where most of the money in the Jewish community is being spent. I live in Teaneck, New Jersey. Our Bergen County Federation makes two or three million dollars a year and our local schools spend about five million dollars a year.

"Why isn't there a national newspaper about Jewish education?

"A lot of the stories that do get covered miss the point. When Rabbi David Wolpe gets up and [challenges the historicity of the Exodus] it is only news in a he-said, she-said way. How does Conservative Judaism handle Biblical Criticism is a great story. You call Conservative rabbis and ask them how they deal with these things. What's the deep story behind what Rabbi Wolpe's saying? Do you do conventional he-said, she-said stories or do you do New Journalism and let the story speak for itself?

"I wrote a damning profile of a guy I considered a nudnik and the guy said, 'wow, what a great story. You told it like it was.' I read the story and think the guy is a nudnik, but if you like him, you really like the story.

"Tom Wolfe says this is America. *Life* Magazine doesn't talk to me about these hot-rodders or these other subcultures. These are people who speak a language *Time* magazine can't comprehend. We need tools to do it.

"How well does somebody who reads the *Jewish Journal* know about the Persian or Israeli community in Los Angeles? Who's telling the Israelis about the Americans?

"If I were the editor of the *Jewish Journal*, I'd pitch the publisher to come out with several editions—Orthodox, Persian, Israeli, and unaffiliated. We'll swap the best stories. Rather than trying to be all things to be all people.

"Bernie Weintraub covers Hollywood for *The New York Times*. His wife, Amy Pascal, is a studio executive. The unaffiliated Jew like Bernie doesn't want to read an umpteenth debate about the settlers in Gaza. Rabbi Dov Fischer [frequently published in the *Jewish Journal*, Larry clashed with him in their student newspaper days] has been writing the same things over and over again. That's not news. A baseball player such as Shawn Green (latest *Jewish Journal* cover story) is not news either. He has no interesting ideas. [University of Judaism Talmud professor] Aryeh Cohen has interesting ideas. Has he made the cover of the *Jewish Journal*?"

"No."

"Jewish academia hasn't made its way into the Jewish newspapers. They're living off ideas that are decades old. David Twersky and J.J. Goldberg had some new ideas in the 1960s. We had a couple of new ideas in the 1980s. I don't see any editor shouting at his reporters, 'Hey, kid, give me a new idea.'

"I'd ask, could this story have been written ten years ago? If so, why do it now?

"Without a clear conception of who your communities are, and how you can keep all of your readers excited at least some of the time, you just end up with something that inoffensive and uninteresting. If you have a New York paper being edited by a Modern Orthodox Jew living in a Modern Orthodox community [Gary Rosenblatt of *The Jewish Week*] and has reported from a Modern Orthodox perspective, you are not going to be inside baseball enough to interest people in the Modern Orthodox community and it's not going to be interesting enough for people on the outside.

"Gary Rosenblatt doesn't know why he's doing it this way. Mark Joffe (editor of the JTA) doesn't know why he's doing things this way. Seth Lipsky did something that was not done in any other Jewish newspaper. He had regular Thursday morning meetings after the paper came out. I sat in while I was being courted by him. I occasionally got these great job offers from him that required a change in location and a cut in pay.

"He would criticize the headlines and the stories and he was teaching his staff. He had people come in and commit good journalism under him and go on to commit great journalism. Philip Gourevitch. Jeffrey Goldberg.

"Elsewhere, there's not the self criticism and there's not a goal. Until you have a mandate to do great journalism, it's not going to happen. If the head of the Federation placed calls to editors at *The LA Times, Variety, Hollywood Reporter*, to get them to critique the *Jewish Journal* to make it better, they would do it. The magazines that I like are the ones that tell me something that I don't know. When was the last time you read something in a Jewish newspaper that you didn't already know?

"Everything Seth Lipsky would tell you would be a scoop, no matter how trivial. If Luke Ford brings me the first coverage of the important new Philip Roth novel coming out, that's news. I learned about this from you. Philip Roth has become the definitive Jewish novelist of the 20th Century.

"If you're writing for a paper with the idea of getting scoops, you will get things.

"*The Jewish Week* can't take ideas seriously. The story about bacteria in the New York water is probably most the important Jewish story so far in the 21st Century. *The Jewish Week* treats the story as a silly joke. They put it on page three with silly things where they called the Health Department for comment. It's a big story in the history of halakha in the 21st Century.

"*The Jewish Week* ought to be able to cover this story better *The New York Times*, which will cover the halakha and the science seriously."

"Who do you think is doing the best work in Jewish journalism?"

"I'm reading it less and less. I'm finding it harder to do more than leaf through the Jewish newspapers.

"The only paper I find generally interesting is the *Forward*. The Arts section is worth looking at. Occasionally there's an interesting story in *The Jewish Week*. I was Jewish news junkie. Now I read about new technologies."

"How much do you think the Internet is influencing Jewish journalism?"

"It's changing the environment in ways that haven't been caught up with yet. The Jewish community hasn't taken advantage of it. Jewish newspapers haven't reacted to it. Andrew Silow-Carroll repackages Web logs on page three for his community. Web logs will always be read by a minority, but can serve a useful function in the news pyramid. Paul Krugman is a conduit for Web logs to get into *The New York Times*."

"Were you ever offered bribes?"

"I wish. If I were, I might've stayed there.

"I got some comment from Malcolm Hoenlein, when Larry Cohler was coming to *The Jewish Week*. He said I was the 'Good Larry' in Jewish journalism. It sent chills up my spine and made me feel dirty. It probably motivated me to write a nasty JTA anti-Presidents Conference article (how the Conference was silent on the Peace Process).

"There were occasional orders from on high at JTA. I got taken off a beat once when the head of the Council of Jewish Federations complained about a story.

"The closest I ever got to a bribe was that Chabad's PR guy Zalman Schmotkin who was kind enough to study the rebbe and Chasidus with me once a week for about a year. He gave me a lot of understanding of Chabad. Not one word of that ever turned into journalism.

"I remember a gay congregation (Beit Simcha Torah) wanted to march in the Salute to the Israel parade. The Orthodox didn't want them to and threatened to pull out. The Orthodox parents couldn't understand the big deal. The Orthodox leadership said, oh no. These are gays. They're violating Torah law. The parents said, what about Reform temples? They're not violating Torah law? You had ideology on high. If you ran the story with the ideology from the gays and the Orthodox, you had one story. When you spoke to real people, there's tolerance. Yes, they're going to hell, but they're going to go to hell anyway for not having a mehitza.

"*The Jewish Week*'s story this week on the upper West Side. You have one factoid, two anecdotes, and one pop sociologist. Give me ten facts. I don't see the editor screaming at the cub reporter, 'What about this or that?'

"Look at some of Gene Lichtenstein's stuff from a year out. He had a way of telling community stories in a distinct voice. Talk of the Town (*The New Yorker*) but briefer. This got frittered away over the years. They ran press releases and lost their voice. Who's going to read it if there's not a voice?

"If I want to connect young people to Israel, then I'll do it in a way that will offend everybody over 55. You want to be involved with Israel because it is a sexier, crookeder, funnier, nastier, more backstabbing, more backbiting, crazier, more psychotic than Hollywood. If you think Ronald Reagan and Charleton Heston were senile old men, let me tell you about Shimon Peres. Let me not run week-by-week updates on Ariel Sharon and his bribes. Let me out-tabloid everybody else. You should go to Israel because they have the most provocatively-dressed women of any parliament on the planet. They're sexier in the Knesset than in Sacramento.

"You keep asking about bribes of money, drugs and whores. Israel is filled with that. You like prostitutes? Israel has a ton from Eastern Europe. The Federation wants people to like Israel as a cause to give money to. Well, maybe you should like Israel because it produces the best Ecstasy on the planet.

"Let's have a gossip column about Israel. Let's tell the story of Israel through gossip. The profiles that *The LA Times* won't dare run.

"Psychedelics had a huge impact on the Jewish Renewal movement and everything that is vibrant in the past generation. You take a bit of drugs and you take Heschel and Buber and Abbi Hoffman and chant the Zohar in English and you have the Renewal movement.

"Abe Foxman gambled big and gambled wrong on *The Passion*. I haven't seen a story stating this and suggesting we fire him. Imagine a giant headline: 'Abe Foxman: His Passion, His Mistake.' It doesn't matter whether it is fair or unfair to him, true or not true, but it's interesting. Abe Foxman's a grownup. He can take it. Abe Foxman's board knows the whole story anyway. You don't have to be fair to Abe Foxman. You need to make waves.

"If you write about a crime in the Persian community, use it as a peg to write about the community. Any time you have a synagogue fighting, it is always about a clash of cultures. It's not a story about why they're firing this rabbi because a certain percentage of the shul got fed up with him. That's the peg. Now you ask what's the difference between the half who likes him and the half who hates him? It's not that so-and-so says he was not a good rabbi and so-and-so says he was diddling the secretary. Liking the rabbi is just a marker of the two different groups in the shul. Is it the Left and the Right? The old and the young? Behind every synagogue battle is a real story and that story is never written about.

"They just fired the rabbi at Lincoln Square Synagogue. So some board members found him obnoxious. Why does the rabbi have defenders? Why do people hate the rabbi? The story isn't about the rabbi sending out silly emails, not understanding 20th Century technology. The story should be—what's the culture of Lincoln Square?

"What's the last high profile split in LA?"

"Ohr HaTorah (R)."

"What's it ostensibly about?"

"That the rebbetzin made half the kids in sixth grade cry."

"That is a great story. It is going to break down over the question of how much do we build the self-esteem of little suburban kinderlach and how much do we call it like it is. It's probably an argument in part about parenting styles. You should pitch this story to *The LA Times* or the *LA Weekly*. This is a story you can pitch from inside the community to outside the community. It's a great way to talk about raising kids, Jewish parenting values, authority. A

Hebrew school is not like a public school where you are bound by bureaucracy and nobody expects you to do a good job.

"There's an inverse proportion between flashy and important. The General Assemblies of the Federation are flashy. There's real news happening there but a lot of the time it was happening in the back room. Decisions made about hundreds of millions of dollars. Those meetings may have been boring. Five hundred pages of particulars from the NJPS (National Jewish Population Study) may be boring but they are substantive. If the Federation puts out a report by some well-meaning bureaucrats, it's probably going to be boring, but if you sit down and read the damn thing, you'll find interesting facts in there.

"Most press conferences are unproductive. One exception. On my last week on the job, I got to hear an American rabbi (Abraham Hecht, a fool) call for the assassination of Yitzhak Rabin. I got to see Herschel Schachter, who is prominent, say no comment when I asked him about it. He just sat there saying nothing when the psak [ruling] was given.

"There's less press release journalism that there used to be. Every segment of Jewish life is going to complain about a story told about them because it will be incomplete, unless you go in deep. If you make it a conventional news story, they're going to feel ripped off.

"The real nasty stuff is where the money is. There's been no great coverage of the kosher food industry or the bodies in Harlem River. Moving the kosher meat industry out of New York was the OU's (Orthodox Union) way of moving the industry away from organized crime. It also affected the quality of the kosher meat. Kosher steaks are not as good as kosher steaks were a few decades ago. Where are you going to publish this story? It's a month of research. Ten thousand words. The *Jewish Journal* might pay you a $1000 for it. It's not worth your while if you're not 20 years old anymore. *Moment* magazine will pay a similar pittance. Will *Moment* run the story? Maybe.

"If you want to reinvent Jewish journalism, you have to figure out how to reinvent the demand side. How do you make it worth someone's while to pay reporters. Let's make a business case for why someone should invest a million dollars in Jewish journalism. There are simply stories that can't be told through the current mediums. It may be time to reinvent the funding mechanism, because it is not going to pay for itself. Things that are good for you do not pay for themselves. Things pay for themselves in the long run because they get people more involved in the Jewish community.

"Chabad will have someone learn with you for free, and treat you with the same respect [other Jewish institutions reserve] for the millionaire. Chabad gives away adult education classes. They make it up in the long run through good will and donations. It's the same principle for Jewish journalism.

"*Heeb* had a good idea but they're trying to be the cultural object rather than report on the culture object. The sign of a good editor is one who finds a cultural object and nurtures a cultural moment. *Commentary*, *Judaism*, *Tradition* magazines in the '60s not only created movements, but captured moments. *Wired* and *Whole Earth* magazines in the '80s and '90s did the same thing.

"One of the dirty secrets of Jewish journalism is that none of the Jewish professionals read a single word I wrote. If I wrote that the Orthodox Union used Klingon telepathic technology to make mashgichim (kashrut supervisors) more effective and was considering applying this to Jewish day schools, and two years later spoke to the head of the Reform movement, he would say, 'I just read this article about Klingon technology in *The New York Times*.... I was thinking of using it for our Hebrew school teachers.' While I thought I was helping the movements, in fact they couldn't be bothered opening up the newspapers.

"I'm curious what you will do with this. Will you self-publish and make $20? I share Larry Cohler and Andy Carroll's skepticism of this turning into a book. Then again, if we were the types who believed that books were easily published, we might have published books. Yossi Klein Halevi is the only one of us who's written a book. I remember him in Israel in 1991 telling me to look for stories to break out of Jewish journalism to write for *The New Republic*. Now he's on the masthead. One of his Op/Ed pieces in *The LA Times* is equal to 12 Op/Ed pieces in the *Jewish Journal*."

22

Yori Yanover

July 8, 2004

"I don't think a muckraking Jewish newspaper would make it. *The New York Times*, *The Los Angeles Times* are muckraking Jewish newspapers.

"I started writing when I was 17 in 1971 in Tel Aviv (for a paper put out by Shalom Cohen, on the left edge of the Zionist camp). They still owe me money. They paid mostly in hash.

"In the Army, I was a standup comic. I wrote for a monthly paper of the IDF, *Bamachaneh Nachal* [on the political Left].

"I lasted about two years at NYU Film and Television School. I produced shows for Pacifica's WBAI in New York. I became frum (Orthodox) in 1983. It happened through writing. I was hired as a dialogue writer on the fourth rewrite of a never-produced Israeli-co-production in Toronto. The producer was frum. It was supposed to be named Esther and was about Mossad and Biblical prophecies.

"I tried to do frum radio in New York City. I worked with Dov Shurin. He was the only guy in Jewish radio who made money. He bartered with everybody up and down the block and fed his family and paid his rent and put money aside for aliyah. He was a colorful and sweet man. He had a show motzei Shabbos that was 50% commercials and 50% editorial content. He helped me do my show. We lost all the money people invested in my show.

"I became the first DJ of Arutz-Sheva on the high seas (radio station operated off a ship off the Israel coast) in 1988. They needed someone who was frum, knew radio, and didn't mind being on the high seas. My wife (since 1976) gave me permission.

"*Yedioth* stole me from my local paper in 1993. I had that local star quality. I felt like a football star sought after by a rival team. They had a corporate strategy of going for the jugular of a competing newspaper. Drive them out. Then drop all the stars and local salaries you picked up.

"Everything was changing about Jewish journalism in 1995 with the Oslo Accords and the Yitzhak Rabin murder and the election of Benyamin Netanyahu in 1996. Your bosses rarely bother to read what you wrote. They prefer to hear from people who complain about what you wrote. I wrote a lengthy six-part article about Rabin after the assassination.

"I waited on the article until after the 30th day of his death. I did not know that they were going to commemorate his death on the 40th day in Madison Square Garden. His widow Leah was here and somebody made sure that she saw the article. All she saw was the critique at the end. I had said his political career was not remarkable and reflected the policies of his masters. If his master was Ben Gurion, he did that. If his master was Begin, he did that. If his master was Shimon Peres, he did that. I said Rabin deserved to be forgotten but because of this idiot Yigal Amir he will be commemorated forever.

"Leah Rabin went directly to the owner of the paper and told him that somebody in his New York supplement wrote that it was a good thing that Rabin was murdered. I was suspended. The next time there was a complaint about my column (that I was a Holocaust denier, which is strange because all my family was burnt in Auschwitz), they fired me.

"By that time, I was an editor for the Jewish Communication Network, the first online Jewish magazine. It was an amazing adventure from 1994–98 (funded by Niv Bleich and Adi Ben Jacob). They devised a Jewish AOL in English. An intranet rather than the Internet. There was no real business plan behind JCN other than to attract users. When the intranet idea failed, JCN was headed for failure.

"In 1998, I was hired away by the Lubavitch News Service (which became Chabad.org). In 1994, I had published a book in Hebrew on Chabad with *Nadav Ish-Shalom—Dancing and Crying*. It was about the last two years of the Lubavitcher Rebbe and his community as he was dying.

"The book does not turn to an outside source. It's all about what the Lubavitchers have to say about themselves and the incredible political wars that were going on, down to real fist fights between the Messianists and the anti-Messianists. Even though I am not a part of the Lubavitch movement, I see them as incredibly positive.

"USAJewish.com was for three years an extensive daily review of everything about Jews and Israel. I keep hearing from Jewish reporters that I should start it again. All you had to do was go there to get your stories.

"I don't think I was as partisan as [Matt] Drudge. I've managed to retain my friendships with most of the people on the Right and all the people on the Left. The one person I don't get along with is Binyamin L. Jolkovsky [of JewishWorldReview.com]. I hired him for a few articles on JCN. We had a major falling out over [Joseph] Lieberman. I thought he was vicious in his attacks on Lieberman. He thought my reaction was out of line. I asked his forgiveness. At this point, it's a relief not to be in the world of Jewish journalism. Some of those things are not as painful as they used to be."

"What were the greatest obstacles to doing good journalism on Jewish topics?"

"Money. Nobody is interested in expensive investigative journalism. Whenever you see attempts to do good well-researched articles, you see organizations going into bankruptcy.

"The *Forward* launches occasional interesting and hard-hitting articles. Don't press me to cite one. *Moment* and *Jerusalem Report* occasionally come up with that quality article. It may not be investigative journalism, but it is a fine well-researched article. In general, people don't get paid enough to write [investigative] articles."

"What do you think of *The Jewish Week*?"

"It's still in an identity crisis. I'm never comfortable reading it. I read my friends. New York newspapers write about Israel all the time. Is it because it is the most important thing or is it because it is the most convenient thing?

"Today I do a local publication [GrandStreetNews.com and also in print]. It is all about the needs and interests of people here on the Lower East Side. It's written with a touch of sweetness. I see my readers every day. I feel that I am serving the needs of a real community. We're in color. We're in the black. We make money. Everybody is happy with us. I don't have to deal with the Malcolm Hoenleins and all that mishegos."

"What did you love and what did you hate about your time writing on Jewish topics?"

"I hated that many of the disagreements between communities and religious movements inside Judaism were based on ignorance and self-centeredness.

"I love that we're a family. I see that reflected in Jewish journalism. It can be schmaltzy and amateurish, but it is needed like oxygen. I can come to your house and I can see in your eyes that we are brothers."

"Any good stories?"

"We had this fake newspaper. It was adjacent to JCN18.com. It had its own fake Web site. It was called the *Petah Tikvah Times Herald*. The most impossible name combination. In 1998, we had an article making fun of the Bible Codes. We wrote an expose of a code discovered in the Ten Commandments regarding the death of Princess Diana. Anybody who understands anything understands this is fake. 'If you count every fifth word, it says, princess will be killed with rich Arab prince.'

"We have it online. I get a phone Friday morning from Larry Yudelson, who used to be my coeditor. He says, 'Open *The Jewish Week*.' It was the summer. *The Jewish Week* editor stole the piece and he didn't even attribute it. They just stole it and published it as their own news story.

"During Hanukkah while I was at Arutz-Sheva, it was motzei Shabbat. I was on the boat with my wife and my teenage sister. An Israeli Navy speedboat came up to the boat. They wanted to light Hanukkah candles. We went down to the public quarters and opened the portholes and told them that first they had to do Havdalah (ceremony marking the end of the Sabbath). Then we lit Hanukkah candles. They sang Ma'oh tzur with us. There wasn't a dry eye. Everything good about this nation was right there."

23

Benyamin Cohen

July 9, 2004

Cohen (frum from birth on April 22, 1975) works three jobs. He edits Jewsweek.com (debuted May 1, 2001) and *Atlanta Jewish Life* magazine (bimonthly) and oversees Jewishcontent.com.

He's having a bad day. His car won't start. His computer won't work. And his air conditioning is broken.

"I come from a family of Modern Orthodox rabbis. I'm the only non-rabbi. My family sees what I'm doing as promoting the Jewish cause."

Benyamin's father, Rabbi Herbert Cohen, (has semicha from YU, and a PhD in British Literature and was the principal of the Yeshiva High School of Atlanta for almost 30 years) lives in Denver. Benyamin's mother died of a brain aneurysm when he was 13.

Cohen went to Jewish day schools until college (Georgia State). "I went to YU for one semester but I can't stand New York or YU. What do I not have against YU? It's too much of a clustered environment. It's too much of a good ol' boys network."

"Why do you put so many pictures of shiksas on Jewsweek.com?"

"My philosophy on Jewish journalism is that most Jewish journalism sucks. It turns assimilated Jews away from Judaism because all it talks about are boring things such as Federation politics. My goal is to get people jazzed about Judaism. I feel that putting Madonna in every issue and doing irreverent things like that is a way to get people interested in Judaism."

Jewsweek comes out about 40 times a year. "The biggest obstacle we face, obviously, is a financial one. We're working on a shoestring budget with few resources to pay writers. Most everybody is doing stuff on a volunteer basis. If one of your star writers is busy paying his rent with his day job, it's hard to ask him to spend time on putting a compelling story together.

"The other challenge is getting mainstream acceptance. Mainstream institutional Judaism has yet to come to terms with the next generation."

"They're not stepping up to the plate to sponsor the site?"

"Not only that, they're not even recognizing it as a viable resource. They scoff at it. They laugh at it."

"You've gotten a fair amount of media attention over it."

"Yes and no. Not compared to *Heeb*. While we have published about 125 issues in three years and gotten three or four press mentions, they've published five issues and received triple the amount of press attention, which boggles my mind.

"I find non-Jewish magazines much more compelling than Jewish publications."

"Do you read the *Jewish Journal*?"

"Online. The only thing that is different about them is that they have the occasionally interesting celebrity profile because they are in LA. Aside from that, I don't see anything exciting about it."

"I think they skew younger because they have younger writers."

"Yeah, but it is hard to find the good nuggets when it is muddled by all the other stuff."

"Why isn't there more compelling Jewish journalism?"

"Lack of creativity and funding. Lack of creativity by those who do have money. There are plenty of people like myself and the guy who does Jewschool.com who are doing great blogs who are in their 20s who are not given the resources to make their projects grow."

"I want more reasons for why it is so dull."

"They've been following the same formula for years. No other niche market does that. You take a look at any popular magazine, it evolves over time. You have to stay on the edge or people are going to find you irrelevant. The younger generation of Jewish readers don't care about what is going on in Israel or which philanthropist gave their money to which cause or most of the stuff these Jewish weeklies are reporting on."

"Many of the journalists for the Jewish weeklies tell me that people read a Jewish newspaper for a different reason than they read their primary newspaper. It's to reaffirm their Jewish identity and their belief that Israel is right."

"That's a horrible reason to read a Jewish newspaper. If they have a brain, they should be able to do that by reading a regular newspaper. That's a lazy way to be Jewish. People should read Jewish newspapers to find out information that they are not getting elsewhere. There's so much Jewish news to report out there. If they're only going to report the bomb in Israel this week with a sympathetic view towards the Jewish people, that's horrible journalism and lazy Judaism."

"Tell me about JewishContent.com."

"Most Jewish weeklies don't have enough staff. My editor at the AJT (*Atlanta Jewish Times*) would tell me to go on the Internet and find some content to fill the paper. We only had three staff writers. I thought, wouldn't it be great if there was an online store where I could just buy content. It's taken me five years to take that idea to fruition with the help of Jewsweek publisher Reuven Koret. The JTA service is archaic. Eventually, I think, people will move over to our system."

"What's the most controversial thing you've done at Jewsweek?"

"When we were first started, I wanted to get a name for ourselves, so I published a list of the 50 Most Influential Jews in America. In additional to the usual suspects, I put people influential in their own towns."

"Let's say you walked into a prominent Jewish institution and you saw a prominent Jewish leader diddling someone who was not his wife, how would you handle it? Would you think, this is not good for the Jews?"

"No, I'd write the story. Why wouldn't I?"

"Because your father would give you hell for it."

"My father would give me hell for 100 other things before he gave me hell for that. I don't think before every decision, what's my family going to think. My family is proud of Jewsweek. Is it something they would produce? Probably half of it is. That's the beauty of Modern Orthodoxy. You can see the value in things, even if you don't agree with them."

"Do you often think before publishing a story, is this good for the Jews?"

"Not at all."

"Is that more of a generational question?"

"Absolutely."

The most interesting part of my interaction with Benyamin came after our interview. We exchanged a contentious series of emails on Sunday, July 11.

I've found that a large number of people I interview, such as Benyamin, suffer from the misapprehension that I seek their approval at the cost of my work. They are wrong. Any friendships I develop from my work do not come at the expense of my work.

Saturday night I sent Ben a transcript of what I wanted to use from our interview. I did not seek his permission to publish it, nor did I promise that I would accommodate all of his requests for changes.

I am under no journalistic obligation to give Ben or anyone a transcript of our interview. Not only is this not journalistic practice, it is the opposite of journalistic practice. Occasionally, to get an interview, I will promise a subject that he can approve any of his quotes. I do this only when I have to and I did not give any such assurance to Ben.

He gave me a bunch of changes. I was fine with most of them.

Almost everyone I interview welcomes the opportunity to amend things they've said. I usually go along with their changes, but not always. In fact, I can't think of any time when I've accepted every change requested. Until Benyamin Cohen, everybody I've interviewed has understood that it is up to me to accept or reject changes.

I started to run into problems with Ben before 8 a.m. I asked him for contact info for his journalist friend Vincent Coppola. He replied, "Why?"

I replied: "Because I want to ask him out on a date.

"Why? I want to interview him for my book on Jewish journalism."

Ben replied: "Yeah, but he's not a Jewish journalist. And he only worked at a Jewish paper for a year."

I replied: "Ben, I don't tell you how to run Jewsweek. Don't tell me who I should or should not interview for my book. I get this all the time and I'm sick of it. If you don't want to give me his email, why don't you email him and ask if he'd be willing to talk to me. He could be a black lesbian Buddhist for all I care, so long as he has worked in journalism on Jewish topics. That he is not Jewish makes him all the more interesting to me, sheesh, why do I have to explain something so elementary."

Ben replied: "Luke, Relax, man. I just wasn't sure you if you knew that he wasn't Jewish. That's all. Truth be told, in my opinion, he knows more about Jewish journalism than most Jews do."

Ben sent me about a dozen more emails when I did not go along with every one of his requested changes to his transcript. I agreed to most of them but I wouldn't change the word "sucks" to "stinks."

Ben had said on Friday: "My philosophy on Jewish journalism is that most Jewish journalism sucks."

I emailed Ben that I preferred to keep "sucks." It was more pungent.

He replied: "I would prefer it to the other way please."

I replied: "Nope."

He replied: "Huh?"

I replied: "I am not making the change you requested."

He replied:

> Luke, I don't think that's appropriate. I'm asking you again to make that change. If you do not, I will have to ask you to delete my interview completely.
>
> Before I agreed to the interview with you, I asked Andrew Silow-Carroll if he thought it was a good idea. He said it's fine since Luke will let you read the transcript and change things if you want.
>
> I guess I was under that false impression.
>
> I rarely, if ever, use words like "suck" (ask my friends, it's not in my character).
>
> You caught me at an extremely perturbed time and I think now you're taking advantage of it.
>
> Look, it's your site and you can post whatever you want. I just think that (a) you're doing a terrible disservice to your readers by showing them a Benyamin Cohen that doesn't really exist; and b) as such, you're losing credibility in my eyes.
>
> [...]
>
> If the wording doesn't change, I will not be able to help you any further with any project you may be working on and I will dissuade my colleagues from helping either.
>
> I am the moderator of the AJPA listserv and I will be sending out an e-mail to all the editors later today to tell them of my unprofessional and discourteous experience with you.

I replied: "Go for it."

He replied: "FYI, I have told Vince not to speak with you. As well, I have sent out an e-mail to all the Jewish newspaper editors advising them not to talk with you."

I replied: "May I have a copy of the letter you sent out about me?"

He replied: "Nope."

I replied: "You're such a brave man."

He replied: "C'mon. Why would I give you that kind of professional courtesy when you treat me the way you did?"

A few hours later, I find Ben's letter posted on Steven I. Weiss's blog:

> To all editors,
>
> If you have not already, you will probably be contacted soon by a guy named Luke Ford, a writer from Los Angeles. He is currently writing a book about Jewish journalism and is asking for interviews with several AJPA members.
>
> Like some of you, I agreed to be interviewed by him. In a transcript he showed me of our conversation, he ended up taking my words out of context and later started acting very discourteous and unprofessional.
>
> Besides this Jewish journalism project, he's been involved in some shady projects in the past (some pornographic, some evenagelical, etc.) I would highly reccomend to anyone who has yet to speak with him to NOT DO SO. You may come, like I have, to regret it later.
>
> All the best, Benyamin Cohen

Marc S. Klein, editor and publisher of the San Francisco Jewish weekly, emails me an hour later: "Luke: It has been suggested by one of my colleagues that I should not speak to you. I'm sorry but I must take that advice."

Vince Coppola stopped returning my emails.

Andrew Silow-Carroll replies to Cohen on the AJPA listserv: "A number of us have been interviewed by Ford. He is a character, but I found that, after posting a transcript of our interview on his Web site, he was open to my corrections and emendations and quickly changed the transcript to reflect them. And because he posts the full transcript, there's no defense that any of us were quoted 'out of context.' Ford clearly has his point of view—he thinks Jewish journalism is lousy and wants those in the profession to explain why. But so far, the interviews—with Larry Cohler-Esses, Rob Eshman, Jonathan Sarna, Michael Berenbaum, and others—make for fascinating and sometimes sobering reading about the state of the profession. I also think it is never a bad idea for journalists to experience what it feels to be on the other end of an interview. So I'll have to disagree with Benyamin—take Ford's call, weigh your words carefully, and enjoy the debate that he is engendering with his project."

A day later, Klein changes his mind and gives me an interview.

Steven I. Weiss writes on his *Forward* blog: "I can't tell you how many Jewish journalists contacted me to ask me about Luke Ford's interviewing them. That they did strikes me as profoundly disturbing relative to their potential to legitimately carry Jewish journalism forward."

Allison Kaplan Sommer writes on her blog:

> Cathy [Seipp] and her daughter [Cecile du Bois] act as important character witnesses for Luke Ford. I've had quite a few bloggers who he's taken a slightly obsessive interest in and a people I know in real life that he's contacted for his book research ask me if he's nuts in a harmless way, or might border on dangerous.
>
> Cathy and Cecile seem like pretty sensible people, and they are friends of someone I know from college. So I tell the people who ask that if Ford were truly a stalker/axe murderer type, I doubt they'd be taking him along on road trips.
>
> I think that Cathy and Cecile should use their show biz connections and create a television show based on their lives—I envision an edgy right-wing-Jewish-California version of the *Gilmore Girls*, with Luke as their charming but insane former Seventh Day Adventist converted to Orthodox Judaism turned showbiz/porn journalist/blogger friend.

24

Marc S. Klein

July 12, 2004

Marc has edited and published San Francisco's Jewish weekly since 1983. It's now a magazine called *j. the Jewish news weekly of Northern California*.

"What are the biggest obstacles to putting out a compelling paper?"

He thinks for about ten seconds. "I'm not sure the Jewish community wants a compelling paper."

Marc's voice is rich and vibrant. "I've heard from my colleagues over the years that we put out one of the best Jewish newspapers in the country. Does that mean we're compelling or does that mean we have a lot of compelling stories because we're in the San Francisco Bay Area? I can't answer that one.

"Jewish newspapers would be more compelling if Jewish readers wanted a more compelling paper. I can't tell you how many times over the years [out of 23 years in Jewish journalism] that I've heard readers say, 'I read your paper on Shabbat. I don't want to be disturbed. I just want to read nice Jewish news. I don't want things to make me angry. I don't think you should say anything that's going to hurt the Jews.' That makes our role that much more difficult."

"I'm guess there's a generational issue here. I'm guessing that you don't hear that as much from younger Jews."

"We don't hear much from younger Jews period. We redesigned our paper last September into a [weekly] magazine format. The idea was to get younger readers. We have gotten more subscriptions. Unfortunately, we're losing just as many on the other end, either dying or moving away. Mostly dying. Virtually all Jewish newspapers have readerships that are getting old. The young people, especially here in the Bay Area, didn't have bar or bat mitzvahs of their own, or came from intermarried families. On the East Coast, you will find a husband and wife who were bar and bat mitzvahed, sending their kids to Hebrew school like their parents sent them to Hebrew school, but you see that less out here. If they are not going to be sending their kids to Hebrew school, chances are they are not going to be getting a Jewish paper. Even if they do send their kids to Hebrew school, they may not get a Jewish newspaper.

"What we hear a lot is, 'There are so many things going on in the Bay Area. I've got too much to read. I just canceled my *Time* subscription. I just don't have time to read.' We're not only fighting the issue of people's Jewishness and interest, we're fighting the decline of reading. I use public transportation every day and I am almost the only one reading a newspaper. In years past, young families sending their kids to Hebrew school, often got a Jewish newspaper, at least on the East Coast. What we're experiencing here, the East Coast will experience some time later. California sets trends."

"Is San Francisco the most assimilated large Jewish community?"

"Certainly one of the top. We've had estimates of up to 80% intermarriage. You can talk to Conservative rabbis here who say that a large proportion of their congregation is intermarried. The last demographic study (about 13 years ago) found the Orthodox to be about two percent of the general Jewish population. While there are a number of Orthodox congregations, none of them have a large membership."

"How many papers do you print each week?"

"Twenty thousand. We have almost 19,000 subscribers."

"You're not giving away a lot of your papers."

"We could never do what LA is doing because we don't have Jewish neighborhoods, condos, delis. Our readers live far away from each other.

"Until lately, we've always been four to eight pages bigger than the LA paper."

"They print 53,000–70,000 copies a week."

"They give away the bulk of those copies. I know that would never work for us."

"Are you a Federation paper?"

"No. We're kind of like LA. My boss is my board of directors, which is self-appointed. Four members of the 19-member board come from the Federation. The Federation has never even tried to control the paper. The Federation buys about 85% of the papers that we mail. The paper is deeded to the community."

"What does that mean?"

"Everyone has always asked us that question. We don't know. None of the lawyers know what that essentially means. It would only mean something if, God forbid, we went out of business."

"What would you guess is the median age of your readers?"

"I think Jewish newspapers are all the same—low 60s. Anyone who starts giving you better figures is not being totally truthful."

"I had Rob Eshman tell me it had gone down by 12 years since he took over the paper because he's got great young writers."

"I hope Rob's right. It's good for all of us if he's right."

"Are you doing anything to attract younger readers?"

"We're putting out more of a magazine with stories to attract them more. But I have my doubts whether there's anything you can do. If you are a young person who's not involved in anything Jewishly, why would you read a Jewish paper? Every study shows that fewer young people are getting affiliated with the Jewish community. If you look at Federations across the country, and even if you are privately owned, your readership base is affected by the Federation, Federations aren't growing. So we don't grow."

"I can tell just by talking to you that you retain tremendous passion for what you do."

"It's been a lot of years. I've been president of the American Jewish Press Association on two occasions. I worry about these issues. I have a feeling that I am of the last generation of editors that will see thriving weekly newspapers."

"I see a lack of New Journalism techniques in Jewish journalism."

"I have three writers here. I'm sure you know how large the Bay Area is. There is no way we could put out a paper if our writers were out in the field. Once in a while, it's imperative that they see the person they talk to, but for the most part, they do their stories sitting at their desk. You know the traffic jams in the Bay Area. You could lose a day going out for one interview."

"Malcolm Hoenlein says Jewish newspapers shouldn't report dissident voices because it weakens the community."

"He doesn't want to hear from Michael Lerner anymore than a lot of our readers do. He doesn't want to give the left-wing Jewish voice much credibility in the community. Jewish leaders want to hear from them, but they want to keep their earplugs in while they're hearing. We try to report dissident voices as much as possible. We try to bring in the Berkeley voice. One of our reporters is very liberal and a lot of the people in those organizations are her friends. She comes to me with stories and I'd say she gets 60% yesses from me. We probably cover the Left voice more than most Jewish newspapers do in the country."

"Because you have more of a Left voice in San Francisco."

"More of a Left voice that can make itself heard. Does the rest of our community like that? I don't think so. The letters that come in when we do the Left voice are numerous. The letters from the Left side hardly come in at all. Readers sometimes complain that our cover story is on the liberal end. Most of the letters then either attack what somebody [liberal] said or attack the paper for covering it. You get few letters that say, right on!"

"Rob Eshman recently published a cover story of two men under a chuppah getting married. He told me he didn't think any other Jewish newspaper would do such a thing. Would you put a same-sex marriage on the cover of your paper?"

"We have many times. Way before Rob was doing it. We were doing stuff like that 18 years ago. We've always covered the gay population. A gay synagogue gave me an award a few years ago. They've never felt slighted here. The rabbi from the gay synagogue is on my board of directors. She loves what we've done for the gay community.

"The complaint that I get constantly is that we have too many stories about gays. We feel we should cover them. Even the Federation is reaching out to the gay community. There are a lot of natives out here who didn't like the hippies years ago and don't like the gays today."

"What do you love and what do you hate about your job?"

"The hardest part of the job is personnel—retaining, hiring, firing. The daily job of running the staff. You deal with people's daily emotions. The second hardest part of the job is dealing with people on the phone yelling at you.

"What do I like about it? I like the grind of getting out each week's paper. I love the challenge of the deadline. I was in daily newspapers. I've been living with deadlines since college."

"How is the Internet and blogging affecting Jewish newspaper if at all?"

"In 1995, we started the Jewish area on America Online. Keyword Jewish. We went on the Web with Jewish.com. We eventually sold it. When the dot-com bust happened, we couldn't afford to keep it running. We decided it was too hard to do an international Web site from San Francisco and run a newspaper at the same time.

"It's harder to get ads for the Internet the smaller your audience gets. We weren't serving the Jewish community. We were serving the Jews who were interested in the Jewish community. We saw tremendous hits come on Passover and Hanukkah for recipes. The rest of the year, we got a decent amount of traffic, but nothing close to what our friends in the Christian community were getting. I don't think it is a sustainable business to run a Jewish Internet site.

"Do I think the Internet is going to take over? It's hard to say. I know people who rely on getting online every day and reading the Jewish news. But a lot of them also get our paper. In all the years I've run the paper, I think I've had three emails say, 'Save the trees. I'll read your paper online.' It's not like we're losing readers over the Internet. As long as most Jewish newspapers have a readership [of people over 60], the Internet is not going to cause a problem. But it will for the next generation. When I and my peers turn 60, 70, we're going to be Internet savvy. There may not be many Jewish weekly newspapers outside of New York and the big cities."

"Is there one Jewish newspaper that has influenced you the most?"

"The *Baltimore Jewish Times* when Gary Rosenblatt was running it. It was compelling. Gary did a lot of investigative stories and fantastic features that were interesting no matter where you lived. I don't think any paper has replaced what Gary did there."

"I don't think he's as interesting at *The Jewish Week*."

"No, he's not. We've talked about it. He's serving a different readership there."

"It feels to me that *The Jewish Week* is edited by a Modern Orthodox Jew from a Modern Orthodox perspective for a Modern Orthodox community."

"I can't disagree. If you look at the pictures, there are a lot of pictures of beards in the paper. Gary feels that a magazine works better in Baltimore than in New York. I'm not so sure that in the future they won't have to seriously consider changing to a magazine format."

"Do you find AJPA conferences compelling?"

"I don't think I do. I've been around so long. I stay up on the news. So if Malcolm Hoenlein comes to speak at AJPA, I like seeing him because I've known him for years, but what he has to say, I've read already. There's little at this stage that I find compelling."

"I've only been to one for about an hour but it was a giant snooze."

"It's hard to program. You can't program for my level or Gary's level or Rob's level. Rob didn't come to this last one. He said that he mostly comes to see his friends and chat around the hallways. That's what I do. But we have to program for the small paper whose editor hasn't been in the business long, who hasn't been exposed to daily newspapers. For whom everything is new.

Who doesn't get out of her small town. We have two different levels of people at these conferences but we have to serve the level that needs the most help."

"**My favorite Jewish singles columnist, Teresa Strasser, worked at your paper.**"

"Teresa Strasser was one of my three writers. She covered features and news. She wasn't writing a singles column. She's a helluva writer. She could be very difficult. She'd be in the hair of my copy editor, looking over every single word to make sure it wasn't touched."

Marc gives me a parting thought. "There's plenty to criticize about the Jewish press, but when you look at other religious newspaper, we are way ahead. That just shows you how difficult it is to serve a religious community."

"**It's just another part of community journalism, whether it is for Latinos, blacks.**"

"Blacks are more of a rage and rant type community paper than a Jewish newspaper will ever be."

25

Yossi Klein Halevi

July 12, 2004

My favorite Jewish journalist turned out to be my most disappointing interview.

Through his film *Kaddish*, his books *Memoirs of a Jewish Extremist: An American Story*, and *At the Entrance to the Garden of Eden: A Jew's Search for God with Christians and Muslims in the Holy Land*, and his work in *The New Republic*, *The Jerusalem Post* and *The Los Angeles Times*, Yossi Klein Halevi is a Jewish journalism star.

He's at his best writing about himself.

His first book describes his journey from hating goyim to falling in love with a shiksa.

His second book ends with Yossi wrapping tefillin in a church and imitating the Muslim manner of prayer.

Both are riveting reads. *The New York Times* described the first as "a drama central to the very soul of Jewish life." *Publishers Weekly* described the second as "exuding yearning for commonality and love."

Klein moved from a childhood obsession with killing goyim to praying with Christians and Muslims.

In his youth, Yossi terrorized his fellow Jews who wouldn't join with him in JDL violence. In his 50s, he declared gentle Charedi Uri Lupoliansky too intolerant to be mayor of Jerusalem because he would not meet with a group of Reform rabbis.

Orthodox screenwriter Robert J. Avrech attended Brooklyn Talmudic Academy with Yossi in the 1960s. He says about *Memoirs*: "It was accurate and exactly mirrored my experiences. I knew who he was, but I kept my distance because he hung out with the Betar, JDL guys. They used to go to the basement, behind the lockers, and smoke cigarettes and discuss how they wanted to kill Arabs and goyim. All of them were children of Holocaust survivors. Their collective pathology was so naked, so raw that we who had American parents kept a fearful distance."

Kaddish "is a bio-doc of Yossi Klein Halevi's early years [in New York]," says a Jewish journalist, "his pathological family history, produced by a horrifying world history, and also, the contemporary events that formed his paranoid-visionary consciousness. It's one of the earliest examples of children-of-Holocaust-survivors literature (though it's a film). It was a genre just then emerging from a cohort recently aware of itself. It does have one curious blank spot; while it deals with his Soviet Jewry activism, including his chaining himself to the Soviet emigration office in Moscow's Red Square, it slides over that he did much of this as one of the founding members of Meir Kahane's Jewish Defense League."

"Yossi personalizes almost every story he writes," says a peer. "He has a spiritual vision he incorporates into his journalism. Yossi is one of the few Jewish journalists who's seriously thought through the conflict between secular journalism and the demands of Judaism's laws against lashon hara."

By 1975, Klein had moved out of the JDL and decided to become a journalist. He submitted a story on the JDL to the *Village Voice*. He was told to develop it.

To learn to write characters and scenes, Yossi studied fiction at City College of New York (where he met his future wife). The techniques he learned there flow through his writing to this day.

At the beginning of his two books, Yossi notes that while the events and characters in his books are real, some of the names and identifying traits have been changed. Unfortunately, Yossi never lets us know when he is inventing names and traits.

With friends such as Jonathan Mark (now with *The Jewish Week*), Yossi created *New Jewish Times* in 1980. The paper came out a few times and folded within a year.

Halevi and his wife moved to Israel in August 1982. She converted to Orthodox Judaism, taking the name Sarah. Their first child, Moriah, was born in 1985.

Yossi got crazier. He fantasized about winning back what the Nazis had done.

He moved to the south of France to find equilibrium. He was largely subsidized by *Long Island Jewish World* publisher Jerry Lippman and his peers. Halevi could write about whatever he felt like. Writing like a novelist, free from the mundane concerns of regular journalists who wanted to break stories, Yossi focused on himself, his feelings, his visions, and the movement of his God in history.

It was 1989. The Berlin Wall fell. Yossi traveled throughout Eastern Europe, countries he'd demonized for years, interviewing people. His soul stirred. His paranoia lifted. He wanted to reconcile Jews with non-Jews. He wrote some of his best stuff.

He returned to Israel, and wrote for *The Jerusalem Post*.

He got a non-Jewish female Indian guru in Jerusalem. He uncovered a community who were mainly born as Jews but were now leading halakhic lives as Christians.

In July 2004, we exchanged email. From Israel's neo-conservative Shalem Center, Yossi wrote: "I looked up your Web site and have to admit to being troubled...by the lashon harah aspect of your work. Why is it important to know the private lives of Jewish leaders? Would that make better Jewish journalism? What is Jewish journalism? Does it have a commitment not only to truth but also lashon harah?"

I reply: The private lives of Jews and non-Jews become legitimate fodder for journalism when they affect the community at large. For instance, if a Jewish leader has an affair that affects and weakens his work, it becomes legitimate. It becomes particular legitimate when the subject is a master at using blackmail to bully people into doing his will. Midah k'neged midah (measure for measure). Alcoholism, gambling, sexual sins, temper, rudeness, etc, all become legitimate when they affect the general public.

Yossi replies: "I think that Jewish journalists need a serious internal discussion about the ethics of the profession and lashon harah. It's not at all as straightforward as you put it—especially the notion midah k'neged midah, which is not in our hands but in God's hands to do."

I reply:

> It is much easier to accuse another of lashon hara than to spell out a definition of lashon hara that one's own work can then be examined

by. If we held by the Chofetz Chaim, most of your work, as well as mine, would be forbidden.

Where do you draw the line on reporting the private lives of public figures? When someone's drinking problem affects their public work, and therefore the public, how do you decide when to report on it?

Yossi responds:

> I recently wrote an article about the Kabbalah Centre which was full of lashon harah—I felt it was a necessary warning against fraud and even evil. But clearly one man's warning is another man's lashon harah. My criterion would be whether we really need to know the personal lives of our leaders—unless they are moral leaders, for example, say a rabbi who preaches taharat hamishpacha and is cheating on his wife. That becomes a public need to know issue. If the head of a Jewish organization is cheating on his wife, I fail to see how that impacts on the community. That's where I draw the line on journalists and lashon harah.

Interviewing Yossi was like squeezing blood out of a stone, as I had to write several emails for every one he'd grace with a brief reply. It turned out that he didn't want to talk to me because I'd published embarrassing personal details about a Jewish leader with whom he had "good relations."

With a mind to Yossi's concerns about lashon hara, I gorged on his work and found it was chock-full of riveting details of personal weakness. As far as lashon hara is concerned, it was indistinguishable from other journalism. For instance, this paragraph on page 208 of his *Memoirs* about the poor sucker who funded Yossi's *New Jewish Times*:

> Marv Steinhartz was what they called in Yiddish a chazir fesser, a gluttonous consumer of pork, an expression that described not merely his diet but his being. Marv was always on the make—for quick bucks, quick lays, quick highs. A cigarette dangled from his thick lips, a Humphrey Bogart effect ruined by traces of spittle.

Evidently Yossi's concerns with lashon hara only apply to the work of others. (Yossi confirmed via email that none of the characteristics above, except for the name, were invented.)

Yossi's friend, Jonathan Mark from *The Jewish Week*, wrote to me a few weeks later:

> You can't bust Yossi for writing lashon hara about "Steinhartz" at *New Jewish Times*. Yossi was using a pseudonym for the real individual, who was every bit as sleazy as described. That Yossi doesn't use the person's real name can only testify to Yossi's discretion, a remarkable kindness in this instance. You can't "lashon hara" someone if you hide that someone's identity.
>
> Second, not all "scoops" are the same, and it's meaningless to hold Yossi to an arbitrary standard for what a writer should be writing. Knocking Yossi for not having scoops is like busting DiMaggio for not dating redheads. Give the man credit for what the man's done.
>
> In the mid-1980s, when I was senior editor at *the Long Island Jewish World* and Yossi was sending in pieces there, I remember some of his essays that foretold the Intifadah when most everyone in Jewish journalism was still writing about the West Bank like it was Willy Wonka's. Yossi, better than anyone else, gave a clue that the West Bank was about to blow. In the Jewish World, and elsewhere, he wrote essays from Europe that were startling, journeys through the end of the old Eastern bloc, and the Europe we knew, or thought we knew. Over the years, he's written about the Jewish Defense League and the Soviet Jewry movement in ways that were a revelation, and before anyone else. He's been able to explore the souls of Jews, Christians and Moslems in Israel in stunning prose and reporting that ought to be studied—proof that no one can write, or interview, about the landscape of the soul as well as he can. His analytical pieces in this current war have been consistently wise—free of rant, party or predictability. In each of these areas he was either first, or as good as anyone in the ring. Just because he doesn't look for front page stories on schemes and scams within Jewish organizations and Jewish leadership (I'm glad that others do) doesn't mean Yossi ought to be questioned on not "breaking stories" in the simplest sense of the term. Instead, Yossi has broken through and illuminated every key Jewish turning point of the last 40 years, with a clear, distinctive

writing style, a voice all his own. It's a tremendous loss for this book not to have had a serious conversation with Yossi about what Jewish journalism ought to be about.

Yeah, I'm his friend, as I'm friends with a lot of people in this book, and a lot of them have inspired me, but when his collected works are published it would be the first book I'd hand out in journalism class, Jewish or otherwise.

Each of us has a special relationship with someone in the Jewish community, or a special respect for someone, and, like O'Henry's story of the cop who didn't want to arrest the old friend he met under a street light, we'd prefer that another journalist do what has to be done. There are limits to the benefit of being an outsider and an alien within the community. The best of us are in and of the community. That's where we get a lot of our stories and where we learn about the life and issues that our newspapers should be covering. You have to pick your spots about when and whom to jeopardize.

If in the big and tough world of Jewish journalism not one other journalist can do the story, if not a single publisher chooses to publish the story, if no members of an organization care about abuses of leadership or management, then Jewish community doesn't deserve to have the story done, and our community can die a corrupt and dull death.

We should be more in alliance as a journalistic community. If a story can't be published in New York it should be published in Philadelphia or Phoenix, with a byline or without a byline, or on a blog if that be the only venue. There's no reason any story shouldn't get out, somewhere. If a Jewish leader wants to pressure a journalist, fine. We ought to be able to be pressured and not give a damn. But if any one journalist, not backed up by his publisher, can't stand up under personal or financial pressure, also fine. I understand. Another newspaper or journalist surely can be found to step up and get the story out.

If we invested as much energy in figuring out how to share stories and support each other, we'd have more power than any Jewish leader.

And if we weren't so patronizing and condescending to the idea that we have of our readers, if all of us were instead the kind of newspapers that earned the love and devotion of our readers, and showed on a consistent basis that are devoted to our readers in return, than no Jewish leader would dare pressure us because we'd have the Jewish people on our side and no leader could stand up to that.

But how many of us can say we are devoted to the Jewish people, both as journalists and in our private life? How many of us can use the word "love" in conjunction with Jewish journalism, and keep a straight face? How many of us can say we are loved by the people? When the readers believe that they are loved by us, and that we understand them, that we are them, then they'll trust us when we write about what's unpleasant because the reader will know, from years of trust, that what we're exposing or investigating is being done for the holiest of reasons. On the other hand, when so many of our week to week stories are silly and unsophisticated, we lose that essential trust and reservoir of good faith that we need to call upon in a tough spot, or when under pressure. We've convinced readers and leaders, who read us regularly, that our papers are silly and unsophisticated and alien, and therefore can be pushed around.

It reminds me of a story from some old Democratic convention. A rally had started on the floor for a candidate, with a marching band roving through the aisles and placards waving in the air. The chairman boss of the convention began to gavel the convention to order: "Will the guests of the convention please come to order!" Bangs the gavel. "Will the guests of the convention please come to order!" Everything quieted down. Then one guy in the balcony screamed into the quiet—"Guests, hell! We're the people!" And the arena exploded with excitement and the boss with the gavel didn't stand a chance.

The trouble is, not enough Jewish journalists today are "the people," but are "guests" at the convention. Imagine walking into *The Wall Street Journal* and declaring yourself a journalist who doesn't understand or know anything about business, or doesn't care about the future of business. You'd be laughed at.

Imagine walking into *The New Yorker* and telling them, without shame, that you never heard of Fitzgerald because he wrote 70 years ago, or that you don't like reading. You'd be told, "Kid, this isn't your kind of job."

A sports reporter would be laughed at if he walked into *The Sporting News* and said he didn't like going to games, or didn't know who Bob Feller was, or about the Giants-Colts sudden death game in the 1950s. Imagine trying to cover any team and not being conversant with that team's history. Yet, aside from the Gary Rosenblatts, J.J. Goldbergs and some others out there, many Jewish journalists and editors, especially the younger ones, couldn't tell you who Achad Ha'Am was, or who Jabotinsky was, or who Itzik Manger was. They don't go to shuls—of any denomination—and they don't send their kids to Jewish schools. They don't know Israel's landscape and they don't know Jewish neighborhoods, other than their own, if indeed they even live in one. They couldn't tell you anything about chassidus or the Lubavitcher Rebbe except "outreach" and the messianic crap of the 1990s.

The Rebbe was arguably among the most important rabbis in the last 500 years, let alone the last century. And yet these journalists couldn't write one paragraph, not one paragraph, on the Lubavitcher Rebbe's ideas and policies in the 1940s, 50s, 60s, 70s or 80s. They couldn't write or refer or understand the echo of most any Jewish idea that happened the day before they showed up for their first day of work in a Jewish newspaper. But these same journalists walk in like the cock of the barnyard and want to write about the Jewish people, the rabbis, the Jewish arts.

But they're like sportswriters who don't love the game, and it shows in their writing and in their editing.

People get into Jewish journalism because it's journalism, but they don't know the team, and they don't know the fans. They don't know where the bodies are buried and they don't know where the treasure is buried.

You look at the choice of stories, the absence of savvy, the absence of communal memory, the many writers who cover Jewish communities as if the writer just landed from Mars, and you tell me: Are we the guests or are we the people?

Answer that question honestly and you'll understand why many Jewish newspapers and Jewish journalists are insecure.

When all of us, not just a few of us, are as immersed in community and know as much about the community as Malcolm Hoenlein does, and have cared about the community as long as Malcolm has—going back to his teenage days in the Soviet Jewry movement—and are as sure of our place in the inner Jewish community as much as Malcolm is, and are as personally invested in our synagogues, in our neighborhoods and in our schools as Malcolm is, and if our readers knew that, and if Jewish leaders knew that, then we could deal with any Jewish leader with so much Jewish pride and dignity that pressure would be powerless.

26

David Twersky

July 12, 2004

"I co-founded the JSPS [in 1971] with David Kaufman.

"I lived in Israel for twelve years (1974–86) and edited an English-language journal of the kibbutz movement *Shdemot*. For four years (1982–86), I founded and edited a magazine for the Israeli labor party called *Spectrum*. It was for distribution among parties of the Socialist Internationale in Europe.

"In 1990, I came to work for the *Forward* as Washington bureau chief. From 1993–2002, I was the editor of the *New Jersey Jewish News*.

"I don't miss the sense of working for the Jewish community and having to worry about where the chips fall.

"There are many different financial models for Jewish newspapers. Some are owned by the Federation. Some are financially dependent on the Federation. Some have a sour relationship with the Federation, such as the Minneapolis paper. That independence hasn't manifested itself in any stellar contribution to journalism.

"The Federation provides the most complete mailing database for a subscription list. Invariably, even if the paper begins with the best of intentions, inevitably Federation looks at it through the prism of what's good for the [fundraising] campaign and what's not good for the campaign.

"If you look at any small-town paper, they also do a lot of honorifics. Someone elected president of the Elks Club. So-and-so baked pies for the high school reunion. That tends to be a dimension of the Jewish paper as well."

"Are we any different from the Catholic and Protestant press?"

"Yes, we're better. The Catholic papers are bad. They're basically newsletters."

"Which Jewish newspapers would you read for fun?"

"The *Forward* obviously. I look at *The Jewish Week* every week because I live in the New York area. And JTA."

"Do you look at the *Jewish Journal* of Los Angeles?"

"I look at it sometimes. They've got some good people. They do some interesting stuff. No question about it."

"Such as?"

"I don't know. I haven't looked at it lately. LA is an interesting community."

"What are the biggest obstacles to doing compelling journalism on Jewish topics?"

"People are usually more interested in a superficial telling of their story. There's a small constituency that is interested in all the passion and all the depth of the Jewish story. The *Forward* in its current incarnation is 14 years old and still has fewer than 30,000 subscribers. They make a valiant effort. There are a lot of intelligent, articulate, well-educated Jews who simply don't care about what to them is inside baseball. They connect with the Jewish community occasionally. They may just want a local superficial what's-going-on-in-my-community paper.

"The problem with running a national paper is that it is hard to get ads. We made money in New Jersey off of banks and real estate and car dealerships. Those are local. You need a mass of readers in one area. Are there enough people interested in a national Jewish newspaper?"

"If you told a compelling story, there'd be more people interested."

"That remains to be seen."

"What are the biggest stories you never got to publish?"

"There are two stories that I blew. One was about Jesse Jackson trying to become the leader of the NAACP. I had the scoop and didn't do anything with it. And I knew about the blind sheikh Abdul Rachman before anybody else. I will never forgive myself for fucking that up."

"What about scoops that you couldn't get in the paper?"

"Nothing worth talking about. In the Jewish news, the more local, the more problematic. If you had a scoop that affected somebody locally, then it raised eyebrows. If you had a great scoop about Israel or Washington, nobody would care.

"There was a scandal in the Jewish Federated community."

Marty Kraar was the married head of CJF (Council of Jewish Federations) for ten years. He had a sexual affair with a woman in her 20s, Liz Hollander, who worked under him. After he ended their affair, she threatened a lawsuit in 1999 against Kraar and the Federation. The suit was spearheaded by her New Jersey father, Sandy, a lawyer with The Jewish Agency. News coverage was slow. Liz moved to Israel and had at least one more affair with a married man in Marty's Israel's office, breaking up a family south of Beersheva with four kids. Then she had a relationship with a Holocaust survivor who worked for the Jewish World Service. In most, if not all, of the press coverage, only Marty, not the woman, were named. Marty remarried. Liz apparently resented that. The Federation gave her about $60,000 to go away.

David: "Gary Rosenblatt wrote a signed editorial about it. Marty was furious. He said to me that I had to write a response. I wouldn't do it. The woman involved, her parents lived in MetroWest [David's district]. I thought there was no point in dragging them through the mud on this. There's no higher goal here. Marty Kraar's done. He's not going to become the head of this new entity UJA. I can't save him or do him in. It's been aired in a gigantic Jewish forum. If I go after this any further, I am going to do to that particular [Hollander] family what Philip Roth did to the parents [Patimkins in the novela] of the girl in *Goodbye, Columbus*. There are still people in my synagogue who do not forgive Phil Roth.

"I know people close to that family who are furious that he would write a book about screwing their daughter."

"Yeah, but it was worth it because it was such a great book."

"That's what Philip Roth would say."

"What would you say?"

"I would say it was worth it but I didn't know the people. He writes a lot about people who people really know. The Swede in *American Pastorale* lives in South Orange, a mile from me. His nickname is the Swede. They went to high school together. We interviewed him. He was happy with the book. It's not true that his daughter went underground. *I Married a Communist* was mostly literally true. It was based on something that his homeroom teacher told him about his younger brother the communist. I called the teacher and he was still so blown away by the McCarthy period that he wouldn't talk about it. But he talked to Roth about it and one of the things he and Bellow are so great at is recording and imitating the way people really talk.

"It's one thing to write an article in the *Forward* and screw somebody because you out them on some issue and it's another thing in a local community where you have to live with the people you're outing. You have to see them at the UJA meeting next week or the kosher butcher.

"When Mort Pye was the editor in chief of the *The Star-Ledger* in Newark, he published this thing on the front page of the Jersey section on some wealthy Jew from the Wilf family, one of the Holocaust survivor families that went into building. Lenny Wilf, a big Jewish philanthropist, was having a nasty divorce. His wife leaked to the paper what she estimated his net worth at. She was going to get 50% of whatever X was. He printed the estimate. It just so happened it made the front page. It was supposed to be buried. It was in the Sunday paper. Everybody saw it.

"Mort Pye walked into his club and nobody would talk to him. Everybody turned their back on him in the locker-room. It's like when the Jewish lawyer in the OJ case (Robert Shapiro) went to [Wilshire Boulevard Temple] on Yom Kippur [the day OJ was found not guilty in the criminal trial] and everybody moved away from him."

27

Debra Nussbaum Cohen

July 12, 2004

Raised Reform and married to a man raised Lubavitch, Debra and her family now belong to a progressive Conservative synagogue.

"My father, a Holocaust survivor, was born in Germany. My parents were from traditional backgrounds. They kept a kosher home because they wanted their parents to be able to eat there but they let go of it when my sister and I began wanting to eat at McDonalds.

"My kids go to a Jewish day school. We are fairly observant and wholly committed. A lot of that has come through my work in Jewish journalism.

"I bumped into my friend Allison Kaplan Sommer at a 1989 pro-choice rally in Washington D.C. I wanted to take a picture of two older ladies wearing straw boaters labeled 'Hadassah Ladies For Choice' but they were talking to someone, so I waited. When the third woman turned around, it was Allison, interviewing them for JTA, and the rest, as they say, is history.

"JTA had an opening, so I applied. They hired me in 1990. A few months later I got married [and added Cohen to her name].

"JTA was revamping its domestic coverage. They put me on the beat of Jewish life. I traveled from one end of the community to the other. I was there almost ten years.

"I cut down to almost half time. I had two kids. The salary was cut to half but the expectations weren't. I was ready to move on.

"Larry Cohler had just left *The Jewish Week*. Gary hired me for a half-time job working mostly from home, which is perfect."

"My impression is that you are most famous for your JTA series on rabbinic sex abuse."

"It was the first writing on the subject. I worked on it for a long time. It was a challenge to get people willing to talk about something difficult at a time when this issue wasn't at all part of the culture in general.

"As were getting ready to roll the series out, JTA and I were threatened legally by the Skirball Institute (which had hired disgraced Reform rabbi Robert Kirschner). They huffed and puffed mightily. JTA didn't handle it as I wished they would've.

"I was thrilled that all the major Jewish papers coast-to-coast carried the series in its entirety. I had feared that nobody would touch it."

"Who else has tried to make it difficult for you to do your job?"

"In the mid '90s, Sheldon "Shamai" Englemayer was doing communications for JTS. I'd done a story about Rabbi Joel Roth [a leading halakhic expert in the Conservative movement and a staunch opponent of ordaining openly homosexual rabbis] about something inappropriate between him and a [male] rabbinical student. Engelmayer was so offended that he sent around an article to all the Jewish newspapers, making it look like a JTA story from me in which he made things up in a skewed effort to do what he considered repair work. He also put something in all the mailboxes at JTS impugning my shul as 'progressive.'"

"Who are some of the other biggest sleazebags you've dealt with?"

"I was writing about Lubavitch. The rebbe was dying. The messianist thing was at a boiling furor. Somebody in that community sent out an article making it look like it was by me and making things up.

"I take great pride in having a reputation for being fair. Rabbi Avi Shafran from Agudath Israel congratulated me for a story I wrote on the Conservative movement where I quoted a Conservative Jew who copped to the fact that he wasn't observant. He congratulated me on having the courage to do that. I thought, that's ridiculous. There was no courage involved. I was just doing my job."

"Has it been difficult for you to get access to the right-wing Orthodox world, being a woman?"

"Yes. By the same token, being a woman given me access to people and places that men wouldn't have. Women are a lot more powerful and influential, in some ways, in Charedi communities than people are often aware of. When I've gone to things in that community, I know how to look the part. Not 100%, because I'm not wearing seamed stockings and a sheitl in Williamsburg, but I can wear a hat and long sleeves. There are journalists who don't mind sticking out as a journalist but I think it is far more effective not to."

"What are the obstacles you've had to overcome to produce compelling journalism on American Jewish life?"

"There's an endemic, institutionalized fear of offending powerful people. That has filtered down to a level I find ridiculous. It has made it not possible to do stories that seem so parve to me. There is a tendency not to be sharp. There's a fear of running into the people who control the money."

"Have you lost friends over your journalism?"

"No. There have been moments that needed clarifying with friends over things that I've written. When you live in the community you're writing about, you also become friends with some of the people you write about.

"People sometimes assume that they know me because they've read my writing. Some people assume that I'm Orthodox because I write about that community. Some people assume that I'm gay because I've written on gays. Some people think they know my politics because of some of the things I've reported, which they don't."

"What are some of the bravest things you've had to do?"

"Asking Michael Steinhardt some hard questions, knowing I was arousing his ire. He's one of the most powerful people in the community, and knowing that I might alienate him, and he might remember, that prompted me to take a few deep breaths.

"When I was at JTA, one of the most important rabbis in the Jewish world lied about what he'd said because it had bit him in the ass politically. This was a moment of spiritual disappointment for me. This happened by the time I had gotten back to the office from the press conference where he'd spoken. He absolutely lied about it. Thankfully, Gary Rosenblatt was there with a tape recorder. What disappointed me was that my editor at JTA did not just trust what I was telling him was true but felt the need to verify it.

"When I subsequently saw this rabbi at conferences, I wanted to approach him about it for a long time. When I finally did, a year or two ago, he said he didn't remember. If true, that would make it even sadder. That would make it not extraordinary.

"Rabbis lie as often as anybody else. They're just human beings. More gifted in some ways than many, but also more flawed. We expect so much of our rabbis. They're invested with so much responsibility."

"Do you find any stereotypical differences between the religious movements?"

"I find that the less observant the movement, the more fabulous a venue it chooses to hold its conventions at. I've always enjoyed going to those really great resorts for the Reform rabbinical conventions. There's an inverse relationship between the frumness and the quality of the hotel."

"What do you love and hate about your work?"

"I love how rich, deep, and meaningful it is. I love that what I do touches lives. I love the consonance between my life and my work. I hate the lack of courage among top editors who are occasionally afraid to make waves. I've had some great ideas I couldn't get in the paper out of fear of alienating advertisers or funders.

"The other thing I hate is how undervalued we [Jewish journalists] are. People in the community will talk about the importance of Jewish journalism and the impact it makes, then do nothing to back that up. Journalists in general are poorly paid. I've written about Jewish continuity but [many of the organizations touting the Jewish continuity agenda] will do absolutely nothing to pay for parental leave, to provide enough of a salary so that people can afford to send their kids to Jewish day school. I find that painful."

"What about status? Is it closer to that of a day school teacher?"

"I think it is much higher. I think it's a pretty glam job. I enjoy seeing my byline and I enjoy, when I meet people, having them say, 'Oh, I read you all the time.' Who wouldn't enjoy that? Part of what makes you a journalist, as opposed to some other kind of writer, is wanting to see a byline. The status, however, is not matched by money.

"I had a friend who went from working for a Jewish paper to a secular paper. She was shocked by the lack of respect that journalists for Jewish papers get from the people in the community. I haven't experienced that. She was struck by how much more respect from sources she received at the secular daily."

"Do you still participate in pro-choice rallies and the like?"

"What I do as a private citizen is private."

28

Steve Rabinowitz

July 15, 2004

A source at the *Forward* says: "Steve worked as a press aide for umpteen Democrats up to and including Bill Clinton. He knows how to deconstruct an article and more about how to report one and put it together than most Jewish journalists. He is the Democratic strategist most interested in the Jewish press—it's part of his business model—and the PR professional who has most touted it as a 'market.' He boosts us, but at the same time, often busts our chops."

Steve says: "[The Jewish press] serves a purpose. It's not everything that a journalism professor would want it to be."

"**Eve Kessler told me that we are all a bunch of mediocrities.**"

"It's difficult for me to dump on these guys too much because of my relationship with them."

"**But you'd really like to if you could.**"

"I'd really like not to be quoted as saying so. So many of these Jewish editors are friends, and if not friends, I can't afford to make them enemies.

"You get what you pay for. A lot of the Jewish papers are free. The Federation owns them. The good news is if there is anything major in the community, it will be in *The New York Times*.

"I'm frustrated by how poor the circulation of the *Forward* is. It's a great newspaper. The *Forward* is the closest thing we have to a national Jewish paper. It has influence, but not a wide reach."

"**How do you tell when you're dealing with a sharp reporter?**"

"You can tell if they are knowledgeable about a beat from the questions they ask. The follow-ups are a measure of a good reporter. Whether or not the next question comes from your answer or is like a chess move, already anticipated before the answer.

"One of the problems with Jewish papers is that few have reporters who can become expert in their beat [because they have to do so much general reporting]. They invariably have to cover issues they have little background in. They're vulnerable to being led by sources and having to write superficially."

"How often do you encounter a reporter from a Jewish paper who is as sharp and knowledgeable about his beat as a reporter from *The New York Times*?"

"It's just a different animal. If you compare them to African-American weeklies or other ethnic papers, Jewish journalists would stack up well. If the Jewish reporters were of the same caliber as those for *The Times*, *The Times* would scoop them up. A lot of Jewish journalists are looking to make the jump to mainstream.

"Then there's James Besser. He's totally at peace with where he's at. He's a lot better of a journalist than many of the papers he writes for. He's got a family and he's happy. It's the youngsters who are trying to climb."

"What are some stories the Jewish press is missing?"

"I think the unaffiliated Jew doesn't get covered. First of all, he isn't reading the paper. It's a difficult person to define. Young people haven't been covered. There are painfully few young Jewish readers of traditional Jewish media.

"This becomes cyclical so you have community papers such as Jewish papers just reporting on themselves. Like local society magazines, the people who read them are the people who are in them.

"The same sources get quoted over and over. If I had a nickel for every time Norm Ornstein (American Enterprise Institute) or Larry Sabato (University of Virginia) had been quoted about politics, I'd be rich. It seems to be worse in the Jewish community, and I say that as a frequent source for some stories.

"Something big will happen in the world that's not about the Jews and the Jewish media will always want to immediately write, 'What will this mean for the Jews?'

"A few days ago, my wife was coming out of the bathroom with a local Jewish newspaper. She said, 'This is the most ridiculous story I've ever seen.' She pointed to a headline that was the lead story in the paper about John Kerry's selection of John Edwards as his running mate. And what does it mean for the Jews? I said, 'Hey, I'm in that story.'

"I know that a lot of journalists hold their noses when they write these stories, but they are compelled to write them, not just because their editors assign them, but because they will absolutely be published and read. At the end of the day, we love to read these 'What does it mean for the Jews' stories and the counting Jews stories (how many Jews in Congress, on the Boston Red Sox etc).

"We're missing trend stories. Where is Jewry headed?"

29

Tom Tugend

July 18, 2004

It takes Tom just a few minutes to size me up. "You don't want Jewish journalism," he says. "You want an orgasm."

He then proceeds to give me the most mind-blowing interview I've had all day, leaving me spent yet exhilarated, with renewed faith in God, Torah and the *Jewish Journal*.

["This is the first time I've been accused of renewing anyone's faith in God and Torah," Tom writes later, "but if you say so."]

We meet at Elysee Boulangeries in Westwood. Tom's just finished his daily swim at the UCLA pool.

"I was born in Berlin in 1925. My dad was a pediatrician. He came from a line of assimilated German Jews. This all changed in 1933 when they discovered with all the other Jews that they were indeed Jews. My mother became president of the Women's International Zionist Organization for Germany. I belonged to a Zionist youth group. First I went to a Montessori and then to a Jewish school. I have an older sister.

"My dad left in 1937 and became a lecturer at Bryn Mawr College in Pennsylvania. That allowed us to get out of Germany in April 1939. We felt no sense of urgency. My father kept writing to tell us to leave and to forget about the furniture and so on. The feeling was that there wouldn't be any war. Stockholm Syndrome. Hitler would get what he wanted and there wouldn't be any war.

"I went to a school in suburban Philadelphia. As soon as I turned 18 and had a chance to get away from home, I went into the Army [early 1944]. I was still in high school. Whatever your skills or IQ [141], they needed infantrymen. I fought in France and Germany. Towards the end of the war, I was transferred to the counterintelligence corps when they discovered I spoke German.

"I supposedly educated German prisoners of war about democracy. I was offered an opportunity to translate at the Nuremberg Trials but I was sick of the Army and wanted to be transferred back. It's one of those things I regret I didn't take up.

"I was discharged in May of 1946. I started going to UCLA on the GI Bill. I wanted to go into journalism. UCLA didn't offer that major. I went to UC Berkeley in 1947 where they had a journalism school.

"In 1948, I left Berkeley and went to Israel for the War of Independence. I fought in an Anglo-Saxon unit, the Fourth Anti-Tank Unit. I was a squad leader. I worked on a kibbutz after it was over. I finished up my degree in 1950.

"I was recalled in the service for the Korean War. The Army was never more fucked up than in the Korean War. They were sending in old guys, wounded guys. Fortunately, they needed somebody to put out a newspaper at the presidio in San Francisco. I spent a year editing the *Foghorn*.

"After I was discharged, I got a job as a copy boy on the *San Francisco Chronicle*. That was one of the few ways to get in. If you made it, they made you a reporter. I was a copy boy for nine months. Herb Caen was there. Pierre Salinger. Other copy boys included a former philosophy professor and a socialite lawyer from New York. All oddballs. The most intelligent group of people I've known putting carbon sheets between sheets of paper and getting coffee for the reporters.

"As a reporter, I mainly covered the police beat and the court beat in Oakland. After three years, I overdosed on Hemingway and decided to go to Spain for a year.

"I came home. I married an Israeli girl in 1956. We have three daughters and eight grandchildren. I got a job at McDonnell Douglas for a year as a technical editor (and worked on the copy desk of *The Los Angeles Times* at night]. Then I got a job for 30 years (until 1989) at UCLA as a science writer and communications director. That meant interviewing the different academics about their research and then trying to translate it so that the average news–

paper reader could understand it, based on the theory that as their taxes paid for it, they were entitled to know. It would be sent out to the general press.

"In 1957, I started working for the *Jewish Heritage* newspaper. Herb Brin was the publisher and editor and advertising manager and everything else. On Saturday, we generally put the paper together. Whatever I wanted to write about, he published. I did a lot of theater and politics and Hollywood. In the best of times, he printed about 30,000 copies. He had papers in San Diego, Orange County, Central Valley and LA.

"I spent a year in Israel as the head of PR for the Weizmann Institute of Science. When I married my wife, I promised her that we'd try to make aliyah. They gave me a job. Now, all the people I had worked for at UCLA were goyim and good goyim. They didn't pound the tables. If there was a problem, we talked about it. I'm not confrontational.

"When I was in Israel, they started sending me letters, when are you coming back. I really missed the goyim. My theory is that if there were no Jews, life would be dull. If there were only Jews, I'd be climbing up the wall.

"I started as the Los Angeles correspondent for the *Jewish Chronicle* of London around 1970 and shortly thereafter for *The Jerusalem Post*."

"Was the *Heritage* the biggest circulation paper in LA?"

"No. The *Bnai Brith Messenger*. Around 40,000. I don't know. They all cheated like crazy. They weren't audited. There was one paper, *Israel Today*, which said it had a circulation of 65,000 when it really only had a few hundred copies."

"Did any of them run a real gossip column?"

"No. The papers in the '50s and '60s were really dull. The *Heritage* was not a dull paper but it was not balanced. Herb had three marriages. Our relationship lasted longer than any one of them [from 1957 until Tom went to work for the *Jewish Journal* in 1993]. If he liked you, you were not just a good journalist, you were the greatest journalist whoever lived. And if he hated you, you were the most miserable sonofabitch."

Tugend has been the Los Angeles correspondent for JTA since 1984.

"Gene Lichtenstein used to pick up my JTA stories. Every once in a while, he'd ask if I wanted to work for the *Journal*. I felt loyal to Herb and I said no. Finally, in 1993, he made me an offer I couldn't refuse. The *Journal* was getting better and I thought it would be nice to work for a paper that more people read and was less a reflection of one man's personality."

"What is the difference in the *Jewish Journal* under Rob Eshman?"

"It's generational change. Rob has angled it to a younger and hipper audience. I can do without all the singles columns but I see that you are looking for a wife, so.... Rob once said he wanted me as a counterbalance to the kindergarten [set]. At the staff meeting, it's mostly young girls. I have a certain institutional memory. I think it's become a livelier paper.

"I am not primarily an investigative reporter. I try to get both sides. I'm old school. You keep it as balanced as possible."

"He-said, she-said."

"Correct. I know that's not terribly fashionable. I think that if I do a critical piece, people say that I did not do it out of malice or to win a Pulitzer Prize, but out of fairness."

We talk about the Museum of Tolerance and its ilk.

"One swastika painted on the door of a synagogue and the ADL, Wiesenthal Center, and the American Jewish Congress will say there's a Holocaust around the corner. But in the 1940s, there really was solid anti-Semitism.

"A Jewish reporter criticizing Israel in the 1950s and 1960s was like going into Beth Jacob [Los Angeles Orthodox shul] and saying there was no God. It wasn't done. American Jewish society has changed. You can now criticize Jewish organizations.

"I did a story about the most influential Jews in town. I started out with ten. I ended up with about 130. Most important rabbis, industrialists, politicians. I made 130 friends and about 10,000 enemies.

"On the one hand, people say the *Jewish Journal* is a rag. 'What do I care? I'm above these things.' One academic friend who I left out of the list stopped talking to me for two years until he published a book. I mentioned this to somebody. He said, 'How ridiculous. How childish.' But if we left that guy out, he'd react the same way.

"Somebody once said of journalism is that it is the last refuge of the vaguely talented. If you are a tremendous genius in music or art, you focus on that. If Jewish journalism had the same pay scale as the general media, you'd get top talent.

"There's an old Yiddish saying that a man should live, if only to satisfy his curiosity. I've never lost my curiosity about human beings, including all the mishegos of the Jewish community. I still sweat over every story. One of my struggles as the LA correspondent for different overseas papers is that they really only want to hear about the mishegos: what nubile starlet and what orgy took place.

"There was an old story about *Time* magazine that if they wanted something about finances, they called the New York bureau. If politics, the Washington bureau. Academic life, they called Boston. Agriculture, Chicago. If they wanted something off the wall, they called LA.

"The *Jewish Chronicle* would be happiest if I just wrote about Hollywood and is Paul Newman really half Jewish. Is so-and-so one-eighth Jewish. Part of my educational effort is to say that California and LA are the most interesting social laboratories in the world."

"Who are the sexiest starlets you've ever interviewed?"

"Barry Levinson? When I write about a film, I try to interview the director."

30

J.J. Goldberg

July 19, 2004

J.J. edits the *Forward*.

"**What are the biggest obstacles to providing compelling journalism on American Jewish life?**"

"The biggest obstacle is that most Jews don't want compelling journalism on American Jewish life. The Jews who look to Jewish journalism tend to want to be anesthetized. They want journalism that will make them feel great about being Jewish and remind them of how much the Jews have overcome and how horrible their enemies are and how cool it is to be Jewish. The ones who have distance from that have so much distance that they don't want to put any effort into it. Critical loyalty is nearly gone except on the right-wing where they are critical of the rest of the Jewish community for not being sufficiently observant and appreciative of the Torah. That's the biggest obstacle. Everything else is secondary. If that didn't exist, there would be more interested readers and more tolerance and more people would be coming and trying to do this stuff. The stuff that is done, including the community weekly journals, against the odds, is sometimes pretty good."

"**When did you first start writing on Jewish life?**"

"I was doing it as a teenager in the '60s. I was involved in the [left-wing Zionist] youth group *Habonim*. I used to write manifestos about the community, civil rights, and oppression, in our newsletter. In college, I was part of an editorial collective that put out a weekly radical student paper *The Other Stand*.

"I'm a rare bird who hasn't changed his views much since he was a teenager. I'm more nuanced and, I hope, a little more grown-up, but my outlook on the world is left-of-center and Zionist and I still keep kosher.

"My first reporting job on the Jewish community was in LA in 1981 for a Hebrew weekly aimed at the Yordim [those who've left Israel] community. That lasted a year. After two years working outside of journalism, I came to New York for journalism school."

"Can you give me any turning points in your career? Times when you've decided to tell the truth in something and known you were going to lose friends?"

"That happens all the time. Many of the people I've been friends with over the years [came] from out of the Jewish student movement, the Jewish Student Press Service, friendships with people who are now senior officials at Jewish organizations such as my oldest friend David Twersky. We've lived on kibbutz together. We've been in newspapers together. The friendship goes in and out as the roles change. John Ruskay, Steven M. Cohen, on and on. Even people that I'd been reporting on for so long that they'd become relationships and then one day you've got to bite them in the ass and they really don't like it and they're not your friends anymore. That's hard. There are weeks where it is very hard to go to shul because everybody is mad at you.

"A year ago when I translated the Avraham Burg essay (former speaker of the Knesset) that was transformative in how upset people got. He wrote a piece in *Yediot Ahronot*, Israel's largest-circulation newspaper, last August about the occupation [of the West Bank and Gaza Strip] and its corrupting influence on Israeli life. He wrote that it was destroying Zionism.

"I read it in Jerusalem. I ran into him that morning. I said, 'Do you mind if I translate this into English?' He said sure. It got reprinted within two weeks all over the world, in the *International Herald Tribune*, *LeMonde*, the *Guardian* of London, *The Baltimore Sun*. It spun around the Web. The day before Yom Kippur, the Syrian ambassador was on CNN quoting from it, to show how corrupt Israel supposedly was.

"I went to my [Conservative] shul on Yom Kippur. We don't have a rabbi in my shul (though a big percentage of the members are Conservative rabbis). Every week, there's a different person giving a dvar Torah. Somebody got up and talked about how awful it is that some members of our community are providing ammunition for the enemies of Israel. Friends of mine almost walked out in protest. You go to shul and expect not to be attacked from the bima. That was transformative."

"Any one article you've done where you lost the most friends?"

"Almost 15 years ago, there was a wave of firings of executive directors at Jewish organizations. My curiosity started out because the head of the National Conference on Soviet Jewry was suddenly dismissed after 20 years on the job. He almost created the Soviet Jewry movement. Somebody said to me, 'Look into this. There's something going on.' I looked into it and it was about lay people. The older generation of lay people [who were big donors] were garment manufacturers [and from other businesses that did not require an extensive formal education] who would write checks and let the staff run the organization. A younger generation of lay people were lawyers and consultants [and] had time during the day. They were micro-managing the organizations and telling the staff what to do. The staff was fighting back. Things were getting ugly. Careers were being brought to an end for no reason.

"I quoted somebody who called it a bloodbath. There were people who were forced to resign. I didn't realize that if you write that somebody was fired when they were merely forced to resign, they will sue you. Years later, over Shabbos dinner, I would run into people who had been friends and who still didn't want to have dinner with me because I had written they had been fired when they had agreed to resign. It still sounds like a silly distinction to me.

"I was struck by your discussion about human feelings with one editor. You were, get the story. This person was, what about *rachmones* (mercy)? *The New York Times* worries about this too. Is the damage you are going to do to this person's personal life deserved?

"Ernie Michel was on that list. A Holocaust survivor, he had been the executive director of the New York Jewish Federation. He was beloved among his colleagues and clients. He was one of the founders of the Holocaust survivors' movement. Thirty years ago, survivors didn't have meetings and issue statements. They nursed their wounds, raised their children, and historians wrote about the Holocaust. Israeli politicians talked about the Holocaust. Ernie, along with Elie Wiesel and others, organized a world gathering of Holocaust survivors in 1981. He was one of the first Holocaust survivors to achieve a position like director of the New York Jewish Federation.

"Around 1987, I heard that he was eased out. There was a big restructuring of New York Federation and they were bringing in younger people. He was in that article.

"My career has been a crossover between the bureaucracy and the journalism. But he'd always been warm to me. The first time I went to interview him. These people always have pictures on the wall of themselves shaking hands with Richard Nixon, etc. He had a picture of him with Harpo Marx. For this world, that's a great thing. He was a good egg.

"He let me know through every avenue possible, other than by talking to me, that he had never been more wounded in his life. There was one time when I really needed a quote from him because he was the only person who knew what I needed. I called him. He got on the phone and said, I just want to remind you that I told you that I was never talking to you again, and I'm sticking to that.

"You would expect it [these rupturing of friendships] to be about something big in the world and it is always seems to be about these little things.

"Ernie Michel mellowed out after a couple of years."

"What always struck me about your weekly columns was how nice you were."

"I tried to be gentle. I was more interested in nailing the issues than the people. My general assumption is that most people do their best. Most things that go wrong are because either something is too hard for the people involved or because there's a genuine clash of interests.

"There's this whole thing with social justice work. Young people doing pro-choice work, anti-hunger work. It is to oppose the policies of the Republicans. The assumption being that Republicans are against social justice. They are not. They have a different way. In their minds, they think that what they do achieves greater social justice. If you stop giving poor people money, they will find jobs and there will be more justice. I don't agree but I don't think they are against social justice. A lot of people assume that if you don't agree with my methods, you must oppose my goal. There's a whole lot of anger and demonization that goes on. 'That John Kerry isn't against terrorism.' 'That George Bush doesn't believe in freedom or civil rights.' I don't agree. I think most people mean well."

"Do you believe that if Orthodox and non-Orthodox Jews socialized together more, do you think that they would hate each other more or less?"

"It's hard to imagine them socializing more together because then they'd want to date. I think Orthodox Jews would do well to understand what it does to other people when you don't want to socialize with them. I think they assume that because they're doing what God told them to do, everybody else needs to understand it. A lot of Reform Jews think they believe in pluralism, that everybody is entitled to their own form of Judaism. Now, Orthodox Judaism teaches that halakhah is Judaism. Reform Judaism doesn't believe that the Torah commands anything. It recommends. By definition, an Orthodox Jew cannot believe that Reform Judaism is an authentic interpretation of the Torah. If you are really a pluralist, you have to believe in the right of Orthodoxy not to accept Reform Judaism.

"The Reform are always pressing in communal situations and organizations for resolutions [calling on Israel to accept the legitimacy of Reform Judaism]. There have been a couple of national Jewish councils that have fallen apart, the Orthodox resigned, because the Reform managed to get a majority to adopt a resolution calling on the Israeli government to accept the legitimacy of Reform Judaism. If they had sat down and thought it through, they would see that the Orthodox can't live with that. If you don't want the council to exist, fine. But if you want there to be a council where everybody sits around the table, don't shoot a hole in the floor of the boat."

"What are you the most proud of since taking over and where do you think you have the furthest to go?"

"What am I most proud of? My daughter learned to ride a bicycle a few weeks ago. She's ten. I also have a seven year old son."

"With the *Forward*?"

"Lipsky created a national journal worthy of the name that became must-reading, that became a platform where the Jewish community of all views had to come together to talk to each other. I have managed to maintain that. Some people think I have raised the level. I turned around the political direction without losing the quality of journalism. You know what they say about turning around an aircraft carrier while you are traveling full steam. I think the Opinion page has become a real forum for exchange on Jewish stuff. I think the Arts page is expanding the boundaries of what is Jewish. The things that Jews are interested in are Jewish things. That could mean everything in the world, but somewhere between that and a narrow interest in Israel, the Holocaust and the Torah is a broad middle area that we're looking for. We're groping in the dark. It's evolving. I'm proud of finding people who are good at what they're doing and letting them do it.

"We have a couple of reporters who are just stars. I get a kick out of the fact that I can find these people."

"I miss Eve Kessler's reporting on religion."

"We don't do enough reporting on religion. Eve was a really interesting religion reporter but she is a brilliant political reporter. She is the kind of journalism you like—go for the throat.

"That serves the political world better than the religion world. In Judaism, there's so little debate, that if you shut down the sources, if you burn everybody, you get one good week and then there's no more. If you can find a way of doing it so that people want to continue the discussion.... The Lakewood business [a yeshiva student from Lakewood self-published a book that argued for the racial superiority of Jews], there are times when you have to let it all hang out. But there are other times, when you look for the negative, look for a way of making people look bad, just for entertainment value, you don't gain that much.

"We're a small paper. We don't have too many resources. I think there's so much going on in the world of religion that I would like to talk about it with depth and intelligence and not just smarts. Some of her stuff was great. In what she's doing now, all of her stuff is great.

"Now that I think about it. I'm listening to you and I'm listening to myself, and it might just be time.... She's gained a whole lot of depth in the last couple of years. That might not be a bad idea to bring her back to the religion beat.

"For getting the paper read, the stuff that she's done on politics the last two years has gotten us more buzz than any other single thing. To the extent that we have grown 50%, part of it is marketing, direct mail, and spending money, but part of it is word of mouth. A lot of that has to be just her getting quoted because she comes up with these great stories. When you're talking about stuff that everybody is interested in. The moment you talk about ethnic ghetto narrow Jewish stuff, the involved Jews will be grateful and everybody else will tune you out.

"Hillel had this debate about how to structure their buildings where you have the kosher lunch and Torah lessons upstairs and downstairs you have the general stuff that will bring people in. If you have the hardcore stuff by the entrance, then other people will never get in the door. If you want to design a newspaper to get read as widely as possible, the theory would be to have really good coverage of something that a lot of people are interested in.

"The other thing that is hard about doing good Jewish journalism, is that there are not many people who are informed on Jewish affairs, have an open mind so that they can fairly listen to varying Jewish points of view, who appreciate both Jewish tradition and culture and politics, who get into the Middle East and the Jewish communal world, and the religion. The people who tend to get that stuff tend to be conservative. The people who get that stuff and are what I'm looking for, center-left, are rare. The people who are left are frequently left-wing. I'm not looking for ideologues. The subset who are left who also know how to do journalism are a small group of people.

"If you look at the staff we have working here, most of them are good at something. They're not that interchangeable. The hardest thing is to find somebody who can cover Jewish religion intelligently. Ami was the best but he's also the best news editor. That was his triage. Now I'm looking for somebody else [to cover religion]. Somebody who understands Orthodoxy and can cover Reform. If you know anybody, send them along."

"What do you think about using some of the techniques of New Journalism in your paper?"

"It makes the articles longer. If you can do that and still tell the truth, then it makes for a better read. We've had a couple of reporters who were able to do that. My rule is first, give me a credible news report. Then, the more charmingly it is written, the more people are going to want to read it."

We talk about bullies.

"It's a chess game. Everybody is out there to block each other's pawns. Our funding is internal. When the *Forward* was a major metropolitan daily, it acquired a lot of assets. Now we're living off the interest. We're lucky. *The Jewish Week* is more dependent on the views of its audience.

"One of the freest reporting positions I ever held was when I was at *The Jewish Week* [1987–90, after which J.J. moved to the *Forward*]. Nobody ever told me what to do. Before that, I'd gone to journalism school and then to work at a daily newspaper in New Jersey. I was frustrated. I was a low-level editor watching the Iran-Contra thing go by and knowing a lot of the big players because I'd been involved at a high level in Israeli politics and thinking I could be writing stories better than this. Then *The Jewish Week* offered me an opportunity to do that.

"I'm skeptical of [blaming the] Federations [for dull journalism], but the pressure you get from your readers and advertisers is serious. You hear occasionally about a Federation editor who hears from the Federation [that] you can't write that about a donor.

"There are a million stories in the world. I could write 15 stories about the block outside my window. So if I can't write that story because it would end the career of my newspaper, big fucking deal. If the most important thing I need to do is to piss in the pool I'm swimming in, I'm probably in the wrong line of work.

"On Israel, the people who raise money for it have very strong views. It's not so much the Israelis as their big fans. These real estate guys and lawyers…have intense feelings. They want their community to reflect what they think is right. I got dropped from the Philadelphia *Jewish Exponent* for writing something bad about Mort Klein [right-wing head of the Zionist Organization of America]. Now, I'm still friends with Mort Klein. He made calls saying, 'This is ridiculous. He wrote an article. I didn't like it. It's over.' The people who run the [Philadelphia] Federation were people I was friendly with. They had intervened in the beginning to get my column into the paper. But there were a couple of big donors who did not want my type of column in the paper. That sort of thing happens all the time. When big donors call up and say, if that sort of thing happens again, you lose my gift. The bullying mainly happens from donors."

"**What would you guess is the median-age of a *Forward* reader?**"

"A little under sixty. That's down a decade since I took over. We're trending younger. Our new acquisitions from our new advertising who emphasize more of the irreverent stuff. We had this event in the East Village last week. The 100th anniversary birthday bash for I.B. Singer. It was a hip bar. It was packed. The average age was well under 30."

"**How is the Internet and blogging affecting Jewish journalism if at all?**"

"I have no idea. I don't understand it. There are people who follow that stuff. I don't see much crossover. I see a whole lot of gossip passed around as though it were news. There's no fact-checking. It's impressions. I'm old-fashioned. Journalism is get the facts and tell the story. Find out what the other side thinks.

"I had an Op/Ed piece submitted a few months ago. The author wrote: 'This person who issued this statement, I have no idea why he said that.' I sent the piece back to the author. 'Find out why he said that. Give him a call, for Chrissake. His number is in the phone book. There is no reason not to know why he said it.'

"Some blogs I read obsessively because they give me a lot of information I didn't have. Mainly blogs by journalists—Josh Marshall, Eric Alterman, Andrew Sullivan, Mickey Kaus. But blogging is not the same thing as journalism."

"**How hands-on an editor are you?**"

"I don't sleep much, if that helps. Mostly, I leave a lot of it to Ami [Eden, national editor], Wayne [Hoffman, managing editor], Alana [Newhouse, Arts], Oren [Rawls, Opinion]. They work with reporters. I go back when I notice something. I go through everything just before the paper goes to press, if I can."

"I hear stories that 'J.J. wasn't here all week and then he shows up just a few hours before the paper is to go to press and he goes crazy.'"

"I've gathered that it is always better for someone else to pass on bad news than me because I tend to get impatient. The kindly persona that I tried to create in my columns doesn't seem to come across when I'm airing my wisdom with people. It seems to work best when I don't share. I want English to be good English. I don't want dangling participles. I don't want upper cases to be lower case. I hate misuses of the word 'for.'"

"How often do you come in to the office?"

"I'm in every day. I don't come in all week? I was in Israel for a week. I meet with people."

"What do you love and hate about your job?"

"I hate writing the editorials, I guess."

"Then why do you do them?"

"I do it well. People seem to like them. It's hard for me. It's always the last minute. I'm always against deadline. Writing on deadline is a physically painful thing for me. Having written is one of the most gratifying things.

"Management stuff is my least favorite. When you've got to let somebody go. You've got to mess up somebody's life. I hate that.

"Somebody gets off the phone and they've just nailed something, such as why a Jewish agency is cutting a budget. They jump up and there's a look on their face. That's magical. The whole newsroom lights up for five minutes. You just know the front page is going to be great next week.

"Sometimes there's a Tuesday morning when we're putting together a front page. I'm proud of how we remade the front page to have that colored section on the left with the non-news stuff. I'd like that to be bigger but I haven't figured out how yet. I've pushed the balance of news and features a little more towards features and still make it feel like a newspaper. I don't know quite how to do that.

"But there are moments on Tuesday morning, right after we've finished the front page, when I know we're going to have a great issue."

"Some people say that you push a lot of front page anti-Bush stories that don't have much to do with the Jewish community."

"I don't think there's anything in the paper that doesn't have anything to do with the Jewish community. The *Forward* has a two-part mission—Jewish culture and social justice. It's 106-years old. I'm not going to apologize for that.

"When [Seth] Lipsky was editing the paper, he was pushing a lot of stories about privatizing the nation's economy and lowering the capital gains tax.

"There are a lot of poor Jews. The median income for a lot of American households is around $40,000. The median income for American Jewish households is around $50,000, which means that half of the Jewish households in America are living on less than $50,000 a year.

"The American Jewish Committee did a study in the mid '80s of the cost of Jewish living. If you have two kids and you want to put them through day school, belong to a synagogue, send the kids to summer camp, make a modest donation to Jewish charities, is out of range of 90% of the Jews in America. How do they set tuitions? How do they structure Jewish life? The boards of major American Jewish organizations are all made up of people who make more than $200,000 a year (from a study a decade ago by Steven M. Cohen for the Israel Democracy Institute). How would they know how people live?

"You meet with these people and ask them how people will manage and they'll reply, 'They'll manage. I manage.' A chair of the nominating committee of the New York Federation Board told me in the late '80s when I was at *The Jewish Week*, 'We're not limited to rich people. We recently took a new member onto the board whose annual gift is $5000. That's not rich.' That's the poverty faction.

"I think these [issues of poverty] affect Jewish life. Most Jews are sorta interested in Jewish stuff but they're interested in a lot of other stuff. If we only do the narrowly-defined Jewish stuff, we're not doing what most Jews are interested in. It's a delicate balance. So we talk about comic books. We talk about administration policies.... I write editorials around holiday time, such as Shavuos, where you are not allowed to cut the corners of your field [to provide for the poor]. The Torah outlaws extracting full profit from your enterprises. It's not yours. The idea that the government can't tax you because the money is yours? George Bush says you can keep your own money. It's not your own money. The Torah says so. Why is that not a Jewish issue?

"I've been doing Jewish journalism for 30 years. I don't get to write this stuff anymore except for the editorials. I'm trying to get editors to work with writers and develop this stuff and a lot of people have no idea what I'm talking about. Most young Jews don't think about economics and poverty that much. When they think about progressive, they think about gender, race and war and peace issues.

"You've heard that I have a temper and I bark at people. Partly, I throw out ideas and hope they stick. Partly, I do a bit of assigning myself and work directly with writers on stories I'm particularly interested in. Sometimes I say, do a story on that topic and we'll worry about the Jewish angle next month. Sometimes we don't do it because we don't see a way to do it."

"Do you have any right-wingers on your staff? Conservatives?"

"Republicans? Probably not."

"Would you be a better paper if you did?"

"Possibly. We have some Orthodox Jews. We have some hawks, doves, Democrats and we may have one Nader supporter. We probably would be a better paper if we did."

"What drove you to start putting blogs on Forward.com?"

"Staff people said, I'd like to put a blog on Forward.com. I said ok."

"Did you have any concerns?"

"We're responsible. We get a lot of attention from lawyers whose clients don't like what we wrote. The minute the lawyer writes you a letter, you've got to get your lawyer to write them back, so it's costing you money. You don't want to get involved with lawyers. You're spending money on lawyers anyway to review articles that might get you in trouble. We've got a lawyer on retainer who reads the articles he needs to read. That's grown-up newspapering. Bloggers just write whatever is in their head. Generally speaking, it is not practical to have a blog read in advance by an editor. Blogging is in real time. They could write something. It is on our Web site. And the next thing I know, I'm in court.

"Even if that doesn't happen, the blogger expresses an attitude. The blogger then goes back to their day job as a reporter, writes an article. Somebody comes back with their lawyer and says, 'You were trying to fuck me.' 'Oh no, we were just reporting the news. We have no agenda.' 'What do you mean you have no agenda? The writer in his blog expressed this attitude and now he writes this article to twist the facts to advance that attitude?' The blogger is revealing his state of mind.

"*The New York Times* has a rule that staff members are not allowed to go to demonstrations. There was a big pro-choice demonstration in Washington a couple of years ago. Several of their staff members went and were disciplined. Because you've got to be a monk.

"Once I decided to go in the direction of blogging on my Web site, I'm moving into unknown territory. I'm holding my breath. I'm hoping for my best. I'm hoping it enriches the discussion."

Goldberg says the geographic distribution of *Forward* readers mirror that of the Jewish community in general in America. About 35% are in New York. About 15% seem to be Christians.

"Have you ever killed an important story?"

"I don't think I've ever killed an important story for any reason other than it wasn't ready to go. There are important stories I would love to run that would piss a lot of important people off but we haven't been able to nail because we're not big enough. We don't have enough people to do deep research.

"I recently found out that a story I was waiting for was on the backburner because people were under the impression that I wouldn't want it because it was going to embarrass a politician I liked. That hurt my feelings.

"There was a review [by Lawrence Grossman] of Rabbi David Hartman's new book on J.B. Soloveitchik. Somebody really roasted him across the coals. I saw it Tuesday night, on the boards, ready to go to the printer.

"I thought: Gee, this is really harsh. It doesn't really address his ideas. It psychoanalyzes him.

"[Rabbi Hartman] was my professor for years. I love the guy. I visit him when I'm in Israel. For a while, he wouldn't speak to me."

"Because you ran the book review."

"That's happened to me a couple of times. But you have a contract with the writers that they get to do honest journalism. At times, I will say, this is stupid. Write an article about what he thinks. Don't psychoanalyze the guy. If I had read it on Monday and we had time to remake the page.... I'm kicking myself because it changes my life because I read it on Tuesday night instead of Monday morning. I couldn't make everybody stay up all night to remake the page and write another review to put there so this could be rewritten next week.

"Frank Rich at *The New York Times* would write reviews and plays would get killed. For all these people, their livelihoods were finished because he didn't like the play. We have a little bit of that influence in the Jewish world. They have a million [subscribers] and we have 30,000. I try to have more rachmones.

"This is where we started. I want to know that the person deserves this. If they don't deserve it, find another way to do it. If somebody calls me up and tells me you better not do it, I'm more likely to say, fuck it, rachmones is out the window."

"How would you handle a story about a leader of a major Jewish organization who is involved in an ongoing extramarital affair that is disrupting his work life but he's not doing anything illegal?"

"It came up. Rabbi Sheldon Zimmerman. We ran the story. I hear he hates me."

"But you didn't run any details on what he did wrong."

"At the time, we couldn't find out. Once we got the details, we did."

"You got sexual indiscretions. Everybody wants to know what they were."

"By the time I found out, it was ancient history. The guy's already dead. Why shoot him again? At a certain point, it becomes pornography. The issue is, what's going on in Jewish life. If we had known that week what had gone on, we would've printed it. But everybody clammed up on that. Nobody wanted to talk. My family and friends who are involved in these things [Jewish organizations, not necessarily sexual indiscretions], and they won't tell me. Everybody is afraid to talk to me.

"It took weeks and weeks to find out what it was about. If it is only interesting because we can find out who stuck what where, then in it is pornography."

"He is now at a major Jewish position. [He's vice-president for Jewish Renaissance and Renewal at United Jewish Communities.]"

"And we wrote about that. He's really mad that we wrote about that. Now, it turns out that what I gather he did is so unexceptional. It wasn't with children.

"If it is [a certain type of sexual indiscretion], we'd have to have it lawyer-proofed. Maybe they don't sue bloggers because bloggers don't have any money. It's amazing how many more letters we got from lawyers once newspapers reported we had sold our radio station for $70 million. Suddenly everyone is interested in the details of what we wrote. I can't [publish] anything I can't prove in court."

"How good of a job are you doing covering all the sex abuse scandals rippling through the Jewish world?"

"Not much. There are a number of things we don't do as well as we should and that is probably one of them. We've covered a few of them. *The Jewish Week* was ahead of us. It's not one of the things we do best. Along with religion, Jewish education, and a few other things."

"What can you do to cover Jewish education better?"

"We need a reporter who's going to make that his beat. Most of the coverage we give to it is in the back of the paper in a feature-kind of way. If it is going to be on the front, it's going to be hard news. It is sometimes hard to see the hard news in what goes on. People have a new idea on how to run a school. They have a conference that brought teachers together to talk about teaching. It's a yawner. To the people involved, it's their life and we need to report and I haven't found the answer to that yet."

"Rabbis in particular want it both ways. They want to go on television, be the spiritual heads of their congregations as well as CEOs, preach from the pulpit, and yet not be covered as public figures."

"For most American Jews, their Judaism is a leisure time activity. They've been trained to regard themselves as authorities regardless of how much they know. They're proprietary about it. Everything sets off Holocaust imagery. Jews are sensitive about their Judaism. I think Catholics are sensitive about their Catholicism."

"Is there a generation issue here? I don't hear younger Jews worrying about what's good for the Jews."

"Research shows that younger Jews worry less about what's good for the Jews because they're less interested."

31

Wayne Hoffman

July 20, 2004

The 33-year old *Forward* managing editor has a brother who's a Conservative rabbi.

"I've been a professional journalist since I was 18. I was a music critic for the *Washington Blade*."

"**What is the *Washington Blade*?**"

"It's the oldest gay newspaper in the country, founded in 1969.

"I freelanced for many gay newspapers. I got a Masters from NYU in American Studies (specializing in gay pop culture). I finished my course work for my PhD [but] quit to form New York's largest gay paper, the *New York Blade*."

"**What's it like for you publishing stuff that will upset members of your community?**"

"It's less of an issue for me working at the *Forward* than for some other people who work at the *Forward* [and are more involved in Jewish life than Wayne is]. It was a larger issue for me working in the gay press. I largely live within the gay community. I don't live within the Jewish community. I live in Greenwich Village, not the Upper West Side. I go to gay bars more frequently than I go to synagogues. I go to shul once a year, on Yom Kippur. I don't believe in God."

"**Have you ever lost friends over what you wrote?**"

"No. J.J. told you about going to his minyan and having people get angry at him. I don't have a minyan. So if people in J.J.'s minyan are mad at me, I don't know them.

"I came on board the *Forward* at the beginning of 2003. I've always done work on Jewish topics. I wrote a piece on queer yiddishkeit that got syndicated and won an award. I'm also a travel writer and I've written about Jewish travel. I've covered two books for the *Washington Post* on gay life in Israel and two memoirs about the Holocaust."

"Do you feel a visceral hatred for those who hold that your lifestyle is an abomination?"

"My lifestyle? You mean that I get up and go to work every day? I think that is an abomination. Or do you mean that I'm gay?"

His voice rises into incredulity.

"That you are a practicing homosexual."

Wayne laughs. "Practicing homosexual? If they used language like that any time after 1965, I would be more amused than anything else. Do I have a visceral hatred of those people? No. That there are people who think that I am an abomination before God? I don't value their opinion. Let them think that. It doesn't bother me as long as it doesn't affect my civil rights and my rights as a citizen."

"Is the journalism better on Jewish life or on gay life?"

"There's writing on Jewish life from a thousand different perspectives. The variety of experience is not reflected in gay writing yet."

"What's more compelling? Gay journalism or Jewish journalism? Let's take someone who is neither gay nor Jewish and you give them journalism from those communities, how much would interest him?"

"If you were neither gay nor Jewish, the vast majority of gay and Jewish journalism in this country would not interest you.

"But just because most community papers don't have earth-shaking journalism doesn't mean they're not important. My parents are traditional Conservative Jews in their mid 60s living in suburban Maryland. Well-educated, left-of-center. Traditional but open-minded. In addition to the *Forward*, they also read community newspapers and find them extraordinarily compelling. Both the one from where they live and the one from where they're from, North Jersey. They read it voraciously every week. It's very important to them to know what happened to the community in which they grew up.

"I'm curious about what's happening in the Jewish community of Washington where I grew up but it doesn't keep me up at night. But for my parents, it is urgent, even 40 years after they left Jersey."

"The intended audience for Jewish papers is dying. The average median age of a reader of a Jewish weekly is about 60. You don't see young people getting excited about what's in the latest Jewish weekly."

"You don't see young people getting excited about what's in *The New York Times* either."

[According to *The Times*, the median age of its readership is 43. According to surveys conducted by Scarborough Research in Manhattan, the average age of a newspaper reader is 53.]

"Is there something you are failing at, that's not bringing young people in to the *Forward*?"

"There are things we are trying to do, particularly in culture coverage, we can make our pages younger. Paying more attention to pop culture and the large cultural scene that is youth-driven.

"The gay press has had the opposite problem. It has tried to attract older readers."

"Does the *Forward*'s circulation of about 30,000 bother you?"

"No. The job I had before the *Forward* was at *Billboard* magazine. Have you heard of *Billboard*?"

"Yes."

"It's famous. Yet it's circulation is not noticeably larger than the *Forward*. Numbers aren't the issue. The question is, how important are you? How much do you stand out in your field? How much do people turn to you as an authority? *Billboard* has never relied on numbers. Both papers have a [century old] history. Knowledge of issues from the inside. People take them seriously because they have credibility."

"Did you find that moving to the *Forward* was moving from one trade paper to another?"

"No. Working at the *Forward* is similar to the experience I had working at the *Blade*. What drives the publication is different from what drives a trade. Here editorial drives the product. You hope advertising follows. At a trade, it's the opposite."

"What do you love and what do you hate about your job?"

"I love my job because of the people in the newsroom. The collection of people at the *Forward* is unique in the number of people I respect. Being a managing editor to Ami Eden, Alana Newhouse and Oren Rawls is a breeze because they do their jobs so well. Even though I have more experience as a journalist than any of them, they do their jobs in such a way that I've never once stood back and said, I could do this better.

"What I hate about my job is trying to get the paper out. I'm the only person at the newspaper who has that as a primary goal. J.J.'s interest is to make the paper reflect his vision as much as possible. Ami's is to get as much news in as well as possible. Alana's is to get as much arts and culture coverage as well as possible. Oren's is to get the biggest names on the editorial page and the most interesting discussion going. The art director wants to make the pages look the best. He wants to get better photos. He wants to have more space for photos. Everyone has competing interests. I'm trying to get them all out the door."

"Do you have a whole vision for the *Forward* if J.J. disappeared tomorrow and you took over?"

"If J.J. disappears tomorrow, I will call you and tell it to you."

"I can just imagine being in your position and hoping that one day you will get the chance to execute it."

"I don't have that much time on my hands to think about what I would do if J.J. met his unfortunate demise. I'm busy thinking about how many stories we can get in the paper and what the headlines are going to be."

"In the list of your ten biggest fantasies, is that one of them?"

"J.J.'s unfortunate demise? That is not on my top ten list of fantasies."

"What about presiding over the paper?"

"That is also not on my top ten list of fantasies. In fact, none of my top ten list of fantasies involve Jewish journalism.

"Before I started the *New York Blade* in 1997, I was a gay activist. I was screaming in the streets and going to gay protests. Then we launched a newspaper. People said to me, this is great. You will have this opportunity to push your opinion. I said, that's not what the newspaper is about. I wanted the *Blade* to be a place where everybody felt free to express themselves and to disagree. Our reporters didn't back down from challenging people but we gave column inches to people whose views I despised.

"Yeah, I have political opinions about some of the issues we cover, but that's not the point."

"Were you one of those activists who stormed into churches and threw blood?"

"I was not. I did not storm into a church and I did not throw blood but I was 'one of those activists.' I was in the group that did those things."

"Do you think that was a little strong? Throwing blood and storming into churches?"

"In the face of hundreds of thousands of people dying of AIDS? No. They didn't kill anybody. When I was at Tufts, there was a protest of this type, which involved going into the Catholic church on campus and greeting your fellow parishioners and shaking hands. This was considered a campus outrage. That they had gone too far by invading a church. Something that should've been off limits to political protest. I said, bullshit.

"In the face of tens of millions of dead today, was it over the top? No. It was quite under the bottom. It should still be going on right now."

"How do you see yourself primarily? As a man? A Jew? A homosexual? An American?"

"Can we please stop using the word 'homosexual?'"

"My primary identity depends on the minute of the day."

"Is being gay or being Jewish more important to you?"

"It depends on the context. I've never been at a point in my life where I didn't think about being Jewish. And I've never been at a point in my life where I didn't think about being gay. I'm also conscious of things like gender, race, class, geography, educational level, and my politics and being an atheist."

"What do you dislike about the word 'homosexual'?"

"It's outdated and misses the point."

"So you think 'gay' is infinitely superior?"

"They're different. Homosexual is what you do as an act. It's not an identity. In year 2004 in New York, let's use 'gay.' It's the lowest common denominator. No, not all homosexuals are gay. Not all gay people are queer. I think all gays are homosexual but you never know these days."

"What's the difference between gay and queer? Is it like Reform vs. Conservative?"

"No. It's more like the difference between being Jewish and being Zionist. They are related, but not synonymous. In a similar way, gay is a personal identity and queer is a political stance."

"Like, we're here and we're queer and get used to it."

"A lot of queers are not gay. Transgenders, some lesbians, bisexuals do not identify as gay."

"On almost any sexual issue (homosexuality, same-sex marriage, abortion, pornography), Jews are more liberal."

"I think that's great. In 1989, when I was 18, I took a semester off and worked on Capitol Hill for the Human Rights Campaign Fund, which is the largest gay political organization in the country. We were working on various legislation, such as the Americans With Disabilities Act, which passed. We also worked on the Employment Non-Discrimination Act, which is still not law. We still don't have civil rights in employment in the United States. Even though only a tiny portion of Congress people had signed on to the bill, numerous Jewish groups had already come out in favor of it. They were at the front of the line.

"Going to pro-choice marches, Jewish groups were there in force. Going to gay rights marches in 1987, 1993, Jewish groups were there in force. That always made me proud.

"Coalition building is always a challenge. Often you see groups doing a tit-for-tat exchange. 'We showed up at the divest-in-South Africa march last month, so this African-American group should show up at this pro-choice rally this month.' That's coalition-building that will never last beyond next week.

"Jewish groups have always seen the connection between other groups in terms of social justice without any expectations. It was never a tit-for-tat exchange. Hadassah never called up the Human Rights Campaign and said, 'We will come out for gay rights if you come out for moving the American embassy to Jerusalem.'"

"How do you think America would be different if we eliminated all anti-discrimination laws? You could hire who you wanted. Rent to who you wanted. Play golf with who you wanted. Would we have a radically more hate-filled homophobic society?"

"It would be explicitly those things. Would you have country clubs that didn't allow Jews? Yeah, about ten minutes after that passed. Would you have neighborhoods that did not permit blacks to rent apartments? Yeah, in about one-and-a-half minutes. Would you have gay people being fired from their jobs left and right? We already do. Would it be easier for that to happen? Yeah. Would gay parents start losing their children? We already do."

He laughs. "It would be like it is now, except even more. It would be disastrous. More importantly, what would it be like in 20 years?"

"You see the law as holding back a dike, plugging a dike?"

"It's not so much that it is holding back a flood but it is creating a boundary, saying that this is something as a country we don't do. We don't discriminate. You don't have to like each other. You can think what you want and say what you want. You can publish a newspaper about it and refuse to print dissenting opinions. Law creates the edge past which behavior is not acceptable.

You're talking about eliminating the edge. Will people give in to their inner drive towards discrimination and bigotry? Of course. Then, people who didn't feel strongly one way or another will see that, 'Yeah, it is better this way. I won't rent to black people either. I'll have the gay teacher in my school fired too. I'll bring Christian prayer back to public schools and the Jews can go fuck themselves. It's a great idea. It never occurred to me, but now that you mention it, let's do it.'

"It's not about the PC Police or the Thought Police, like so many people created this bizarre bogeyman of the Left. You can say whatever you want. You just can't discriminate."

"Would you like to see same-sex marriage?"

"Yes. Is it my number one issue? No."

"Do you think everyone on the *Forward* staff supports same-sex marriage?"

"My guess is most."

"Do you fear more getting beat up because you are gay or getting beat up because you are a Jew?"

"Gay. But I don't spend that much time worrying about either one."

"Have you ever been beaten up for either?"

"No. I've had my share of verbal harassment for both and I've been pushed around as a gay person physically."

"Have you received more insults for being gay or for being Jewish?"

"No contest. For being gay. A hundred fold. In elementary school, I wasn't out as a gay person but it didn't stop people from calling me faggot. When was the last time I encountered anti-gay harassment? Two days ago. When was the last time I encountered anti-Semitism? Many months ago. I can't think of one."

"What's the most serious anti-Jewish thing you've had done to you?"

"There was a kid in elementary school who used to harass me regularly. He'd call me a dirty Jew, a kike, and a hebe. He kept bringing up that the Jews had killed Jesus and that the Jews had killed the Pope. That was pretty bad."

"What's the most severe anti-gay thing you've had done to you?"

Wayne laughs, "Other than being denied my civil rights? Beyond that? Other than that, actually being pushed in Boston by a stranger. He was calling me faggot and that I was going to get AIDS and that I needed to get the fuck out of the city. It was on Harvard Square. It was 1988. I was walking down the street with a pink triangle pin on my jacket. At that moment, I was not being a practicing homosexual, but I was being an out gay man. Also, I was borderline queer. See the difference?"

"How do you feel when gay people call themselves faggot?"

"I call myself faggot sometimes. It depends on the context. It's fine. Do you want me to call myself a faggot? I'm a faggot."

"Does it annoy you that black people can call themselves nigger but you can't?"

"No."

"What about the terms shiksa, shaygetz and shvartze?"

"Shvartze bothers me. Shaygetz is not used that often so it doesn't have as much of a charge as shiksa. I can at least imagine the word shiksa, because I've experienced it, being used ironically. Using it in a purely derogatory way is crappy. I can't imagine using the word shvartze in a way that's anything but really horrible."

"Let's say I say in a unironic tone, man, my place was robbed by shvartzes last night. How would you react?"

"I would call you on it. That's racist."

"What about if I said with no inflection, I went out with this great shiksa last night?"

"I would probably call you on that too. I'd be quicker to call you on shvartze."

"Well, thank you. I've enjoyed this. I'll send you a transcript."

"Am I the first faggot you've talked to?"

"You are the first in this book."

"But hopefully not the last."

"You are the first identifying gay person I've spoken to for this book."

"The first left-wing atheist faggot you've interviewed for the book?"

"Almost everyone has been left-wing. I use the term 'homosexual.' I'm old fashioned. I'm also right-wing. I don't like the word 'gay.' I think it has been hijacked. I come from Australia. 'Gay' meant happy."

"It still does."

"But it's primary meaning has been hijacked to mean what it means."

"It just means happy. That's how I use it.

"The most recent time I encountered an anti-gay incident was two days ago. I was on the New Jersey transit coming back into the city from visiting a friend. Someone was walking down the aisle. A man wearing some kind of freakish attire you really only see in New York. Long black robes. Red leather headgear. Some kind of alien priest. I don't know if he was referring to me or the guy across the aisle from me or just talking in general. He said, 'Oh man, there are sodomites all over this train.'

"I thought, 'sodomites. That's the one word we haven't taken back yet.' Then again, this remark came from a man wearing a dress."

"Do you think 'sodomite' is a nasty term?"

"It is so archaic as to be hilarious."

"I have such a hard time using 'gay.' I hope you will forgive me."

"You'll come around in 20–30 years, when we're on to our next term."

32

Alana Newhouse

July 22, 2004

According to my source, Alana is "absolutely gorgeous."
I call her in the morning.
"Are you ready for your close-up?"
She groans.
"What clique did you hang out with high school?"
"The JAPpy (Jewish American Princess) clique. I grew up in Lawrence, Long Island, and I loved it. To this day, I can do a better French manicure than any French manicurist you can get in Manhattan. I can put lip liner on in a dark cab. I was pretty focused. I'm a well-honed JAP."
"How do you reconcile your desire to be JAPpy and your desire to be tznious (modest)?"
Alana laughs hard. "I don't. There's no problem. There was a woman in my neighborhood who had everything perfectly covered but she was the most immodest woman I've ever met in my life. Modesty is a character trait."
"What about length of skirts?"
"I don't wear only skirts. My skirts tend to be pretty short. Tznious as a ritual observance—I don't observe that ritual. If I go into a shul, I'm going to be dressed appropriately. But I walk around in pants and shorts. I feel like modesty is more about your character than about what you wear."
"What does modesty mean to you?"

"I don't really know. It's a very personal thing. You didn't ask whether modesty as we understand it is a good trait. It should be ok to talk about yourself when it is helpful for someone else.

"There are ways that you can cheapen yourself, and make people feel that you are usable in any number of ways—professionally, emotionally, psychologically, sexually. That is what I mean by immodest."

"How many inches above the knee would a dress have to be before you would consider the wearing of such in the *Forward* office to be a sin?"

"A skirt more than four inches above my knee might make the people I work with uncomfortable and, as such, I'd avoid it. Not because I believe it's a sin against God—I don't think God is scandalized by my thighs—but because it's a sin against fellow human beings."

"What were you expected to become?"

"Married with a baby.

"I think I was expected to become a writer."

"Where did you go to college and how did you get into journalism?"

"I went to Barnard College, graduating in 1997. I majored in American History and Political Science. Writing was one of my first loves from high school. I grew up in a Modern Orthodox home and I went to Orthodox day schools. I went to Hebrew Academy of Five Towns in Rockaways. I'm a Long Island JAP. When I went to Barnard, the whole world opened up for me. I fell in love with politics.

"When I was a Junior, I met David Garth, a big political consultant in New York. He gave me a job after college. I worked for him for a couple of years. I burned out on politics. I went to Columbia Journalism School and graduated [with a Masters degree] in June 2002.

"I was interested in magazine journalism. I asked a professor what I should do for the summer. He said to go to Thailand or Europe because nobody was hiring. There was an ad for an internship with the *Forward*. I met with Andy Silow-Carroll. I immediately felt like if I had the opportunity to work with him, it would be a great experience. I ended up staying. I became a reporter in the Fall. I was covering religion and ideas. In April of 2003, I took over the Arts section."

"Are you still Orthodox?"

Long pause. "I don't want to respond to that question because I am not sure of the answer. I am certainly not as observant as I was when I was growing up. I'm in a weird phase of my life. I'm betwixt and between."

"Did you pay attention to the *Forward* before you worked there?"

"My father was a charter subscriber to the English edition. My father and I read it on Friday nights together. Jeffrey Goldberg wrote for the *Forward* and I was completely enamored with him. And Jonathan Rosen's art section."

"Did you read any other weekly with equal joy?"

"No."

"What are the primary obstacles you face in putting out the best Arts & Culture pages you can?"

"I know there is great stuff going on in the rest of the country but I need writers in those cities who have their ear to the ground and can tell me the great cultural things going on. I want to know about a great underground Jewish ska [Jamaican-type music] scene in Detroit. I want to know about a cool literary series going on in Houston. I'm acquiring a stable of freelancers to do that work."

"How was your journalism school education? A benefit or minus to your career as a journalist?"

Long pause. "It's a benefit but if I had to do it all over again, I'm not sure I would've gone."

"The more you learn about arts and culture, the more does it tug you away from Orthodox Judaism?"

"No, the two are not related."

"How often do you run stories you couldn't give a hoot about?"

"Once every six weeks. One of the great things about being an editor is that I choose what I want to run."

"Do you choose it on the basis of what excites you?"

"Yes. Literature is my first love but I learn from my writers. I'm not really interested in dance, but Joseph Carman did such great writing about all sorts of Jewish dance—Israeli folk dancing, the Jewish origins of Flamenco. Everything about my section excites me, at least in its idea. It may not be executed as well as I want it to. There are times you have to salvage a story."

"Who are the great Jewish writers?"

"The children of immigrants from the Soviet Union are going to be an unbelievably fruitful generation of fiction writers. David Bezmozgis's short story 'Minyan' is infused with a sense of Jewish life. Dara Horn, who is a great writer of journalism and fiction. She's steeped in Jewish life. She lives it and you can feel that. Even when she's not writing about anything Jewish, she feels Jewish in the best way.

"The masters are still at it. Philip Roth has a book coming out in October. I love it. I think he's going to win the Nobel Prize for it."

"Do you read a book a week?"

"It's hard. I read the first chapters of lots of books. That's why I don't review a lot. I believe that writers of every kind should fetishize beginnings. Make it amazing because so many people will never get past it if you don't."

"What's your favorite part of your job?"

"I've fallen in love lately with layout. My favorite is probably text editing."

"What's your least favorite?"

"Writers can be difficult to work with. Some are prima donnas and they need hand-holding and coddling. Some have been presumptuous about my time. Some will send me 2000 words for an 800-word story. I know I can cut it but I don't want to cut it. I want you to hand in a story of 800-words. Generally speaking, I don't work with those writers again."

"Do you think writers as a group tend to be misanthropic?"

"Yes. The best writers need to escape the world to think hard to create art. It's almost a survival mechanism. You turn on your misanthropic stance when you need to leave the world to analyze it."

"How do you determine if a story is Jewish enough to go into your pages?"

"It largely depends on the writer. I got an email about an author, Josip Novakovich. He's not Jewish and there's nothing Jewish about his book. But somebody sent me a pitch that his book had I.B. Singer written all over it. I took a look and I sort of saw it. He's Singeresque. I didn't end up running the piece because it would've been for September and I'm too packed.

"The woman who founded Bluemountain.com, where you can get e-cards, is Jewish. I was sent her autobiography. It looks like an interesting story but there's nothing about her being Jewish that made her start a greeting card business. It just didn't feel like a *Forward* story.

"On the other hand, there's a guy who's half Italian and half Jewish who's starting a Jewish chi-chi tenement hotel on the Lower East Side. It's completely formed by his sense of Jewish culture. He could've been a Roman Catholic, and it would fit. It's more feel."

"How do you balance high culture vs. low culture?"

"I just do it. I know the difference between the Beastie Boys and Isaac Luria and I try to have both of them in my section. I go on what I would want to read. I read *Page Six* and I read *The Times Literary Supplement*. I am a high-low girl."

"Are there any great Orthodox novelists?"

"I don't know which writers identify themselves as Orthodox. Rebecca Goldstein? Nessa Rappaport? Jonathan Rosen is certainly affiliated with Judaism but I don't know that he is Orthodox."

"From your knowledge of the Orthodox community, what are the obstacles, if any, between being Orthodox and being a great artist?"

"Everything. Art is seen as a waste of time that could be spent on Torah. That [attitude] is depressing to me. I see the world as one thing and religion as another. I don't know that Orthodox communities encourage kids to look at art or to understand music. Maybe they should get out and see God in art? You can see art as taking away time from Torah or you can see art as a different way to learn Torah, a different way to connect to the divine."

"What about the communal pressures towards conformity?"

"Now you're getting really nuanced. I don't know how you'd even address that. Yes.

"It's very difficult for certain religious people to see power in something other than religion and God. There are religious people who are able to reconcile this wonderfully. It can be very frightening for religious teenagers who are taught that everything is God and religion to see power in art.

"When I got into politics, I thought there was a weird perception of that, that I was out in the world of shtus (foolishness)."

"Have you spent much time wondering about whether Orthodoxy can be reconciled with Modernity?"

"Yeah. I think about that every day."

"Do you tend to be more pessimistic or optimistic on that question?"

Long pause. "As an idea, I know it can be reconciled. In practice, I *think* it can be reconciled. I just don't see it happening in practical terms."

"How do you reconcile Biblical Criticism with the Orthodox approach to sacred text?"

"Luckily, I don't have to."

"Why not?"

"You mean in my life?"

"No, in your head. The traditional way of studying text in a secular sense is to ask three questions: Who wrote this document? When was it written? For whom was it written? When you apply those tools to the Torah, you get results radically different from the understanding of text in the Jewish tradition. So how do you deal with that?"

Long pause. "You're asking me a question about my personal views. I have writers who express both ideas, who venerate the Bible as literature and those who venerate the Bible as the word of God. Personally, I don't know. I don't know how to answer your question. When I first learned the Bible, I learned it as the word of God. It was only when I got older that I started seeing it as literature. It's like I have two distinct brains. I can see it as both. When I come to a place in my life, which I am coming to whenever, where I feel like I need to reconcile what I want to practice in my daily life and what I believe, I may need to come to terms with this.

"Every time I close a Bible, I kiss it."

"If you were to lead a normatively Orthodox life, could you do a similarly good job as you are doing now?"

"Yes."

"Well, thank you very much."

"You sound exhausted. Did I wear you out? Go get some sleep."

"I didn't get a good night's sleep. I was racking my mind for questions to ask…"

"Arts and culture in Jewish journalism."

"Tossing and turning and crying out to the Hakadosh Baruch Hu…"

"What is Jewish literature?"

"What is tznious? What would the Kotzker Rebbe say?"

"What *would* the Kotzker say?"

33

Ami Eden

July 23, 2004

"When I was a kid, I wanted to become a disco dancer, or president of the United States.

"Both my parents are lawyers. I used to be argumentative. So I guess they figured I'd become a lawyer or a politician. They weren't disappointed when I became a journalist. My mom reads several daily papers. My mom reads all of the *Forward*, even the stuff I don't read. My dad reads it selectively.

"I come from a long line of knowledgeable heretics, Labor Zionists. I went occasionally to a Conservative havurah. I started to move towards Modern Orthodoxy towards the end of college and I finished that move a year after college.

"I had started dating a girl who was Modern Orthodox. It was like a suit I had in the closet that I would put on from time to time. I was always comfortable in the suit and started wearing it more often. I ended up running with it on my own. I ended up marrying the girl [and having three kids]."

"Do you find much support for journalism in the Jewish tradition?"

"I think about that all the time. Am I just engaged in idle gossip? Then I look at the Torah. It exposes all sorts of things that would be considered yellow journalism, all sorts of sexual stuff that we don't even print at the *Forward*. There's a clear message in the Jewish tradition that power is not a shield against criticism. I heard Rabbi Saul Berman say that the Torah gives every detail of what the priests are supposed to do during the sacrifices not because the priests wouldn't know, but to remove all mystique, any sense that the masses would think that the priests are doing something secret and have special power. We are not supposed to be blindly subservient to authorities. They are supposed to be checked and examined."

"Have you ever checked with a rabbi for halakhic guidance on how you should go about reporting a story?"

"No. The only time I did something like that was when I was dealing with a personnel issue."

"Is your journalism and your Orthodoxy separated or integrated?"

"Sometimes it is integrated. I've written columns from my religious perspective. To some degree, it's always helping me frame the variety of questions I'm going to be asking."

"Let's talk about lashon hara that is accurate and true and what is legitimate to put in the newspaper?"

"This is the problem. I'm not a rabbi. I don't think you can justify any article if you simply ask, does this meet the criteria of lashon hara? Truth is not a defense in lashon hara. I believe that you need to have a value that trumps lashon hara, such as the public's need to know and to keep institutions honest.

"There was the head of a seminary [Sheldon Zimmerman at HUC]. Did we want to get into the details of what he did? I was not sure how important the details were. The guy had been severely punished [fired from his job for sexual sins with adults]. Everybody seemed to agree that the Reform movement dealt swiftly and responsibly. He's accepted the punishment. There's no sense that the person who made the complaints is now complaining. Did we need to get to the bottom of what this thing was? I don't think so. From a lashon hara perspective, getting into the sordid details would be crossing the line. What's the justification?"

"The problem by not spelling out what his sexual sins were is that everybody then wonders what were his sexual sins. Now he's in a responsible position somewhere else."

"That's a valid point. I don't think anybody cracked the nut about what he did. It's not like anybody was sitting on a pile of info and didn't publish it. When he got a new position, I said to myself, I didn't think that through. Maybe I need to reevaluate it. Then again, maybe the people who hired him for his new position did due diligence. Then again, that's not my role as a journalist.

"In the Rabbi Baruch Lanner story, the details were important. You had a situation where an entire bureaucracy had spent two decades covering something up. It wasn't like the OU dealt with Baruch Lanner and then we were trying to get into the details for no reason."

"How come *The Jewish Week* broke that story and you didn't?"

"Gary lives in New Jersey where that story happened. He has the persona of being both a journalistic leader and a person in the Modern Orthodox community. If you were a victim, he would be an obvious person to go to. My sense is that he knew about it for a while."

"**Do you have any doubt that you are working for the best Jewish weekly in America?**"

"No. The only reason somebody would pick any other newspaper over the *Forward* would be for the communal focus. I worked at the *Jewish Exponent* (summer of 1997 to summer of 2000) for three years and it became clear to me that the most important thing people wanted from their local Jewish newspaper was to find out who was born, who got Bar Mitzvahed, who got engaged and who got married. I can't give that to them with the *Forward*. I can't even give them the second most important thing—what events are going on at the shul."

"**What stories couldn't you put in the *Exponent*?**"

"You get a good idea of what you are going to be able to handle. I would always pick areas to cover that I would be able to cover legitimately. We would never cover Federation the way the *Forward* covers UJC. Sometimes we could do stories that covered debates over funding issues. If we are able to do those stories, you are very careful to be [he-said, she-said] rather than compelling eye-catching boil-it-down-to-one sensational point to tell the story which is the way *Forward* does it. Definitely the Federation did not get covered as the dominant institution of the community should get covered. They own the paper. You are not going to do any enterprising reporting about the Federation."

"**What about enterprising reporting on the biggest donors?**"

"You are not going to have that though Jonathan Tobin [current editor of the *Exponent*] and his predecessor Buddy Korn established the precedent that the news is not going to be ignored.

[In 1999, Akiba Hebrew Academy in Philadelphia refused a $2 million gift from Raymond and Ruth Perelman rather than rename itself after the donors.]

"We ran all [those] news stories. They were important donors who were very embarrassed. There were people who said we should've ignored that story but we didn't. It was news and we covered it.

"You'd be amazed at what upsets people. It's the most local and most irrelevant things that upset people. I wrote a string of stories about the way Israel was dealing with Ethiopians and whether the JDC (Joint Distribution Committee) was doing enough. There were no complaints. It wasn't seen as stepping on anybody's toes in Philadelphia. But if you do a story on a rabbi in one neighborhood, the question becomes why didn't you do the other rabbi in the other neighborhood? That's what would cause a firestorm.

"Federations are built around the culture of fundraising. Fundraisers have their own way of seeing the world. They think that the donor must always be kept happy. I thought we foisted low expectations on the donor community. I've heard about Federation people calling to apologize to a donor before the donor complained. If there is a general expectation that a newspaper operates like a newspaper and doesn't play favorites, I think donors can be educated to accept a paper like that and not going running and crying to the Federation over whatever problem they have.

"I was sympathetic to the anxieties of the Federation people. Their task is to raise as much money as possible to take care of people with desperate needs. I spent more time thinking, if I run this story in the *Exponent*, and they lose $10,000 because of it, I can talk all I want about journalistic freedom but that's $10,000 of meals for senior citizens that they just lost.

"In reality, there were people who pulled contributions because they didn't like the things we ignored. Buddy and Jonathan said, 'Do your job as a journalist. Everything is on our shoulders.'

"I was at the *Exponent* when [J.J. Goldberg's column was dropped for criticizing Mort Klein, a Philadelphia resident]. It happened in a vacuum between Buddy Korn and Jonathan Tobin. There was no editor. It was the worst thing that happened while I was there. What made it so embarrassing was that we ran the column and then we had to make all these apologies [and discontinue J.J.'s column]. Every paper has to spike a column every once in a while."

We discuss the book, *The New Rabbi*, which we both loved.

"I'm not sure that synagogues should be covered like a regular beat. I believe that we should cover the Federation like it's the Whitehouse. But a synagogue, that's like assigning a writer to a family. I don't think congregations should be covered aggressively step-by-step. Should I write that I know that 15 people in the congregation are unhappy that the rabbi didn't thank that person? If you started covering synagogues like that, you'd destroy them.

"But a book is different. It comes out once. It's not every week. If I was at the *Jewish Exponent* and I was doing that every week to your congregation, I'd destroy it. He was getting cooperation. He told people he was writing a book. I thought it was a pro-rabbi. The rabbi [Perry Rank] who was angry at [Fried], it wasn't the rabbi who looked bad but the board for turning him away because the kipa hung by the side of his head.

"I believe rabbis are public figures. If somebody told me that the rabbi of a congregation was having an affair, I'd be slower to think that was a story we needed to write about as opposed to a rabbi who got up on TV and gave a weekly show on morality.

"I remember once I had to wait a week to write about a major rabbinic firing where they were negotiating a severance. The Federation donors wanted it not to be in the paper until it was settled. That annoyed me as the reporter but the story was in the paper a week later.

"It always happens with the senior rabbis, the congregations want to push them out. If you have a rabbi who's been there 35 years and there starts to be a groundswell against him, do you write it just because five percent of the people start saying he's old and batty?"

"Most Charedi rabbis flee from TV cameras, as opposed to a Shmuley Boteach who embraces them."

"If there was ever a rabbi who would merit a full-blown article about his marriage and love life, it would be Shmuley Boteach. He's putting himself out there as an expert in the way you should do it. If I was the editor of the *Jewish Exponent*, I would never assign a reporter to find out what a regular rabbi's sex life is like."

"How is blogging affecting Jewish journalism, if at all?"

"Right now, not much at all. The bulk of people who read Jewish newspapers I can't imagine are hooked into blogging.

"The creation of the *Forward* had a much bigger impact than blogging. When I was at the *Exponent*, I felt there were many stories I ended up doing because the Lipsky *Forward* did them (maybe a little over the top). It moved the goal posts in what we were allowed to write. The Lipsky *Forward* was constantly trying to stick its thumb in the eye of the organized Jewish community. So when we suddenly did a balanced story about a serious issue, Federation types said, ok, you were fair. It created a range of debate because it was such a counter to the liberal assumptions out there. It covered all Jewish organizations so aggressively, people got used to it. If you are a macher and you read the *Forward*, then you read a real news story in your local paper, then it doesn't seem as jarring. Now you're used to seeing articles having Abe Foxman answering for his actions."

34

Leslie Katz

August 1, 2004

After eight years of writing for the *Jewish Bulletin of Northern California*, Leslie quit in September 1999 to work as a copy editor for TechTV.

"I was starting to feel shackled by Jewish journalism. I felt sometimes like I was writing the same stories over and over again. It was time to branch out. The Jewish community in the Bay Area is vibrant and diverse but small. I knew all the players. I wanted to cover a new world."

"What did you love and what did you hate about your years in Jewish journalism?"

"You get access to interviews you might not get if you were a general assignment reporter in the general press. Yitzhak Rabin (Israel's Defense minister) came through when I'd been at the *Bulletin* a month and I got to interview him. It's being a big fish in a small [pond].

"I loved the sense of connection between the paper and the community. I love that when I go to a Jewish event, people knew who I was and wanted to give their opinions about what they loved and hated about the paper.

"Working for a Jewish paper became a prism through which I explored my own Judaism. I felt like I lived in Israel. I didn't have to make any concerted effort to lead a Jewish life. I was around Jewish people all day long. I was writing and thinking about Jewish subjects. It was only after I left a Jewish paper that I started thinking joining a Jewish synagogue, which I did in 2000 (Conservative)."

"How often did you get to leave the office for your stories?"

"Not often enough. Because we short-staffed, we had to do a lot of our reporting on the phone. You discover things in the field that you can't over the phone. In addition to being a reporter, I was a layout editor, so I was in the office more than other reporters."

"So what did you hate about your time in Jewish journalism?"

"I hated doing stories that felt forced. I hated doing stories about someone just because they were Jewish. Let's say someone was in circus and they were Jewish and we had to find some forced connection between being Jewish and being in the circus. I loved the stories that were implicitly Jewish. About someone exploring Jewish life or doing something Jewish or creating art that had a Jewish motivation or theme vs. someone climbing Mount Everest and happened to be Jewish.

"If you are going to do a story like that, don't force it. Don't say, so how does your being Jewish affect your being a clown?

"Sometimes, someone just being a part of a community is enough to be in the Jewish press. It is a community paper. Like the gay and lesbian press will often write about someone in the community and not necessarily ask them to make the connection. Just, they're one of us, so we're telling you what they're doing.

"There are a lot of politics in the Jewish community and sometimes they can…hinder your feeling of freedom as a journalist. There are people who contribute a lot to the Jewish community and have a certain sway over the editorial content of the Jewish press. Because the Jewish world is small and incestuous, there were times I felt we were shackled. I wish we didn't have to worry so much about making everyone happy. There was a sense that if we had done stories about the far Left in Israel, we should balance it out with a certain number of stories on the far right. Sometimes that informed our sense of what we covered more than it should.

"We had to be careful writing about the Federation. We weren't a total Federation paper but we did get a certain amount of money from them. That's one of the biggest obstacles that stand in the way of some Jewish papers being as vibrant and free-minded as they could be.

"Another obstacle is that the readership tends to be older. They've read their Jewish paper for years and they're resistant to change. I'm concerned that the audience for the Jewish press is petering out. The Jewish press needs to find creative ways to make their papers multimedia, online interactive, and find ways to get young Jews engaged in their Jewish news outlet. I don't see that happening.

"There were times when I felt like I would've liked to have written the story differently. I would've liked to have gone further with it, a little edgier. When I was writing my column, I knew there were things I couldn't write about. I had to be careful. It was a different voice than I had when I wrote for TechTV. It was more of an edgy, youthful, in your face style. I had to tread carefully while writing my column because I knew that kind of voice would not go over well with some readers.

"For TechTV, the audience was broader. We had to be careful [at the *Bulletin*] because we needed to get our funding [from the Federation]. There was care taken to not offend the funders. If someone was a prominent member of the community, involved with the Federation, a respected member, a board member of Federation, we might be careful if that person was getting bad press in the general press. We might tone down our coverage of that. It was viewed that this was the place where they should feel safe from criticism.

"People would often say, 'I'd like to read the story before it goes to press. I'd like you to run the quotes that you use by me.' We had to be pretty stringent [against doing that]. There was a sense that we were their paper and therefore we would adhere to different standards from the regular press."

"If you had been the editor of the *Jewish Bulletin*, how would it have been different?"

"I would've liked to have seen more risks taken. I would've liked to have seen more of an effort made to attract younger readers. To do different kinds of stories. I sometimes felt we did the same stories, only put on different headlines. The column that I ended up writing after I left the paper, I wanted to bring that voice to the paper while I was there and didn't get a chance. It's the personal, human, nitty gritty of being Jewish. I know we have to cover a lot of organizational happenings but I would've upped the amount of average-Jew-doing-this-or-that type of story."

"If you were writing a book about your time in Jewish journalism, it would be called?"

She thinks for a few seconds. "*Jew?* Our joke among the reporters at the *Bulletin* was that because we were always on the lookout for stories, anytime we would come across someone in the world, we would say, 'Jew?'"

35

Robert Cohn

August 3, 2004

"I grew up in St. Louis. At age ten, I put out the *Cohn Times*. It had a circulation of four—my own family. In college, I was editor of *Student Life*, the undergraduate newspaper. I later became editor of my law school paper, *The Writ*.

"I graduated from Washington University with a degree in English in 1961. I got my JD [doctorate in law] in 1964. I subsequently earned additional bachelor degrees in Political Science and Philosophy.

"Out of law school, I worked for five years for a county elected official as a press secretary, speech writer and staff attorney.

"In 1969, I was offered an opportunity to take a job at the *St. Louis Jewish Light* for a couple of years as a stepping stone. Here I am 35 years later.

"I took over July 1, 1969."

"Are you a Federation paper?"

"We are affiliated with our Jewish Federation. From 1947–63, our publication was called the *St. Louis Light*. It was a house organ. It was directly published by the Communications department of the Jewish Federation. It didn't pretend to be anything other than a vehicle to promote the campaign.

"In 1963, some high powered people in the Communications department and in journalism recommended we follow the model in Pittsburgh and Philadelphia in which Jewish Federation papers would have their own autonomous boards. So there would be a layer of authority in between the Federation and the editor. That arrangement was put in place in March of 1963 and we became the *St. Louis Jewish Light*. I don't report to anyone at Federation. My boss is the board at the *St. Louis Jewish Light*."

"What have you loved and what have you hated about your career in Jewish journalism?"

"I've even loved the stuff I've hated. I'll be retiring at the end of this calendar year. What I've loved is to have my words taken seriously. If I had worked at *The New York Times*, I might've been assigned one beat for 35 years. Here I've been able to do editorials, hard news, interviews, reviews of books, plays and films. When people in my generation pass away, and I've known them since high school, I'm able to do a more personal obit.

"When you first start out, you only want to do the glamorous things. You realize after a while that every aspect of your job can be interesting and challenging if you just have the right attitude.

"But obviously bureaucratic pressures, being caught in the middle of things, occasionally being targeted by different groups in the community.... There was a serious challenge in the 1980s over Operation Moses and Operation Solomon. The Ethiopian and Sudanese governments were looking the other way as their Jews were getting out [to Israel]. The Jewish press was warned that if we broke that story, it would stop that immigration. I was president of the American Jewish Press Association. I encouraged my colleagues to respect the request. Unfortunately, a little West Bank newsletter broke the story. That was picked up by Jewish papers in New York and Washington. Then *The New York Times* and *The Wall Street Journal*, which had been respecting the embargo, broke the story and it stopped the immigration for a couple of years.

"I came up with something called Jews Before News. An effort that was successful for two years was blown and people starved to death as a result.

"There were a few in the organization who felt that news was news and we shouldn't be directed by Jewish bureaucracy. While I would normally agree, this was an exception. I was supported in this view by Gary Rosenblatt, certainly one of the more independent-minded editors around."

"Gary seems to view Jewish journalism as another form of Jewish service, such as working at the Federation."

"He's worked on both sides of the aisle. He worked for the *Baltimore Jewish Times*, which was the flagship independent paper. It is owned by the Buerger family. They were successful commercially and [publisher] Charles (Chuck) Buerger gave Gary carte blanche to go where the news was. He did an aggressive investigative report on the Simon Wiesenthal Center that was a finalist for a Pulitzer Prize. He won countless journalism awards. He has the credentials to make those comments."

Robert, who served as president of his Reform temple (Shaare Emeth, the largest synagogue in St. Louis), says he's fulfilled his vision for the paper. "I wanted it to be more of a literary intellectual paper with Op/Ed pieces. I resisted all kinds of pressure not to cover Meir Kahane when he was in town or people on the far Left. I'll be leaving from here to cover a group from the International Solidarity and Stop the Wall movement and a counter-demonstration. We covered an American Nazi party rally and there were a group of communists counter-demonstrating."

"What's unique about the St. Louis Jewish community?"

"That most people grew up in St. Louis. The old cliché is that it is more important where you went to high school in St. Louis than where you went to college. There are about 60,000 Jews living in St. Louis. The majority are natives. There has been an influx of Jews from other parts of the country and from the former Soviet Union. It's a fairly unified community. There's cordiality between the different streams. The Orthodox chief rabbi, Shalom Rifkin, is a kindly person who gets along well with his non-Orthodox colleagues. We don't have a lot of the bitter divisiveness that may characterize other communities. The issues between the old German and Russian populations was pretty resolved by the mid '50s. The *Our Crowd* group that Stephen Birmingham describes set up all the institutions and then you had a later influx like my mom's family from Eastern Europe. There are 22 congregations ranging from Agudath Israel to Jewish Renewal."

"How did you like going to AJPA conferences?"

"I loved it. I have three families. My own immediate family. My staff at the Jewish Light. And all these people you interviewed, particularly Gary Rosenblatt and Marc Klein, are among my best friends. When you've traveled around the world and to Israel 18 times with people like Marc and Gary, you get to be tight with them. I've been to about 30 different countries, including Brazil, South Africa, Egypt, Lebanon, Syria, Jordan, Soviet Union. I was president of the AJPA nine times."

36

Rabbi Shmuley Boteach

August 3, 2004

After hosting his radio show, Shmuley's biking with his kids while talking to me on his cell phone.

"You've had a lot of interaction with journalists over the years. What have you come to love and hate about that interaction?"

Shmuley asks me to repeat the question.

"The love part is the privilege of bringing your message to a wide audience. The hate part is when its a tabloid story or you don't feel you are being treated fairly by a journalist."

"How often has that bad experience happened to you?"

"Thank God, seldomly."

"How many journalists are there that you will not return their calls because you regard them as unethical?"

Shmuley asks me to repeat the question.

"I could count them on one hand."

"What do you love and hate about journalism on American Jewish life?"

"I can barely hear you. Sorry. I'm on a cell phone."

I repeat the question twice.

"I think the quality of American Jewish journalism is very good. I think it's honorable and it is not tabloid."

He talks to his child. "Hold on a second. We'll stop and do that."

He returns to me and then his cell phone loses connection.

A minute later, he calls back. "It focuses on issues. I don't see them muckraking or creating artificial disputes within the community. Some of the Jewish publications are respected well outside of the Jewish community."

"Who do you think is doing the best job?"

"I like *The Jewish Week* in New York. I like the *Forward*. I like the *New Jersey Jewish Standard*, which is the one I read weekly. I think JTA does a very good job. I like *Moment*. Those are the things I read religiously."

"Have you noticed any differences between dealing with journalists from Jewish publications and dealing with journalists from secular publications?"

I hear kids playing in the background.

"Hold on one second, Luke."

"Come on, sweetie.

"Have I noticed a difference? Not really. If anything, Jewish journalists tend to be more serious. You don't have tabloid Jewish journalism."

"Do you feel safer when you are dealing with a journalist from a Jewish publication?"

"No."

"When is it legitimate to report about the private lives of public figures?"

I have to repeat the question three times.

"I guess when it directly impacts on their communities, on their politicians, on the nation."

"Let say someone saw you at a gambling wheel..."

"I can't hear you. What?"

"Let say a journalist saw you at a gambling wheel at Las Vegas or New Jersey or wherever they have those sorts of things and you were sitting there for hours gambling. Would that be a legitimate news story?"

"Me personally?"

"Yeah."

"You want me to deal with hypotheticals?"

"Yeah."

"It's a bit of a strange question. Why is it being personalized?"

"Ok, let's just take a generic Jewish leader."

"Again, I can barely hear you."

"Take a generic Jewish leader. I'm just trying to figure out specifics on when it is appropriate to report on their private lives."

"Hold on one second.

"Chana, come this way!

"Hello?"

"Yes. Take a generic Jewish leader and you see the person is a chronic gambler. Do you report on it? Do you not report on it? What sort of protocols should go through a journalist's head?"

"Luke, it's really breaking up. Repeat the question again. I'm sorry. Can you hear me?"

"I can hear you perfectly fine."

The connection dies on Shmuley's end.

He calls me back. "I don't understand what you are doing here. Who's your publisher?"

"I don't have a publisher for this book yet. The publisher of my first book was Prometheus. I've interviewed every editor of a major Jewish newspaper and about 40 other prominent Jewish journalists."

"I'm not an expert in Jewish journalism. I'm a talk radio host."

"You're the most public figure in [Orthodox] American Jewish life."

"I remember you warmly. I want to help. I'm reluctant to talk about subjects I don't claim expertise in. To call me the most public Jew in American Jewish life is flattering but preposterous. I'm not Steven Spielberg."

"In American religious life…"

"I doubt that."

"I interviewed Ami Eden, the national affairs editor for the *Forward*. Here's a quote he gave me: 'If there was ever a rabbi who would merit a full-blown article about his marriage and love life it would be Shmuley Boteach. He's putting himself out there as an expert in the way you should do it.'"

"Why does it have to be about me? You're not asking about my expertise. That's why I'm asking what is this for and who is this for? You're not asking about my expertise. You keep personalizing it."

"Your expertise is that you have dealt with more journalists writing about you…"

"That has nothing to do with this. You're asking about the fact that I write books on marriage. When you're dealing with editors in the Jewish world, that makes sense, but I am not an editor of any Jewish publication."

"Do you feel that by putting writing such books and putting yourself out there as a public figure, do you fear what that could do to the sacred part of your life?"

"I don't believe in living in fear of anything. My next book is called, *Face Your Fears*. It's about living courageously. I'm proud of my books on marriages and relationships and if I can strengthen people's marriages, I will endeavor to do so."

"Is there any area in reportage on American Jewish life that is missing? Are there aspects to the story that are not being told in its depth and passion?"

Long pause. "The real story of assimilation. Why it is that so many Jews don't find the tradition compelling. What alternatives they're finding and how best to engage the next generation of Jews. I think that people scratch the surface on it."

"Could part of the reason be that there is little compelling journalism on leading a religious Jewish life?"

Shmuley asks me to repeat the question.

"That's possibly one of the answers. I'm doing far more mainstream stuff. I don't think I could speak about that authoritatively. No doubt great journalistic minds should be brought to bear on the great questions of Jewish existence."

"Have you changed in your approach in how you deal with journalists? I'm thinking of your book on heroes and it seemed to mark a change in you."

"That book was a personal statement of my core beliefs that we have to get back to an ideal of heroism of doing right because it's right even when no spotlight shines. I wouldn't think of that book as marking a change in my interactions with journalists. I think that book marked a change in my ideas about celebrity. Before that book, I believed that celebrity could help espouse a positive message. I came to believe that the problem with celebrity was that it would ultimately drown out the message. It would be about the personality rather than about the message.

"These days I'm almost a journalist. I'm a radio host."

"Has it been your experience that journalists are among the most secular groups in America?"

"No."

"Would you still do the Howard Stern Show?"

"It depends on which subject. He's a mixed bag. If it were on a substantive subject, probably. I try not to do non-substantive stuff anyway. If he wanted to talk about facing your fear, yeah, if they invited me on, I probably would do it. He has been very respectful to me in the few times that I was on, respecting me as a rabbi. I didn't feel compromised.

"Howard Stern is Jewish. He's a proud Jew. But he does things that can't be condoned. Particularly the degradation of women, something that I speak out against and write about all the time.

"It's a tough call with Howard Stern. As a person, there's an essential decency to him, which is why he has great popularity. In my interactions with him, I've seen that essential decency. I saw him recently at a birthday party. He came over to me and said hello. He's not one of these arrogant celebrities. There are substantive things that he can represent. He speaks up proudly for Israel."

"How do you reconcile Jewish demands of tzniut (modesty) with publicly speaking about sex and have you changed in this regard?"

"No. I speak about it in a modest way. That's how I reconcile it. I'm not explicit at all. It's an important subject."

"Have you feared the encroachment of the hedonistic secular entertainment world into your life as you have so frequently interacted with it?"

"With the exception of having befriended Michael Jackson, I barely encounter it at all. I'm not part of that world. I lead a simple homely existence. My life revolves around writing, teaching, broadcasting. I'm home almost every night with my kids. While I'm speaking to you, the reason this has not been the easiest conversation is that I am riding bikes with my kids, but I didn't want your call to go unreturned."

"With fame, comes public criticism and ridicule. How has it been for you dealing with your vociferous critics?"

"First, I am not famous. I am known within the Jewish community, but not outside. Yes, I have a lot of critics. I guess everybody wants to be loved but it is more important to do what you believe to be right. I try to be more interested in ethically examining what I stand for than wondering whether I'm pleasing people."

"Do you have a home in Orthodox Judaism?"

"Definitely. A very warm one. I get invited to Orthodox communities around the world all the time. I'd like to believe that people who believe in what I do outstrip critics by orders of magnitude."

"You recently made a sharp attack on Madonna. When do you decide to write about an idea and when to make it personal?"

Fifteen second pause. "I don't often write about celebrities. I write about celebrity culture. With Madonna, it came down to the *New York Post* story…"

Shmuley runs off to look after his kids. He shouts, "Hang on, hang on. Wait, wait, wait.

"Luke, I'm going to have to go soon.

"The story that said she was going to simulate sex with another woman and have Hebrew letters all over her show and to promote kabbalah. The intermixing of kabbalah and publicly simulated sex is not acceptable. I'm glad she's into kabbalah but she should not be a spokesman for it."

37

Evan Gahr

August 3, 2004

"When were you born?"
He chuckles. "I don't want to tell you."
I guess it was around 1966.
"Where did you grow up?"
"New York. Upper East Side."
Evan Gahr was fired from the conservative Hudson Institute in April 2001. Here's the *Washington Jewish Week* May 2001 report by Eric Fingerhut:

> Do conservatives have a speech code? Will they refuse to tell the truth about one of their own if the truth is uncomfortable? Evan Gahr thinks so. Gahr has been fired from his job as a senior fellow at the Hudson Institute, only a few weeks after calling longtime conservative activist Paul Weyrich a "demented anti-Semite" because of an Easter column in which Weyrich blamed Jews for killing Jesus.
>
> Officials at the Hudson Institute angrily deny that Gahr's termination had anything to do with his statements about Weyrich, saying that the think tank does not apply a litmus test to anyone's views. Institute vice president and Washington office director Ken Weinstein said Gahr's termination was an internal personnel matter and that his immediate supervisor found it "impossible" to continue working with him. And the group's president, Herb London, said Gahr has acted in an "unprofessional way" by using curse words in

an interview with the *Washington Post*—words that were not printed, but replaced by "bleep." London also cited Gahr's "bizarre behavior" in a televised debate with conservative writer David Horowitz, in which he used stuffed animals, including a chimp named Louis E. Chimpstein, as props to make some of his arguments.

"The only bizarre behavior is Hudson's apparent willingness to implicitly paint Weyrich as the most righteous gentile since Raoul Wallenberg," said Gahr. "I was the Hudson Institute's golden boy until I publicized the odious words of Paul Weyrich," whom his immediate supervisor, conservative columnist Mona Charen, "considers a friend."

"Is that why after months of praising my work and being asked to write a chapter in her book, she now finds me impossible to work with?" Charen did not return a call seeking comment. Gahr accuses his bosses at the Hudson Institute of "carrying water" for Weyrich, and points out that no other prominent Jewish conservative—or non-Jewish conservative—has sided with Gahr.

London, who said he had written letters to Weyrich and Horowitz stating that Gahr's views were his alone and not the views of the Hudson Institute, said he was "not in a position to defend Weyrich," but he had "never seen any evidence of anti-Semitism" on the part of Weyrich. Meanwhile, Gahr is considering legal action.

"Did you go to private schools?"
"Private. Columbia Prep. Other journalists who graduated were Jeff Toobin, Andrew Rosenthal (son of Abe), Nat Hentoff's daughter, and the avuncular and genial John Podhoretz."
"College?"
"University of Pennsylvania. History major."
"You graduated what year?"
"I don't want to tell you. I like to keep my age a secret."
I bet it was around 1988.
Evan has never married and has no kids.
"Did you read that Mona [Charen] thought I'm gay?"
"Have you ever batted from the other side of the plate?"

"No. I don't mind if she thinks I'm gay so long as she doesn't think I'm a Jewish conservative."

"How were you raised religiously?"

"Shiksadox, meaning don't marry one, but you can violate the other rules. That's unfair to my mother, father and grandmother. They clearly instilled in me an important sense of Jewishness, otherwise I wouldn't be doing some of the things I do."

"How often did you go to synagogue during the year?"

"Just on Rosh Hashanah and Yom Kippur."

"Do you and your parents believe in God?"

"Yes."

Evan's parents are conservative Democrats. "My father still calls feminists 'women's libbers,' even though that slang went out in the 1970s."

"You're a rich kid."

"Everybody at school had money but nobody had the need to flaunt it."

Evan voted for Reagan in 1984 and George Bush in 1988. In 1992, 1996, and 2000, he voted for Ralph Nader. "In some ways I'm conservative. The people I've gone after have defiled conservative values. I go after people on their own conservative nostrums. They say they want public shaming when someone does something wrong. I do my own version of public shaming by humiliating them via mass email and they can't stand it.

"After college, I trained at the *National Catholic Reporter* in Washington D.C. It's a leftist paper based in Kansas City. I was there for six months. Then I went up to John Podhoretz and said that I had gone to the same high school as him. I did one article making fun of all-women health clubs. They're illegal but no one cares. Then he hired me for *Insight* magazine [from August 1991 to January 1995]."

"That's the Moonie funded thing?"

"Yeah, but people say that less and less, especially with *The Washington Times* [also funded by the Unification Church].

"*Insight* was wonderful. I had never been surrounded by so many like-minded people. It was so exciting being around people I had only read about in *The New York Times*. I was ecstatic I didn't even get a bed for six months. I just used this mattress on the floor in Roslyn."

"What was your beat?"

"Liberal bashing. That's what I did for ten years straight until my thought crimes against humanity. I broke the House bank story a month after I was there. Then *Roll Call* stole it. In 1992, I broke my Hillary—PLO story. I reported that when she was at the New World Foundation [leftist], she had funded PLO front groups. I gave it to *The Washington Times*. They did an editorial. Then Seth Lipsky's *Forward* did a story. Then Eric Breindel at the *New York Post* did a big editorial. It meant the whole world to me to pick up the *New York Post* and read that 'Now Evan Gahr at *Insight* magazine reports…'

"After *Insight*, I went to the *New York Post* editorial page to work for Breindel. I wrote editorials and a press column."

"**What work were you best known for at the *New York Post*?**"

"Liberal bashing. Going after Al Sharpton. *The New York Times* for being soft on commies. That kind of thing."

"**How long were you at the *Post*?**"

"Two years. I tell people that I used to work for Eric Breindel and sometimes feel like I still do. I try to emulate him every day. When I did the AFM (Alliance For Marriage) story its supporters being in cahoots with radical Islamic terror groups…

"It took two months from when I reported it in the *Jewish World Review* until when the *Washington Post* picked it up. That was his time span for when he'd do an exclusive editorial before the rest of the media would pick it up. He was brilliant. His articles were pure logic. There was no way you could refute them, which is why people called him names when he said certain groups were soft on communists. His mother and father were Holocaust survivors, plus he had an excellent sense of humor."

"**Do you still have friendly relations with him?**"

"No, he expired in 1998 at the age of 42. Liver problems.

"Scott McConnell came in and bounced me from the *Post*. Then I was freelancing for *The Wall Street Journal*, *The Washington Times*, *National Review*, and *The American Enterprise* magazine.

"In March 2000, I met with William Bennett's then chief of staff Pete Wehner. He told me that Mona Charen was looking someone to help research her new book with the Hudson Institute. I contacted her. She'd already quoted from my articles on Al Sharpton and Hillary and the PLO. Then the guy from *American Enterprise Magazine*, Carl Zinsmeister, more recently known as Carl 'Mona thinks you're a fag' Zinsmeister, or Carl 'Fuck you with your lawsuit, Evan' Zinsmeister, recommended me for a job with her. She asked him if I was gay. To anyone who knows how I dress or what my apartment looks like, that must be very ironic.

"Despite her fears that I swung from the other side of the tree, I got the job."

"Was this an ongoing fear that she had with you?"

"It seemed to be an ongoing obsession. She told me that when she interned at *National Review*, it was all homos. Then Ken Weinstein, the Hudson Institute Washington director asked me if Eric [Breindel] was gay. It's just a form of bigotry that has its parallel in another generation's attitudes towards blacks. They sneer at gays behind their back and in print say they don't want any special privileges for gays. Just no marriage. No special privileges like breathing. It's very ugly despite the humor of Mona thinking I'm gay. She's just a dumb cunt.

"Everybody's curious but in our society, you don't ask something that explicit. First of all, asking me if I were married is illegal under federal law."

"Did she ever catch you in a position where it could've looked like there was some homosexual activity going on?"

"No. Again, it shows what a dumb cunt she is. Because I wasn't married, I was gay. She's supposed to be a big observer of the social scene. As a result of the sexual revolution, men are getting married older. Unlike women, there's no pressure on men to marry. There's no biological clock.

"People find this surprising given how I write or act on the phone, but I'm really kinda shy, or as Eric said, reserved. He had the right word for everything. I started telling some girls I met online that I was gay. That I just wanted to be friends. But it didn't last long because I started asking them what sized dress they are. Then one lie led to another. Then I had to say that I wanted to wear the dress. It just didn't work. But I tried it."

"What age girls are you chatting up?"

"Twenty-something."

"Not like 13?"

"No. Though when she used that analogy, I think these people are the moral equivalent of pedophiles. They see someone who's just lost his job and they know they're doing something horribly wrong.... They're dealing with someone they think is vulnerable and they think they can get away from it, then they get a rude surprise when I embarrass them in front of everyone and don't just wilt in the face of their abuse."

"Can you honestly say that your relationship with Mona Charen was entirely platonic?"

"It was hateful. I find her sheer stupidity combined with banality fascinating. She's a bigger bitch than Lillian Hellman and a much less skillful liar. What does it say about the conservative world that somebody with no particular talent and is utterly pedestrian in every way can get this far and be on TV and all that. It shows that conservatives have affirmative action for women just like liberals have it, just that conservatives don't admit it.

"I sent around these emails. 'Why did you think I was gay? Were you worried I was going to have my way with your dog?' A reference to Rick Santorum. She ignores them for like two years. I figured she would just deny it and then I would leave her alone.

"I say I'm David Brock without the poodle but I don't have a credibility problem.

"She didn't deny it. Then I started just ridiculing her all over New York and Washington. Finally, I call her up. I wanted to ask her something else. About the circumstances of my dismissal. I said I had some questions to ask her. She said, 'I'm not interested in your sexuality. That's not what I want to talk about.' What does that mean? That I think you're a fag but I don't care that you're a fag?

"These people live in the world of ideas. She acts like everything is a *Crossfire*, a *Capitol Gang* show. She was busted. You'd think that she'd say it was a misunderstanding or a joke. That she found out I had lots of girlfriends."

"How long was your telephone conversation with her?"

"It lasted until she had to get on to her broomstick and fly off to another appointment. Less than five minutes. None of these people can stay on the phone with me.

"You know the game 'Beat the Clock?' I'm going to play 'Beat the Jew.' Who can stay on the phone longest with Evan Gahr without yelling, cursing or calling his father."

"Who is Michael Horowitz?"

"Michael has the singular accomplishment in modern Washington of being the only person ever to badger and frighten the father of another player in the political stew."

"What's his day job at Hudson?"

"He saves persecuted Christians around the world but he wasn't too concerned about the Jew around the corner from his office.

"I started working for Hudson in July 2000 in New York. I relocated to D.C. right after Labor Day in September.

"The White House, according to Weyrich's written statement was asking questions about the matter of my employment on May 2nd. I was fired May 4th."

"Why was the White House concerned with you?"

"A press release from the American Jewish Congress linked Paul Weyrich to the White House. They were worried about the political fallout from me calling him an anti-Semite. They called him and asked him to cool it. He said, 'If you can't handle this, how are you going to handle a real controversy?' There were two people to shut up, him and me. They couldn't do it to him because he doesn't get federal contracts.

"On that Tuesday night, Herb London [president of Hudson] swore to the *Forward* that he wasn't going to fire me. Thursday he fired me."

"What is the Hudson Institute?"

"It is a conservative thinktank that has relied on government contracts since its inception, thus the vulnerability to White House pressure.

"Weyrich and I are now pals. He wrote to me right after I was fired and asked to meet with me. He made clear that he regretted the harm he had caused Jews. Then he accepted my invitation to go to the Holocaust Museum and went despite horrible physical pain from having about eight back operations that year. He essentially admitted within six weeks that he had been a demented anti-Semite but the Jews are still defending him.

"I asked [Weyrich that] he get press coverage but he refused. I also asked most every Jew conservative in D.C. to accompany us and the only one who would was Michael Ledeen.

"My transgression here—for which they still abhor me—is saying something that they thought would upset their kosher coalition between neo-cons and the Christian Right, which is pure political expediency and enforced by those such as Bill Kristol, a malevolent liar, who actually, contrary to their supposedly fighting liberal prejudice, have utter contempt for the Christians they embrace as evidenced by Kristol privately telling Marshall Wittmann (senior fellow at Hudson) and Ken Weinstein that [Weyrich's] remarks were a shocking outburst of bigotry then lying to the *Washington Post* and saying it was no big deal.

"Then you have those with condescending attitudes such as Michael Horowitz, who told Marshall Wittman when he was saying Pat Robertson is anti-Semitic that these people—Christians—are 'the salt of the Earth.'

"What a fool, sounds like an earlier era of condescending liberal saying 'the negroes are gentle people.' Salt of the Earth as if they all plow their fields with the churches in the yonder.

"I asked Kristol and Horowitz repeatedly if the Jews killed Christ. They wouldn't answer. Very condescending. They think Christians would be offended by what they believe (no) but the reality is Christians would understand that Jews don't believe that otherwise they would be Christians, duh.

"I was a columnist for David Horowitz's FrontPagemag.com. I was busting on assorted black people, much to his delight. I originally did an article about Weyrich and submitted it to FrontPage. He spiked it. I then gave it to *The American Spectator*. They used it. I then sent it to the *Washington Post*. Then they called me. I described what had happened with Horowitz. They wrote an article that Horowitz has spiked it. So for all this yelping that Horowitz was mad at me for being unfair to Weyrich, the reality is just that he was furious I had told the *Washington Post*. The issue was him, not Weyrich.

"Did I send you the thing about [a prominent conservative] who doesn't wash his hands when he takes a piss? I know everything from their bathroom habits to their lying to the *Washington Post*. That's why they scream and curse and call me crazy. They can't engage my arguments."

Linda Chavez emails August 3: "Evan, Does it occur to you that your obsessive behavior might be responsible for your being 'blacklisted'? You send out weird email messages to people, harass them on the phone, and then accuse people of blacklisting you. You need help."

"It's quite fascinating that all my mental problems went unnoticed when I was going after feminists, fags and uppity negroes for ten years. I once spent two straight days in the *Yale Daily News* building going through every single issue from Hillary's Yale Law School days to look for incriminating material. For that I was a tenacious reporter.

"Notice that her email contains—to use an Eric expression—assertions not arguments. She doesn't explain why I'm not well and what the specific problem is.

"Her husband Chris Gersten is assistant secretary for Health and Human Services. In the beginning, she had been supportive. After the White House [got Evan fired], she explained she wouldn't say anything bad about Hudson. I kept asking her, did the White House say anything about me? She called me delusional."

"Have you ever dated a black girl?"

"Yeah. I went to the *Washington Times* party in 1994 with this black girl. There was no racial tension except from other black women who didn't like her going with a white guy. With two notable exceptions, I've never heard any derogatory or sneering attitudes towards blacks in conservative circles. It's just towards gays. It probably was towards blacks earlier.

"One was *New York Post* editor Bob McManus. He used to call this self-help group 100 Black Men '100 Black Men With Their Parole Officer.' There are always little truths in humor. I do think that Jill [Abramson] is cute and soft and fluffy.

"Someone at *Insight* magazine [Charlotte Hays] would always make racist remarks to another Southerner, Steve Goode, thinking he would appreciate them. He found it disgusting and shocking."

"Father Richard John Neuhaus. Do you have a relationship with him?"

"I did until I went after him on the AFM story. He was cool. He was the only one who wouldn't hang up on me. I could ask him any question I wanted. On the first Muslim one, he talked to me. He said it was just the nature of alliances. But this time he wouldn't talk to me. It was post 9/11. It was more sensitive. I'm going to do more satirical calls. I'm going to call him and he's going to say, 'Who's this?' And I'll say, 'It's Pope John Paul II. I'm calling to confess for lying about Jews.'"

"Have you considered Scientology?"

"No, I'm Jewish, and this has made me a more serious Jew. The religion is congruent with me intellectually. I call myself a Jewish journalist. Actions matter more than thoughts. I've never done journalism reading minds. I've stuck to the written records."

"Why do you think there are so many Jews in journalism?"

"There are Jews in everything. Somebody at Columbia Prep said Jews have an elitist quality. My father said, that's because we're the best."

"Is Ann Coulter a slut?"

"It's on my Web site that she did two guys in one night when she was out in California talking about Clinton's moral depravity. I don't believe in the concept of slut.

"Ann blocked my emails right after I asked her about David Brock's charge in his book *Blinded by the Right* that she indulged anti-Semitism.

"Conservatives always talk about promiscuous homos? But they are silent on promiscuous 'breeders' just shows this argument and others is a proxy for bigotry. So I decided to 'out' promiscuous heterosexuals."

"Lawrence Kaplan?"

"Lawrence 'the girl' Kaplan. He's now a senior fellow at the Hudson Institute. I asked him about the circumstances of my dismissal. Conservatives are usually informed but there was a big gap in their reading habits in mid 2001. They all missed 30 publications who did articles about this. They don't know anything about it. He said he didn't know anything about it. He then provided my contacts to someone at Hudson who then gave them to Hudson's lawyer (Bob Brame) who favors capital punishment for homosexuals caught in the act. He was long tied to a Christian reconstructionist group (American Vision) who favored just that."

"What do you think should be the punishment for homosexuals caught in the act?"

"They should have to look at naked pictures on Mona Charen.

"That's the one topic my views have changed post-Weyrich. I used to be very anti-gay. Marty Peretz (publisher of *The New Republic*) told me not to be a right-wing gay basher. Then I learned the hard way that the real abomination before God is not at DuPont Circle (largely gay section of D.C.) but a few blocks south, colluding with Christian anti-Semitism and radical Islam. All the lies, and mean-spiritedness that I associated with the Left is crystallized in Jewish conservatives attitudes towards gays."

"Sounds like you were naive thinking that conservatives would be better than liberals."

"Yeah, I was naive in thinking that dishonesty was limited to one part of the political spectrum. I saw the Left as the repository of lies and intolerance. For a while, it was. In the 1970s, if you were a black conservative like Thomas Sowell, you were treated to real abuse. Now you can be a black conservative who has no talent like Armstrong Williams and you can get your own TV and radio show.

"The stated values of conservatives are good ones but they're not applied consistently. They're always yelping about how the truth is under assault from feminists and Afro-centrists on college campuses. Fine. The truth is under assault from the Vatican for lying in their document, 'We Remember.' It should be called, 'We Forgot.' About the history of anti-Semitism. It's a bigger lie than Clinton ever told. The cover-up is the same as what the Left would do with the Soviet Union and Alger Hiss."

"When did you become a registered Democrat?"

"I've always been a Democrat. My father told me to be a Democrat so you could have an effect on the elections. There were no Republicans elected in New York. I'm nostalgic for the traditional Democratic party."

"Marty Peretz?"

"He has been a mentor since 1992. Nobody knew I was his biggest fag protege since Andrew Sullivan. He recommended me for numerous jobs. He called Conrad Black on my behalf. Then I discovered that *The New Republic* was part and parcel of this whole cover-up.

"Right after I was fired, Franklin Foer knew I was fired. He wrote an article glorifying the Hudson Institute, Marshall Wittman, and Bill Kristol as defending free expression against conservative intolerance when they had just enforced the prime speech code of the Jewish Right, which is no criticism of the Christian Right. Until I spoke out, there had not been a single instance of one Jewish conservative or neo-conservative denouncing a member of the Christian Right as an anti-Semite or denounced their language as anti-Semitic. How can you say Kristol is an iconoclast if Kristol won't condemn Weyrich?

"Franklin Foer likes to show he's so hip. That he's sympathetic yet critical of conservatives. He wrote that after Pat Robertson made some anti-Semitic remarks in 1992, Bill Kristol and John Podhoretz jumped to his defense. First, the anti-Semitic remarks were in 1991. Second, there's nothing in the database about either Kristol or John Podhoretz jumping to his defense. Kristol was at the White House then as Dan Quayle's chief of staff. It's entirely counterintuitive that he would've been speaking out on his own. If he did, it would've been all over the news. John Podhoretz didn't do it either. Franklin Foer has a problematic relationship with the facts, as Eric Breindel would say. If Foer is making things up about this, does he do it on other cases?"

"How did all this affect your relationship with Marty Peretz?"

"I haven't talked to him since [2001]. I don't know what to think. I'd like to think he's better than all these people. It must be a painful for him that his magazine became an adjunct to the only anti-Semitic fascist purge in modern Washington."

"You are calling what happened to you an anti-Semitic fascist purge?"

"Yeah. It had the power of the government."

"*The New Republic* has declined since Michael Kinsley left."

"The cliché is that journalism is the rough draft of history. *The New Republic* reads like the rough draft of a masters thesis. Every article is—conservatives are right to criticize liberals but conservatives are wrong.... There are 300 million people in the US but only the twelve boys of *The New Republic* know how it really is. Peter Beinart is a partisan putz. They always have to show that liberals and conservatives are both wrong and only they know how it is. In the last election, Peter wrote about conservatives yelping that the Democratic party has a quota system. Then he said, yeah, but Republicans have their own quota system. He quoted some obscure provision of Republican delegate selection to make his point. Fine, it's probably there, but anybody who knows this issue knows that Democrats have a notorious quota system dating back to

1972. It's nothing compared to the Republicans. When he quotes it to show that he's smarter than everybody, he's showing his own ignorance. I just happen to know this issue real well. I wonder if he does this with other issues."

"**Leon Wieseltier.**"

"He knew all about me from breaking the Hillary—PLO story and for working for Eric but I never talked to him until that fateful night when he accused me of shitting up his magazine. I called him and said, 'Hi, this is Evan Gahr.' He said, 'Evan, I'm not talking to you.' He hung up. I called ten minutes later. I said, 'Why can't you stay on the phone with me?' He said, 'Oh Evan, you've caused a lot of shit at my magazine. Don't ever call me again. Do I make myself clear?' Then he hung up the phone. Big bad Jew. He doesn't scare me.

"These people don't impress me. *The New York Times* impresses me. *The New York Times* are serious journalists. Leon has a PhD in Jewish medieval studies. He made Cornell West his personal negro punching bag. They condemned Cornell West for speaking at a function where there was Farrakhan literature. This is the magazine, by virtue of Lawrence 'the girl' Kaplan, now associated with an organization that purged someone for denouncing anti-Semitism. Cornell West doesn't have that to answer for. They ignored the AFM—Islam terrorism story, even though Peter and Leon's rabbi is Barry Freundel, who was a leader of the AFM coalition. The rabbi won't talk to me.

"In an article on Eric Breindel, Marty said he relished a good fight. So do I, but nobody will stay on the phone with me. The only people who will stay on the phone with me is the so-called PC intolerant *New York Times* because they've done nothing wrong.

"Jonathan Chait writes about the Iraq war yet he can't even stay on the phone with me? He has to use the office manager to intercept his calls? This is the person who has to make sure no one takes too many AA batteries. Now she's doing double-duty resistance.

"Lawrence 'the girl' Kaplan writes about foreign affairs but he can't give out his fax number."

"**Have you threatened physical violence on these people?**"

"Never.

"I'm a threat to their status, stature and prestige because I tell the truth about them.

"Leon Kass is at AEI (American Enterprise Institute) now. I tried to interview him for the *Washington Jewish Week*. I asked him about the AEI purge. I was blacklisted by the magazine, barred from the facilities and lost my on-line column.

"Like everyone else, Kass didn't read for those few months and missed it in those 30 publications. Then I asked him more questions and he wouldn't answer. If you can't talk about a quasi-anti-Semitic purge by his own organization, why should anyone take him seriously on these big lofty moral issues about stem cells?"

"Do you read the *Forward*?"

"Yeah. J.J. is a first-rate journalist. He's the only one who followed up on my Holocaust Museum visit with Weyrich."

"Any other Jewish papers that you read?"

"No."

"Do you have any prominent Conservative literati who've remained your friends?"

"I've been blacklisted by the entire conservative establishment with the notable exceptions of *The Washington Times* and *The Wall Street Journal* editorial page."

"What have you been doing for a living the past couple of years?"

"I don't want to answer that question.

"I've been selling.... Oh, I was going to make a Mona Charen joke but it wasn't a good one. All this humor takes a lot of thought."

"Have you spent time with David Brock?"

"We had lunch in Georgetown. We'd had similar experiences. He said that what happened to me was inevitable. It would've happened without Weyrich, which is probably true. It could've happened over the Pope Pious or Mel Gibson controversy."

"What did you think of the movie *The Passion of the Christ*?"

"I'm waiting to see it with Jill Abramson [managing editor of *The New York Times*].

"She answers her own phone. But all the boys at *The New Republic* are so precious, they need all their calls screened.

"It started off as a joke. I started flirting with her in emails, saying I'd burned all my sources at *The New York Times*. Can you be my new source? Can you be my Deep Throat?"

How could any woman not go for an approach like that?

"How did she react?"

"I haven't heard back from her but other people find it funny.

"Tom Friedman late last year smacked a reader after a speech. So I called her. 'Jill, does *The New York Times* have a policy on columnists smacking readers?' She said, you'll have to ask Gail Collins [head of the editorial pages]. 'I did. She wouldn't talk to me. I'm asking you.' She said, 'It's not my department.' I said, 'Yeah, but it's your paper. What is your personal view?' She said in this cute girly sing-songy voice, 'My personal view is not relevant.' Then I started to say, 'Is that like abortion? You are personally opposed to columnists smacking readers but you don't want to impose your views?' By that time, she had hung up on me. I was vanquished. Jill, I was really getting into it and then you stopped. It's not fair. Come back."

"Do you think she will come to her senses one day?"

"What do you mean come to her senses?"

"About what a great guy you are and come see *The Passion of the Christ* with you?"

"I have this whole pretend relationship with her. We've already seen *The Passion of the Christ*. Next it's going to be *Summer of '42*.

"Then I called Andrew Rosenthal [Deputy Editorial Page Editor] and asked him, 'Does *The New York Times* have a policy about columnists smacking readers?' He said, 'You're postulating a series of facts that I am not sure are correct.' That's *The New York Times* crystallized into one sentence. We went back and forth. I wrote up the dialogue. Evan Gahr, insult thinly designed as question. Andrew Rosenthal, right back at you. Evan almost yelling. Then he says, call me at work. I said, this is at work. He said, I gotta go. Good-bye.

"Then I called him ten minutes later. 'Hey Andrew, did your father have a policy on columnists smacking readers? I thought he'd hang up but he just stayed on the phone. We went back and forth. He goes, I've got a paper to put out. Call me tomorrow. Good-bye.

"That's how a man acts on the phone. Jill acted like a soft and fluffy girl. If these Jewish conservatives can't stay on the phone like a man, they should at least hang up like a lady.

"That took slicing my head to get it exactly right. I've got to write it down.

"These Jewish conservatives won't answer their phone. I call up and ask for a fax number, and they hang up. I did an experiment. I called up *The New York Times* editorial page asking for their fax number. She goes, oh, which one? There are two different ones. There was no intellectual fatwa leveled against me. Jill was right. It [Tom Friedman smacking a reader] was just a silly and goofy thing. They had done nothing wrong."

"Where do you want to go from here?"

"I'm working on a book about the anti-Semitism in all this."

"How clued in are you to Jewish life?"

"I got a little more religious. I started to keep kosher most of the time. I started to go to synagogue more often although I stopped."

"Why did you stop?"

"Because all the girls disappeared from the synagogue."

"Are you a womanizer?"

"No. I'm too honest to be a womanizer. Girls always say, 'You're so smart and funny. You can't really be this conservative.' Yes I am. And I write them a 1500-word essay about the evils of feminism. Then I get negated when I tell them my true feelings about abortion."

"Do you think abortion is murder?"

"Ask Leon Kass. He's the great moralist.

"These people live in their own worlds. They can't differentiate between TV and reality. That is not the question up for debate. The question is, since it is legal under Roe v. Wage, should there be restrictions on it?"

"Have you ever encouraged a woman to abort your child?"

Evan laughs. "No. I don't think this sort of stuff should be used to evaluate someone's ideas."

"Have you ever lived with a woman?"

"No, that's bad. Conservative ideals are still good. Studies have shown that people who do that have a higher divorce rate."

"Do you believe in waiting until marriage before having sex?"

"What's good for my penis is not necessarily good for society. Things worked much better when there was that kind of social pressure. That's why people got married quickly. Now people can just fuck indefinitely. That's why 'relationships' go on and then implode. Feminism, for the most part, has been a disaster for women.

"This has made me a better journalist by helping me to look at the Right more critically. For instance, Bork wasn't borked. It's true that the People for the American Way commercial with Gregory Peck was sleazy, but the reason he went down to defeat was what was depicted accurately. Namely, his record opposed to basic civil rights. They went after him, not for abortion, but for being against birth control."

"How do you feel about rubbers?"

"Do you know Jay Lefkowitz (White House Political Director)? He worked for Bill Kristol at the first Bush White House. He worked for Tim Goeglein when Tim was making phone calls about me and Marshall Wittman. Jay lied to me. He knew nothing about my dismissal. He says he hardly ever talks to Michael Horowitz (his cousin) at Hudson, the guy who harassed my father. I used to see Michael on the phone with Jay all the time.

"Jay's wife Elena Neuman (Neuman is a pen name, her real last name is Lefkowitz) worked at *Insight* magazine (getting the job through a connection of his), she got pregnant. She told us the whole story about how Jay came back from the convention in 1992 and took her au natural. These are the people who believe in modesty telling us about Jay's preferences. She also told us how she did David Segal, who's now at the *Washington Post*, before she was married. How she lost her virginity the first week of college when she smoked pot at the same time. I'm going to out her. I'm going to out all the heterosexuals. Show that the lifestyle they live is depraved and perverted because they try to pass it off as normal.

"When Elena and Jay were dating, her mother and father got her her own apartment on the East Side to spend time with Jay. I bet they did more there than light Shabbos candles."

"Have you given up shiksas?"

"No. The other fascinating part of this story is how Weyrich and I became such close friends. He's been providing me spiritual counseling and practical counseling."

"Has he brought you to Jesus?"

"No. If this were a movie, that would've happened. I told him, I found Jesus. He's wonderful but he's yours. I don't want him. He's made me a more serious Jew. He talks about things in Christian terms that I then translate into Jewish terms. We've started calling each other brother.

"Do you and Weyrich call each other nigger? Or aren't you close enough yet?"

"Funny. No, we don't. But the more relevant questions is whether Karl Rove calls Linda Chavez his bitch."

"A friend emails me: 'Good Evan Gahr interview but he sounds like less than a delightful character. Could be me, but I don't think he likes women very much.'"

"No, I like women a lot. Girls are soft and fluffy. Last time I was in D.C., all my friends were girls."

"Why didn't you just lick your wounds and go on to something else after the firing? Did you feel like your whole conservative schtettle ejected you?"

"The dismissal was not some little internecine squabble in the conservative backyard over Jews and chimps. It was the only anti-Semitic fascist purge in modern Washington.

"Everybody says at first, yeah, the White House gets people fired all the time. Do they? When was the last time they got anybody outside government fired? Travelgate was their own employees and that was a ruckus."

38

Debra Rubin

August 4, 2004

Debra edits *Washington Jewish Week* (12,000 circulation).

"I graduated [Rutgers] in 1980. I got a job at what is now known as the *New Jersey Jewish News* where I stayed for 18 years until August 1999 [when] I became editor of the *Washington Jewish Week*. It was time for me to do something else and I liked the opportunity of working at an independent paper rather than a Federation-owned paper."

"Is there a noticeable difference in freedom?"

"Yes. You don't have an executive director looking at articles pre-publication. You don't have the kind of control that can be exerted by a Federation."

"I would bet that much of the censorship was implicit?"

"Different executive directors would handle it in different ways. Some would tell you outright that 'I don't want something in the paper.' Others would ask for changes, to put a quote in a different place, to put a more important person higher up in a story."

"Did that drive you crazy?"

"Yes."

"What do you love and hate about working in Jewish journalism?"

"I love the opportunities, variety, that I have been able to learn so much about the Jewish community and Judaism and been exposed to so many different types of Jews.

"I hate the lack of resources. Sometimes people in the community would rather not see a Jewish newspaper be a newspaper. Why is it that when there's a scandal, someone will be more likely to talk to the secular newspaper than the Jewish newspaper?"

"What's the median age of your readership?"

"About 60."

"Would you like to lower that?"

"Of course I'd like to lower that. What paper wouldn't? We're trying to do a larger variety of profiles. We've instituted a column called Capitol Shmoozing. We have a rotation of four columnists in their 20s to 40s. We're trying to do articles that may appeal to people in different ways. For example, in the past year, we did a feature about single women who, by choice, have become mothers."

"Gary Rosenblatt views Jewish journalism as another form of Jewish communal service, such as working at a Federation."

"When I worked in New Jersey and I was considered a communal worker, I always balked at that description."

"When was the last time you got excited about an article you read on American Jewish life?"

"I can't think of anything in particular. I'm not looking at it the way you said. I'm looking to see what stories are other papers doing, whether we could do a similar story. How did they handle something we already did. What kind of columns are they running."

"How often do you get caught up in the pleasure of reading an article on American Jewish life?"

"Occasionally, I say to myself, I have to take this home and read it. And end up not doing that because I have a pile of other things to read at home. Once a week or so I'll read through the whole thing.

"Maybe there is something about a publication not being a community publication that makes people feel more anonymous. One of our greatest difficulties has been finding people willing to talk. Maybe it's part of community journalism. I will be introduced to somebody as the editor of *Washington Jewish Week* and the person will say, 'Don't quote me.'"

"Did that also happen at the *New Jersey Jewish News*?"

"I don't recall that happening much."

"Because they knew they were safe."

"I don't know."

"The more scared people are, the more respect it shows for your publication."

"We'll start asking questions to see if there's really a story, and we'll get accused of digging for dirt."

"As though that's a bad thing."

"We have people who are still holding a grudge over a series of articles (on a kosher Chinese restaurant) that were done in the early 1990s, four editors ago. It doesn't matter that it is new management and an entirely new editorial staff."

Debra was president of the AJPA from 1995–98.

"Are AJPA conferences hard-drinking occasions?"

"No. I wouldn't know from such things. I'm not a drinker, but I've never come across anyone who's been hard drinking at one of these conferences."

"Have you seen anyone light up a joint?"

"No."

"Snort a line?"

"No."

"Just imagine you look up and there's Gary Rosenblatt snorting a line."

"You're stretching. I'm one of the boring interviews. You're trying to find something…"

"I want to hear, 'Gary Rosenblatt was snorting a line of coke with me at the AJPA conference.'"

"Absolutely not."

39

Charles Fenyvesi

August 5, 2004

"I was born in 1937. During the Shoah, I was in Budapest under another name. I hid in a place maintained by a Lutheran pastor, a friend of one of my uncles. He had these houses for Jewish children and their mothers or other relatives. He maintained 34. My parents survived but most of my extended family did not.

"I came to the United States in 1956 after the October revolution in Hungary. I got my BA from Harvard in Social Relations.

"Since the age of six, I'd wanted to become a journalist. Before I learned to read and write. I've never had any other job (aside from two years on a Fullbright fellowship where I taught philosophy in India). I've been a journalist since 1963. I started out at Foreign News Service in New York (it no longer exists). I came to Washington in 1966 and joined *Near East Report*, a newsletter on the Middle East (and unofficial outlet for AIPAC). I became associate editor. Then, for five years, I became the editor of *National Jewish Monthly*, now called *International Jewish Monthly of Bnai Brith*.

"I did freelance work for *The New Republic* and *The New York Times* and I was the Washington correspondent of *The Jerusalem Post* and *Ha'aretz* and the Jerusalem radio station Kol Yisrael. I went to the *Washington Post* full-time in 1980 for two-and-a-half years. I wrote a gardening column for them for 19 years. They retired me. The *Post* does not like people to stick around if you get to be 65.

"The *Washington Jewish Week* was acquired by its printer Dr. Leonard Kapiloff. He was looking for an [editor]. He made me an offer that was difficult to refuse. It was much more than I was making at the *Post*. I told him right away that I didn't want the job. He made it a paying proposition. He also said he would not interfere with editorial content. He was strictly a publisher. He loved Jewish journalism. He loved Judaism. This would be his contribution to the Jewish culture of the United States. Eventually, I fell for it [1983–85]. It was a mistake."

"**What was your part in the Operation Moses story [a scoop published in** *Washington Jewish Week* **in November of 1984] first?**"

"The story was brought in by Michael Berenbaum, who was then the book editor. I thought it was a good story. I discussed it with a number of people, including some Israeli officials who didn't think it was a good idea to publish it, but they never used the argument of pikuah nefesh. We ran it. It was cited by *The New York Times*. The story blew open.

"Having been a refugee myself, and knowing how insensitive governments are about refugees, that refugees can be shoved aside, put in a box, and nobody needs to hear about them, I thought that sooner or later, this story has got to come out. In retrospective, I don't think it was all that wise, but somebody would've used the story. It was a matter of days, not weeks, before it blew open. That's the nature of a large-scale immigration. You just can't hide it.

"UJA was campaigning, raising money. They had ads in the paper showing Ethiopian Jews. They didn't identify where the immigration came from in the paper, but they did say in public. I had nothing to do with the machinations of the Israeli government. Since then I've heard that they weren't all that displeased with the story coming out, because eventually the government thought there were too many Ethiopians coming to Israel."

"**Do you regret running the story?**"

"Yeah, I guess I do, in retrospect."

"**Do you think that Jews in Ethiopia died as a result of that story?**"

"I don't think so. There was no mention of lives being lost."

"**No mention by who?**"

"By, say, Israeli officials."

"**The Israeli official [Yehuda Dominitz] in charge of it didn't want Ethiopian Jews in the first place.**"

"I think that was part of it."

Edward Alexander wrote in *Commentary* magazine July 1985:

> Official secrecy about Israel's program to rescue thousands of Ethiopian Jews and bring them from famine-ravaged Ethiopia to the homeland obtained until 2 January 1985, when Yehuda Dominitz, director general of the Immigration Department of the Jewish Agency, told the settlers' newspaper *Nekuda* that "a majority" of the Ethiopian Jews were now in Israel. On 3 January the government reluctantly acknowledged that "more than 10,000" of the Beta-Yisrael have been brought to Israel during the last few years. Although Israel's program of rescue had been an open secret in certain circles before January, and Arye Dulzin, Jewish Agency executive chairman, had all but revealed it in a statement to the press in early December of 1984, the American and Israeli press had, in general, showed rare and admirable self-restraint in withholding the story, and—as it turned out—for good reason. As soon as Dominitz and then Shimon Peres acknowledged the truth of these rumors, Operation Moses was stopped—by an embarrassed Sudanese government.
>
> Dominitz was suspended from his duties by his supervisor in the Immigration Department, Haim Aharon. His claim that he had granted the interview to *Nekuda* on condition that it not be printed was greeted with skepticism, especially among those who recalled that back in 1975 Dominitz had said: "Take a Falasha out of his village, it's like taking a fish out of water...... I'm not in favor of bringing them."

According to the Israel Association for Ethiopian Jews:

> News leaks ended Operation Moses prematurely, as Arab nations pressured the Sudanese government to disallow Ethiopian Jews to cross Sudanese territory. About 1,000 Jews were left behind in Sudan, and tens of thousands more remained in Ethiopia. Babu Yakov, a community leader summed up the situation in saying that many of those left behind were the ones unable to make the dangerous trek across Sudan—women, children and the elderly. He continued, "Those least capable of defending themselves are now facing

their enemies." Approximately 4,000 Ethiopian Jews died on the overland, on-foot journey through Sudan.

"Was it your decision to run that story?"

"It was a collegiate decision, but I guess if I had said no, we wouldn't have run it.

"Within a week [of being fired by Dr. Kapiloff], I went to *US News* under the new editor Shelby Coffey, who I worked under at the *Washington Post*. He was the most talented editor I've ever met. He was the creator of the section called Style. It was new to journalism. He was groomed to succeed Ben Bradlee [as editor of the *Post*]. Mort Zuckerman had just bought *US News*. He wanted the best editor with the best manners. He wanted to take away somebody who was groomed to become the *Washington Post* editor.

"Shelby thought of me. He wanted to redo the magazine as I had wanted to redo the *Washington Jewish Week*.

"I was at *US News* for 12 years. Within a year, I became editor of a very important page called Washington Whispers. It was almost the front page of the magazine, which was not very good. It offered inside information.

"I had a few good scoops. I enjoyed the chase. People who had something to say, whistleblowers and otherwise, got in the habit of calling me because they knew I do not distort what's given to me. I am a plain old-fashioned reporter.

"We had advance on the Romanian revolution of 1989. That was a real coup. In the beginning of November, I had somebody tell me that the revolution would happen before the end of the year. Then I got another source. We had a strict two-source rule.

"In the grand perspective, these things are small. But we got them first. After we got them first, you can forget about them. The finest hour of journalism is an hour, and after that, it's gone."

"Who were the biggest Jewish bullies you had to deal with?"

"Arthur Goldberg, the former US Supreme Court justice and UN ambassador. He had a most distinguished career (as Secretary of Labor and shaper of the UN resolution after the Six Day War) and was an absolute sonofabitch. When I was editor of *Washington Jewish Week*, he said he'd run me out of the community. My name will be mud. Nobody will hire me.

"One of the things about American Jewish papers, is that people like Arthur Goldberg think it really doesn't matter. He can say whatever he likes.

He can threaten me and I have to go along or I'll be fired. But he couldn't have me fired.

"Arthur was the worst example, not Malcolm. Hoenlein has an abrasive aggressive manner. His threats were more subtle. He's snakelike. I never felt like I was being targeted or that I should be worried about it.

"My *Washington Post* affiliation helped me. These guys were never sure that I would stay in Jewish journalism. Many of these guys would say, 'How come you are in Jewish journalism? How come you're not at the *Post*? Aren't you happy that you left [Jewish journalism]?

"Some Jewish leaders said to me pointblank—how long are you there for? When are you going back to 'regular journalism?' Or 'mainstream journalism' was a more polite way of putting it."

"They meant real journalism."

"Yes, real journalism was what they meant. I said, 'I'm doing a story. We can discuss my career, the two of us, one of these days, but I'm interested in what you have to say about this.' I'm a polite person. I seldom strike back."

"You're saying that the Jewish elite view Jewish journalism as the retarded stepchild of real journalism."

"Yeah. They believe that you are in their pocket. Many Israeli politicians feel the same way. That you [should] do as told. They are surprised when these things don't work out that way."

"They have abundant reason to feel that way."

"Yes. I fear that is still the case. When I was in Jewish journalism, you were essentially the messenger. You were at best a chronicler. 'I tell you what you write.' The word *maskir* in the Bible means chronicler. In today's Hebrew, the word means secretary. It's a subordinate position to the leadership and Jewish interests as defined by the leadership. You have to do their bidding."

"Were you happier working for Jewish publications or secular publications?"

"I had a tough job at *Washington Jewish Week* because my publisher turned out to be an unbalanced person. On Mondays and Wednesdays, he was left-wing in Israeli politics. On Tuesdays and Thursdays, he was right-wing. Especially the extreme. One day he'd think the settlers were the heroes of our day. Another day, he thought they should be run out of Israel. Running a story for or against the settlers would normally only agree with him once a week. Otherwise, it would be, 'How could you run that story?'

"He was a personality on the edge. I couldn't completely ignore him. He never apologized. He was good at praising certain articles. One week, he'd say a certain article was good. The next week he'd say it was terrible. The same article. He had friends who supported him and watched what you were doing. He had a nasty way of doing business."

"When I was with the *Post* and *US News*, there were other pressures. It was difficult to get story ideas past management. You had to fight through a phalanx of editors to get your ideas approved. When you work for a magazine, you have 25 competing reporters coming up with stories. You really have to hustle, which I do not like."

We talk about Raoul Wallenberg, a Swedish diplomat who saved the lives of thousands of Jews during World War II and then either died in Soviet captivity in 1947 or languished for decades in Soviet prisons until he lost his mind.

"People accused me of besmirching Wallenberg's name because I called him an American spy. The word 'spy' for a CIA asset was irresistible and my idiotic editor insisted on it. It was WW II. The guy was helping the Allies achieve victory over the Nazis. That would never occur to me that that was besmirching someone's name.

"I didn't go into the [American government] archives with the notion that I was going to prove he was an American spy. I found the material.

"Did I write my story about the fall of the Romanian regime with the idea that I would save Ceausescu or kill Ceausescu? No. It was a story that came to me."

"What do you think happened to Raoul Wallenberg?"
"That's a terrible story. I think Wallenberg survived until the 1990s."
"In Soviet prisons?"
"Yes."
"Even after the fall of the Soviet empire?"
"Yep."
"He died of old age?"
"We don't know. He would be 92. Yesterday was his birthday.

"In 1995, he no longer knew who he was because of all the drugs and all the treatments given to him by the KGB.

"The man who was convinced that Wallenberg was alive [in 1995] was his best friend from Budapest Per Anger (a modest man). Per started out giving passes to Jews, a piece of paper that said this person was connected with the kingdom of Sweden. He gave about 100 or so to people who had something to do with Sweden, business connections.

"Then, when Wallenberg came in, he said, that's terrific. Let's make something that looks like a passport. It was in color with the Swedish crown colors."

"Per Anger became Swedish ambassador to all sorts of places including Canada and Berlin. I interviewed him in 1995. He was the same age as Wallenberg. He was still in good shape. He told me that he was convinced that Wallenberg was still alive but that he no longer knew who he was."

"Why would the Soviet Union hold on to him?"

"Because it would enormously embarrassing for them to release him. It would be much easier for them to say, we can't find him. Or, we killed him, which is what they eventually said, then to release a broken man whose mind was no longer there."

"Did the US try hard to get him out?"

"No, because the damn Swedes said they would do it. President Truman offered. He was told no, we will handle it."

"Why didn't we, the US, apply more pressure to get him out?"

"According to my best source in the State Department, we never made it clear to the Russians that it would be in their best interest to release him. There was no US intelligence on where he was. The Swedes knew where he was."

"The Swedes found him an embarrassment?"

"Yes. It was their fault that the Swedish government did not press rigorously enough for Raoul's return. If he returned a broken man, can you imagine what would the reaction have been? Why didn't you do this sooner? Why didn't you get him out? It's a very nasty ugly story. The Swedish government behaved abominably."

Fenyvesi belongs to a Traditional shul (mixed seating, but with the Orthodox prayer book]. He keeps Shabbos and kashrut and studies the Torah. "I have a daughter. She could only read the Haftorah for her bat mitzvah [not from the Torah]."

"How do you reconcile Judaism's laws about lashon hara vs. the need to do journalism?"

"It's the truth that we're interested in. There is a great deal of value with the Talmudic rabbis attached to the truth. The Prophets showed how important it is to find the truth, tell the truth. I don't consider the kind of journalism I've been doing lashon hara. I don't malign people. I'm a kind and gentle journalist. I'm careful in print. If somebody is a no-goodnik, let's find out. Remember Natan telling King David, thou art the man!"

40

Neil Rubin

August 5, 2004

Neil is senior editor (number two man behind Phil Jacobs) at the *Baltimore Jewish Times* (17,000 subscribers). It's one of America's top five Jewish newspapers along with the *Forward*, *The Jewish Week*, *Jewish Exponent* and *j. the Jewish news weekly of Northern California*.

"I grew up in Baltimore. I remember in sixth grade I read a lot of history books. I noticed they were often written by journalists. It seemed that the best way to learn was to write about something. The word 'writer' was always more important to me than 'journalist.'

"I went to the University of Maryland for my BA in journalism (graduating in 1985). I have a masters degree from Baltimore Hebrew University in Modern Hebrew Studies. I am currently a PhD student there for the next 500 years. I'm taking a course a semester.

"I spent a year in Israel after my undergraduate degree. Then I came home and got a job writing PR for Bnai Brith International. I remember sitting down one day and trying to figure things out. The books I like to read are on Jewish things. The movies I like are about Jewish things. The articles I like to write are about Jewish things. I really need to be writing Jewish things.

"I was a freelance writer for the *Baltimore Sun* but I was writing on Jewish things.

"The first time I wrote on a paper full-time was in 1990 when I had a freelance contract for the *Washington Jewish Week*. I moved to the *Atlanta Jewish Times* in June 1991 [until October 1998]."

"I think the *Baltimore Jewish Times* under Gary was a better paper than *The Jewish Week* today. They certainly did more investigative journalism."

"They are different. The Baltimore paper, because it wasn't under a media spotlight and had a real community to work with and had people who were involved with national organizations but weren't beholden to them, it was able to do things that I don't know if you can do in New York now. The New York papers, the *Forward* and *The Jewish Week*, primarily report on Jewish agencies. It's inside baseball. The Baltimore paper had a lot more space. Even now, we run 100–130 pages each issue. The *Baltimore Jewish Times* then was 160 pages in a regular week. You could run a 10,000 word article. We can't do that today."

"How many Jews do you have in Baltimore?"

"About 100,000."

"We have 500,000 Jews in Southern California but the *Jewish Journal* of Los Angeles only runs 40 pages."

"There's geographic concentration in Baltimore. The people reading *Baltimore Jewish Times* aren't just reading it for Jewish news. It's community news. Back then, there were more mom-and-pop operations. There were corner pharmacies and hardware stores. Now with Home Depot, Wallmart, those small businesses are either going out of business or do not have an advertising budget anymore. The national chains do not advertise in Jewish newspapers or any weekly newspaper."

"What have you loved and hated about your time in Jewish newspapers?"

"The pettiness is insane. We deal with the real world. It's maddening, deadening, inspiring, boring. There are rabbis in town who, when they call me, I want to pick up the phone and say, 'Hi rabbi so-and-so, what's the problem today? What's wrong now?' People have no idea how to have a relationship. I liken it to editing a newspaper on your family that's honest, and then showing it to your neighbors and not telling your family members about it, and then them finding out and freaking out about it.

"I've been approached in a men's room about why we didn't write a certain story. People have lined up at kiddish on Shabbat just to say [their piece about the paper]. Nice people will say, do you mind if I talk to you about work? And I will say, 'Yes, I do. Can't it wait until Shabbat's over?' Then they will say, 'Ok, but such-and-such.' It goes with the territory but sometimes it drives me nuts. You're a quasi-public personality, particularly if you write a column with your picture in the paper.

"What I do like is that I can get any book I want. I can interview almost anybody I want. I can ask any question I want. On a good day, I'm sitting with Adin Steinsaltz and he's explaining to me his new commentary on the *Tanya* and we're going off on a million tangents. I was able to go to Camp David and cover the peace talks in 2000."

"Have you been amazed that leaders in Jewish life tend to get most upset at you over trivial things such as picture placement?"

"No, because those people are trivial people. Real leaders don't care about that stuff. We have a good photographer so we don't do the grip-and-grin stuff. We spend money on freelance too, photographers and reporters.

"We have one full-time reporter on staff, one three-day-a-week reporter and one regular freelancer who does our Arts and Life section. We have four editors and [they] all write."

"Why are you getting a PhD?"

"Because it's stimulating. I always wanted to get a PhD. I've always wanted to sink into a topic. One of the things that is frustrating about journalism is that you know a little about a lot. I'm fascinated by the concept of religion in the peace process. Every time we get serious about the peace process we talk about land and water and refugees and borders and Jerusalem. Everybody says religion is a problem but nobody deals with it. I'm researching Jewish text to find out if there's spiritual possession of the land vs. physical possession. What does it mean to give up land? Religion is a concept that political science bypassed until the Iranian revolution [1979]."

"Do you guys do same-sex marriage announcements?"

"We have considered that and debated that. We have only been asked to do one. We decided not to do it but we wrote a cover story about it. In the last year, we've published eight-to-ten stories about it. We felt the need to sensitize the community first. It ain't a big issue here. Baltimore is a conservative town. In Atlanta, I did run same-sex announcements."

"Is the *Forward* better or worse under J.J.?"

"It's different. Clearly, it has gone back to a neo-socialist perspective. I don't know if the columnists are as good as they were under Seth. I don't know if the culture stuff is as good as it was. You have to look at it and *The Jewish Week* every once in a while to know what is going on. I think it is fantastic they have competition in New York. I wish we had competition here. I think we would be a much better paper.

"We had a horrible situation a few months ago. A non-Jewish family living in an Orthodox Jewish neighborhood had three of their kids murdered by having their heads decapitated. Some family issues. We wrote a story about a memorial ceremony for these kids that the neighborhood leaders put together and how no Jews showed up. The Orthodox community was outraged at us.

"I'm giving this as an example of people caring what happens in their neighborhood. This is a void in most Jewish newspapers. We're lucky. We have Jewish neighborhoods. It ain't so easy in Atlanta.

"I live in the Jewish neighborhood of Pikesville. My neighbors are all Jewish. I walk to shul. I struggle to be an observant Conservative Jew."

"Do you find much support for what you do in Jewish text?"

"It depends on how you look at it. I look at what we do as a humble low earthly continuation of the Talmud. The Talmud records the debates of the Jewish people. There's a reason it has minority opinion. Every so often, it says teyku, meaning, this will be decided when the Messiah shows up. I believe in discussion with integrity. Last night I was at a right-wing event. Today I had lunch with two left-wing Israeli professors at John Hopkins University.

"James Besser is our Washington correspondent. *The Jewish Week* and *Baltimore Jewish Times* split Jim."

"He's with the *Jewish Journal*."

"He takes his directions from us. He writes an analysis column each week just for us. He sends it out to other people, but Jim and I confer every Monday morning. We talk several times a week."

"So what's the benefit in running Jim's column?"

"Because he's damn good."

"Damn good at what?"

"He's an excellent reporter. He's respected by everyone across the spectrum."

"Umm."

"Yes. I know you are going to tell me now that some people think he's a left-wing commie pinko. I disagree. I edit Jim's analysis column. Jim is definitely center/center-left in his personal views. I don't see it coming across in his reporting."

"With the relentless bashing of the Christian Right?"

"He's definitely obsessed with the Christian Right. Is that Jim doing that or is he following the Jewish community's interests?

"I'm studying this stuff for my dissertation. I happen to believe that evangelical Christians are the most underreported issue in the Jewish community. I just wrote a cover story on the relationship between evangelical Christians in

Baltimore and the Jewish community. Under my instructions, Jim writes about that topic a great deal."

The Baltimore Jewish community is 20% Orthodox, which is twice the national average. About half of Baltimore's Jews are born in Baltimore.

"You're not going to ask what music I like? You've asked everything else."

"Top five records of all time?"

"Springsteen, Springsteen, Springsteen, a little Rolling Stones, more Springsteen."

"Did you like his editorial blasting Bush in *The New York Times* today?"

"I'm disappointed he's getting into politics."

"Top five movies."

"*Star Wars: Return of the Jedi*. I have a daughter named Leah. *Field of Dreams*. The *Star Trek* movie with the whales. *The Wedding Singer*. *Uncle Buck* with John Candy."

"What five books would you take to a desert island aside from Jewish sacred text?"

"I wouldn't necessarily take any Jewish sacred text. I would take Milton Steinberg's *As a Driven Leaf*. *The Power of One*. *The Foundation Trilogy* by Isaac Asimov. *Operation Shylock* by Philip Roth. *Portnoy's Complaint* is dated and didn't do as much in character development. This book was so existential and so bizarre. I might toss in *Catch 22* by Joseph Heller."

"Which Hollywood actress would you take?"

"Nicole Kidman. Maybe Jerry Seinfeld's wife [Jessica Sklar]. Is she an actress? I'll take her anyway."

"He took her from his best friend [when they were newly married]."

"It's only fair that I take her from him then.

"How long would I be on this island?"

"Eighteen months."

"Ahh, my wife might find out. I better just take some more books."

"You should get married. Why should we suffer alone?"

"You ask in your column: When a popular rabbi gets fired for allegedly having an affair with a congregant, is it news?"

> Of course it's news. A) People are talking about it B) S/he's a public figure C) Isn't it news when it happens in other religions?
>
> You can always argue over context and timing and that's very fair for our readers to do (and what they should do more of).

Whether or not you're going to accurately get the story in a way that's printable and that you won't get sued is the issue. Rabbis are public figures. We write stories about them when they show up saying they're the greatest thing since sliced challah, and then we let them sneak out of town at midnight? To the best of my knowledge this has not happened while I was an editor in Atlanta or Baltimore. The closest I came was in Atlanta when I had to write a few articles about a rabbi [Juda Mintz] who had founded a congregation 17 years earlier and did not have his contract renewed. There were rumors of poor fiscal accountability, basically not that he stole, but that he could not account for things he bought for the shul via receipts. He said he bought them from dealers in Jerusalem that didn't give receipts. I happen to think he was just not that bright in this area. The hitch: He had performed my wedding a few years earlier. After it all happened, we went out to lunch. He looked at me and said, "Kakha hayah." (This is how it was.) In other words, I didn't lie and wrote a fair story. I'm proud of that, but still sad I had to write that story.

When a Jewish federation macher is sued for illegal business practices—on the eve of being reelected federation president—how should a Jewish newspaper respond? That's a tougher one.

In the abstract, I'd say yes but I have to honestly say it would depend on particulars and I do wonder how I would respond. If he were accused of financial improprieties, then you have to write about it. The guy can't be asking for millions, have that cloud hanging and have nobody write about it. Talk about your kosher elephants in the corner of the room.

In Atlanta, after I had left, my successor [Cynthia Mann] wrote a story about the President of the Federation who was being sued by his business partners for business practices. The *Atlanta Jewish Times* wrote a gutsy story about it.... and took tremendous heat. The relatively new editor found out very quickly the cost of writing such stories as some of the verbal responses were personal, digging into her own family situation (details of which I will not reveal).

I do not buy the argument that writing about this will damage the community via fundraising. The real question is would we consider the story fair? Is it important news for our community? (After all, anyone can sue anybody for anything in this country. There's also an issue as to whether you would break the story or not.)

It's for the editors to decide, in consultation with a publisher and the paper's libel attorney. Another mark of a good paper: Do you have a libel attorney that you show stories to? If not, perhaps you're not writing gutsy stories. As our editor Phil Jacobs likes to say, 'Apologies to my wife, but nobody helps me sleep better at night than our libel attorney.'

We seem to have a much more difficult time recruiting people today than we did ten years ago even in Baltimore. At one point, we were offering good salaries compared to other newspapers. However, newspapers have taken a general dive in that period in circulation and ad revenues. That means that salaries have not rise that much. At the same time, fewer people want print journalism—which I believe actually weakens broadcast journalism as well because in print you truly learn to be an effective communicator and collator/cruncher of large volumes of information.

41

Walter Ruby

August 9, 2004

"It was 1974. I was in graduate school at the University of Wisconsin [doing] a masters. I had married too young. I was depressed. I went to a shrink. I was saying to him, I really feel like I need to do something creative. He said, you'll come up with a specific task to move this forward. I said, I'd like to submit an article to the local newspaper (*The Capital Times of Madison*, a daily). He said, you have to sign an agreement [to do it] by whatever date, [or] you have to pay me $100.

"A few months before, I'd been to this town in northern Wisconsin and met this old man who was running a historical museum. I said, that will be a good article.

"Let me go up and interview him and write the article. I went up and did the interview. I came back thinking they'll never publish it. I had an inferiority complex. But I had to do it or I'd lose $100. So I did it. I went to the newspaper and walked in the room and found an editor and said [hurriedly], 'My name is Walter Ruby. I wrote this piece. You probably won't like it. But anyway.' I put it into his hands and ran away thinking, good, at least I won't lose $100.

"At my next session with my shrink, I walked into his office and he had this enormous grin on his face. He took out the newspaper and there it was.

"I made aliyah [moved to Israel] in the beginning of 1976. My wife was a Midwestern Baptist. She ended up leaving me for an Arab. I can't totally blame her because I discovered Israeli women along that period.

"Somebody told me they had all these great teaching jobs in Israel. I found out there weren't any great teaching jobs. The only jobs available were in tough towns with terrible pay amidst rough conditions with tough kids. I did a little practice teaching and I thought, I really don't want to do this.

"I managed to see the editor of *The Jerusalem Post*, Irwin Frankel. He looked at my resume. He saw I hadn't written anything except for a few freelance pieces. He said I should do a few freelance pieces. I was starting to leave the office. He looked at my resume again. 'Wait a minute. You went to the University of Wisconsin. That's my alma mater.' He found me a position in the Haifa bureau. He said, 'There are these two difficult guys who run the bureau. We've sent about five guys up there already. The deal is they have to take you for three months. Then they can fire you. I'm sure that's going to happen to you too. They're impossible but these are the union rules. But if you want to give it a shot?' I said yes.

"Three months later, I was fired. They were impossible people. I think Irwin Frankel felt some guilt about it. He put me on a small retainer and said, 'We'll look favorably on whatever freelance stuff you submit.' The next year was the best year of my life. I was this roving freelance feature writer who traveled around Israel. I did the first story in the English-language press about being gay in Israel.

"I got involved in a peace project with Israelis and Palestinians. I got excited in the mid '90s about the possibilities of the Internet for inter-group communication and reconciliation. I started a Web site called Encounter. In 1999, I lived in Berzeit teaching computer skills to young Palestinians. I'm a strong peacenik. I want to find a solution for the conflict that will be win-win for both peoples. I have this warm and fuzzy dream that one day we can create an ethos where the two peoples can love the land together. Some of this has made me not very popular within certain precincts of the American Jewish community. I've been called a self-hating Jew a lot.

"I've been writing a lot about the Russian community for *The Jewish Week*. I was just back in the Ukraine for the JTA."

"How did you lose your great gigs [*The Jerusalem Post, Ma'ariv, Forward*] in the early '90s?"

"*The Jerusalem Post* moved to the right. I was a marked man. As soon as Russian and Israel established relations, *Ma'ariv* were able to get their own man in there. My main employer was the *Forward*. I did not get along with Seth Lipsky. His politics are really Neanderthalish. Things got mixed up and he decided to get rid of me. I lost all my positions within a few months.

"I said, fine. There are all these books I want to write. Then I came back and found I didn't have any books I wanted to write. I don't have anything to say. I guess I'm really a journalist. I would love to be able to make a living with a column but that hasn't worked out. In the meantime, I play reporter. I try to be a peace advocate where I can."

"Did you remarry?"

"There was a second wife from whom I'm now getting divorced. She was from the Soviet Union. I met her in 1980. That's how I got my whole Soviet connection. Now I'm with another woman who I may marry. She's from the Ukraine. The second wife was Jewish. The third one is a wonderful woman."

"Any great stories you haven't been able to get into a paper?"

"Sure. Many.

"In the late '80s, I talked to a gentleman named Barry Gurary. [He was the son of Rabbi Shemaryahu Gurary, Rabbi Yosef Yitzhok's elder son-in-law, married to his eldest daughter. Menachem Schneerson beat out Rabbi Shemaryahu to become the leader of Lubavitch.] There were books at 770 Eastern Parkway that he claimed belonged to him. Lubavitch claimed they belonged to them. He took the books and sold some of them. That led to a court suit. He was found guilty and forced to pay back much of the money.

"Barry sent me transcripts of fabrengens that the rebbe had preached that these books were like living documents, pieces of flesh, and that anyone who would sell them, it was like killing somebody. After the rebbe delivered one of these fabrengens, one of his young followers went upstairs, knocked on the door of Barry Gurary's mother and knocked out her eye. She was 85 years old. The fellow who did this was put on the first plane to Israel before they could prosecute him.

"The police didn't come around very fast, as a local [black] police sergeant in Crown Heights said to me, Mayor Kotch doesn't put a high priority on looking into this as the Lubavitcher Rebbe delivers 40,000 votes to him every election.

"This story was laid on my doorstep. I submitted it to the consortium of Jewish newspapers. Then I went on a long trip to Russia in late 1989. When I came back from Russia, I found that I had been fired. One of the editors [Jerome Lippman] had showed the thing to someone in Chabad who had threatened to sue. Then I was going to sell it to *New York* magazine. I didn't get around to it. I did see it published in *New York* magazine by somebody else.

"You can't expect the rebbe to apologize. He didn't tell the guy to go up and beat this old woman to death but his words caused it."

"**Did you have any dealings with Malcolm Hoenlein?**"

Walter laughs. "The story got published and almost 20 years later, Malcolm still doesn't speak to me.

"Around 1986, Cardinal John O'Connor, the late Catholic Archbishop of New York, had gone to Israel and he was doing some diplomacy. The Presidents Conference people were unhappy because he seemed to be saying some mildly critical things about Israel. For me it was almost indiscernible but for them it was a shanda. The Presidents Conference ruminated for several days about issuing a statement. Hoenlein wanted to get this statement out before Shabbat. It was already Friday morning. They couldn't hammer it out. So he went ahead and wrote the statement and wrote the names of every one of the 53 president of the major Jewish organizations.

"Cardinal O'Connor returned to New York. Reporters were waiting for his response. He looked at the statement and blew up. He said it was outrageous. How dare they? I do everything for Israel and now they're attacking me....

"Monday morning. I was writing for the *Long Island Jewish World*. Editor Jerry Lippman called me. He said he was getting all kinds of calls from presidents of Jewish organizations saying they never signed that letter. He asked me to look into it.

"Until now, I had had a decent relationship with Hoenlein. A month earlier, my editor at *The Jerusalem Post*, Ary Rath, had been in New York and Hoenlein had made a point to say to him, 'Walter's a wonderful reporter. You are so lucky to have him.' I guess he figured he bought me with that.

"I call him. I told him I'd heard from about 20 of the 53 presidents who said they had never signed this document. The first thing Malcolm said was, Walter, this would be a terrible thing for the Jewish people if you published this. It would cause grievous damage. I was like, Malcolm, come on. Give me a break.

"I thought about it for a day. I asked the editor if we should go ahead with it. He said yes. I called Malcolm back. I said, 'We're going to press tomorrow. We'd like some response.' He said, 'If you publish this, I will fuck you for the rest of your life.'

"And he did. A month later, he and the chairman of the Conference, Morris Abrams, the Mort Zuckerman of his era, went to Israel and had lunch with the editors of *The Jerusalem Post* and asked that I be fired. David Landau, who was then managing editor, said your ass was hanging by a thread, but they couldn't stomach it. They felt Hoenlein was so right-wing and they were liberal left. On the other hand, they said, why do we need the tsures?

"Later on, there were moments when I felt like he was hurting me behind the scenes. Years ago, when I was in Russia, the JTA position in Moscow opened up. I was the only logical person for the job. They offered it to a young businessman who was not a journalist. He said to the editor of JTA, why wouldn't you offer it to Walter? And he [editor Marc Pearl] said, according to the businessman, 'Walter Ruby has no credibility in the Jewish community.' That felt like the hand of Malcolm Hoenlein.

"In 1998, Jeffrey Goldberg, who has gone to great things with *The New York Times* and *The New Yorker*, wrote in the [4/17] *Forward* how Hoenlein had threatened him."

> Several years ago, at one of the money-wasting general assemblies the Jewish federations fete themselves with, Malcolm Hoenlein, the major American Jew who runs the Conference of Presidents of Major American Jewish Organizations, spotted me in a hallway and called me over for a huddle. It turned out that Mr. Hoenlein had a warning for me.
>
> I had just written a story that appeared on the front page of this newspaper disclosing the salaries of 10 of the country's top professional Jews. As an exercise in reporting, the story was no great shakes—it simply entailed collecting figures from a series of public IRS filings. In the secular press, a story detailing the salaries of muckety-mucks usually lands with a yawn. But in the self-righteous and hypertouchy world of Jewish officialdom, the story elicited weeks of whining about the damage the *Forward* was doing to the Jewish people, it being common for professional Jews to conflate their own problems with those of their people.
>
> Though [Hoenlein] didn't even make the list, he felt obligated to warn me that my future in what he referred to as "Jewish journalism" was looking dim. "You really should be careful," he said. "You can alienate a lot of people with stories like that." At the time, he served on the board of the UJA-Federation's New York organ, so I assumed he was speaking officially. I thanked Mr. Hoenlein and went on my way, armed with further proof of something I have long believed: that the men and women who serve as Jewish "leaders" today are by and large incapable of grappling with unvarnished truth. Their spinelessness is reflected in their inability to deal straight-on with nearly every issue that confronts them...

"I know other reporters who have gone through that with him. I wrote a long letter to the editor narrating my experiences at the hands of Malcolm Hoenlein, a serial abuser of Jewish journalists."

"Is journalism a good way to meet women?"

Walter laughs. "Certainly. When I'm doing a story, I'm interviewing women. I met my second wife playing journalist. She had just arrived from the Soviet Union. I was sent by UJA/Federation to interview her. I did PR for a year or two. I am shy with women and it is a good way to break the ice. My present girlfriend too. I was working on doing a book about the Russian community in New York. Probably most women I've met in my life have been that way."

42

Yosef I. Abramowitz

August 16, 2004

"In 1992, I became a senior editor at *Moment* magazine under Hershel Shanks. We pushed the envelope and won tons of awards. The economic situation of the magazine turned around during that time. We did an issue on Judaism and homosexuality, which won a first place GLAAD (Gay & Lesbian Alliance Against Defamation) award. We beat *The New Republic*, the *Atlantic*.... We were the first to cover the issue of Orthodox women rabbis.

"Even though people thought I did a good job, I was fired by Hershel. He called me to his home, which is where he does most of his work. He said, 'Yossi, you're doing great. You're winning all these awards. But I bought this magazine to have fun. Ever since you came on board, I'm not having fun anymore.'

"What would happen is that I would have a different opinion on cover stories and what was covered and I would get the rest of the staff to agree with me.

"I learned magazine editing and publishing under Hershel. It was hard for him. He was not as successful as he should've been. That's when I realized I needed to do my own thing.

"I started a parenting magazine. It failed but it led to an empire (JFLMedia)."

Yossi has four kids with his wife [Reform] rabbi Susan Silverman.

"When did you do your Jewish National Fund story?"

"The story came out in September 1996. It was an expose of one of the top icons in Jewish life. It was brutal. The smear campaign against me on page one of the *Forward* came out before my articles were able to come out. In the end, we won. They lost $12 million that year. They had to close 15 offices. They threw out their entire professional management team. They threw out most of their lay leadership. They brought in Ronald Lauder as their president and streamlined their organization so that most of their money goes to Israel. It's the one case in modern American Jewish life where an article brought down an institution. I was nominated for a Pulitzer.

"On my wall here is a dozen American Jewish Press Association awards, if that means anything.

"The articles appeared in a dozen Jewish newspapers, beginning with *The Jewish Advocate* (Boston). Everyone was under pressure from JNF not to run the articles. The people at *The Advocate* knew me. They basically said, this is an award-winning Columbia-trained journalist whose ethics and motivations we trust. After them, the others followed."

"Which major papers which you would've expected to have run the series, did not?"

"I brought the story to Gary Rosenblatt's operation. You would think that would be the place. I came with a wheelie. Those luggage wheelies. With four binders packed with all of my sources. Everything to back it up. They had read the story the day before. I came in. I was chewed out for an hour [a senior person] about all sorts of terrible things. Why I was wrong. Who put you on the story? What axe are you trying to grind? Do you have a sister who worked there? It was unbelievable.

"They then had to assign their top investigative journalist, Larry Cohler-Esses, to do his own story, which confirmed what I did. Every year for the past few years, Gary Rosenblatt has told me that he won't publish me. And he won't talk about why. We know why. I unearthed probably the biggest Jewish organization scandal. They were wrong about it.

"After I left the story, everyone was forced to write about it. JTA did a series.

"When [JNF CEO at the time of Yossi's investigation] Samuel Cohen died [in 1999], *The Jewish Week* did the obit. Without naming me, they said a journalist brought him down. I felt that for them, it was a confession.

"I was greatly hurt and surprised that *The Jewish Week* and Gary did that."

"Was part of *The Jewish Week*'s problem with your JNF story was that they are a Federation paper?"

"They are several steps removed from the fundraising. *The Jewish Week* is still one of the top three Jewish newspapers in the country. They still break a lot of stories and the writing is excellent, comparatively. There were Federation people who were implicated. A top lay leader of JNF was a big NY Federation person. Whether or not they carried my story is immaterial, but how I was raked over the coals and chewed out and discounted, that I didn't respect.

"Because I am a combination activist and journalist, people assume my journalism is yahoo. They forget about Columbia. I took my training seriously. I apply the highest standards. The community is not used to that. History has now vindicated me on a number of major stories. I don't write that often. You can't make a living as a freelance journalist."

"Tell me about the smear campaign."

"They had to bring me down. They had to question.... They called me names. They said I was in league with.... It was beyond people's comprehension, therefore it had to be negative aspirations. I said, what do you mean? Every week my kids go to school and put their quarter into the JNF cans. Less than a penny of that goes to Israel. It's fraud. I have planted trees and done all that stuff. It's fraud against the Jewish people. They have smeared the good name of the Jewish National Fund, for which they have to redeem themselves by their actions. I'm sorry to be the messenger, guys. I was the messenger long after people in Houston tried making changes internally.

"I was trying to start a Jewish parenting magazine at the time and I was boycotted, and still am, by some people because I had smeared publicly the good name of a Jewish institution.

"You asked about the obstacles to doing compelling Jewish journalism. It's impossible to make a living doing the kind of stuff I was doing for several years. I was living off my credit cards. It needs to be supported in another way.

"I'll give you another example of censorship and retribution. I was trying to raise money for Jewish Family & Life (JFL)! I was told that if I did an investigative story on another Jewish issue, they were going to kill my money. I did the story and they killed my money.

"I did an official interview with the head of the institution. I asked for permission to tape. They also taped it at the same time. The interview ended. I put the tape recorder in my pocket without turning it off, just to make some small talk. Instead, I got called to a room and basically got raked over and threatened. I have it on tape.

"I'm an independent. We reach more people than any other media operation in Jewish life. I'm not dependent on the usually mediocre American Jewish press and its censorship possibilities. We have independent funding. We have independent means to get the story out. We have national credibility. *The Wall Street Journal* did a page one story on one of our issues of *Sh'ma* last year.

"It used to be that Jews were not allowed to challenge God. God is all mighty, all knowing, all everything. It was blasphemy, heretical, hence the excommunication of Spinoza. With the Enlightenment, you can say whatever you want about God. The next thing we were not allowed to challenge or question was Israel. Israel was always right. It was the role of the American Jewish community to always support Israeli policies no matter what they do, Sabra and Shatilla. There were people who paid a heavy political price for challenging Israeli policy, and were ostracized by the mainstream. Ariel Sharon today is for a two-state solution. Those people weren't visionary? Now they can say anything they want about Israel. What's left? Jewish institutions. They're holy. We can't question whether they should exist. We can't ask for transparency. We've come a long way from God, Israel and, in my case, the JNF. We're creating golden calves. The role of the independent thinker, which was the prophet in ancient days, or the intellectual in the Enlightenment days, or [the] investigative journalist today.

"There's only so much that kvetching accomplishes. There's only so much that writing about things changes things on their own. I made the leap to trying things myself on my own Web. It's harder than it looks. I have greater sympathy and understanding for the lack of risk taking that characterizes Jewish institutions."

"I've spoken to 50 Jewish journalists and editors and you are the only one who is willing to criticize Gary Rosenblatt on the record. Are you surprised?"

"So first there was God. Then there was Israel. Then Jewish institutions. Then Jewish leaders. Then people who control mind share and some resources."

"Now Gary Rosenblatt."

"I'm not dependent on Gary for anything."

"He's the Dean of Jewish Journalism. The epitome of Jewish Ethics. Mr. Investigative Journalism. All in one."

"They have broken many stories."

Almost every Jewish journalist I interview tells me that *The Jewish Week* has broken many stories. Then I ask them:

"Can you name any of them, aside from Baruch Lanner?"

Long silence. "I don't know. Nothing of that magnitude. Larry Cohler was on a roll. I just don't remember what they were. Larry was paid by Gary."

"He also had his balls cut off by Gary."

"That's a separate thing I'm not free to comment on.

"I'm sorry to hear that. Not because of Gary Rosenblatt. Because if journalists are going to be the prophets, the independent thinkers, self-censorship, even within our own realm, is sad.

"The Jewish press has totally failed to do a deep enterprising story about what Madonna has been studying, how deep does the stuff go. Everyone reduces this to shtick and kitsch. The secular press is only going to go to a certain level. This is an entertainment story to them, not a religion story. The Jewish press has missed a historic opportunity to go five levels down on this thing. It's not seen as Jewish journalism.

"I went to the Reinvention Tour. Within that tour are revolutionary seeds for the world and Jewish life. She gets the meaning of kabbalah..."

"What kind of kabbalistic message was sent when she had writhing people simulating sex on stage at her concert?"

"I saw her concert three years ago. It was god awful. I didn't want to be there. She was trying to provoke. I saw her Reinvention Tour. I could've taken my two daughters aged 11 and 9. And I'm a big time censor [to protect their innocence]. She kept her clothing on. She was hitting major messages that I would want anybody who was concerned about social change to hit. It was a deeply Jewish experience that was filled with integrity and made amends for her concerts three years ago and indicate a certain maturation in her own path. If I had the time, I'd be writing that one."

"I've never heard anyone voice that."

"I'm independent. I have an essay unwritten in my brain about this but I can't do it now."

"I only hear the pat put-downs."

"Of course. The Jewish establishment has to do that. Anybody who sees himself as a Jewish religious or organization leader has to discount this because saying otherwise would be taking a risk, and reducing their own claim to leadership. She knows something that they don't about reaching children. She knows something they don't about aspirations of Judaism. She knows something they don't about how to unite people and bring the world together. That's really dangerous. Heaven forbid that she should have any legitimacy. But their kids fall for her stuff."

43

Mark Silk

August 26, 2004

The founding director of the Center for the Study of Religion in Public Life at Trinity College in Hartford, Connecticut, Mark has published the books *Unsecular Media: Making News of Religion in America* and *Spiritual Politics: Religion and American Society Since World War II*.

"I think the Jewish press is pretty good when compared to in-house coverage in other denominations. A fair amount of it is independently owned. A lot of the larger places are good, led by the *Forward*. It has no competitor. It stands alone as the national weekly. Their coverage of intellectual stuff has increased since Lipsky left and is quite impressive. For anyone who wants to keep up with Jewish stuff, it's essential reading.

"It was quirky under Lipsky. It was more conservative, which, to my taste, is less good. It's more predictable now. It was a Likud operation. It was odd, and for the people who booted him out, it was too odd to have a Jewish publication that far right. Editorially it is where most Jews tend to be.

"The Jewish weekly press [aside from the *Forward*] is not especially interesting. They're reluctant to attack the local Jewish establishment or to even look closely. Even if they are independently owned, they are still dependent on advertising and tie-ins on circulation. They tend to be defensive of any criticism of Israel in ways that make for not interesting reading.

"The Catholic press is all run by the archdioceses. They're all house organs. They don't have independent weeklies like the *Baltimore Jewish Times*, *Detroit Jewish News*, *Atlanta Jewish Times*. There are large parts of the country where you have more Baptists on the ground by orders of magnitude than Jews but they're all in different churches. Their sense of denominational identity [is not strong]."

"Two big reasons for the superiority of the Jewish press is the peoplehood component of Judaism and its nonhierarchical nature."

Mark agrees.

"My impression is that coverage of Jews and Judaism has been light in recent years in the secular press. Jews have been a familiar part of the American scene for a couple of generations. I think there's been an editorial reluctance to get involved in the current American Middle Eastern situation. They get screamed at by the Jews for anything that doesn't seem supportive of Israel. And there are now vocal Muslims who get upset on the other side. I think there's a tendency not to do it anymore than they have to, compared to some earlier times when it was felt to be part of American pluralism to cover folks other than Christians, and that only meant Jews.... Now there are other folks who receive that attention.

"I think a significant under-covered story has been the Lubavitch movement. People have not wanted to look closely at the messianism and the local political hardball. They're tough actors and I don't think they get a significant amount of serious scrutiny.

"There's a tendency to regard Messianic Jews as pariahs and not worthy of attention. The secular press is not entitled to disregard them as beyond the pale of respectable religion. It's a religious judgment to say that their combining of Judaism with Christianity is non-kosher but Presbyterians and Baptists are kosher.

"There's the ongoing story of the weakening of Jewish communal agencies and their difficulty finding leaders of the stature that there used to be. That the American Jewish Congress has to go to an Israeli to head it is extraordinary.

"Madonna's Kabbalah thing has not been covered seriously with the exception of one good article by Yossi Klein Halevi. He went to services at the Centre and found them powerful, and he had an explanation for what made Berg's message so attractive. The press tends to regard Hollywood religion is silly. Philip Berg deserves to be regarded as an operator. It's been almost entirely covered as an entertainment story. There's a prejudice against a certain kind of pop religion."

"Don't secular papers normally put their worst reporters on the religion beat?"

"Not at all. It used to be, perhaps. It was certainly a backwater beat for church ladies. Beginning in 1994, with *The Dallas Morning News*'s invention of a faith and values section. That set in train a move towards devoting more resources to religion coverage. With more resources, came first rate reporters. Good reporters get good stories. Ann Rogers out of Pittsburgh. Michael Paulson out of the *Boston Globe*. Teresa Watanabe at *The LA Times* is from a Japanese-American family out of the Pacific Northwest. She was foreign correspondent in Japan. She came back and did a great job on religion for a few years before moving on to other beats. A generation ago, a reporter like that would not have been pushed into covering religion. The notion that the secular press is inherently hostile to religion has never been true.

"My major criticism of the trend towards more coverage has been the preference to do soft stories. To say that religion is becoming less institutional. We have to cover how people feel. I don't think journalists are good at doing that kind of story. It throws them back to repeating whatever this or that academic has to say about more people believing in angels and then finding an example of that on the ground.

"You can't answer questions such as what is the secular press's attitude towards Catholicism. There is no there there. The press tends to not like the abuse of children sexually. It tends to approve of the good works of Mother Theresa. It likes the Pope in some respects and not in other respects."

"What was your reaction to David Klinghoffer?"

"I think he's a dodo. He's ignorant. I've been at the point many times of writing the *Forward* to say, I understand you need to have somebody writing from the conservative standpoint, but he's a dope. It's a real example of a little bit of knowledge being terrible."

44

Dwight Owen Schweitzer

August 29, 2004

In December 2002, I read online two articles from the *Miami Herald* about Dwight Owen Schweitzer. He was the editor and publisher of the now defunct *Jewish Star Times*. He'd been arrested [but never prosecuted] for allegedly kicking a hooker, whom he had befriended three days before.

I laughed and laughed.

Then I forgot about Dwight Owen Schweitzer until this weekend when I read he was suing the *Miami Herald* for defamation. I decided to interview him about his career in Jewish journalism and see if I could gently nudge the conversation towards the things that truly matter—hookers.

"I was a lawyer. A client of mine was a publisher of a business magazine in Hartford, Connecticut, where Alberto Ibarguen [now publisher of the *Miami Herald*] and Willard Soper and I came from. In my early days at the *Miami Herald*, we were referred to as the Hartford Mafia. Alberto started as a legal aid lawyer when I was practicing law. Willard was a banker at Hartford National. Alberto left the law and went to work for Willard.

"Alberto left banking to go into journalism, going from *The Hartford Courant* to *Newsday* to *El Nuevo Herald* to publisher of the *Miami Herald*. Alberto hired Willard to run new business development for the *Miami Herald*. They had launched a newspaper called *The Jewish Herald* in November of 1999. The managing editor, Gerald Schwartz, quit four months later. Willard and I had been close friends for years. He called me from out of the blue in March 2000 discussing this Jewish newspaper. After half an hour, Willard says, I know it's crazy, Dwight, but how would you like to publish this thing? I then knew there was a God.

"I said, 'Send me some issues and let me have a look at it.' I was not impressed by what I saw. I sent him back a memo telling him about the type of paper I'd like to publish. I listed about 20 things I wanted to do with it.

"I had 16 interviews. I think everybody but the local proctologist interviewed me. There were people at the *Herald*. There were people from the Jewish community.

"I was so naive that I never thought of these as job interviews. They came to me. I didn't come to them. I thought I was being introduced around.

"The Jews understood it as a plus that I didn't know anybody in South Florida. The Gentiles didn't understand that.

"*The Jewish Star Times* [renamed from *The Jewish Herald*] is, to the best of my knowledge, the only weekly Jewish newspaper launched by a major daily paper.

"I started at the end of May 2000, and the last edition of the paper was December 13, 2002.

"We started out giving free home delivery to anyone who asked for it. About 28,000 asked for it. The bad news was that the *Miami Herald* charged us 11.5 cents for each delivered paper. That was an expensive bite to my bottom line. We decided to charge for delivery. We got about 6,000 people willing to pay for it.

"In the beginning we had in-paper delivery to targeted zip codes with a high proportion of Jewish households and had racks all over North Dade County. We dropped off [free] copies to condominiums, gated communities…

"I had one full-time reporter and one part-time. I was able to recruit 14 people from the Jewish community who would write features for me [for free] every week on food, fashion, society…. We had anywhere from 28–55 pages.

"I wanted to keep our ad/editorial ratio to no more than 50/50. The *Jewish Journal* [of South Florida] is about 70/30."

In winter, South Florida has about 750,000 Jews. "We're the second highest concentration of Jews in North America behind New York.

"I had a mission for the paper. Because the paper was read by anyone who picked it up, I wanted to stress the commonalties between Jews and non-Jews. Second, I wanted Jews who read it to feel better about being Jewish. Third, I wanted non-Jews who read it to feel better about Jews. Fourth, I wanted to use the paper to introduce the Jewish community to itself. You would rarely see payos or fur hats in my paper.

"I wanted to give a personality to the paper. I felt that the best way to do that was through a 'Message from the Publisher' column. It invariably appeared on page three. It had my picture. It ran the gamut from the profound to the ridiculous. I was acting as a talk show host, giving a monologue at the beginning of the show.

"I wrote editorials. Alberto called me into his office one day and said, you can't write editorials. That was one of my 20 things on my initial laundry list. Alberto said, you are *The Jewish Herald*. People might think you are making editorial policy for the *Miami Herald*. But you can change the name of the paper.

"Without a moment's hesitation, I changed the name of the paper to *The Jewish Star Times*."

"What's been your level of Jewish observance?"

"It did bring me much closer to my Jewishness. I'm Reform. I was bar mitzvahed. I was confirmed. It was a remarkable introduction to my Jewishness coming down here. I was invited to Israel twice. I was invited to Taiwan to cover the Einstein exhibition. I was invited to see the former Jewish heritage in Spain. Spain was the least anti-Semitic country I've ever been to. Everyone wonders whether they are Jewish or not.

"A lot of people felt the *Miami Herald* was an anti-Semitic paper and that anything that was beneficial to Israel was shunted into this Jewish insert. I think the reason they decided to close *The Jewish Star Times* was that Alberto was jealous. He was running into me all over town. For somebody who didn't know anybody in the Jewish community in South Florida, my profile in a short time became large.

"Alberto told a story at a staff meeting that he in Hartford practiced law next door to me. While he was eating day-old bread, he'd walk out of our office building and see my Rolls Royce parked out front of the building. I asked myself why he would tell this story to the executives of the *Miami Herald*. Then it dawned on me much later that he told this story because I now worked for him. Then he began to realize that I wasn't working for him. *The Jewish Star Times* had a separate identity and was becoming a force in Jewish journalism. We scooped every newspaper in the country in finding out Sarah Hughes (figure skating gold medalist) was Jewish. It wound up on the front page of the *Forward*. We scooped every paper, Jewish or non-Jewish.

"As the paper got better, my relationship with Alberto Ibarguen got worse. When I walked into a meeting and he said, 'I thought we hired a publisher and we wound up with a columnist,' I was dumbfounded. I would've thought that was a plus."

"When did the incidents occur that you are suing over?"

"In November, 2002, the month before the paper closed. As soon as it happened, I reported it to Willard. Not only did I tell him the story, I got an email from him a week later: 'Don't discuss this with anybody. You are on a paid leave of absence.' I had practiced law for 32 years. I told him that they had no basis to arrest me. And the case was going to be thrown out. The stories were fabrications of police reports that were fabrications. The police reports were fabricated because they were trying to protect a paid police informant [Cristine M. Brooks]. I knew her as a police informant.

"She had been brought to my house for an open house thing. We got to talking. She indicated she was an informant for the police department. At the party, some things got stolen. She called me the next day. She said she had contacts with the police. She could help me find [the stolen things] and get them back. What she was really doing was setting me up to use my apartment to bust a guy who was a dealer. The whole story [that Dwight kicked her] was to protect her from retribution.

"When I walked in the door and found these strangers in my house, the police arrived within seconds. It was clearly a setup. I got caught in the middle."

"Did you know she was a prostitute?"

"No. It wasn't in my police report either. It was in her's. I think frankly it was just her cover. The [Joan] Fleischman story [in the *Miami Herald*] said she stayed at my house for three days. She never stayed at my house. The police report didn't say that she stayed at my house."

"I remember when this story came out, I found it hysterically funny."

"I never got passed hysterical.

"Even if every word was true, why would my own paper [*Miami Herald*] publish it? My paper [*The Jewish Star Times*] is closing. The decision to close was made in October. One former executive at the *Herald* told me that somebody must've been really pissed off at me. Otherwise, it wasn't news. It wasn't accurate. The police came after everything was over. There were no witnesses other than me and Christine."

"Was she dressed like a hooker?"

"No."

"Was she attractive?"

"Yes. I liked her. I make no apologies for it. She was smart, funny, and fun to be around. That was the extent of our relationship."

"Did you sleep with her?"

"No."

"No sex?"

"None."

"How did these articles affect your life?"

"You can't imagine. In every single conceivable way. Those two pieces are on every search engine that anybody could imagine. Any time someone Googles me, those two stories come up. Jewish men who are accused of kicking women are not popular.

"I came down here with a new wife who divorced me. I was in an automobile accident. I ruptured a disc in my back and tore a ligament in my knee. I'm trying to publish a newspaper where my staff is shrinking. Then this happens. I'm trying to put my life back together. *The Sun Sentinel* were in discussion about whether they would like to hire me. As soon as those things hit the press, I became a non-person.

"People who saw me who were great dear close friends would turn and look the other way. It was horrible. The jobs that were interested in me on Tuesday did not call me back on Thursday. I remember going to a Jewish Federation meeting and I saw a couple I adored and they adored me. I would have dinner at their house. When she saw me, she turned away. It was like I had betrayed a friendship. It just tore my heart out. It happened over and over again. Fifty, a hundred times, in one form or another.

"I wrote Ibarguen more than once and asked him to take those things off the Internet. He didn't reply. But he was able to make my press release about him disappear from his name's Google results within two days.

"Invitations that would be routine just stopped coming.

"My wife and I were in the midst of a divorce. My wife was bipolar. Being down here was not a good environment for her. She was Irish Catholic and she was not particularly embraced by the Jewish community. I was married to a beautiful young smart woman. I'm 61 and she's 34. We married in May 1999 after having gone together for seven years, since she was 22.

"Since the paper folded, I've been writing but I haven't been paid for it. I've been working on two books. One is a novel about growing up in the '60s and the other is a more factual account of my life in the 1990s in Hartford. At the time of the crash in 1991, I was developing real estate. I was forced to go back to being a lawyer again after giving my practice away. For five or ten minutes, I was probably the largest developer of entry-level single-family housing in Connecticut.

"If the *Herald* is found guilty of defamation, and I think they're dead in the water, it raises the question of liability of the search engines."

"I can only imagine what this did to your dating life."

"I've been on the phone with someone and really liked them and they seem to like me and all of a sudden they're going back to their old boyfriend or they're not returning my calls."

"Would you say that about half of potential dates were affected by this?"

"More. Several people who dated me mentioned that they saw it and just couldn't believe it. 'It just seemed so incongruous that I had to meet you and talk to you about it.' But that is rare.

"I said to the police officer in the car, you have my career in the palm of your hand. When you write your report, add that she admitted that I didn't kick her. He said he would and he didn't.

"I was held over night and not booked until 4 p.m. I was with people who scared the living daylights out of me.

"Finding a lawyer down here who's going to sue the police is not easy. I wanted to include the police in the lawsuit because the police reports were false but then there's a question of privilege...

"I kept hoping the whole thing would go away but instead it kept biting me everywhere I turned.

"Finding a lawyer wasn't easy. The *Miami Herald* is the gorilla that sleeps wherever it wants.

"For the first six months after this happened, I was agoraphobic. Here was somebody who was being wined and dined by heads of state on Tuesday and was a hooker-beater on Thursday. I'm proud of what I've done with 99% of my life and to have that be the capstone was horrible."

"Should you have been able to tell she was a hooker?"

"No. And with all the time we spent together in those three days, which wasn't much, I'm not sure I would've cared. And down here with the way women dress, give me a break. You can walk down the street and take your choice. The governor's wife is on one side and who knows who is on the other and they're wearing the same dress or no dress. This is South Beach."

"Why did you stay in Miami after all this?"

"I didn't want to be seen as leaving with my tail between my legs. It would've seemed like an admission. It took me a while to believe that I had become a pariah in a community that had adored me. They loved the stuff I wrote. I'd run into people on the street who'd recognize me by virtue of my picture being in the paper.

"To have this done to me by my paper and by my friends. I had known Alberto for 32 years. I had been his lawyer. When he had a problem, he came to me. I know this article was run by him before it was published. I didn't return Fleischman's calls because I knew if there wasn't corroboration for the stories, they couldn't run them. The police had no information. Christine Brooks had gone to parts unknown. Yet she wrote that story as if they were facts from the police reports."

"How come South Florida can't support a good Jewish weekly?"

"Many of the people down here are transients. You've got every stripe, from ultra-Orthodox to Reform. They don't mix and mingle. They're spread out. You can't focus a newspaper geographically. Finding common denominators was tough. They're not intellectual here. While there were people who liked the paper, they were not the people who advertised."

45

Jason Maoz

September 2, 2004

In his book, *Memoirs of a Jewish Extremist,* Yossi Klein Halevi writes:

> Every Friday, as if to subvert the approaching peace of Shabbos, *The Jewish Press* arrived in the mail. More than just the voice of Brooklyn's Orthodox Jews, *The Jewish Press* was a cosmopolitan digest of disaster. It probed the world, looking for woe.... The editorials, cartoons, letters to the editor, and blue-and-red headlines all merged into a single cry of "GEVALT!"—a great cry of alarm. Stories were said to continue on non-existent pages or ended mid-sentence, as if some calamity had suddenly struck its author. *The Jewish Press* was a newspaper with a mission and had no time for the formalities of grammar; its typos were the stutter of an urgent messenger. *The Jewish Press*' implicit motto was: No threat can ever be exaggerated.

Seven years at *The Jewish Press,* Jason has served as editor for three years. Frum from birth, he's 44.

"Those passages of Halevi's describing *The Jewish Press* of the 60's are among the funniest things I've ever read. They are a perfect description of some of the paper's shortcomings during that era."

The Jewish Press averages over 100 pages with a 50/50 ratio between advertising and copy. About 70,000 copies per week are printed. Jason says that "due to family size and pass-along rate, our readership is around 350,000, numbers reflecting actual interested readers, not just copies printed and sent to names on a Federation mailing list.

"*The Jewish Press* has been a Modern Orthodox weekly since January 1960. It was geared to a national Orthodox audience though New York was the base. It was the only Orthodox newspaper in English. Yiddish was dying out. The standards were different then. If you look at just about any Orthodox publishing endeavor in the days before ArtScroll, the aesthetics were less sophisticated. *The Jewish Press* has maintained its format since 1960, though we've been doing some graphic improvements of late.

"*The Jewish Press* has long been a target of criticism—some of it justified, much of it not—from precisely the kind of people who frequent Protocols. There's a certain element in the frum community that jumps on *The Jewish Press* for real or alleged sins that are overlooked or ignored in other publications, from typos to factual errors to the massaging of news coverage to suit an agenda. Hell, one guy [Avraham Bronstein] even posts 'stupid letters of the week' from *The Jewish Press* on his blog—'stupid' being anything he disagrees with—ignoring the fact that no other Jewish publication has as open and freewheeling a letters section as we do.

"It seems like we're more appreciated in born-again Christian circles (a church in Tennessee recently bought one hundred subscriptions for its congregants) and among Jews outside the Orthodox community (Sid Zion buys *The Jewish Press* at his local Manhattan newsstand first thing Wednesday mornings, Seth Lipsky is a longtime subscriber, and Mort Klein says we provide the best coverage of Israel among Jewish weeklies) than we are by those pseudo-intellectuals who look down their noses at us but who when pressed for specific reasons for their disdain invariably resort to name-calling, obfuscation or outright lies.

"A lot of non-Jews are hungry for a Jewish viewpoint that isn't the typical liberal secular ACLU *Forward* type. They are surprised when they find Jews who not only share their views on Israel, but also their cultural views.

"The paper has always been right-of-center, particularly on Israel. Meir Kahane was a columnist for many years. He started in the early '60s. JDL (Jewish Defense League) was his creation started through columns in *The Jewish Press*. Over the years, he veered away considerably from the initial goals of the JDL—to combat neighborhood anti-Semitism in Brooklyn."

"Did the paper ever attack Kahane and say he had gone too far?"

"I don't think they ever attacked him, but there were times, not that often, when his column was held back, and he was told to tone something down.

Meir Kahane was extremely popular with *The Jewish Press*'s readership. Even if management didn't agree with a particular viewpoint he espoused, unless it was something over the top, they weren't about to muzzle him.

"Because the paper was identified with that right-wing camp, the perception became that the paper was wild-eyed and radical.

"In 1999, David Luchins, a former assistant to Senator Pat Moynihan, told the *Forward* that *The Jewish Press* 'wished for and welcomed the assassination of Yitzhak Rabin.' We went back and looked at issues several months before the assassination and not only was there nothing to be found approaching what he was describing, we had editorials strongly condemning the assassination. We used to carry columns by Yitzhak Rabin.

"Certain people in the Jewish establishment press vilified *The Jewish Press* because we were the only voice from day one of Oslo that hammered away at [the peace accords], highlighting what Yassir Arafat would say in Arabic on the one hand and in English on the other. This is when everybody was falling all over themselves celebrating Arafat, the newborn peacemaker.

"We challenged Luchins to find something to support what he said. Needless to say, he didn't. Luchins represents a certain prejudice in the Modern Orthodox community towards *The Jewish Press*. You see his mentality in certain blogs, such as Protocols—a mentality that tends to combine a hyper-politically-correct liberalism with Orthodox practice.

[*The Jewish Press* was the only American Jewish newspaper to endorse George Bush in 2000.]

"There is a YU-type blogger who is conservative politically and agrees with *The Jewish Press* down the line yet he made a hateful post about *The Jewish Press*. He said the community would be better off it didn't exist. I emailed the guy and went down the line where we agreed. I pointed out some of the improvements the paper had made over the years. I asked him to be more specific in his criticism. The guy emailed me back immediately and sheepishly admitted that he hadn't looked at *The Jewish Press* in some time.

"There was a prominent YU rabbi who was in the habit of constantly denigrating *The Jewish Press*. One day, somebody called him on it. The rabbi admitted that he was talking about *The Jewish Press* as he remembered it years ago.

"People who've come to *The Jewish Press* in the last few years appreciate it for what it is now, rather than for what it may have been 20 years ago."

"Is there room for improvement?"

"I'm still bothered by our typos. A lot of people aren't bothered when there are typos in *The Jewish Week*, the *Forward*, *The New York Times*, but when there's a typo in *The Jewish Press*, it seems to take on monumental proportions. 'Oh, typical *Jewish Press*.' That is probably why I am super-sensitive to it.

"I had a woman call me and criticize my writing for starting paragraphs with 'And' or 'But.' She said she had taught English for 30 years. I asked her if she had a copy of that day's *New York Times* handy. She did. I had a copy. I went over that day's front page, and I found several paragraphs and half a dozen sentences that started with 'And' or 'But.' When I pointed it out to her, there was silence on the phone. She said the rules of grammar must've changed since she taught school.

"An infamous story about *The Jewish Press*, mentioned by Gary Rosenblatt in a public symposium years ago, was that during the first week of the Yom Kippur war in 1973, *The Jewish Press* had this huge headline on the front page, 'Israel Wins.' The joke is that obviously Israel was in a precarious state the first ten days of the war and here we were cheerleading.

"When I started working here, I went through all the bound volumes from the '60s and '70s. The headline is true. The Yom Kippur war broke out on Saturday. We go to press Tuesday. The line that Israel was putting out then was that this was no problem. They were calling up reserves. They had it handled. It was only later during that first week that the perception began to change, that Israel had a problem.

"If you look at the daily news reports from that time, at *The New York Times*, *New York Daily News*, *Washington Post*, the reporting was almost all from the Israeli vantage point that this was no problem.

"The next week our coverage changed. It was cautious optimism.

"With any other paper, that story would've been long forgotten. But 25 years after that, people were still using that as an example that *The Jewish Press* is untrustworthy.

"Does Gary Rosenblatt regard you as a peer?"

Jason chuckles. "I've only spoken to Gary once and it was before I started working at *The Jewish Press*."

Jason chuckles again. "I know that Gary is regarded as beyond criticism. I think he did a great job with *The Jewish Week*, at least at first. When he took it over, it was a graveyard of press releases. He certainly injected a new tone and brought in some good writers. I think it's gone down in quality in the past few years.

"*The Jewish Week* is a competitor. I used to look forward to reading it. It was good for a few interesting profiles. But the paper is obsessed with Orthodox feminism. It's about the only Orthodox thing it covers in a positive way. *The Jewish Week* is the house organ of the Orthodox feminist movement. You won't find any negative copy about it, even though it's such a fringe phenomenon. The Jewish Orthodox Feminist Alliance boasted about getting 1500 people at one of their biannual conventions. *The Jewish Week* treated it as something unprecedented in Jewish history.

"When one of the Modern Orthodox synagogues hired a female rabbinic intern, you would think, from *The Jewish Week*'s coverage, that the Sanhedrin had come to life and ruled that women could become rabbis. You are talking about a handful of synagogues on the furthest edge of Modern Orthodoxy.

"I don't think Gary considers me anything. I don't think that publicly he would admit to anything good about *The Jewish Press*.

"I have no relationship with J.J. Goldberg. I've never sat on a panel with these men.

"Part of it is my fault. I'm extremely busy throughout the week. Even taking a vacation is a problem. My only vacation is Passover. Maybe I should participate more.

"*The Jewish Press* is a member of the AJPA. That's a whole other problem. Someone who had dealings with the organization told me that it was dominated by people who would never do anything to offend people like Gary Rosenblatt. The whole organization is in thrall to him, or to his mentality, and they would never give *The Jewish Press* any recognition.

"About seven years ago, we joined. For the first couple of years, I submitted stuff for their annual awards. Most of it was my stuff. I do a weekly 'Media Monitor' column that has been quoted widely and reprinted in several venues. I submitted a number of those columns for consideration. A couple of years went by, not only did we not win any prizes, but no honorable mentions. I'm looking at the stuff that won and a lot of it was pedestrian.

"We still belong to the organization but we don't bother submitting for the awards. It's a pain. You have to do everything in triplicate. I'm not going to do it if I think it is not going to be taken seriously."

"Have you gone to any of their conferences?"

"No. And that's a reason why.

"We are the only Modern Orthodox weekly out there with a mass readership. We are the only one trying to hold a line against all these chumras, against this mass move to the right that's been going on in the Orthodoxy community in the last 25 years, while still championing a vibrant Torah Judaism. Some yeshivish readers of *The Jewish Press* left us for [New York-based papers that launched around 1990] *Yated Neeman* [20,000 circulation] and *Hamodia* [25,000] because they felt we were too Zionistic, too modern, we had pictures of women in our advertisements, too much prominence given to women columnists. *The Jewish Press* was instrumental ten years ago in getting a get [Jewish divorce] law passed in New York. That sealed a breach between the Charedi world, Agudath Israel particularly, and *The Jewish Press*.

"We've had to accommodate certain shifts in the Jewish community. William Helmreich, a Modern Orthodox sociologist, said that back in the 1950s, Orthodox publications would run ads from Hebrew National meat, which today is not considered kosher by Orthodox Jews. It is not glatt kosher. Glatt has become the standard. Until 30 years, non-glatt was considered an acceptable standard for Orthodox Jews.

"Now *The Jewish Press* would never take ads from Hebrew National, nor would any other Orthodox publication. In the 1970s, the Orthodox press would take ads from Israeli nightclubs where they would advertise belly dancers (without photos). We would be out of business if we did that today. We have to walk a fine line. We can't offend either end of the spectrum.

"We don't cover the more scandalous things that happen in the community. We have a family matters section covering sexual abuse, agunot [women who aren't granted divorces by their husbands]. People were complaining it was not something they wanted in their homes. So a few years ago, we put the family section in a pull-out so that parents could remove it easily and their kids wouldn't see it.

"This whole Charles Kushner thing in New Jersey [he pled guilty to hiring a prostitute to try to smear his brother-in-law]. We have not covered that. Until he pled guilty, it was charges. Would it have been lashon hara to cover that story? Many of our readers would have thought so.

"The *Forward* recently had a front-page story about [an Orthodox rabbi accused of sexual harassment]. With things like that, he-said, she-said, we don't cover it. As it is, we constantly get complaints from readers who think we cross the line into lashon hara with what we do publish. Then you have people on the other end of the spectrum who think we should cover everything like the *Forward* and *The Jewish Week*. They think it marks us as less of a newspaper that we don't.

"We are not a newspaper in the ordinary sense. We are always cognizant that people regard us as a Torah publication, and that we are held to a different standard than a secular publication.

"A few years ago, there was a horrific car accident. The family was coming home to Brooklyn from visiting the husband and father who was incarcerated in an upstate prison for some financial crime. We included a line that they were returning home from visiting the father in prison. We were inundated with complaints. The family just went through this horrible tragedy and you had to put in that they were visiting the husband in prison. It was common knowledge in the community, which is so close-knit. Everyone knows who's in jail and who's not. Who's going through scandals and who's not.

"We had an editorial the next week apologizing if we offended anyone. We said we didn't mean to extend the family's suffering."

Fulltime, *The Jewish Press* has two reporters, two editors, and one Israel correspondent. They have a bunch of stringers.

"Steven Weiss, whom I greatly admire, mentioned to me that other Jewish editors and reporters look down on *The Jewish Press*. Even if *The Jewish Press* had a staff of 30 and was able to cover every story without fear or favor, just that we're on the other side of an Orthodox/secular, liberal/conservative divide would arouse hostility and a sense of otherness among secular and liberal Jewish journalists. I don't know how if I were more personally interactive with those people that would change anything."

Steven I. Weiss emails: "I've never heard a Jewish journalist comment positively on *The Jewish Press* as a whole, and I've heard a fair number of prominent J-journalists comment negatively upon it as a whole."

"You wouldn't have run the Baruch Lanner story, even if you had it nailed down like Gary did?"

"I don't know what we would have done if someone would've come to us with concrete proof. After it came out that Lanner was culpable to at least some of the charges, people were asking why is *The Jewish Week* lunching out on this? For months afterwards, they were doing constant follow-ups and updates. It was obvious to many of our readers that they were really enjoying this. Even a year later, an article would pop up on the front page of *The Jewish Week* revisiting the Lanner situation. In retrospect, there was certainly justification for the exposure they gave the initial story but our readership felt *The Jewish Week* was using this as another means for bashing the Orthodox community.

"When we started running domestic abuse stories, there was a lot of resistance to it, even by those who might've had first-hand experience with it. They felt it was not the position of an Orthodox paper to air the community's dirty laundry. As someone who likes to think of himself as a newspaperman, I obviously don't agree with that. If I were at a non-Orthodox paper or a secular paper, I would have no qualms doing things that I am constrained from here.

"I am not complaining. Never once have I been told to change anything I've written. I don't think a writer at *The Jewish Week* or the *Forward* would be able to say that. The paper is owned by the Klass family. Rabbi Sholom Klass, who died in 2000, was the founder of the paper and longtime publisher."

In September 2004, Jason responded to several critical posts on Protocols:

> The bit about Lubavitch advertising is typical. Are we supposed to start turning down ads from certain groups within Orthodoxy? For better or worse, Lubavitch is such a driving force in Jewish communities across the country and around the world. Of course they're going to advertise their activities in an Orthodox paper like *The Jewish Press*. And of course we'll cover many of those activities. Look at the JTA's coverage of Jewish life in foreign countries. Almost invariably when they quote an Orthodox rabbi in south America, Europe, Asia, etc., that rabbi is a Lubavitcher. You can't cover the Orthodox world without giving Lubavitch an inordinate amount of ink. And by the way, contrary to some dumb rumor posted by an ignorant twit on some blog recently, there is not one Lubavitcher in any editorial decision-making capacity at *The Jewish Press*.

> As for the 'Kahanist rag' comment—obviously a retort made by a retard. There may be some columnists we feature who share some of Kahane's views, but they're in a minority—and certainly don't reflect the official editorial positions taken by the paper in recent years.

> As to the comment about our being heavily feature-and-commentary-oriented at the expense of hard news, of course that's true. A weekly publication in the age of the Internet and 24-hour cable news must by necessity focus more on background and features. *Time* and *Newsweek* realized this years ago and began to go more in the direction of lifestyle-type features. It would be presumptuous for us to think that most readers look to a weekly of any kind as their primary news source. It's even more ludicrous to expect a weekly newspa-

per—one that goes to press Tuesday and that most people don't read before Friday and Saturday—to contain breaking news stories.

I don't think I need to elaborate further on the Lubavitch issue other than to ask the poster named Sidney if he would be kind enough to take a few moments—from what I'm certain must be a busy and challenging schedule of intellectual pursuit—to explain what he means by "Lubavitch slant." Yes, as I noted in my Friday comments, we take ads from Lubavitch organizations. And we do have a few Lubavitcher columnists—among the dozens our regular columnists and contributors who cover the spectrum of Orthodoxy from Modern to yeshivish to chassidish. (We also frequently feature pieces by secular Jews and non-Jews; I suppose this means we have a "secular slant" or a "Christian slant" to go along with that alleged "Lubavitch slant.")

So please, Sid (you'll pardon the informality), ads and opinion columns aside, tell me where exactly you detect that old-time Chabad religion in our news stories or our editorials. I'm sure someone blessed with your Alpine intellect knows the difference between reporting on a Lubavitch-affiliated institution or event and, as you so strikingly phrased it (tell me you write for Yated and I promise I won't doubt it for a second), being a paper "that allowed/s Lubavitch 'Christians' to still proclaim their leader as the second coming [sic] messiah."

One more thing, Sid. Show me when and where we turned Baruch Goldstein into a "Jewish saviour." (Shhh—don't tell the Lubavitchers; we wouldn't want them to think we practice a polytheistic form of messianism.) If nothing else, your timing is exquisitely bad, since this very week in our Letters to the Editor section, one of our frequent contributors, Steven Plaut, strongly admonishes two readers who saw fit to defend the actions of the same Baruch Goldstein you posit as one of our paper's designated "Jewish saviours." Since I oversee the Letters section and solicited Plaut's rejoinder to the aforementioned readers, I'm afraid that makes me the house heretic. Stoning commences immediately after Mincha tomorrow. (Bongs optional.)

Which brings me to the poster known as Mike Da Kike—(my, the time and thought that had to have gone into formulating such a sensitive and literate moniker)—and his story about "interviewing for a job" here.

Remember that marvelous scene in *Annie Hall* where Woody Allen (as Alvy Singer) encounters a blowhard on line in a movie theater spouting off about Marshall McLuhan? Woody/Alvy summons forth the real Marshall McLuhan who shuts up the pretentious bore by telling him, "You know nothing of my work." At which point Woody/Alvy turns to the camera and says, "Boy, if life were only like this!"

Well, life is like that, at least in this instance, as I have the luxury of summoning myself to question the claims of Mr. Kike, who, when he made them early Friday, had no idea I would involve myself in this little discussion. I happen to be in the unique position of knowing that we have not had an editorial opening at The Jewish Press for at least five years now. There was a spot open about five, maybe five and a half, years ago, but we hired someone very quickly. Before that, there was an editorial hire in 1997—me. So unless Mr. Kike was one of the four or five interviewees who didn't get the job five and a half years ago(and I believe all of them were women)—or unless he interviewed before 1997, which would make his story irrelevant at best because The Jewish Press was a far different paper from what it is today—his story doesn't hold up.

(In reviewing Mr. Kike's post, I see he doesn't describe the position for which he supposedly applied, and so perhaps I jumped the gun in assuming it was related in any manner to editorial work. We have filled a couple of custodial positions over the past few years, and perhaps that is what he is referring to—which, come to think of it, makes perfect sense when one considers the quality of his prose.)

Finally, poster Benjy throws around some IQ figures. I'm thumbing through the last few issues of The Jewish Press where I see such notorious exemplars of low IQ as Jonathan Tobin, Joseph Schick, Phyllis Chesler, Victor Davis Hanson, Dr. Yitzchok Levine, Ed Koch, Rabbi Dovid Goldwasser, Rabbi Moshe Meir Weiss, Rabbi Steven Riskin, Marvin Schick, Professor Louis Rene Beres, and arts critic Richard McBee (none of them Lubavitch and all of them, I'd wager, considerably more intelligent than Benjy). Not a bad lineup at all, and one that definitely can do without the services of Mike Da

Kike. But do send us an updated resume, Mr. Kike—those custodial positions tend to have a high turnover rate, and you never know when you'll get lucky.

A veteran Jewish journalist on the right says:

> *The Jewish Press* was nuts but not inaccurate. Because they had exclusivity in English-language Orthodox journalism, nobody could do anything against them. Since Rabbi Klass left this world, the paper has become responsible. He ran it as a stranglehold. Nobody could start up with him. Whatever he said went.
>
> It's probably the most financially successful Jewish newspaper in America. It nets more than a million dollars a year.
>
> A lot of the things they said were correct, just the world wasn't ready to hear it yet. That made them appear to be nuts. They were so far ahead of the time that people looked at them as if they were crazy. A lot of what they predicted, such as about Arafat, came to fruition.
>
> Seth Lipsky once spoke at a prominent Manhattan Orthodox shul. He was head of the editorial board of *The Wall Street Journal*. He was asked what Jewish papers he read. He said *The Jewish Press*. People rolled their eyes, snickered, and waited for the punchline. He said he was serious. *The Jewish Press* is 100% correct.
>
> *The Jewish Press* was not sophisticated and few people [outside of Orthodoxy] were ready to listen to them [on Israel, the peace process, that Republican presidents are better for Jews].
>
> A lot of what Kahane said was right. He just said it at the wrong time. The packaging was off.
>
> *The Jewish Press* does not have the mainstream credibility of an ADL or a Simon Wiesenthal Center. People saw them as these meshuganah Orthodox Jews with their accents and black hats and black suits. The product looked shoddy.
>
> People used to pick up *The Jewish Press* for the same reason many people in a different society pick up the *Village Voice*—for entertainment purposes. Now there's substance. They started buying news

services such as *The Jerusalem Post* and the JTA. There's a lot more competition now in the Orthodox community.

In recent years, they've added Charedi-type rabbis to the paper. They've remade their paper to keep up with the tilt to the right.

Rob Eshman emails:

I've read [*The Jewish Press*] all the way through maybe twice, so it wouldn't be fair for me to offer an opinion. (Now, here comes my opinion): The times I have flipped through it, my impression was it seems to cater to a certain niche of American Jewry, and it seems to do that quite well.

I don't think anybody is in Gary's thrall, handsome and funny and brilliant as he is—uh oh, maybe I AM in his thrall. Seriously, Gary's a very good editor and he puts out a very good paper. There are a lot worse role models out there for editors of any paper, but he's not the boss of anyone at AJPA.

The Jewish Week serves its audience, and certainly has taken on tough stories in a responsible way. No one editor or one community Jewish paper is going to please all the Jews all the time. Papers like *The Jewish Week* and the *Jewish Journal* have to appeal to a large and broad Jewish audience to fulfill their missions and stay solvent. We don't have big backers, an endowment, a niche Jewish market to serve or relatively homogenous Jewish populations. We try to serve the needs of hundreds of thousands of Jews in each issue: smart Jews, simple Jews, wise and ignorant, right, left, rich, poor, traditional, freaky. The result can be articles that are sometimes too safe and predictable and middle of the road, but all of the good editors I know push beyond that as much as possible.

APPENDIX A

A History of Jewish Journalism in the United States

By Dr. Jonathan D. Sarna, copyright Jonathan D. Sarna

The history of Jewish Journalism in the United States presents something of a challenge.[1] Traditionally, historians like to recount the story of progress: development onward and upward from primitive origins to flourishing contemporary success. The history of Jewish journalism in the US, by contrast, represents, at least until recently, a story of marked decay.

From a period when they were independent, innovative and national in scope, American Jewish newspapers declined in quality, lost their independence, and became far more consensus oriented and narrowly focused. Admittedly, recent decades have witnessed some great improvements in American Jewish journalism and a new willingness, at least among some newspapers, to tackle sensitive and controversial issues. It is nevertheless worthwhile to understand why the earlier, prolonged decline took place, because the reasons shed light on problems that are endemic to American Jewish journalism, and I suspect to all minority group journalism; problems that plague the field to this very day.

First, some background. The oldest Jewish newspaper that we know dates to 17th century Amsterdam. Traditionally, the *Gazeta de Amsterdam* (1675) was considered the first Jewish newspaper; recently it has been argued that the paper was only printed by a Jew, and that the first paper published for Jews was the *Dinshtagishe un Fraytagishe Kurant*, published in Yiddish in 1686–7.[2] I cannot resolve this question, but I do want to observe that, from the very beginning, Jewish journalism has not been easy to define: does a Jewish publisher make a journal Jewish, does a Jewish readership make it Jewish, does a Jewish language make it Jewish? I am going to focus on newspapers that defined themselves as Jewish newspapers, but it is worth recalling that Jewish journalism might also embrace a broader field, particularly since Jews (indeed a disproportionate number of them) have been involved in the field of journalism from its earliest days.

Why Jews have been so involved in journalism is in itself an interesting question. I do not want to take us too far a field, but I suspect that the opportunities found in journalism (especially during its period of rapid growth), the fact that it offered practitioners a great deal of independence, and the comparative advantage that people with cosmopolitan backgrounds, like Jews, enjoyed in the field all help to explain the phenomenon. Even early on in American history, when the Jewish community numbered no more than a few thousand, Jews played a disproportionate role in journalism. Their importance in the profession has, in the intervening years, in no way diminished.[3]

In the United States, the earliest newspaper with a Jewish name is Cohen's Gazette and Lottery Register (1814–1830), published by Jacob I. Cohen, Jr. While published by a Jew and read by Jews, this was hardly a Jewish newspaper; it was, in essence, a gambling sheet.[4] A journal of a different sort was published in 1823–1825. Its title was *The Jew*, and its subtitle explained that it was "a defense of Judaism against all Adversaries, and particularly against the insidious Attacks of *Israel's Advocate*," which was a missionary journal. *The Jew* adumbrates one of the major functions of every vernacular Jewish newspaper: to defend Jews against their adversaries. But one can scarcely imagine anyone actually reading *The Jew* for news. The only significant news that it printed was a series of scoops about scandals within the American Society for Meliorating the Condition of the Jews, the society dedicated to converting Jews to Christianity.[5] Jewish news was published in various American newspapers, particularly those edited by the distinguished Jewish journalist-politician, Mordecai M. Noah. But like today's *New York Times*, Noah's dailies were designed for a broad audience. They never claimed to be Jewish newspapers, even if they did devote disproportionate attention to Jewish matters.[6]

Jewish journalism as we know it in the United States dates quite specifically to April 1843 and the publication of *The Occident* by Isaac Leeser, chazzan of Cong. Mikveh Israel in Philadelphia and the most significant Jewish traditionalist religious leader of his day. Leeser was influenced by a range of factors: the development of national Jewish periodicals in Germany, France and

England, the evident need to unify the far-flung American Jewish community (a need made painfully evident by the Damascus Affair of 1840), the emergence of newspapers as instruments of Jewish enlightenment, and most immediately by the need to respond to a new missionary journal published in New York entitled *The Jewish Chronicle*, not to be confused with the distinguished London Jewish newspaper (1841–) of the same name. Publicly, Leeser described his journal as an "advocate" for Jewish interests (the full title was *The Occident and American Jewish Advocate*), and its announced aim was "diffusion of knowledge on Jewish literature and religion"—in other words, communal defense and Jewish education, two principal aims of Jewish journalism forever after.[7] To carry out these aims, *The Occident* published news from American Jewish communities, and from abroad (often reprinted from foreign Jewish publications), as well as sermons, editorials, historical articles, book reviews, innovative policy proposals (for schools, Jewish colonies, unity etc.), religious philosophy, and controversial (or apologetic) articles leveled against missionaries and other enemies of the Jewish people. Leeser admitted into his pages many writers with whom he disagreed (sometimes he mentioned the disagreement in an introductory paragraph), and he published many verbatim documents.

Especially in his early years, he saw his as the newspaper of record for the American Jewish community, and he opened its pages to a wide range of contributors, including non-Jews.[8]

The Occident was a quality production, and it remains a magnificent historical source: one of the finest journals that the American Jewish community has ever produced. There were nevertheless significant limits to what it was prepared to print.

"On no account can our pages become the vehicle for violent denunciation or unfounded aspersion," Leeser wrote in his introductory remarks, and he naively urged readers "never to send us any thing which may require contradiction or amendment in a future number."[9] Although he understood that controversy and error were unavoidable, he hoped to project an image of Jewish consensus—a projection of the community as he wished it to be, rather than the community as it was. In this, I think, he adumbrated a problem that has long plagued the field: a tension between the Jewish journalist as a reporter of news and the Jewish journalist as a shaper of community. In Leeser's case, this explains why he mostly closed his columns to divisive debates over slavery and the Civil War: he feared that such debates would be harmful to the Jewish community (and perhaps also to himself since he personally sympathized with the South and supported the idea of compromise for the sake of Union.) But, as the slavery issue demonstrates, self-censorship comes at a price: Jews who sought to debate the hotly-contested issues of slavery and union had no regular Jewish forum in which to do so.

The success of *The Occident* generated a spate of new journals on the American scene, published in diverse locations, including New York, New Orleans, Cincinnati and San Francisco. Already by the 1850s one can discern a movement in American Jewish journalism parallel to what we know in American journalism generally, a movement away from all-embracing national newspapers and toward local or regional papers that were narrower in focus and more circumscribed in their ambitions and aims. Most of these newspapers were weeklies, not monthlies like *The Occident* (which became a weekly for a brief and unsuccessful period), and they modeled themselves after American religious and family newspapers, rather than highbrow magazines. As a result their format was different from *The Occident*'s: they looked like newspapers (some were printed on cheap newsprint), and they aimed to be much more entertaining than it was; at least one of them, for example, published chapters from a serial novel each week on its front page. I am not able to deal with every newspaper from this period, but let me briefly mention three that represent to my mind different directions, or options, for American Jewish journalism to follow.

The first, which was also the first significant Jewish newspaper to be published in New York, was entitled, the *Asmonean*. It was edited on business principles by a (failed) New York Jewish businessman named Robert Lyon, and perhaps for this reason it was livelier, bolder, and much more diverse in its subject-matter than other 19th century Jewish newspapers. The *Asmonean* billed itself as "a family journal of commerce, politics, religion and literature devoted to the interests of the American Israelites," and represents a model of American Jewish journalism not seen again, at least in English, until our own day: a journal for American Jews but by no means limited to Jewish subject-matter. It lasted for nine years (1849–1858), until Lyon's death, but the absence of a follow-up suggests that most English-speaking American Jews conceived of Jewish journalism in more restrictive terms. Just as they compartmentalized their lives into secular and Jewish realms, so too their newspapers.[10]

A quite different direction was followed by the first Jewish newspaper in Cincinnati, now the oldest continuous Jewish newspaper in the United States: *The Israelite*, renamed the *American Israelite* in 1874, and published by the pioneer of American Reform Judaism, Rabbi Isaac Mayer Wise. Here we have the first example of an American Jewish newspaper committed to advancing a particular ideology and unafraid of controversy in defense of that ideology. Wise was blessed with a lively pen and an engaging often biting style, and his newspaper, which was much more entertaining than *The Occident*, gained a wide national readership. So long as Wise was alive, it was recognized as his semi-official organ representing the Reform movement in American Judaism.[11] Although the *American Israelite* lost this mantle after Wise's death and steadily deteriorated into a run-of-the-mill local newspaper, a pattern had been set. Thereafter in American Jewish life, we have many examples of significant, movement-sponsored periodicals. In the best cases, the idealism, energy and commitment that stand behind the movement are reflected in its journal. Such was the case, for example, with the *American Hebrew*, the vibrant weekly created in 1879 by religiously traditional young Jews (ages 21–29) hoping to revitalize American Jewish life.[12] Later, we see this same pattern in such journals as the *Menorah Journal*, *The Reconstructionist*, *Jewish Frontier*, and in the Boston student newspaper, *Genesis II*.

The third model that we have beginning in this period is the foreign-language Jewish newspaper. Several of them appeared even before the Civil War, *Sinai* and *Die Deborah* being the most famous, and all of them were published in German. This is not the place for a full-scale discussion of the foreign-language Jewish press in America.[13] Suffice it to say that significant Jewish newspapers were published in German, Hebrew, Yiddish, and Ladino, and they deserve a separate analysis. A whole documentary film, in fact, has been produced just on the Jewish *Daily Forward*. For our purposes, however, let me confine myself to four salient points:

1. Foreign language journals consisted of two types: intellectual (high brow) journals and popular (low brow) ones. The former, like *Sinai* (in German) and the *Di Tsukunft* (in Yiddish) addressed immigrant intellectuals, the latter like *Die Deborah* (in German) and *Der Hoyzfraynd* (in Yiddish) were directed to the masses and especially to women (although it was widely recognized that men read these journals as well).

2. Foreign language Jewish newspapers were much less compartmentalized than English ones. Like the *Asmonean*, they presented secular and Jewish news as well as features. One can see this clearly in Abra-

ham Cahan's *Forward*; it remains true even today in the newspaper produced for Israeli immigrants, *Yisrael Shelanu*.

3. The foreign-language press was much more focused on issues of immigration, Americanization, and developments in the old country than the Anglo-Jewish Press. The Yiddish press, in particular, covered developments in Eastern Europe with a depth not seen in parallel English language Jewish newspapers.

4. Finally, foreign language Jewish newspapers were often bolder and more critical of American and American Jewish life than English-language ones. This is especially true of the intellectual journals and the Hebrew journals that had a small, well-defined readership and editors far less fearful of the journal "falling into the wrong hands." Intellectuals, to be sure, tend to be alienated no matter what language they write in, but the secure sense that they were being read by a select and sympathetic audience made it possible for them to criticize people, institutions, and social trends in a way not often found in the parallel English-language Jewish publications that were more widely circulated and that gentiles sometimes perused as well.

So much, then, for the early decades of American Jewish journalism, when so many of the central trends and central tensions that characterize Jewish journalism in this country were determined. Now it is time to move on to the question with which I began: why did the once varied and vibrant world of Jewish journalism in the United States deteriorate into the so-called "weaklies" that Jewish leaders like Stephen S. Wise used so regularly to deride. Let me suggest three major reasons:

First, the proliferation of local Jewish newspapers, while probably unavoidable given the character of American journalism generally, changed the focus of Jewish journalism from the kinds of national issues that dominated the *Occident* toward a much narrower local-oriented journalism with a strong component of boosterism. Local Jewish newspapers, especially those outside of major population centers, could not attract the kinds of contributors that a national newspaper could, and their goals became proportionately more modest and consensus-oriented. Primarily, they sought to convey information, promote local communal involvement, and if necessary defend Jews against their enemies. Only a small number of local newspapers like New York's *American Hebrew* which, as I mentioned had a larger objective—to revitalize the American Jewish community on a more traditionalist basis, or, to take an example closer to home, Boston's *Jewish Advocate* which under Jacob De Haas had the larger objective of promoting Zionism—only these ideologically motivated newspapers managed to stave off the narrow parochialism that affected so much of American Jewish journalism in the Twentieth Century. Unsurprisingly these were also among the most vibrant and significant Jewish newspapers of their day.

Second, financial pressures led to the deterioration of Jewish newspapers. Most proved unable to break even, especially in smaller population centers, and like it or not they came to depend on financial backers. Beginning in the 1940s, in cities like Philadelphia, the local Jewish Federation stepped in to cover the annual deficit. Inevitably, this financial dependence impacted on the ability of local Jewish newspapers to remain independent—as we say in Hebrew, Baal ha-meah, baal ha-deah (translated idiomatically, that means "he who pays the piper picks the tune"). In Philadelphia, where the subject has been studied, criticism of Federation-supported Jewish agencies, and even widely-available negative news concerning these agencies stopped appearing in the Jewish newspaper (or in some case found mention only long after news was widely available elsewhere).[14]

In smaller communities, even independent editors found that they dared not alienate subscribers or advertisers, so they played it safe. Faced with the choice of having a bland Jewish newspaper or no Jewish newspaper, most editors understandably chose the former. They justified their journalistic compromises as necessary to keep their local Jewish newspapers alive.

Finally, anti-Semitism, particularly in the period between the wars, had a chilling effect on the Anglo-Jewish press. As fear stalked the Jewish community and conditions for Jews domestically and abroad deteriorated, newspapers became frightened of controversy, scandal or of other news that reflected badly on the Jewish people, and they worked all the harder to promote an image of consensus and sobriety, lest they unintentionally play into the hands of Israel's enemies. While there was no shortage of intra-communal controversies or scandals during this era—witness the fierce debates over Zionism, the tactical debates over how best to respond to anti-Semitism, or the many scandals connected with Prohibition violations—these were not by and large reflected in the Jewish weeklies. Even anti-Jewish violence such as regularly occurred here in Boston only rarely found mention in the press. To write about such violence, Jews feared, was to risk stirring up trouble and making the situation worse.

Once again, then, the press exercised considerable self-censorship. It did so, I think, with the best of intensions; it believed that it was serving the larger interests of the Jewish people. The result, however, was a loss of credibility. Jews seeking accurate and reliable Jewish news turned elsewhere.

Where did they turn? For years, many Jews read the Yiddish Press or in far fewer cases the Hebrew Press, which as I indicated felt less constrained than the English-language weeklies; they were a much better and more accurate source of news. Others Jews subscribed to national Jewish magazines which then (and by and large still today) were much more vibrant than the local weeklies and did open their pages to debate: one thinks of the *Menorah Journal*, *The Reconstructionist*, *Jewish Frontier*, the *Contemporary Jewish Record Commentary*, *Midstream* and many others. The number of English-language national Jewish periodicals proliferated in the twentieth century. There were a grand total of four such periodicals in 1900: one for "Young People" (*Young Israel*), one for "the Jewish Religious School and Home" (*Helpful Thoughts*), one for Hebrew Union College students and alumni (Hebrew Union College Journal), and one, *The Menorah*, the official organ of B'nai B'rith. Today, by contrast, the American Jewish Year Book lists more than sixty such periodicals, not including those for religious schoolchildren, catering to the widest array of ideologies and interests. As a result of this exponential growth, Jews dissatisfied with local Jewish newspapers, who want more serious and indepth analyses, have in the twentieth-century been able to find alternative publications to read.

Finally, I should mention two other sources that American Jews began to turn to for reliable news: First, the Jewish Telegraphic Agency, founded in 1917 to provide world Jewry with news about the World War from a Jewish point of view. Its cable service, set up in the 1920s, soon became the dominant provider of worldwide Jewish news for most American Jewish weeklies, improving the quality of their Jewish news. Yet this development also created a certain uniformity of perspective, as almost all American Jewish newspapers came to rely on the same source—"the JTA"—for Jewish news from around the nation and the world. Moreover, as a Jewish sponsored agency, the JTA faced some of the same tensions that local weeklies faced: its commitment on the one hand to journalistic detachment, and on the other hand its very strong attachment to the American Jewish community to which it has always been beholden.

Second, *The New York Times* became increasingly influential within the American Jewish community. Purchased by Adolph Ochs, the son-in-law of

Rabbi Isaac Mayer Wise, in 1896, it consciously paid special attention to news of Jewish interest both because of its Jewish ownership and because Jews comprised a substantial percentage of its New York readership. In return, Jews rightly or wrongly came to perceive *The Times* as the ultimate authority on substantial news stories of Jewish interest. *The Times*, in reporting such stories, has always projected an air of objectivity and detachment that no Jewish newspaper can match.

Recent years, as we all know, have witnessed a considerable revolution in the world of American Jewish journalism. This is not the place to analyze this revolution—especially since so many of the revolutionaries are participants in this forum—but I think it is fair to say that Jewish journalism's long downward slide has during this time period begun to be reversed. The strong national emphasis on journalistic independence in the wake of Vietnam and Watergate have echoed in the halls of Jewish journalism, and almost all major American Jewish newspapers have been affected by this revolution. As a result, a new high-quality national Jewish newspaper, the English-language *Forward*, has been established that sets a new standard in the field, while the best local Jewish newspapers have displayed a willingness to tackle controversial issues that would just a few years ago have been shunned.

Rather than ending on this happy and uplifting note, however, I want to close by restating in question form three central problems that seem to me to have plagued American Jewish journalism over the past century and a half, problems that help to account for its decline early in the century, and problems that remain on our agenda today, even as we hope that Jewish journalism is improving.

First, what is the mission of Jewish journalism? Is its mission primarily to inform? To educate? To defend? To support one or another Jewish ideology? To promote community and continuity? And if one insists that its mission embraces all of the above, what happens when two or more of them come into conflict?

Second, what are the responsibilities of Jewish journalism? Should the "good of the Jewish people" (or the good of the local Jewish community) be the highest goal, or should "truth" be the highest goal? What happens when these two come into conflict?

Finally, what compromises should a Jewish newspaper be prepared to make in order to ensure its survival? Should it seek private or communal support? How much independence should it be prepared to sacrifice in return for such support? Where must it forcefully draw the line?

These are not easy questions. Nor do I pretend that history provides us with sure answers to any of them based on past experience. What I do believe is that the quality of Jewish journalism depends on our willingness to confront these questions honestly—and to wrestle with them continuously.

NOTES

[Earlier versions of this paper were delivered before the Brinn Forum at Brandeis University and at the Board Institute of the *MetroWest Jewish News*.]

1. The literature on this subject to 1983 is reviewed in Robert Singerman, "The American Jewish Press, 1823–1983: A Bibliographic Survey of Research and Studies," *American Jewish History* 73 (June 1984), pp.422–444.

2. Joel Cahen, "Amsterdam, Cradle of the Jewish Press?" Proceedings of the Symposium on the Jewish Press: Why? Past, Present, Future (Amsterdam: *Nieuw Israelietisch Weekblad*, 1985), pp.17–23.

3. Jonathan D. Sarna, *Jacksonian Jew: The Two Worlds of Mordecai Noah* (New York: Holmes & Meier, 1981), pp.5–6; Stephen J. Whitfield, *Voices of Jacob, Hands of Esau: Jews in American Life and Thought* (Hamden, CT: Archon, 1984), pp.180–207; Stephen J. Whitfield, *American Space, Jewish Time* (Hamden, Ct: Archon, 1988), pp.129–150.

4. Extant numbers of this journal are available in the American Periodical Series, reel 93. On Cohen, see Isaac M. Fein, *The Making of an American Jewish Community: The History of Baltimore Jewry from 1773 to 1920* (Philadelphia: Jewish Publication Society, 1971), pp.22–24.

5. George L. Berlin, "Solomon Jackson's The Jew: An Early American Jewish Response to the Missionaries," *American Jewish History* 71 (September 1981), pp.10–28.

6. On Noah's newspapers, see Sarna, *Jacksonian Jew*, passim.

7. Naomi W. Cohen describes early American Jewish newspapers as "Pioneers of American Jewish Defense." See her article by that title in *American Jewish Archives* 29 (November 1977), pp.116–150.

8. The best study of Leeser, including his newspaper, is Lance J. Sussman's *Isaac Leeser and the Making of American Judaism* (Detroit: Wayne State University Press, 1995). On the origins of *The Occident*, see Jonathan D. Sarna, "The Impact of Nineteenth-Century Christian Missions on American Jews," in *Jewish Apostasy in the Modern World*, ed. Todd Endelman (New York: Holmes & Meier, 1987), pp.242–243. The journal's first number is reprinted with an introduction in Abraham J. Karp, *Beginnings: Early American Judaica* (Philadelphia: Jewish Publication Society, 1975).

9. Occident 1 (April 1843), p.5.

10. Cohen, "Pioneers of American Jewish Defense," pp.133–140; H.B.Grinstein, "The 'Asmonean': The First Jewish Weekly in New York," *Journal of Jewish Bibliography* 1 (1939), pp.67–71; Henry S. Morais, "Robert Lyon," *Eminent Israelites of the Nineteenth Century* (Philadelphia: Edward Stern & Co., 1880), pp.221–222.

11. Cohen, "Pioneers of American Jewish Defense," pp.140–149; Sefton D. Temkin, *Isaac Mayer Wise* (Oxford: Oxford University Press, 1992), pp.112–124.

12. Philip Cowen, *Memories of an American Jew* (New York: The International Press, 1932), pp.40–111; Charles Wyszkowski, *A Community in Conflict: American Jewry During the Great European Immigration* (New York: University Press of America, 1991), pp. xiii-xvii.

13. See, inter alia, Arthur A. Goren's analysis in his thoughtful survey of "The Jewish Press" in *The Ethnic Press in the United States*, ed. Sally M. Miller (New York: Greenwood Press, 1987), pp.203–228; Joseph Gutmann, "Watchman on an American Rhine: New Light on Isaac M. Wise," *American Jewish Archives* 10 (October 1958), pp.135–144; Mordecai Soltes, The Yiddish Press: An Americanizing Agency (New York: Teachers College, 1925); Michael G. Brown, "All, All Alone: The Hebrew Press in America from 1914 to 1924," *American Jewish Historical Quarterly* 59 (December 1969), pp.139–178; and Marc D. Angel, *La America: The Sephardic Experience in the United States* (Philadelphia: Jewish Publication Society, 1982).

14. Maxwell Whiteman, "A Century of Jewish Journalism: The Jewish Exponent, 1887–1987" *A People in Print: Jewish Journalism in America* (Philadelphia: National Museum of American Jewish History, 1987), p.19–20.

APPENDIX B

The Economics of Jewish Journalism in the United States

By Neil Rubin

As the adage goes, "If a tree fell in the woods and no one heard it did it really fall?"

In journalism, it's been adapted to read, "If a tree fell in the woods and the media was not there to record it, did it really fall?"

At North America's Jewish newspapers, it should be rewritten a bit further. "If a tree fell in the woods, and Jewish newspapers didn't write about it, fearing it fell in a prominent philanthropist's forest, one who would be angry if the article were reported in the local Jewish paper, did it really fall?"

Bizarre as that might sound, Jewish journalism in North America, commonly known as the Anglo-Jewish press, is indeed a complex and at times difficult to understand topic. It varies widely in scope and quality from city to city. To date, the vast majority of research on these publications has dealt with several main topics:

- The general history of a particular publication, often articles or monographs put out by those publications, or state Jewish historical societies, to coincide with publication anniversaries;

- How American Jewish newspapers dealt with the powerful and chilling mounting realities of the Nazi Holocaust (a source of a number of doctoral dissertations);

- How ethical dilemmas have been handled—such as the 1984 controversial decision by the *Washington Jewish Week* to expose the previously secret airlift of imperiled Ethiopian Jews to Israel, resulting in the temporary halt in that human pipeline.

Despite that study, and despite the general explosion of interest in academic Jewish studies over the past three decades in America, the topic of Jewish newspapers and how their editors seek to shape the general Jewish consciousness—knowingly or unknowingly—has been ignored by scholars.

Indeed, study of the Jewish press—and certainly its economics—is basically non-existent. Among the reasons: the difficulty of attaining Internal Revenue Service tax filings and the reluctance of editors/publishers to share such information.

This paper begins to explore the intricate and diverse world of the economics of Jewish journalism. Research primarily consisted of sending 14 editors of small, medium and large market Jewish communities a survey about their economic situation, plans and experiences. Those were: Atlanta, Ga; Baltimore, Maryland; Boston, Massachusetts; Detroit, Michigan; Birmingham, Alabama; Chicago, Illinois; Cleveland, Ohio; New York City, N.Y.; Palm Beach, Florida; Phoenix, Arizona; Philadelphia, Pennsylvania; Pittsburgh, Pennsylvania; San Francisco, California; Seattle, Washington. Their responses are understandably varied, reflecting different markets as well as models of ownership, which we shall explore.

This paper also relies on my personal experiences as a 15-year veteran of Jewish Journalism. I am senior editor of the *Baltimore Jewish Times*. I served as assistant editor for 18 months and then editor for six years of the *Atlanta Jewish Times* (1991–1998). I also served as contributing editor to our sister publications (now sold): the *Detroit Jewish News*; the *Palm Beach and Boca/DelRay Jewish Times*; and the *Western Jewish Bulletin* (serving Vancouver, British Columbia).

In each case, I worked closely with publishers. One drilled into my head the reality that "your work has a direct impact on the bottom line, which has a direct impact on your future resources, not to mention your salary."

Now, as vice president of the American Jewish Press Association, I constantly discuss all facets of our field with various editors and publishers. Economic/financial concerns—from the salaries of reporters, to rising printing and mailing costs, to federation subsidies, to circulation woes—are always part of the agenda.

THE PROFESSION TODAY

Today, Jewish Journalism in North America is a profession. Editors and reporters are often sought by professional employment recruiters. The professional association—the American Jewish Press Association—is active. It hosts several conferences a year (in both the editorial and business tracks), is addressed by speakers such as Sen. Joseph I. Lieberman and Harvard Law School Professor Alan Dershowitz, has a regular newsletter and maintains a Web site (www.ajpa.org). It even lobbies Congress, with other minority publication groups, about the impact of postage increases, via the Coalition of Religious Press Associations.[1]

As for the publications themselves, in the course of a year numerous ones now sell more than several million dollars a year in advertisements. Almost all of these papers are weeklies. Unlike in previous decades, they no longer need to "Americanize" new immigrants. Rather, the goal is to maintain a broad sense of community, and to be honest purveyors of the news. The vast majority are in English, but specialty publications exist in Russian, Hebrew and Farsi. The *Forward*, has a Yiddish as well as a Russian weekly.

These publications are staffed by trained journalists, not the passionate community activists that once formed their staff's core. They compete with secular weeklies as well as dailies on all levels—staff recruitment, delivery of top news stories and the selling of ad space. Jewish newspapers can be financially viable in Birmingham, Ala. and New York City, in Kansas City, Mo., and Las Vegas, Nev.

At times, the economic competition between papers within larger communities such as New York City and south Florida is fierce. Some, such as the *Long Island Jewish World*, have run large announcements attacking the Federation subsidies of a competitor, *The Jewish Week*.

Almost all of these papers are weekly, arriving in people's homes on Fridays to provide Shabbat reading. The World Wide Web has brought a new sense of timeliness to the gathering of Jewish news. This has created headaches for papers facing early deadlines. The *Atlanta Jewish Times*, due to its printers' schedule, currently has a Monday deadline for getting its pages to the paper, but the paper is not delivered until Friday. But there also are exciting challenges in the creation of new products. Numerous papers now have Web sites, often updating local stories throughout the week and providing daily updates via the Jewish Telegraphic Agency (known as "the Jewish Associated Press").

But to readers, what usually counts most is not the latest spin from an Israeli politician, or the Jewish angle on Washington's partisan infighting. Rather, is the local news fix—particularly the cradle to grave life cycle announcements—that is eagerly read. Readers will tell you that they scan b'nai mitzvah announcements, engagements, obituaries and the like regularly to keep in touch with their divergent community's important events. Such realities help drive story selection as well as advertiser recruitment.

Mass publishing—Jewish or otherwise—is expensive. Distribution costs can run hundreds of thousands of dollars a year, or more (depending on size and market). More money is spent on marketing than ever before. In the past decade, numerous papers have opened a marketing/circulation department.

That effort can pay off. The more successful publications can gross more than $10 million a year. As such, they need quality staff, which costs money. It is not uncommon to see a handful of people on advertising staffs earn more than $100,000 a year. Top editors in a handful of markets approach the six-figure limit. Most earn substantially less; they often offer entry-level positions at between $18,000 and $25,000 annually.

Always close to the surface is the existential dilemma of the Anglo-Jewish press. On the one hand, to quote Tevyeh the Milkman of Sholem Aleichem fame, the job is to spread the good news about the community. On the other hand, the traditional journalism's role of watchdog must be upheld.

Jewish institutions must be challenged when necessary, and voice must be given to those who feel disenfranchised by organized Jewish life. Jewish newspaper editors must raise unpopular questions, ones that will anger readers and influential community leaders. And that must always be done at the right moment and in the right way—no easy task.

And it's not so simple:

- It cannot be when major newspapers (and particularly minor ones) are owned by the establishment itself—the Jewish Federation.

- It cannot be when major advertisers—whose budget can have a major impact on profitability—have to be approached with great sensitivity.

- And it cannot be when one is not merely a journalist, but a Jewish journalist.

We are community journalists to the extreme. Our job is to be accessible, to be communal leaders. People have lined up at Shabbat kiddish to berate, praise, suggest or nudge me about what has (or has not) appeared in print. I once was confronted in the restroom of a movie house. And when a Jewish newspaper editor walks into a kosher establishment in America, he or she does a quick check of the mental body armor before swinging through the door (and, depending on the week, putting on dark sunglasses).

There is not one editor of a quality Jewish newspaper who has not had a serious clash with a Federation director. In Atlanta, I was regularly threatened with withdrawal of Federation advertising funds—some $50,000 a year—were coverage not favorable.

As one editor, who requested anonymity for obvious reasons, said, "The phrase, 'he who pays the piper calls the tune' is very much alive and well in the Jewish press." What is being painted here is the natural tension—in good times—between the business side of Jewish journalism and the integrity of its editorial product. Or as the editor of *New Jersey Jewish News* puts it, "The Chinese wall should stand. Nevertheless, I don't see how editors can escape concern about economic viability."[2]

THE OWNERS

A quick review of the ownership of the Jewish press in America says much about its economic standing. Not surprisingly, editors and publishers are reluctant to give out specific information. All interviewed for this paper did so on the condition that the information would not be used elsewhere. They fear a backlash of people demanding that subscription and ad rates be lowered if much money is being made, and they fear demands of raises by staff.

As such, the Jewish media commits the sin that it often accuses others of—not being open and candid about its inner workings (particularly hirings, firings and expenses).

We who control the print media (and now electronic additions through the World Wide Web) simply do not publicize profits or losses. Due to U.S. Postal Service regulations, we must print once a year the details of ownership as well as circulation. Advertisers look closely at those numbers—if they see it on the one week it's published. Those advertisers, by the way, are sometimes given inflated statistics by sales staff seeking to impress perspective buyers with the publication's alleged reach.

That said, there are two main types of owners of Jewish newspapers. They are primarily independent or Federation owned.

Privately owned

Sometimes, as with the *Baltimore Jewish Times*, these newspapers are family-owned. At times, they also have boards, which include extended family members and close friends of the controlling family. For example, the current publisher of the *Baltimore Jewish Times*, Andrew A. Buerger, is a fourth-generation publisher of the *Baltimore Jewish Times*. The company, Alter Communications, is controlled by a board of family members and a few close friends.

In the past decade, wealthy Jewish communal leaders have entered the Jewish journalism fray. In particular, the *Forward* (New York) and *The Jerusalem Report* (locale obvious), are being underwritten respectively by Michael Steinhart and Charles Bronfman. While the latter is seen as an "Israel publication" it makes substantial effort to market itself in North America, and aggressively seeks paid advertisement from there. (*The Jerusalem Post* makes a similar case with its Internet edition, but is overwhelmingly Israel-based in advertising in print.)

It's well known that both publications lose money. Yet, they are quality works whose resources enable them to attain a certain "buzz" in the Jewish world as well as some of the profession's top staff.

Federation owned

Numerous Jewish newspapers are actually owned and operated by Jewish Federations, the large philanthropic central agencies that are the lynchpins of every American Jewish community of size. The offices of these publications often are housed in Federation buildings; their staff are part of the Federation communications/media relations department.

Some of these papers do produce excellent articles, particularly on social needs. The Philadelphia *Jewish Exponent*, the *New Jersey Jewish News* (which has several editions) and the *JUF News* (Chicago) are prime examples. Sometimes they are forced to cover controversial stories dealing with Federations or Federation agencies if a story breaks first in the general press. After all, the house organ needs to address what people are talking about. Yet those papers do strive to shape the content of those conversations.

On their own, these newspapers will rarely if ever conduct the serious investigation needed of their Federations and their agencies. In addition, major donors of the Federation who can be controversial in the general community, have a general sense of immunity from these publications. That is an important economic lesson that virtually all editors of these newspapers learn quickly.

In 1999, my immediate successor at the *Atlanta Jewish Times* ran an article about the president of the local Jewish federation who was being sued by former partners over business matters. Despite the topic having been reported first in the local business weekly, and much discussed in Jewish circles, the Atlanta editor found herself receiving numerous furious telephone calls and angry face-to-face conversations.

The Jewish Week receives a hefty subsidy from UJA-Federation of Jewish Philanthropies of New York, Inc., but has primarily operated as an independent publication in recent years, at times criticizing major communal figures—and causing substantial headaches for the sponsoring Federation. The current editor of that paper, Gary Rosenblatt, is widely seen as the profession's dean of ethics and is fearless in reporting the news.

The editor of Chicago's *JUF News*, a monthly owned and operated by the Jewish United Fund/Jewish Federation of Metropolitan Chicago, reports that the paper reaches about 50,000 homes, or more than 50 percent of the metropolitan market.[3] That is outstanding because at any given time usually no more than 40 percent of a community is considered affiliated. The editor adds that while there may be some stories that his staff will not write, they refuse to exaggerate or print false material.

THE IMPACT OF NEW FORMS OF PUBLICATIONS

Magazines

Hadassah is the widest circulating Jewish publication in North America. It has hundreds of thousands of readers, often the husbands of Hadassah members.

Newer, independent publications, such as *Moment* magazine, answer to no one but their publisher. There are a plethora of smaller circulating academic, intellectual or spiritual journals. They include *Sh'ma* (an American Jewish thought magazine), *Lillith* (Jewish feminism), *Tikkun* (liberal) and *Commentary* magazine (conservative, despite being published by the liberal American Jewish Committee).

While these publications often have circulation numbers lower than community weeklies, they make an economic impact in both advertising and editorial. Because of their larger circulation area—literally coast to coast—they attract a different type of advertiser. Mainly, they gain revenue from major food products being marketed to the Jewish community, travel agencies and organizations promoting Jewish heritage tours, summer youth trips to Israel and Jewish camps.

These publications often keep operating expenses relatively low by using freelance writers. They are known to pay freelancers much more than the local weeklies. For example, $500 to $1,000 is not unheard of for a feature story in these publications. Obviously, that's a better use of time—and a more prestigious place to be seen—for a freelance writer. Local weeklies may offer $35 to $200 for a feature (although cover stories can go as high as $1,000 in a few places).

Electronic Media

Since the advent of the World Wide Web, publishing has gotten substantially cheaper. Virtually every Anglo Jewish newspaper either has or is developing its own Web page. These have opened new opportunities, based on the resources of those publications.

For example, the *Baltimore Jewish Times* Web page, www.jewishtimes.com, sells advertising and pays for itself (in part because existing staff, such as myself, coordinate its contents). One example of new opportunities is the daily update of obituaries. For that section of the Web site, Jewishtimes.com has sold an ad to a deli that offers trays to be sent to a house in mourning. The theory is that if someone from Baltimore now lives in Florida or elsewhere, they can periodically check to see if someone they know has had a death in the family and respond as they see fit.

An unanswered internal argument is whether putting news on Web pages before it appears in print, damages the weekly. To date, this is not a major problem; a majority of readers still want to physically see a story in print. And few readers check their Jewish newspaper Web site for daily updates. Rather, they take an occasional look at the page.

Some impressive operations, such as Jewishfamily.com, exist solely on the Web (although there was an initial print publication experiment). That company now publishes a host of Web-only publications (FamiliaJudia.com, JBooks.com, JVibe.com, GenerationJ.com, InterfaithFamily.com, SocialAction.com, Sh'ma.com and JewishSports.com).

Such Web sites often have grants from foundations to help pay the bills. This is the case outside of Jewish journalism as well, such as with the popular Beliefnet.com (which features a Jewish section).

Then there are Web zines. Often the brainchild of one interested Jew, they spring up almost daily. They are often personal homepages and rarely attract advertising. Yet, they serve as a stepping stone for some people hoping to get "published." Ironically, such "clips" can help an aspiring writer land a job, or at least a freelance assignment, with an established publication.

WHERE THE MONEY COMES FROM

As has been hinted at numerous times, advertising revenue is a huge factor in the economics of the Anglo-Jewish press. There simply are no benefactors lining up to make donations to independently owned papers—nor should there be. If they are independently owned, they sink or swim on their own. If they are federation owned, they have a solid base, but still try and sell ads to expand their news hole.

Some editors and publishers estimate that about 90 percent of the funds come from advertisements. These paid announcements—as opposed to the plethora of free community ones run—include the broad scope of businesses found in all publications. In a regular week, ads for car dealers, jewelers, restaurants (including numerous non-kosher ones), and small business owners selling services and so on are found. Even movie companies now advertise main stream films, not just ones of specific Jewish interest. There also are, of course, the specific advertisements from synagogues and Jewish agencies targeting their focused audience with information on upcoming programs and new initiatives.

Around election time, a host of politicians pay for notices. A number also advertise greetings for joyous holidays in issues just prior to Rosh Hashanah, Hanukkah and Pesach. (In Atlanta, politicians as diverse as former U.S. House Speaker Newt Gingrich and current House Minority Whip John Lewis were careful to never miss such an opportunity.)

The advertising patterns themselves reveal fascinating portraits of what the general market believes captivates the interest of area Jews. Thus, there often are numerous ads for high-end clothing and furniture stores, travel agencies, etc.

Advertising sales staffs at various Jewish newspapers, such as the ones I have been with, promote the need for such stores to market their wares in Jewish publications through the use of extensive (and not inexpensive) readership surveys, which often include professionally run focus groups.

And everyone knows that there are annual cycles to advertising. For example, it dips in the summer when there is little Jewish programming (and thus little need for Jewish agency advertising). Three big boosts are just prior to three major holidays celebrated in America—Rosh Hashanah, Hanukkah and Pesach.

For Hanukkah, there are special gift guides, which bring in substantial revenues. Some publications I have been involved with have ballooned from a usual 68 pages a week to 176 pages. Much of this comes from holiday greeting ads as well as food and gift advertisements.

Yet, despite Jewish newspapers being well-established, they have great difficulty attracting advertising from national chain stores. The advertising for such companies often is run by ad agencies that prefer to place large announcements and even inserts in mass circulating dailies. Targeting the Jewish community, and any other ethnic group, is generally seen as a waste of time since members of those communities overwhelmingly also look at the dailies.

In Atlanta, even a Fortune 400 company such as Home Depot—based in the city and created by two philanthropists highly involved in the Jewish community—will not advertise in the *Atlanta Jewish Times*.

Indeed, the independent business owner has been the backbone of paid advertising for Anglo-Jewish weeklies. The 1980s were seen as a golden period for tapping into such revenues. The papers were expanding in quality and Jews were participating in the general growth of wealth in the country.

But by the mid-1990s, with recession gripping America, many of these small businesses were closing up. Often they were bought out by mega-national chains springing up. The result is that today most newspapers are smaller—also a result of rising printing and mailing costs.

In Pittsburgh, the Jewish newspaper was "deeply affected by the decrease in the number of independent merchants," said the paper's long-time editor. He also confirmed that there is little or no success in getting national chains to advertise.[4]

However, the lost of such businesses has been offset by other revenue seeking opportunities, ones that are now making a major impact on the bottom line of some publications.

In recent years, numerous publications also have started other publications, usually in slick, glossy magazine format that publish from several to six times a year. They can range from being primarily Jewish, such as *Inside* magazine from the Philadelphia *Jewish Exponent*, to *Style Magazine*, a totally secular lifestyles publication, that publishes in Baltimore and Detroit.

And these days, virtually every Jewish newspaper in a market of size publishes a "Guide To Jewish Living" for their area. They include a few general articles about Jewish life in the area, but their bulk is devoted to extensive listings and descriptions of any and every Jewish operation that would be deemed acceptable to the masses (meaning anything other than Jews for Jesus).

These separate publications play an important and often overlooked role at the larger newspapers—they enable sales staff to make substantial additional money. That's important because it means that Jewish publications can attract quality sales staff in a field where that commodity is quite rare.

Most of newspapers in larger markets have expanded in some way in recent years in addition to new publications. All say that the moves have added to profitability. The *New Jersey Jewish News*, which now has several additions, is a good case study. "We've been profitable (i.e. run surpluses) for the last five years," its editor reports. "We expect to sustain or increase surpluses as we grow the number of editions, pick up total circulation, and create more advertising synergy between editions." [5]

There also have been numerous attempts to cut editorial costs via sharing arrangements between newspapers. Most of these have been short-lived, such as the early 1990s one between the *Washington Jewish Week*, *Long Island Jewish World* and *Palm Beach Jewish News*. Such failures often have as much to do with personalities as the different markets being served.

There also have been attempts by some newspapers to sell stories done by their staff to other publications. The *Baltimore Jewish Times* attempted this in the early 1990s and the *Detroit Jewish News/Atlanta Jewish Times* is again trying to do this. Sometimes, such as in this latest case, the material is often given away in the hopes of raising consciousness as to the quality of the company, which can serve as a recruitment tool for everything from personnel to attempts to buy more papers.

At times, events beyond the control of an editor will spike newspaper and ad sales in one direction or another. Of concern to all publishers and editors are the seemingly endless hikes in printing, paper and mailing costs. San Francisco's Jewish paper has felt the pinch in recent years. Its editor reports that,

"We have reduced the size of the paper, put the job out to bid, used Carrier route sorting and tried to keep the percent of advertising above 50." [6]

Some newspapers in magazine format, such as the *Baltimore Jewish Times* keeps the percentage of the paper to 60 percent for ads and 40 for editorial copy, the *Detroit Jewish News* has gone for a 65/35 split in recent years, while the *Atlanta Jewish Times* shoots for a minimum of 55 percent ads. When one does not heed these rules, the profit margin can rapidly diminish.

Controversial stories make their impact. When *The Jewish Week* (NY) publishes a stunning expose, as it did in the summer of 2000 when a prominent Orthodox rabbi was accused of sexually abusing teens, there is a rise in Web page hits and some newsstand sales. (New York City has a tradition of print media gaining large sales at the numerous newspaper stands on the streets.)

The editor of the *Seattle Jewish Transcript* knows about this. A few years ago the publication's "First Jewish Baby" series focused on a lesbian couple, which happened to have had the year's first Jewish baby. While "dozens" of new readers were gained due to respect for the diversity covered, only one reader canceled a subscript. There was no reported impact on advertising.[7]

Meanwhile, the editor of the *Pittsburgh Jewish Chronicle* added that a letter to the editor printed "highly critical" of a local agency adversely impacted advertising sales.[8]

Environmental factors can have an impact as well. The San Francisco paper had its largest drop in revenue in the months following the 1988 Loma Prieta earthquake. At that point, ad revenue dropped 30 percent for several months—a greater drop than has been felt during prolonged national recessions. The reason: small businesses were recovering and could not put money into specialty publications.[9]

What happens at surrounding media can also make an impact. When the *Detroit Free Press*, the local daily, had a prolonged strike during the mid-1990s, the *Detroit Jewish News* not only picked up some advertising, but some freelance writers as well.

No matter what, by the day's end keeping costs down and profits up is the name of the game. One paper, the *Chicago Jewish News* even fought to receive a "second class requestor" status from the U.S. Postal Service. Combined with other measures—such as having a lighter paper stock—it has cut back on expenses by $100,000 in the past seven years. Some of those savings went back into the publication when it moved to a slick cover and perfect binding—an attempt, of course, to attract more advertisers.[10]

A CLOSING THOUGHT

True study of the Anglo-Jewish press has just begun. While the field has attracted little analysis, it has blossomed into a permanent factor on the American Jewish scene. The best of these publications are partners—formally or informally—with Federations, agencies and individuals seeking to create thriving, healthy Jewish communities. Yet, these publications must walk a fine-line between giving credit to the traditional watchdog role of the media and biting the proverbial hand that feeds it. And they must make money, lots of it via advertising sales.

A strong Anglo-Jewish weekly will make a difference in the health of any community. With all of their inherent tensions, the American Jewish newspapers remains informal meeting places where every Jew of every flavor can meet at least once a week. There, through articles, letters and columns, they share ideas, register complaints and simply learn about one another's life. The economics of how all that comes into being is as complex as Jews themselves.

NOTES

[A longer version of this essay was published May 2001 in *Kesher*, the semi-annual academic journal of the Tel Aviv University and the Andrea and Charles Bronfman Center for the Media of the Jewish People.]

1. "Postal Rate Update: Increases to Take Effect January 7." AJPA Newsletter. December 2000. p. 4
2. Twersky, David. MetroWest Jewish News Editor. E-mail interview, March 9, 2001.
3. Cohen, Aaron. Chicago JUF Jewish News Editor. E-mail interview, March 6, 2001
4. Rottman, Joel. Pittsburgh Jewish Chronicle Editor. E-mail interview February 22, 2001.
5. Twersky, David. Interview.
6. Klein, Marc. Jewish Bulletin of Northern California Editor. E-mail interview, February 15, 2001.

7. Blankinship, Donna. Seattle Jewish Transcript Editor. E-mail interview, February 22, 2001.
8. Roteman, Joel. Interview.
9. Klein, Marc. Interview.
10. Cohen, Aaron. Interview.

APPENDIX C

New Jewish Times

By Jonathan Mark

When Yiddish papers still were dailies, and we were young enough to have grandfathers, my zaydeh took ill and asked, upon entering the hospital, that we save him his papers. My dad or I would go to the newsstand, get the old Yiddish broadsheets, and stash them in the car's trunk. The old man grew weaker, the trunk filled, then the back seat filled too. When he died, it was hard, but throwing out his papers was when we cried.

Then the Jewish papers died, too. The trouble wasn't just that the old Jews were dying, what was dying was the art of the paper. Unlike my grandfather's generation, Jews stopped thinking of the Jewish paper as "my paper," as something to *save* if you missed a week. There weren't writers to love, or that you'd want to punch in the nose (but writers you'd miss, if gone), or stories to clip or bring up at Shabbos lunch.

As Gary Rosenblatt wrote when he came to revive *The Jewish Week* ten years ago, in a world of sinister threats to the Jewish people, the sheer boredom of Jewish life—more exactly, the boredom with which newspapers chose to tell the spectacularly unboring story of the Jewish people—was as sinister a threat as any.

Garrison Keillor, of Prarie Home Companion, speaks of a newspaper trend, even to this day, away from two-fisted, back-alley story telling, replaced instead by articles like "What Is Good About Our Community and Our People," a lot of "unreadable 9th grade term papers about How People From Many Lands Are Working Together To Solve Problems In Our Neighborhoods."

Newspapers, said Keillor, must "depend on crime reporting, exposure of government scandal, and a few irreverent columnists: that's meat and potatoes."

Instead, in the Jewish community, we got sermons. Literally, Jewish journalism, and religion writing in the big city dailies, was reduced to repackaged sermons. In Jewish papers, articles were afflicted with a garden-party tone reminiscent of polite synagogue bulletins in which, at every event, "a wonderful time was had by all." All that, even in the most tumultuous decades in Jewish history that saw us go from refugees and genocide to the attempted Zionist redemption and a Jewish return to history.

These were decades that also saw unparalleled social disruption, with bedrock religious traditions collapsing along with a sense of a common Jewish civilization. It was a remarkable Jewish story—there just wasn't a *Jewish Week*, or any other decent Jewish newspaper in those days, to tell the story, to frame it.

In the glory days of Yiddish papers there was passion, purpose and intimacy—so much so that readers said the magic words: This is "my paper." Not "a paper," but "my paper," not just read on the subways and discarded, but read on the sofa on Friday nights and brought to the table for Shabbos lunch. Jewish writers were accosted on the street, and some writers were even loved.

There was no "my paper" when I was growing up in the 1950s and '60s. When I started to write, in the late 1970s, there were good Jewish writers, like Paul Cowan and others, but they were working in non-Jewish publications. In 1979, I sold some pieces to *The New Yorker* and the *Village Voice*, Jewish pieces that non-Jewish publications thought were fine enough, even as there were no Jewish newspapers to write for.

At the same time, Yossi Klein Halevi was writing brilliantly in the *Voice* about the uniquely Jewish intersection of Borough Park and East Village streets. In 1980, Halevi had an idea for a new Jewish newspaper, *New Jewish Times*, and he recruited me and Israel Lemberg, now a CNN producer in Jerusalem, to edit it with him. The idea—and it was shared elsewhere in Jewish newspapering, as in every good generation—was to break the rules and start all over again.

"We looked for Jewish nightmares," remembers Halevi.

We looked for dreams, lost and found, Jews with stories to tell. Into the pages of *New Jewish Times* came coverage of Jewish murder cases; accounts from homeless Chasidim; Russian Jews who were beat up in Kiev; yeshiva dropouts; Satmar loan sharks; Yiddish characters who whiskey-spiked the coffee of pretty women in the Hungarian pastry shop. We wrote of Israelis conquering their new frontier, and old school paranoids (or so we thought then) who imagined a world of retro Jew-haters.

We did interviews not just with communal presidents but with underground fugitives, such as Abbie Hoffman (who was above-ground posing for our subscription ads). On the editorial staff were veterans of the publishing world, and young unknowns such as Candace Bushnell, who went on to create *Sex in the City*. To reach non-communal types, *New Jewish Times* worked up a radio program on WBAI, featuring editors and guests.

Halevi recalled that the office, a large loft on lower Fifth Avenue, became "a drop-in center for people with obscure obsessions," Jews who kept the passion if not the practice, outlaws and kabbalists, Jews with nowhere to go but who saw in the paper a hometown, the old neighborhood.

We were far from outlaws. On the contrary, we saw Jewish journalism as something sacred, beyond profession. If in light of the last century it is our calling to see every Jew as of infinite value; if Israel, and making the world safe for Jews—uniting Jews, and nourishing Jewish possibility—is the defining challenge of this generation, if the media is the theater for how this story is told, then reporting that story in a uniquely Jewish newspaper, and making Jewish papers financially viable, is equally sacred, too.

New Jewish Times didn't last much more than a year, but around the country new newspapers, such as *The Jewish Week* (refashioned in 1979, but actually a descendent of several merged Jewish papers dating back to *The American Hebrew* in 1879)—began taking this cause to a higher level.

One challenge is telling the Jewish story in a way that is compelling as a story, as journalism, not just as a PR handout. For young Jewish writers coming out of yeshiva, the Torah itself was the model for how to write, even how to write subversively. Of course, much about God is a mystery. We don't know what He looks like. We don't know what He sounds like. But we know the way God writes. Imagine in the dark ages of Jewish journalism, assigning a profile on Father Abraham. How pompous and pious it would have been. But look how God chooses to write the Abraham story. The very first quote attributed to Abraham in the Torah is him saying to Sarah, "Now look, I know you're beautiful. When the Egyptians see you, and know you're my wife, they'll kill me but keep you alive."

That was the first New Jewish Journalism. Some are offended by that kind of approach to writing—but 70 nations rejected the Torah, too, before the Jewish people said yes.

In the Biblical spirit, newspapers have become the prophet speaking truth to the king or high priest, because without a prophet—or an editorial—not only is God voiceless but the people are, too.

The world these days can seem like the opening verses of Genesis, "unformed and void with darkness over the face of the deep." That fear always was right below the surface, even in better times. The first issue of *New Jewish Times* featured nothing but a nuclear mushroom cloud and the headline, "Next Year in Jerusalem." It's seems less crazy now than it was 20 years ago, but for Israeli children the Purim mask gave way to a gas mask.

What would you write about if the world was coming to an end? My inspiration was Emanuel Ringelblum and his band of brothers in the Warsaw Ghetto. They couldn't put out a Jewish paper, but they did the next best thing. Meeting once a week, and calling themselves "Oneg Shabbos"—with equal parts sarcasm and sentimentality—they took to amassing a weekly archive of the Jewish people. Oneg Shabbos collected everything, the ephemeral, the ethereal, Hebrew candy wrappers and chronicles of hunger; children's poems and dead men's paintings; ghetto theater programs and maps of Treblinka. It was essentially a Jewish newspaper delivered not to your mailbox but to the tin boxes and metal milk cans that they buried in the rubble. Who would find it? Who'd be their audience? Would there still be Jews in the world? For Oneg Shabbos, the act of gathering and telling the Jewish story was heroic enough.

At Ground Zero, in 2001, we had an "Oneg Shabbos" experience all our own. In the ruins, people found, and *The Jewish Week* wrote about, the fluttering papers that carried to earth a yeshiva's tuition bill; a letter from a summer camp; stories of people worth knowing—more worth knowing than we might have supposed the day before. In the rubble, someone found a yarmulke inscribed from a wedding, Sept. 9. The ordinary is now extraordinary. In fact, it was extraordinary all along.

Our lives are fragile and fleeting. We are the generation that history will have to walk through to keep the Jewish story alive. These are the days in which Jews are looking to "my paper," a Jewish paper, to tell us who we are, where we're going, and what we have seen and loved.

APPENDIX D

Jewish Sources For Journalistic Ethics

By Yosef I. Abramowitz

> *"The newspaper that is true to its highest mission will concern itself with the things that ought to happen tomorrow, or the next month, or the next year, and will seek to make what ought be come to pass...the highest mission of the press is to render public service."*
>
> —**Joseph Pulitzer, Publisher, Founder, Columbia School of Journalism**

Thousands of years before the invention of the first printing press, Judaism codified within its laws, traditions, governance and values the essential characteristics of classic journalism.

Joseph Pulitzer's description of the role of the newspaper within society was preceded by a rich and institutionalized tradition of moral prophesy in ancient Israel. As early as *Deuteronomy*, the fifth book of Moses, God mandates in the desert the structure of Israelite society once the Hebrews enter the Promised Land. "You shall then set a king over yourself whom God will choose," (*Deut.* 17:15), representing the Executive branch of government. "Judges and law enforcing officials shall you appoint for yourself in all your gates," (*Deut.* 16:18), representing local judiciaries. Judicial appeals were made to the Levites, the priests, who served as a higher court (*Deut.* 17:9).

The court, later referred to as the Sanhedrin, was divided into two sections: The Small Sanhedrin with twenty three judges and the Grand Sanhedrin with seventy one judges. The Grand Sanhedrin had considerable powers; "its decisions had the force of law; it ratified the appointments of high priest and king; and its permission was required if the court's rulings were frequently innovative, it was in effect also a limited legislative body." (*The Torah, A Modern Commentary*, page 1460). It has been compared by some to the U.S. Senate in function.

While a system of governance was mandated, God also institutionalized another voice within the society. "I will raise up for them a prophet from among their own brethren, and I will put My words into his mouth, so that he may speak to them everything that I will command him." (*Deut.* 18:18) While representing an independent moral voice, the Prophet was also God's instrument for anointing a new king. After the anointing, however, the prophet had no formal powers beyond the moral voice to which people, including the king, were expected to hearken.

And, indeed, the first two kings of the Hebrews, Saul and David, were confronted over the moral inequities of their regimes and leadership by the prophets Samuel and Natan.

Melvin Mencher, in *News Reporting and Writing*, writes that "morality is basic to the theory and practice of journalism. The free press justifies its existence in terms of moral imperatives..." (page 600)

"Justice, justice shalt thou pursue" (*Deut.* 16:20) commanded God of the Israelites, and Isaiah was one of the most eloquent of prophets to fulfill his mandate as a voice for justice. Isaiah was commanded to "Cry aloud, spare not; Lift up your voice like a trumpet." (*Isaiah* 58:1) He did, and called on the Children of Israel to "Learn to do well—seek justice, relieve the oppressed, judge the fatherless, plead for the widow." (*Isaiah* 1:17) In modern terms, Isaiah asked that the rights of the most vulnerable parts of society be vigorously protected.

Abraham Joshua Heschel, the 20th Century thinker, said of the prophets: "In a sense, the calling of the prophet may be described as that of an advocate or champion, speaking for those who are too weak to plead their own cause. Indeed, the major activity of the prophets was *interference*, demonstrating about wrongs inflicted on other people, meddling in affairs which were seemingly neither their concern nor their responsibility." As a quality newspaper would do, "prophets remind us of the moral state of the people: Few are guilty, but all are responsible." (*The Wisdom of Heschel*, by Ruth Marcus Goodhill, pages 296, 284).

There is also an inherent distrust of government by the prophets. "Be careful with the government authorities as they do not come close to a person but for their own need." (*Avot* 2:3) Furthermore, the prophet Samuel pleaded with the people not to call for a king. And Isaiah lamented "O, my people, your leaders mislead you, And confuse the course of your paths." (3:12)

The prophets were also the first to bring the written word to the people. "Write the vision; Make it plain upon tablets," commands the prophet Habakkuk (2:2). After the Babylonian exile, the prophets introduced public readings of the Five Books of Moses in Jerusalem thus bringing the written word from the elite of society to the masses. Also institutionalized within Judaism is the ceremony of Hakel, where the king appears before the entire people to read from the Bible. (The practice has been reinstated since the establishment of the State of Israel. Israeli President Chaim Herzog, before a massive crowd at the Western Wall of the Second Temple, read from the Five Books in fulfillment of the commandment of bringing the written word to the people.)

After the destruction of the Second Temple in 70 CE, Jewish life became radically transformed from a temple-centric cult into a community and lifestyle that had to adapt and survive outside of the Holy Land. The laws of this society, derived from the Bible, became codified in the Talmud around the year 400 CE.

The Talmud deals with virtually every issue within a society, including issues of speech. Here we find Jewish ethics to be less in harmony with current journalistic practice.

Immediately in the beginning of creation, the enormous power of speech is demonstrated. "And God said, Let there be light! And there was light" (*Genesis* 1:3), and, subsequently, God created the world by proclaiming each and every thing.

Recognizing the power of speech, God warns in the Book of *Leviticus*: "You shall not go about as a talebearer among your people." (19:16) *Proverbs* has nine major warnings about the power of speech. Among them: "Life and death are in the power of the tongue" (18:21), "The words of a talebearer are as wounds" (18:8), and "he that guards his mouth, guards his life; but he that opens his lips wide will have destruction." (13:3)

Based on the above and other citations, a wide body of law developed elevating the value of a reputation of an individual in society. It was prohibited to say, and later, print anything (often even true) which could damage the standing of the individual. The rationale was that if people were created in God's image, then they must be given respect. The exceptions, based on the Biblical phrase that "You shall not stand idly by the blood of your fellow" (*Lev.* 19:16), relate to warning the public in order to prevent more sins from being committed.

In general, Jewish law commands giving everyone the benefit of the doubt ("You shall judge your fellow favorably," *Lev.* 19:15). Therefore, Jewish law would prohibit the widespread journalistic practice of printing the names of people arrested prior to a guilty verdict in court. However, a strong case could be made that if potentially dangerous people were let out on bail, that the community should be publicly notified.

Even when public speech is sanctioned, it must be accurate. "Sages, be careful with your words.... You may incur the penalty of exile" (*Avot* 1:11), which was the same penalty given for manslaughter. Maimonidies, the great 12th century Jewish thinker wrote, "Watch what you say in public. No expression should be ambiguous and admit several interpretations. Otherwise, if there be heretics in the audience, they will interpret your words in accordance with their own opinions, and the students, having heard it from them, may turn to heresy." (*Insights: A Talmud Treasury*, Rabbi Saul Weiss, page 145). In *Deuteronomy*, we are taught that "You shall investigate and inquire and interrogate thoroughly." (13:15)

Community, based on the foundation of strong family units, is the context for much of Jewish law relating to reputations of individuals. The value of community also creates a journalistic tension within the search for truth.

On the one hand, peace within the community (Shalom Bayit) is a strong value ("One must not perpetuate strife" *Sanhedrin* 110a;) On the other, Judaism is relentless in its pursuit of truth.

The search for truth is a major theological component of Judaism. "Upon three things the world rests, upon justice, upon truth, and upon peace," teaches the Jerusalem Talmud (*Taanit* 4:2). "And the three are one, for when justice is done, truth prevails and peace is established." Truth is also one of God's names, and "The seal of the Holy One, blessed be He, is Truth." (*Shabbat* 55a)

While truth must be vigorously pursued, there is one exception to the rule. In the interests of peace in a household or in a community (Shalom Bayit), the truth may be altered somewhat. (Rabbi R. Solomon Lurie [1510–1573], however, ruled that even for the purpose of Shalom Bayit, the altering of the truth must be infrequent.) While the modern journalist may worry about the negative repercussions of a sensitive revelation, it is likely such a story will end up being published.

Other Judaic ethics which relate to journalism include:

1. Attribution: "Whoever reports a saying in the name of its originator brings deliverance to the world." (*Avot* 6:6)

2. Altering quotes: "He who alters his speech is as though he had engaged in idolatry." (*Sanhedrin* 92a)

3. Op/Ed pages: "Whenever a dispute is for the Name of Heaven, it will ultimately endure." (*Avot* 5:20)

4. Sources: Two eyewitnesses are needed for the Sanhedrin to rule on legal matters, including declaring the new moon.

The advent of the modern press was not foreseen in traditional Jewish text, and so there are no specific ancient laws relating to the industry. Yet Judaism does have a rich moral tradition that upholds, supports and perhaps even inspires many of the ethical norms that exist today in modern journalism.

The prophet Hosea lamented 2,600 years ago that "My people are rejected for lack of knowledge." (4:6) Pulitzer's solution was to popularize the media and create a school of journalism so "That the People Shall Know."

APPENDIX E

What *The New York Times* Tells Us About Ourselves

Ari L. Goldman writes for The Jewish Week
December 3, 1993

This summer, when I was wrapping up my career as a reporter for *The New York Times*, my father told me a joke that I haven't been able to get out of my mind. It goes like this:

A doctor and lawyer sit together every week in shul. And through the davening, people come over to the doctor. "My son has an earache. Can you take a look?" one man says. "What's better, penicillin or tetracycline?" asks another. "Do you know a good cardiologist?" says a third.

In exasperation, the doctor turns to his friend the lawyer and says, "I can't stand it. These people are driving me crazy. I can't even daven anymore!"

"I've got a solution," the lawyer responds calmly. "From now on, if anybody asks you a question, just send them a bill after Shabbos."

"Great idea," the doctor says, feeling a sense of relief.

A few days later, the doctor opens his mail. And in it, there is a bill from the lawyer.

For the last 20 years, I've felt like that doctor. I go to shul Shabbos morning and the questions don't stop. "Why did your paper write this about Israel?" "Why did you write that about Crown Heights?" "Why did you write so much about Israel?" "Why did you write so little about Israel?"

And, in what might be termed "the revenge of the doctors," one of them, a specialist in infectious diseases, berated me for 20 minutes at a recent kiddish about "a terrible" article on Page 1 of *The Times* about Lyme disease. "But I'm a religion writer," I pleaded. He wouldn't stop. "Write a letter, please," I begged. But he wouldn't' stop. He didn't care what I was and he certainly wasn't going to write a letter. He needed to get this off his chest. And I was the recipient.

Ah, if only I could them all a bill, I've often thought since hearing my father's joke. I'd be a rich man today.

Well, after 20 years at *The Times*, the last 10 of them as a religion writer, I've decided to tell all—not about *The Times*, but about the Jewish community.

The Times, while far from perfect, has been very good to me. It took me on as a copy boy right out of Yeshiva College and enabled me to pursue a challenging and fulfilling career as a reporter. And one of the most important lessons I learned at Yeshiva was the principle of *hakarat hatov*—recognizing and acknowledging the good people do for you. So this is not a kiss-and-tell article.

I, of course, also learned to love Israel and the Jewish community at Yeshiva. But this love was never compromised at *The Times*. Despite the charges of Jewish "media monitors," who see anti-Israel bias in every picture and headline, I can state categorically that there is no anti-Israel conspiracy at *The New York Times*.

There are, to be sure, editors and writers who are less inclined toward Israel and others who are more inclined. But the policy of the paper is one of evenhandedness (or should I say evenhandedness with a liberal/Labor bent) and the pro and con voices at *The Times* most often balance themselves out.

Moreover, what seems like hostility is often ignorance. And the level of ignorance, even among Jewish editors, is astounding.

Editors would often bring photographs from Israel to my desk and ask what the Hebrew writing said. This was understandable; not everyone knows how to read Hebrew. But once a Jewish editor brought me a photograph of a sign in Hebrew and asked me what it said. And to my great surprise, he was holding it upside down. Not only didn't he know our people's language, he didn't even know what was up and what was down.

One Sunday several years ago, the metropolitan editor in charge—a newcomer to the paper from the West Coast—decided not to send a reporter to the Salute to Israel Parade. No need to cover it, he reasoned. He didn't cover the Pulaski Day Parade the week before and no one seemed to mind.

When Monday's paper appeared without a word or a picture about the Salute to Israel parade, hundreds of people called to complain. The editors were so embarrassed that they ran a correction in Tuesday's paper saying that they had made a terrible mistake by missing the parade. And they've never missed it since.

On another occasion, I wrote an article about a woman rabbi near Albany who was a graduate of a Reform seminary but was seeking admission to the Conservative rabbinical organization. I wrote that she wouldn't drive on Shabbos, so if the weather was particularly bad, she wouldn't walk the mile to shul, but her congregants "would come to her house."

An editor added: "...and drive her to the synagogue." Luckily, I caught the error moments before it got into the paper. The editor was Jewish, and when I explained to him that some religious Jews don't ride in a car on Shabbos, he said in all sincerity, "I never knew that."

The level of Jewish ignorance in journalism is probably no greater than in any profession, but when this ignorance slips into the pages of *The Times*, it becomes another opportunity for charges of anti-Semitism.

I know this because I've heard from these people over the years, sometimes in shul and sometimes on the job. As a religion writer, it was my job to cover all religions—Islam, Buddhism, Hinduism, the many denominations of Christianity as well as Judaism and its branches. Still, Jews, who account for only 2 percent of the nation's population, made up 50 percent of my calls and letters.

And the Jewish public relations people were, without a doubt, the most persistent. If the publicist for the National Council of Churches would call to tell me about an event on Sunday and I said that I wasn't interested, she'd politely wish me a good day. But if the publicist for the National Jewish Anything would call and I'd say I wasn't interested, the questions would only then begin: Why not? How come you never write about us? Why do you always write about the Conservative/Orthodox/Reform (whatever the caller wasn't)? And then, my favorite: Well, if you can't do it, who else at *The Times* should I call?

You couldn't get them off the phone. Unless, of course, you were asking them tough questions. The late Irving (Pat) Spiegel, one of my predecessors at *The Times* (and, as far as I know, the only other Jewish religion writer in the paper's history) told of calling a Jewish publicist during the nursing home scandals of the 1970s.

Once it was established that the publicist's organization was soon to be implicated in the growing scandal, the conversation went something like this:

"Pat, if you print that, you know I'm finished."

"Don't be ridiculous," Pat said. "We're not talking about you, we're talking about your organization."

"We're one and the same."

"Listen, relax. You'll weather this."

"No, you can't print this. Pat, I want you to know I've brought the phone over to the window. Pat, I've opened the window. Do you hear the traffic? Pat, I'm not sitting on the ledge. And, Pat, if you tell me you are going to print this, I am going to jump. And I'll hold on to the phone so you can hear me scream."

Pat spent the rest of the conversation talking the poor publicist off the ledge.

I came to the conclusion long ago that *The Times* was more than just a newspaper to the Jewish community. It is our common denominator and holds the community together in the way that the old Yiddish papers once did.

Reading *The Times* has become part of being Jewish in America. For many it's become their daily devotion, their tallit and tefillin, their new kashrut. They don't have breakfast without it.

In many neighborhoods, you wouldn't go out to Shabbos lunch at a friend's house without reading it. How would you make small talk? *The Times*' society page has become our social register. Its Op-Ed page, our town square. Its obituaries, our Jewish cemeteries.

My friend Marvin Schick, the president of my other alma mater, the Rabbi Jacob Joseph School, once told me that he proposed to the board of directors of the school that they stop "wasting money" on paid obituary notices in *The Times* for friends and supporters of the school. The proposal met vehement opposition on the board. One elderly man shot Marvin an angry look. "Are you going to deny me my final resting place?" he asked.

Marvin's proposal was resoundingly defeated.

The first week after I quit *The Times*, I went to shul feeling like a man freed of a burden. I walked in, took my seat, opened my siddur and waited for the first question. "How about that Tom Friedman?" someone said. "I don't work there anymore," I responded.

"Where?"

"At *The New York Times*."

"How could you give up a job like that?"

I just smiled and kept on davening.

APPENDIX F

Eleven Problems With Jewish Journalism

By Luke Ford

Here are some of my opinions on what is wrong with Jewish journalism.

#1. Failure of imagination.

Jewish journalism is predictable. It rarely catches the reader offguard. Most of the time, when you read the headline, you know the story. There's no need to read more. It's just the same old actors repeating the same old lines. To hold the attention of an infant or an adult, you have to constantly defy expectations. You have to play peekaboo with the reader.

#2. Lack of clarity on mission.

You can be kind. You can be truthful. You can investigate. You can shape the community. But neither an individual nor a newspaper can do all these things equally well. Jewish newspapers need to decide if they are primarily in the propaganda game (most Jewish weeklies) or in the news game. Is your mission primarily to report the news in your community or is it to act omnisciently in the best interests of the community by frequently withholding the news (the stance of virtually all Jewish weeklies except the *Forward*)? If it is the latter, you must ask yourself what qualifies you to decide what is good for the community. There's nothing inherent in the status of journalist that conveys such wisdom. It's not as though journalists for Jewish weeklies are geniuses. They're not up to par covering their communities. They have no basis for believing they should concentrate on shaping their communities.

#3. Lack of technique.

It is rare to read a Jewish paper and lose yourself in a story. Instead, Jewish weeklies depend on the Inverted Pyramid tradition of newstelling (where the important facts go first), a method appropriate for dailies and reporters tapping out their stories via the 19th Century telegraph.

Jewish weeklies tell stories what happened days and weeks prior to publishing. It is not good enough to simply warm over the facts. To emotionally rivet the reader, you must:

- Go somewhere. You must have a beginning, middle and end to every story and every scene. You must employ scene-by-scene construction moving towards a climax. There must be desire, struggle and realization on the part of your protagonists.
- Realistic dialogue from real people rather than canned quotes from authority figures.
- Abundant attention paid to status details (the various ways people strive to boost themselves above others and avoid humiliation).
- Multiple points of view.

#4. Stuck in the past.

Blogs are an increasingly preferred way of getting news, yet few if any Jewish newspapers offer blogs, or use blogging techniques in their print editions. First person news accounts written with attitude can be more powerful than the familiar objective stance. There's no inherent reason why the journalist writing a story has to be less interesting than the people he's writing on. There's no inherent reason he can not be a character in his stories. Jewish journalism could develop stars by allowing those with talent to experiment with different techniques of telling a story. We need more Yossi Klein Halevis.

#5. Desire to be loved.

Most Jewish journalists fear the wrath of their community. This attitude rarely makes for compelling reading. We need more J.J. Goldbergs who place their commitment to journalism above their desire to be popular.

6. Delusions of grandeur.

Jewish weeklies could do a good job of covering their community if they wanted to, but most of them, particularly the *Jewish Journal*, suffer from delusions of grandeur. They devote considerable resources to national and international stories where they have no expertise. They rarely improve on what *The New York Times* offers, but instead insist on publishing second rate material because it makes them feel like they are big time. Too many editors (that's you Rob Eshman) spend their weekly columns on worldly themes even though they have as much skill at international punditry as their non-English speaking janitors.

#7. Newspapering for morons.

If you have readers who rely on your paper for their news and analysis about Israel (stuff that is offered better and quicker by secular sources), then treat them with the same consideration that you would readers who turn to you first for wrapping the fish.

#8. Unwillingness to treat religion with the same seriousness that it treats politics.

That's where *The New Rabbi* was revolutionary. It gave a synagogue the same treatment other institutions of similar size routinely receive.

#9. Only publishing positive book reviews.

The only Jewish weekly that takes books seriously is the *Forward*.

#10. Placing sensitivity, tact, and restraint above other values.

Though restraint is always the safest option, it is not always the best. Problems hushed up are not necessarily problems solved. By not naming the sexual sins that cost rabbi Sheldon Zimmerman his job at Hebrew Union College, the *Forward* and other Jewish papers left people wondering about his fitness for his current position with United Jewish Communities. By not naming Amnon Finkelstein, dean of admissions at UJ, for his drug-and-sex debauchery that led to the permanent brain damage of a UJ student, the *Jewish Journal* let him and his university off the hook. Instead of inquiring why UJ has been rife with inappropriate relations between faculty, staff and students, the *Journal* took the lame angle of a cover story on "When Bad Things Happen to Good Institutions." My headline on all this would read, "When Good Stories Happen to Bad Newspapers."

#11. A preference for vague generalities over zesty particulars.

A May 30, 2003 *Jewish Journal* cover story on "The New Rabbis" wrote: "Along with the try-anything spirit of youth, these rabbis bring a refreshingly unladen approach to working with each and a determination to quicken the momentum of outreach and spirituality that characterized the last decade."

The story was a waste because it lacked specifics and relied on clichés.

Index

A
Aaron, Joseph xxxiv
Abramowitz, Yosef xxi, 90, 124, 294
Abramson, Jill 266
Ackerman, David xxxiv
Adlerstein, Yitzchok 34
AIPAC 71, 77, 78, 79, 82, 274
Air Supply 38, 39
Alexander, Edward xxxiv, 23, 276
American Jewish Committee 218, 339
American Jewish Congress 49, 207, 260, 300
American Jewish Press Association (AJPA) ii, 40, 41, 71, 117, 140, 145, 175, 176, 180, 182, 247, 248, 273, 295, 313, 320, 334, 335, 350
And They Shall Be My People xxix, 5, 11, 23, 31
Artson, Bradley Sharvit i
Atlanta Jewish Times 173, 281, 286, 299, 334, 335, 339, 342, 343, 344
Avrech, Robert J. xv, xviii, 185

B
Baltimore Jewish Times 182, 247, 281, 282, 284, 299, 334, 338, 340, 343, 344
Beilin, Yossi 72
Beinart, Peter xxxiv, 264
Beis Yitzchok 66
Berenbaum, Michael ii, 97, 98, 177, 275

Berger, David 45
Besser, James xxxiv, 136, 202, 284
Biale, David xxxiv
Blitzer, Wolfe xxxiv
Bloom, Stephen 51, 57, 60, 61, 62, 64
Boteach, Shmuley ii, 156, 242, 249, 251
Breindel, Eric 257, 264, 265
Brock, David 259, 262, 266
Bronstein, Avraham 66, 310
Brown, Tina 16
Bushnell, Candace 37, 349

C
Cad: Confessions of a Toxic Bachelor 37
Carroll, Andy 145, 166
Chabad xxi, 40, 42, 43, 44, 46, 83, 131, 137, 138, 142, 163, 165, 168, 290, 317
Chaim, Chafetz 24
Chait, Jonathan 265
Charen, Mona 255, 257, 258, 263, 266
Chavez, Linda 261, 269
Chicago Tribune xxvii, 53, 57
Chronicle of Higher Education, The 54
Cohen, Aaron xxxiv
Cohen, Benyamin ii, xvii, 171, 174, 175, 176
Cohen, Debra Nussbaum 159, 197
Cohler, Larry xxxiii, 70, 76, 77, 80, 103, 157, 158, 162, 166, 177, 197, 295, 298
Cohler-Esses, Larry 76, 80, 177, 295

Cohn, Robert 109, 246
Columbia Journalism Review xxxiii, 86
Columbia School of Journalism xxiii, 351
Coppola, Vincent xxxiv, 174
Coulter, Ann 262
Cyrulnik, Jason 65

D
Dorff, Elliot xxxiv
Drudge, Matt xix
Dylan, Bob 28

E
Eden, Ami 225, 238, 251
Eshman, Rob xvii, 35, 36, 84, 103, 120, 129, 130, 131, 177, 180, 181, 206, 320, 363

F
Federation iii, xxii, xxiv, xxvi, xxxi, xxxii, xxxiii, 1, 21, 22, 43, 69, 70, 74, 79, 81, 83, 84, 89, 91, 94, 95, 96, 101, 104, 105, 107, 108, 111, 113, 114, 120, 132, 133, 134, 139, 142, 144, 148, 149, 160, 162, 163, 165, 171, 179, 180, 181, 193, 195, 201, 211, 215, 216, 218, 240, 241, 242, 244, 245, 246, 247, 271, 272, 286, 292, 293, 295, 296, 306, 310, 327, 334, 335, 336, 337, 338, 339, 341
Feldman, Leonid 27
Fenyvesi, Charles 98, 99, 109, 274
Fishkoff, Sue 40, 48, 49
Foer, Franklin 264
Forward i, ii, iii, xvi, xviii, xxii, xxiii, xxvi, xxvii, xxxi, xxxiii, 3, 4, 5, 20, 26, 35, 43, 55, 56, 57, 70, 71, 74, 84, 85, 87, 101, 102, 103, 104, 105, 108, 126, 127, 128, 130, 136, 145, 147, 148, 149, 151, 155, 158, 159, 162, 169, 177, 193, 194, 196, 201, 209, 213, 215, 216, 217, 219, 223, 224, 225, 226, 229, 233, 234, 235, 238, 240, 242, 250, 251, 257, 260, 266, 281, 282, 283, 288, 289, 292, 295, 299, 301, 304, 310, 311, 312, 313, 314, 316, 325, 326, 329, 335, 338, 361, 363
Freundel, Barry 265
Fried, Stephen i, xvii, xxii, xxxi, 1, 7, 14, 26, 28, 30, 31, 73, 124, 125, 126
Friedman, Tom 103, 109, 267, 360

G
Gahr, Evan 254, 257, 259, 265, 267, 269
Goldberg, Hillel xxxiv
Goldberg, J.J. iii, xvi, 76, 102, 115, 120, 127, 155, 161, 191, 209, 241, 313, 362
Goldberg, Jeffrey xxxiv, 161, 234, 292
Goldman, Ari xvii, 20, 22, 25, 32, 73
Greenberg, Eric xxxiv
Grossman, Lawrence xxxiv, 220
Grossman, Sue xxxiv, 76

H
Hadassah xxiii, xxvii, 52, 56, 57, 58, 60, 61, 197, 228, 339
Halevi, Yossi Klein xxxiv, 76, 166, 184, 185, 300, 309, 348, 362
Hallmark 55, 56, 57, 58
Har Zion xxxii, 3, 8, 18, 27, 125
Harrison, Josh 66
Hartman, David 220
Harvard 16, 25, 26, 29, 229, 274, 335
Hays, Charlotte 262
Hecht, Abraham 165
Herber, Jacob 28
Hirt-Manheimer, Aron xxxiv, 76
Hoenlein, Malcolm i, xxxiv, 71, 80, 159, 162, 169, 180, 182, 192, 291, 292, 293
Hoffman, Wayne 223
Horowitz, David 255, 261
Horowitz, Michael 259, 260, 269
Hostein, Lisa xxxiv, xxxv
Hudson Institute 254, 255, 257, 258, 260, 262, 264

J

j. the Jewish news weekly of Northern California xxiv, 178, 281
Jacobs, Phil xxxiv, 281, 287
Jacobson, Gershon xxxiv
Jdate 36
Jerusalem Post, The xxvii, xxxiii, 35, 42, 81, 103, 184, 186, 206, 274, 289, 291, 320, 338
Jerusalem Report xxiv, xxviii, 8, 126, 169, 338
Jew vs. Jew xxii, 6, 29, 55, 140
Jewish Exponent xxviii, xxxii, 18, 70, 102, 215, 240, 241, 242, 281, 332, 338, 343
Jewish Journal ii, iii, xv, xvi, xvii, xviii, xix, xx, xxii, xxiv, xxv, xxvii, xxviii, xxxi, xxxiii, 5, 7, 15, 20, 21, 23, 27, 34, 36, 37, 41, 67, 68, 69, 70, 72, 74, 75, 76, 79, 82, 84, 85, 87, 88, 89, 90, 91, 97, 99, 100, 101, 103, 104, 105, 106, 107, 109, 110, 111, 114, 119, 123, 126, 127, 128, 129, 130, 131, 132, 133, 134, 135, 136, 137, 138, 139, 140, 141, 142, 143, 144, 146, 148, 150, 152, 153, 157, 158, 159, 160, 161, 162, 165, 166, 168, 169, 170, 171, 172, 174, 175, 176, 177, 178, 180, 184, 185, 186, 188, 189, 190, 191, 194, 197, 200, 201, 202, 204, 206, 207, 209, 214, 216, 218, 224, 226, 237, 242, 243, 244, 245, 247, 249, 250, 251, 262, 271, 272, 275, 278, 282, 284, 292, 293, 296, 297, 298, 302, 303, 304, 315, 319, 320, 321, 322, 323, 324, 326, 327, 329, 330, 332, 333, 334, 335, 336, 337, 338, 341, 348, 349, 361, 362, 363, 364
Jewish Ledger xxv, 21, 105
Jewish Telegraphic Agency (JTA) xxxv
Jewish Theological Seminary xxiv, 12, 16, 73, 149
Jewish Week, The xxii, xxiv, xxv, xxvii, xxxiii, 21, 67, 76, 78, 79, 80, 87, 89, 92, 93, 94, 95, 101, 102, 103, 105, 123, 126, 127, 141, 142, 145, 149, 150, 157, 161, 162, 163, 169, 170, 173, 182, 185, 188, 194, 197, 215, 218, 221, 240, 250, 281, 282, 283, 284, 289, 295, 296, 297, 299, 312, 313, 314, 315, 316, 320, 327, 335, 339, 344, 347, 349, 350, 357
JewishWorldReview 151
Jewschool 66
Jewsweek 151, 172, 173, 174
Joffe, Mark xxxiv, 161
Journalist and the Murderer, The xv
JSPS xxiv, 76, 158, 193
JTS 17, 198

K

Kalb, Debbie xxxiv
Kalb, Marvin xxxiv
Kaplan, Lawrence 262
Kaplan, Mordecai 16
Kass, Leon 265, 268
Katz, Leslie 243
Kessler, E.J. ii, 147, 153
Kessler, Eve 127, 145, 159, 201, 213
Klein, Amy ii, xvii, xxxiv, 34, 41, 145
Klein, Marc 109, 117, 248
Kosher Sex ii, xxi
Kozodoy, Neal xxxiv
Kraut, Yehuda 65
Kristol, Bill 260, 264, 268

L

Lamm, Norman 67
Lanner, Baruch 27, 86, 88, 100, 123, 156, 239, 240, 297, 315
Lapid, Tommy 72, 84
Lefkowitz, Jay 268
Lenkiewicz, Lisa 105
Lerner, Michael 85, 180
Lichtenstein, Gene 84, 110, 163, 206
Lilith xxv
Lippman, Jerome xxxiv, 290
Lipsky, Seth i, xxxiv, 20, 102, 128, 147, 161, 162, 257, 289, 310, 319

Living a Year of Kaddish 32
Long Island Jewish World xxv, xxix, 76, 157, 158, 186, 188, 291, 335, 343
Los Angeles Times, The ii, xxviii, 114, 160, 167, 184, 205
Lubavitch, 197

M
Maguida, Arthur xxxiv
Malcolm, Janet xv
Manilow, Barry 38
Mark, Jonathan 105, 141, 185, 188, 347
McManus, Bob 262
Meyers, Joel xxxiv, 4
Museum of Tolerance 207
Myers, David xxxiv, 103

N
National Jewish Population Survey (NJPS) 127, 165
NCSY xxvi, 27, 123, 157
Netter, Perry xxxiv, 10
Neuhaus, Richard John 262
Neuman, Elena 269
New Jersey Jewish News xxi, xxvi, 69, 128, 193, 271, 272, 337, 338, 343
New Jewish Times 185, 187, 188, 347, 348, 349, 350
New Rabbi, The i, xvii, xxii, xxxi, 7, 10, 11, 18, 73, 90, 106, 125, 139, 140, 149, 241, 363, 364
New Republic, The 166, 184, 263, 264, 266, 274, 294
New Testament 15
New York Daily News xxxiii, 78, 79, 312
New York Post 8, 21, 253, 257, 262
New York Times, The xxiii, xxviii, 22, 27, 31, 43, 44, 48, 77, 79, 98, 100, 102, 103, 107, 108, 109, 118, 124, 127, 128, 136, 143, 148, 151, 154, 156, 159, 161, 162, 166, 167, 184, 201, 202, 211, 219, 220, 225, 247, 256, 257, 265, 266, 267, 274, 275, 285, 292, 312, 328, 357, 358, 360, 363
New Yorker, The xxxiii, 6, 12, 16, 140, 152, 163, 190, 292, 348
Newhouse, Alana 225, 232
Newsweek 140, 316

P
Passion of the Christ, The 266, 267
Peace Now 69, 111
Peretz, Martin xxxiv
Peretz, Marty 263, 264
Pfefferman, Naomi xxxiv, 117, 120, 143
Philadelphia Inquirer, The 21
Philadelphia magazine 24
Podhoretz, John 255, 256, 264
Podhoretz, Norman 71
Portnoy's Complaint 72, 129, 285
Postville xxi, 42, 46, 48, 49, 50, 51, 52, 53, 54, 55, 56, 57, 58, 60, 61, 62, 63, 64, 106, 126, 139, 140
Project Next Step 34
Protocols xxvii, 65, 66, 67, 68, 74, 131, 251, 310, 311, 316

R
Rabbinical Assembly 3, 4, 23
Rabin, Yitzhak 165, 168, 243, 311
Rabinowitz, Steve 201
Rank, Perry xxxiv, 26, 28, 73, 106, 242
Rebbe's Army, The xxii, 40, 49
Reconstructionist 16, 263, 325, 328
Reform Judaism magazine xxvii, 76
Rifkin, Ira xxxiv
Robertson, Pat 260, 264
Rosen, Jay xxxiv, 5, 7, 12
Rosen, Jonathan xxxiv, 127, 148, 234, 236
Rosenbaum, Jay xxxiv, 5, 7, 12
Rosenblatt, Gary 21, 27, 79, 80, 86, 87, 91, 92, 93, 100, 101, 102, 110, 128, 156,

161, 182, 191, 195, 199, 247, 248, 272, 273, 295, 297, 298, 312, 313, 339, 347
Rosenthal, Andrew 255, 267
Roth, Philip 162, 195, 234, 285
Rothenberg, Jennie 56, 58, 60, 64
Rove, Karl 269
Rubashkin, Sholom 51
Rubin, Debra 271
Rubin, Neil 281, 333
Ruby, Walter i, 76, 288, 292

S

Sacramento Bee, The 58
San Francisco Chronicle 58, 205
Sarna, Jonathan 123, 142, 177
Schachter, Herschel 165
Schneerson, Menachem 290
Scholem, Gershom 35
Schweitzer, Dwight Owen iii, 302
Search for God at Harvard, The 25, 26, 29
Segal, David 269
Seipp, Cathy ix, 130, 131
Sex in the City 37, 349
Shafran, Avi iii, 154, 198
Shamir, Yitzhak 84
Shanks, Hershel xxxiv, 85, 101, 294
Shapiro, Pinchas 65
Sharon, Ariel 72, 163, 297
Silk, Mark 299
Silow-Carroll, Andrew xxvi, 69, 162, 175, 176
Simon Wiesenthal Center 34, 247, 319
Singer, Sam 65
Sommer, Allison Kaplan iii, xxxiii, 104, 177, 197
Stoll, Ira xxxiv, 102
Strasser, Teresa xxxiv, 36, 112, 120, 138, 145, 183
Sullivan, Andrew 216, 263
Supertramp 38

T

Teitelbaum, Sheldon 81, 116
Tikkun xxviii, 71, 101, 102, 339
Tobin, Jonathan 18, 240, 241, 318
Tugend, Tom ii, 81, 122, 204
Twersky, David 120, 128, 161, 193, 210

U

University of Judaism i, xxviii, xxix, 9, 97, 118, 130, 161
Upon This Rock 6, 7

V

Vanity Fair 64, 144

W

Wall Street Journal, The 138, 148, 158, 190, 247, 257, 266, 297, 319
Washington Jewish Week xxii, xxxiii, 70, 74, 76, 77, 97, 98, 99, 100, 107, 109, 159, 254, 265, 271, 272, 275, 277, 278, 281, 334, 343
Washington Post xxii, 56, 77, 99, 100, 102, 109, 224, 255, 257, 260, 261, 269, 274, 277, 278, 312
Watanabe, Teresa ii, xxxiv, 301
Weiner, Julie xxxiv
Weinstein, Ken 254, 258, 260
Weiss, Steven 158, 315
Weyrich, Paul 254, 255, 260
Wieseltier, Leon xxxiv, 6, 265
Wilkes, Paul 5, 6, 12, 31
Winner, Lauren xxxiv
Wittman, Marshall 260, 264, 269
Wolpe, David 9, 160
Wolpe, Gerald 26

X

XXX-Communicated: A Rebel Without A Shul vi, xv

Y

Yanover, Yori i, 167

Yeshiva University (YU) xxix, 65, 66, 157, 171, 311
YU Commentator 65
Yudelson, Larry iii, 76, 157, 170

Z
Zimmerman, Sheldon i, xxxiv, 220, 239, 363
Zionist Organization of America 69, 216
Zuckerbrod, Nancy xxxiv

0-595-33202-1

Made in the USA
Lexington, KY
25 November 2009